I0820504

FASCISM IN INDIA

FASCISM IN INDIA

Race, Caste, and Hindutva

LUNA SABASTIAN

HARVARD UNIVERSITY PRESS
Cambridge, Massachusetts · London, England
2025

Printed in the United States of America
First printing

EU GPSR Authorised Representative
LOGOS EUROPE, 9 rue Nicolas Poussin, 17000, LA ROCHELLE, France
E-mail: Contact@logoseurope.eu

LIBRARY OF CONGRESS CATALOGING-IN-PUBLICATION DATA

Names: Sabastian, Luna, author.
Title: Fascism in India : race, caste, and Hindutva / Luna Sabastian.
Description: Cambridge, Massachusetts ; London, England : Harvard University Press, 2025. | Includes bibliographical references and index.
Identifiers: LCCN 2025013687 (print) | LCCN 2025013688 (ebook) | ISBN 9780674299436 cloth | ISBN 9780674302242 epub | ISBN 9780674302259 pdf
Subjects: LCSH: Savarkar, Vinayak Damodar, 1883–1966—Political and social views | Nationalism—India—History | Fascism—India—History | Hindutva—India—History | Hinduism and politics—India—History | Caste—India—History
Classification: LCC DS480.45 .S227 2025 (print) | LCC DS480.45 (ebook) | DDC 954.03/5—dc23/eng/20250716
LC record available at https://lccn.loc.gov/2025013687
LC ebook record available at https://lccn.loc.gov/2025013688

For Adam

CONTENTS

FASCISM IN INDIA

INTRODUCTION

At the famous stroke of midnight on August 15, 1947, India gained freedom from British colonial rule, but at the price of Partition. It was only the second colony to gain independence from the British after the United States of America some 170 years earlier, and it anticipated the major era of decolonization by more than a decade. During Partition, the country was divided along religious lines. Pakistan was carved out as a homeland for the subcontinent's Muslims, taking the bizarre shape of an eastern and a western wing, separated by a vast expanse (over 2,000 kilometers) of Indian territory. In the so-called Partition violence that has been powerfully reinterpreted as a civil war, fifteen million refugees moved across newly established borders.[1] It was one of the largest and most rapid migrations in human history, and the scale of human suffering was superlative. A million people were killed; up to one hundred thousand women were abducted and countless more raped. In 1971, East Pakistan (now Bangladesh) split from West Pakistan (now Pakistan), belying the two-nation theory—and its claim that all of India's Muslims constituted one nation—on which Pakistan was founded in the first place. From historical first to unimaginable violence, from India's sheer scale to its proverbial diversity, something momentous had happened in India, where the move beyond aping Western political concepts lay at the heart of the nationalist project.

This book is concerned with one addition that India made to political thought: Hindutva, the ideology of Hindu nationalism. The book's title, *Fascism in India,* names its central provocation. At a time when fascism seems globally on the rise again, it argues that India can teach us something new about the "f-word." Hindu nationalism has been linked to fascism for decades, especially since 2014, when the Bharatiya Janata Party (BJP) came to power and began to redefine India, unleashing formidable violence.[2] Nevertheless, the identification of Hindutva and fascism—contemporaries in the first half of the twentieth century—remains controversial, and a book espousing it opens itself up to accusations of polemicism. Certainly, if one defines fascism only through its famous European cases of Fascist Italy and Nazi Germany, then no, Hindutva has never equaled full-blown fascism. It was and is *too different.* But *Fascism in India* has a slightly different concern. It asks what fascism would look like if charted from India instead of Europe. Hindutva was not identical to European fascism—it was *India's* fascism. And it can teach us something altogether new about the concept.

In resolutely turning to history, *Fascism in India* aims to contribute to debates about India's and the global present moment, but it advocates a step beyond drawing parallels and tracing influences. Indian history is more than just a field of application for ideologies and universals produced elsewhere. It is therefore not enough to seek to reveal that India, too, experienced fascism in the sense of German National Socialism or Italian Fascism, which would yield little conceptual gain. Instead, *Fascism in India* challenges the glossaries produced by Eurocentric definitions of "fascism" that have poorly understood not only Hindutva but also decisive features of political thought in Nazi Germany. The book's charting of fascism from India includes a theoretical discussion of the meaning of "fascism" through Indian thinkers Benoy Kumar Sarkar (1887–1949) and Subhas Chandra Bose (1897–1945). Reframing India as genuinely generative of fascist ideas, it uncovers deep conceptual discontinuities between Indian fascism and the more traditional varieties of fascism, thus shedding new light on Nazi thought and "global" fascism more broadly. The key to India's contentious present, *Fascism in India* suggests, lies not in Adolf Hitler's Germany or Benito Mussolini's Italy (let alone Donald Trump's America), but in developments in Indian political thought from the 1920s through 1960. This in turn revises our understanding of what was possible and indeed thinkable in the fascist age.

But what is fascism? One hundred years of deliberation have not ended the debate. In a published exchange of letters with Ernst Nolte, the historian of communism François Furet notes that fascism emancipated the European Right from the "counterrevolutionary impasse" of using revolutionary means to return to the prerevolutionary past.[3] Fascism appropriated the revolutionary idea for the Right and gave it a forward projection. At the same time, fascism developed its "galvanising effect on the masses" through "making the national idea absolute."[4] The fusion of the revolutionary with the national has since come to constitute what Roger Griffin has referred to as the "(now old) 'new consensus'" in fascist studies, echoing his own definition of fascism as "palingenetic" (or revolutionary) "ultra-nationalism."[5] This definition is apt and one that I heuristically employed when conceiving this book, but it is also limited. Other definitions, especially those derived from Fascist Italy, converge on the state as the vehicle for fascist rebirth. Yet these definitions inadequately capture the three points that stood out to fascism's perhaps most original (and irreverent) Indian observer, Benoy Sarkar: first, that the forward momentum of fascism lay in democratization; second, that statism does not contradict this democratizing force; and third, that fascism shared these aspects with communism. Not only that, but as this book's first, theoretical chapter demonstrates, Sarkar and Bose refused to treat fascism as evil or untouchable.

A central figure in this book, Benoy Sarkar was the theorist of the new. The Bengali social scientist was adamant that what he saw as the world's first global century—the twentieth century—had also brought about a transformation in the history of political ideas. Liberalism had utterly lost its power to fascinate. Communism was an alternative proposition that, since 1917, radiated out from Russia and resonated across the colonies. But communism was internationalist: in its utopian formulation, it elevated international revolution over the national sovereignty that was the aim of anticolonial nationalism. Even Bose, the self-declared "Leftist" and socialist in the Indian National Congress, groped around for alternatives, ultimately leading him to cooperate with Hitler and the Axis powers. Regimes called fascist, for all their sins, repatriated the subject of revolution to the nation. As rendered by Sarkar, its unapologetically original Indian theorist, fascism was in fact an improvement on liberal democracy because it mobilized the masses, the "people" proper. With deep resonances in Nazi thought that are explored in Chapter 3, fascism as theorized by Sarkar was a nondemocratic form of popular sovereignty. That fascism also entailed coercive elements did not fluster Sarkar, who saw in it a marriage of popular sovereignty and dictatorship that he baptized "demo-despotocracy." Yet neither Sarkar nor Bose saw fascism as the final word on political philosophy. Rather, as inveterate critics of Eurocentrism, they trusted in India's capacity to produce universality. India would bring about the next creative fusion and put a new political model before the world.

For Bose, fascism was a species of ultranationalism, with which he sided against communism's internationalism. Of course, the suspicion that a potential fascism lurks behind every nationalism pervades the literature on ethnic or ethnonationalism. As an analytical term, ethnonationalism is set against the conflation of nation and state, the ethnic and the civic. It assumes that nationalisms are at their core about the *ethnos*—the nation, tribe, or ethnic group—making ethnonationalism a tautology of sorts. As the current Hindu nationalist dispensation of power is displacing the civic or secular idea of Nehru's India, one may speak of the rise of ethnonationalism in contemporary India.[6] Is fascism just an extreme case of ethnonationalism? Crucially, unlike "ethnonationalism" (and the term "ethnicity" itself),[7] "fascism" is an emic term contemporary with the phenomenon it describes. Sarkar and Bose theorized it, Hindu nationalists flirted with it. Fascism, not nationalism, was the new political model demanding conceptual engagement between Mussolini's power capture in 1922 and the fall of Nazism in 1945. For these reasons, I cleave to it.

Fascism in India assembles an eclectic array of figures: some well-known Indian thinkers like Bose, Sarkar, and archtheorist of Hindutva Vinayak Damodar Savarkar (1883–1966), as well as famous Nazi ideologues including Adolf Hitler himself. But the "great men" in this account are interspersed with a great many lesser-known yet insightful figures, and chapter-length explorations of the thought of one famous political thinker are interwoven with topical chapters whose cast lists run into the dozens. Individuals were included because they were impactful or idiosyncratic, or because they advanced a particular theme—or all three at once. Some of the thinkers explored in this book were chosen early in the book's composition, like Savarkar. The founder of the Rashtriya Swayamsevak Sangh (RSS), Keshav Baliram Hedgewar (1889–1940), or his successor, M. S. Golwalkar (1906–1973), might have been logical next choices, but instead the book focuses on the lesser-known figure of Deendayal Upadhyaya (1916–1968), the thinker-politician who ushered Hindutva into the era of Indian independence and reinvented RSS ideology for a political party. Bose was the usual suspect for Indian fascism, along with Benoy Sarkar—in my opinion, fascism's most original Indian observer. Both had to be grappled with. Others joined the cast of this book as its guiding tropes—race, caste, and sovereignty—emerged. This selection of thinkers is not exhaustive; others might have been included, and it is left to future researchers to explore them. Crucially, all major thinkers that made it into this book are Hindu. Certainly, fascism also resonated with India's Muslims, as evinced by the paramilitary

Khaksar movement of Inayatullah Khan Mashriqi (1888–1963).[8] But a minoritarian fascism cannot win. Only Hindu nationalism had the capacity to become India's fascism. This book traces its development.

The book builds on the recent turn in Indian historiography to "global intellectual history" or "global political thought" that reconceptualizes the Global South as a place from which to theorize. While the history of political thought is overwhelmingly accessed through a European canon (White and male) and for this reason has become the target of students' demands to "decolonize," global intellectual history is inherently "decolonial" and a new and vibrant field, with seminal manifestoes and edited volumes published to establish it only a decade ago, and a flowering of monographs at present.[9] Few if any of the thinkers explored in this book are pure armchair theorists. It has been argued that the impact of political thought on political action in India does not present itself in the same way as in Europe—that since Indian members of the founding generation (active around 1947) were so effective as politicians, we are only beginning to reconstruct them as thinkers now.[10] This is true, but it is also more complicated. Take the case of Savarkar. As Hindutva's theorist, he was undoubtedly influential, and yet his thought was often more radical—unpalatable to traditional Hindus, even—than the movement associated with his name. The translation of thought to mass political action was therefore not the primary criterion for inclusion in this book. Instead, it was the ability to reshape the landscape of political ideas. Rather than tracing the export to India of German or Italian blueprints, *Fascism in India* centers India itself as a producer of novel political ideas that redefined how political community was imagined and political violence performed in the twentieth century.

Fascism in India makes four major interventions. First, it demonstrates how fascism's Indian contemporaries can advance our understanding of fascism. Second, it rethinks the meaning of race and sovereign territory—"blood and soil"—from an Indian vantage point. Third, in exploring the meaning of the term "caste" (*Kaste*) under the Nazis, the book showcases the ability of India to contribute a universal concept to modern political grammar. Fourth, it introduces the idea that there are in fact two distinct strains of Hindutva, whose competition we see in India today. Hindutva was crafted by Savarkar in 1923,[11] but it was only with Upadhyaya in the first decades of Indian independence that Hindutva became definitively religious. Crossing what may appear as a natural dividing point in Indian history—1947—*Fascism in India* theorizes how the horrendous rupture of the mid-twentieth century forced Hindutva to reinvent itself.

Whose Sovereignty?

It is often thought that the "Reader," addressee, or antagonist to Mohandas Karamchand Gandhi's (1869–1948) "Editor" in the Socratic dialogue of *Hind Swaraj* (1909) is Vinayak Savarkar. Anticolonialism, after a youthful infatuation, was ultimately not the aim of Savarkar or the Hindu nationalist movement whose major theorist he became. Whether through the ethical (as in Gandhi), the social, or the communal, few Indian political thinkers at the time retained the purity of anticolonialism aimed primarily at a confrontation with empire. This is not to downplay the fierceness with which the British clung to empire: Indian independence was not an inevitable outcome of World War II but in fact was hard won. Indians' imaginings of their political future exceeded the expulsion of the British—and did so long before the last rounds of imperial negotiations. Muslims, as recently explored by Amar Sohal, had to confront the loss of sovereignty that they had enjoyed in precolonial India, where the major political players had been Muslim. It was Muslim empires—the Mughal empire (at its zenith around 1700) succeeding the Delhi sultanate—that had managed to cover most of the Indian subcontinent's iconic triangular shape, a unification last achieved by the Mauryan (ca. 322–185 BCE) and Gupta (ca. 320–550 CE) empires. For the few Indian Muslim political thinkers who rejected Pakistan as the solution to Muslim minoritization in a postcolonial future, commitment to India required overcoming the nostalgia for Muslim sovereignty and striking a "rare compact with loss for a peaceful future."[12] For Muslims, independence and the institution of representative government in the subcontinent portended becoming a permanent minority at the mercy of a permanent Hindu majority. Demography was fate and a source of tyranny, not under empire or foreign rule but in a democracy: one man, one vote. But for Hindus, the prospect of the withdrawal of British power presented an opening in which sovereignty could be reclaimed and Hindu-Muslim relations remade. In large part, it is this opening that *Fascism in India* explores.

One crucial maneuver was the recovery of Hindu statecraft, as elaborated in Chapter 4. By the time of the British, it was thought that Hindus had turned their backs on questions of power for centuries. They had become repulsed by politics and concentrated on religion instead.[13] The 1905 rediscovery of the

Arthashastra of Kautilya, the ancient treatise on statecraft, remedied this. It opened a vista to an Indian center that did not come as a gift of British or Muslim imperialism and an imperial horizon that stretched far beyond India's shores, thus rivaling both the British masters of the sea and Islam's history of empire. The argument has long been made that India's salience was achieved by the iconography of the map coming together with the Hindu goddess. In contradistinction to this scholarly focus on Bharat Mata (or "Mother India")—the deification of the map of India—*Fascism in India* centers the idea of a "Hindu Crown." This crown was not a defined, sacred space, because what Hindu nationalists needed was not territory per se but Hindu sovereignty. The Hindu Crown was the territorialization of a radically itinerant capacity for Hindu sovereignty, which, under conditions of Muslim and British rule, came to rest outside India in the Kingdom of Nepal. Astonishingly, Savarkar imagined this extraterritorial Hindu polity as a nucleus from which to reconquer all India.

Hindu power was patchy, as India was similarly shot through with Muslim power. From Savarkar to K. M. Munshi (1887–1971), the leader of the Akhand Bharat ("Undivided India") movement and later executor of independent India's takeover of the Muslim princely state of Hyderabad, Hindu nationalism's leaders always suspected that Pakistan did not signify a defined territory but rather the potential and ambition for Muslim Raj ("rule") in all of India. Partition thus staged a battle between rival Hindu and Muslim potentialities for sovereignty in all India. During the civil war of Partition, Savarkar and his party, the Hindu Mahasabha, called on the Hindu-majority states, Nepal, and the Hindu princes to form a united front against the Muslim provinces, spearheaded by Hyderabad and Afghanistan, to fight for sovereign control of India. The nonacceptance of the territorial settlement of Partition was from then on integral to Hindu nationalism.

The problem of Hindu sovereignty was further articulated in respect to religion. Hindutva, when it was coined by Savarkar, was explicitly coined against Hinduism. Savarkar was famously an atheist (or at least an agnostic), as was Muhammad Ali Jinnah (1876–1948), the Quaid-e-Azam ("Great Leader") and father of Pakistan. Without pushing the point of biography too far, it does illustrate that what was at stake in Muslim and Hindu "communalism" in the last decades of British rule was the etching out of identities and a competition of sovereign potentialities, not faith, religiosity, or right observance—in other words, religious fundamentalism. Savarkar had defined Hindutva, or "Hinduness," as the bare quality of being a Hindu, or what was left over after

Hinduism was evacuated from it. His definitional coup, simple and genius, was to prize apart the Hindu subject and the Hindu religion. Hindutva was crafted to overcome the limitations of Hinduism. Beyond its proverbial indefinability, which made it singularly unsuited for anchoring political identity, Hinduism as social theory indexed caste and thus the greatest obstacle to Hindu community (the subject of Chapter 2); philosophically (or, shall we say, theologically), the issue was the Vedanta.

Advaita Vedanta (lit. "the end of the Veda of nondualism") had emerged as the essence of Hinduism through the colonial encounter. This doctrine teaches the total identity of the *atman,* or personal soul, with the Absolute, *brahman.* The appearance of nonidentity, or dualism, is regarded as illusion, *maya.* Consistent with the turn against the political in premodern Hindu thought, Vedantic Hinduism appeared to orientalists as a quietist religion that preached world renunciation as the highest ideal, whose appeal many Hindu politicians in colonial India expressly battled. Not only was Vedanta's monism, or radical nondualism, set against action in general, but it also rendered enmity (as an extreme form of distinction, or nonidentity) definitionally unthinkable. As a theory of enmity, Savarkar's Hindutva therefore had to break with the Hindu religion. Savarkar demanded that Hindus break Brahmanic convention, caste, and social propriety in the interest of unifying them and making them warriors, thus mirroring qualities that their enemies, the Muslims, were thought to possess. If Hindutva is today indistinguishable from Hinduism, this is not due to its original founding but to Hindutva's reinvention after the creation of Pakistan and the geographic fixing of enmity. One of this book's major contributions is diagnosing this rupture, which belies any straight genealogies leading from the religious revivalism of Swami Vivekananda (1863–1902) to Savarkar; L. K. Advani, the architect of the destruction of Ayodhya's Babri Masjid; and Narendra Modi.

The book's final chapter consequently tracks the reemergence of the Hindu religious idiom in a last-ditch effort to avoid Partition and Pakistan through the appropriation of Indian folk devotionalism, which elides the difference between Allah and the Hindu supreme God, Ishwar. But it was Deendayal Upadhyaya, the general secretary of the Bharatiya Jana Sangh (BJS, later the BJP) and a major ideologue of Hindutva after Savarkar, who reconfigured Hindutva as an integrationist matrix that could erase the dualism Pakistan represented. This book gives the first rigorous account of Upadhyaya's concept of Integral Humanism (*ekatma manavvad*), which replaced Savarkar's *Essentials of Hindutva* (1923) as the manifesto of Hindu nationalism at the end of the Nehruvian period. Upadhyaya's Hindutva consigned Pakistan itself to the world of *maya*. The separation that Pakistan represented would disappear along with the disunity in Indian society that had given rise to it. Conceptually depending on the emergence of Indian and Pakistani statecraft, the new Hindutva that was institutionalized in the BJS/BJP nevertheless developed its violence not primarily in geopolitical confrontation with Pakistan but in relation to Indian society itself. Neo-Hindutva therefore weaponized Hinduism's monism to erase diversity or opposition (now rebranded as disharmony) in Indian society, blaming such divisions for the creation of Pakistan. After losing the battle for Akhand Bharat, and consciously set against the moral bankruptcy of fascism and Stalinism, Upadhyaya charted a path to an "integrated," self-regulating society, which would obviate the state by internalizing and naturalizing divine law. The aim was for India to replicate the Kritiyuga, the golden age, when neither kings nor "the people" but *dharma* (religious law) had been sovereign. Hindutva thus took a conspicuously anarchist turn, divorcing sovereignty from the state and recalibrating it as an immanent (but anything but benevolent) power suffusing society. This reading may come as a provocation at a time when the state appears ubiquitous in India for the first time, but it encapsulates how the Hindu state naturalizes itself by reworking society in its image, and it identifies Hindutva's utopian endgame. In contradistinction to totalitarianism and definitions of fascism that center on the primacy of the state, Upadhyaya's Hindutva makes Hindu society, rather than the state, total.

None of this means that Hindutva's founder, though much lauded by Hindu nationalist politicians, is somehow philosophically forgotten today. There are, in fact, two Hindutvas, and contemporary Hindutva draws on them both: Savarkar's Hindutva of enmity and war on Muslims and the "iron" harmony of the Hindutva of the RSS and Upadhyaya that crushes any difference or opposition in the oceanic embrace of its religion and will not stop until Indian society and Hindu society are one. More specifically, today's Hindutva involves the competition of both strains, rather than their smooth combination. Ultimately, both lineages of Hindutva envision their aim as the complete erasure of the dualism that "the other" represents, whether that is the Indian Muslim, Pakistan, or dissent in India.

What, then, is specific about Hindutva's violence? Hannah Arendt, in her deliberations *On Violence* (1970), disambiguated power from violence, with which it is often conflated. In the context of 1968, observing the Left's apparent drunkenness on violence that was sourced from a hodgepodge of Frantz Fanon, Jean-Paul Sartre, and Karl Marx, she rejected the creative power of violence and its status as a source of power. Power, for Arendt, is instead the ability to inspire concerted action (politics). Power has primacy over violence: even violence that destroys a given sovereign order (through revolution) needs power to make a group cohere and act (violently) in tandem.[14] A special relationship with violence has been attributed to modern India, where violence became central to the question of the political and, indeed, sovereignty. Gandhian *satyagraha,* often rendered as civil disobedience but better understood as "truth-force," spectacularly demonstrated the power of concerted action. It demonstrated that power lay with the Indian people, who could shut down the British administration if they acted in concert. Yet Gandhi's nonviolence, as we now know, also functioned through courting (state) violence.[15] Sovereignty, in turn, though long affixed to the legal domain (as jurisdiction), was recalibrated by Carl Schmitt as the decision to suspend the law, and in India's modern political thought, as Shruti Kapila compellingly demonstrates, it was formulated outside the law and the state.[16] The Indian example shows that sovereign power is, in Kapila's words, at its core concerned with "the question of killing and dying."[17] *Fascism in India* considers a different species of violence: absorption. In centering Hindutva's violence, the book explores an unfamiliar yet potent brand of violence that functions not through exclusion of the paradigmatic "other" but through absorption. India's fascism reveals the violence that inheres in the refusal to recognize and respect "the other" as different and nonidentical with the self.

The 2002 Gujarat riots, an anti-Muslim pogrom that claimed over one thousand lives, saw a pattern of mass rape and mutilation of Muslim women's breasts and wombs that was interpreted as an attempt to destroy and pollute their reproductive capabilities.[18] However, rather than destruction, Hindutva developed its genocidal violence through the "occupation" of Muslim wombs reminiscent of genocidal rape in Bosnia.[19] Explored in Chapter 2, Hindutva, as developed by Savarkar and fed into escalating communal antagonism from the 1920s to Partition, deployed a genocidal logic that functioned through life in its gendered capacity for reproduction, rather than only death. Women, though singularly omitted from the canon of Western political thought, were at the crux of Savarkar's political thought, bizarrely anticipating the feminist restoration of women as the foundation of sovereignty and its violence.

Muslim women, for Hindutva's founder, pinpointed the slippage between Hindus and Muslims, who were indigenous converts to Islam and therefore kin to the Hindus. Muslim women also showed the way to restore millions and right a historical wrong: the growth of a rival political subject in the subcontinent. This vision entailed a peculiar conception of race. Indeed, the prime antagonizer of India's Muslims formulated a concept of the Hindu race that was based on mixed, rather than pure, blood and capable of absorbing the Muslim "other" through (forced) intermarriage and sex.

Discussions centered on the United States have cemented the view that race must be about skin color and that racism must valorize purity of blood, a conviction for which Nazi Germany stands as a paragon even more than the United States or apartheid South Africa. But India's manifest diversity required new ways of imagining race. Indeed, Savarkar's founding theory of Hindutva produced a myth of the Hindu race grounded in reproductive admixture. Marshaling Savarkar's prolific published writings and unpublished personal papers, party records, and other archival sources, *Fascism in India* demonstrates that what Nazis and White supremacists at the time considered miscegenation was, for Savarkar, the foundation of the Hindu race. This idea of miscegenation buttressed Hindutva's tremendous violence against Muslims. Jettisoning traditional Brahmanic purity (and proving that Hindutva is not conservatism), Savarkar redefined the caste system as the crucible of the Hindu race, arguing that the endless proliferation of subcastes was a testimony to the long history of intermarriage that had unfortunately expired in the present age. To reestablish the broken bonds of the Hindu race, Savarkar championed intercaste marriage, and he offered the same solution to the "Muslim problem." Muslims, who had carved themselves out of the Hindu race, needed to be reclaimed through conversion coupled with (forced) marriage, sex, and reproduction with Hindus. Yet only Muslim women could be appropriated in this way, as paternity imparted race; Muslim men would be crushed in their potentiality for sovereignty, as well as reproduction, in civil war with the Hindus. The annihilation of Muslims that Hindutva undoubtedly envisaged would come through a vision of gendered incorporation modeled on the capture of women in war, thus attaching a political theory to the abductions and mass rapes of women during Partition.

Finally, while the bulk of the book "provincializes" European understandings of big concepts (race, sovereign territory, political violence, and fascism itself) through centering Indian thought, Chapter 3 demonstrates the potential for Indian thought to yield a universal political concept that makes sense of Western material.[20] This chapter provides the first history of the concept of "caste" in the vocabulary of National Socialism and German political grammar more broadly, which is stitched together from a large array of protagonists and sources ranging from Weimar dictionaries to the *National Socialist Monthly*, from Hans F. K. Günther's (1891–1968) racial hygiene to Richard Walter Darré's (1895–1953) blood and soil, from Alfred Rosenberg's (1893–1946) Nazi theorizing to Hitler's battle speeches. In this argument, "caste," far from designating an Indian idiosyncrasy, was pressed into service for a peculiar vision of popular sovereignty without democracy in Nazi Germany.

Chapter 3 traces the German term *Kaste* from its first occurrence in the context of the French Revolution to the Nazi years, demonstrating how the concept was employed to label the aristocracy as the enemy of "the people," rather than the Indian Dalit or Black slave. To countless commentators in the Third Reich, *Kaste* still designated a cliquish ruling elite that was racially foreign to and derived its right to rule from having conquered "the people," nation, or *Volk*. Thus, *Kaste* marked out the major impediment to the consolidation of the German *Volk*. Only once the *Kaste* of power was removed from the body of the nation, so Nazis and their sympathizers argued, would ruler and ruled be reconciled and rule finally made popular without need of formal democracy. Nazism's Indian interpreter, Sarkar, would have agreed that the German regime was a development in popular sovereignty. Moreover, tracing *Kaste* makes visible a fundamental conceptual tension between Nazi ideas of race and *Volk*. Ideas of *Kaste* figured as positive in only one context: namely, in hopes for a new racial aristocracy, explored in the last part of the chapter. Here, it was above all the reception of Friedrich Nietzsche's master-slave relation that bolstered Nazi ideas of planting German farmers as a ruling *Kaste* into the conquered East. It turns out that "caste" and its relationship to race and conquest that was so problematic among members of the German *Volk* were uncontroversial in the New Order that the Nazis devised for Europe, and particularly the Slavs. If Savarkar's Hindu race pushes us to uncouple ideologies of race from purity and color, reconstructing how the term "caste" was really used in Nazi Germany contributes to our understanding of Nazi ideas of race and—though rarely associated with Hitler's regime—popular sovereignty. It is also a timely intervention against the metaphorical use of India's "caste" in contemporary discussions about racism, especially in the United States.

The Vexation of "Fascism"

By the 1990s, scholars had echoed the intuition of contemporaries of Hitler and Mussolini that German National Socialism and Italian Fascism not only shared considerable ground but represented a wider phenomenon existing beyond fascist states and turned it into a generalized notion of a "lowercase fascism," for which they proposed minimum definitions.[21] As well as an aggressive form of nationalism, they defined fascism as a revolution of the Right that diverged from traditional conservatism and identified liberalism as well as communism as its adversaries. The new paradigm replaced the totalitarianism of the immediate postwar period, which had lumped together Italian Fascism, German National Socialism, and Soviet Communism as experiments in the total domination of human life by the state.[22] A comparative project pushed by Anglophone scholars and today replete with its own journal (*Fascism: Journal of Comparative Fascist Studies*), generic fascism is still resented by German and Italian historians in particular, who tend to insist on the idiosyncratic nature of Italian Fascism and German National Socialism.[23] Given their countries' histories, this is not surprising. Each country has seen historians fight publicly over the meaning of their tainted past.[24] While some scholars still cannot agree that German National Socialism and Italian Fascism were close relatives, the last ten or fifteen years have brought a new turn to "transnational" or "global" fascist studies.

One consequence is a glut of writings on the global "circulation" of fascist ideas and global "responses" to fascism, including in India.[25] Indian attitudes toward Italian Fascism or German Nazism and fascist propaganda in India have equally been explored, complementing older accounts of India's implication in the Nazi imagination (through the Indo-Aryan connection, the swastika, occultism, and orientalism).[26] Studies have suggested Hindu nationalism's particular traction with the Nazis, also considered, though found wanting, by scholars of European fascism as India's offering of a homegrown variety of fascism (a "politicised" or "political religion," "fundamentalism," or a "postfascist" movement, short of the European ideal type).[27] The enigmatic Subhas Bose has been scrutinized, the usual finding being that he, too, did not cross the fascist threshold.[28] At other times, the study of "Indian fascism" has yielded an exposé of the dark underbelly of Indian nationalism.[29] While classical accounts of fascism tend to deny its global reach and newer accounts still often curtail the global to Europe and Japan, the fundamental problem with "Indian fascism" appears to be, first, that it is cast into a dialogic account of encounters or reception histories, and second, that the Indian case studies remain conceptually tethered to the notorious European cases.[30]

And yet it should be evident by now that when ideas travel, they get "cannibalised."[31] Indians did not bother about pedigree when they absorbed ideas. For instance, before becoming Hindutva's founding father, Savarkar appropriated Catholic idioms of martyrdom for revolutionary Indian nationalism with a Hindu bent.[32] Indians took everything, from everywhere, and made it their own. Some even regarded the power to absorb and assimilate foreign material (intellectual or otherwise) as essential tests of the vitality of a nation and a defining feature of their Indian home. Indians may have thought it their special forte, but our current understanding of global history suggests the norm of appropriation everywhere to have been local adaptation, rather than faithful copying. According to one scholar of global fascism, this means we no longer have to labor over fascist minimums and "impossible ideal types." Ideas are global property in this, our shared modernity, and many a creation is only seemingly endogenous, fascism included.[33] For Benoy Sarkar, certainly, the twentieth century dawned as the first global age. "World forces" set in motion in any part of the world had repercussions everywhere else.[34] New political ideas were produced and could be assimilated and made use of globally. Colonizers and colonized finally inhabited the same global now-time.

"Fascism" is no doubt an overused term. Like others, I am uncomfortable with its inflationary use.[35] It is also, and always has been, a polemical term. The word "fascism" derives from the Italian *fasci,* plural for *fascio,* "bundle" or "sheaf." It signifies that something tightly united becomes unbreakable. *Fascismo* was the self-designation of Mussolini's movement, yes, but it was the antifascists that gave fascism its generic, or universal, usage.[36] In the Indian context, as elsewhere, "fascist" was contemporaneously used as a metaphorical allegation—for instance, for the high-handedness of Gandhi and the Congress high command. But metaphors are inherently misleading (they substitute *this* for *that*). It is more productive to inquire seriously, as is done today, whether fascism may in fact constitute a universal political philosophy, like socialism, liberalism, or conservatism, thus having survived its resounding disgrace after 1945 and perhaps on the prowl again today. We would then hardly expect to reach a definition of it that passes the test of mathematical beauty (effectiveness as well as economy). After all, as Nietzsche said, "definable is only that which has no history."[37]

But if fascism has a history and its definition cannot be disentangled from it, then surely this embroilment is what should interest us. Moreover, contrary to the rhetorical work that bandying around the "f-word" does, it is not the case that Hindu majoritarianism in India today turns "bad" if and only if it crosses the fascist threshold as defined by Europe, Nazism in particular (in common perception the paragon of fascism, or pure evil). India's stores of violence and its likely future development in the twenty-first century can be understood through India's own history and the political thought of its founding years. If there was such a thing as "fascism" in India, its contours would be recognizably Indian: an "Indian fascism." If we are indeed witnessing a fascist turn in India today, it is a product of its own thought tradition developed in the mid-twentieth century, which also saw global experiments with fascism and communism, not the afterlife of European catastrophe. An investigation of Indian fascism cannot proceed without the assumption of a shared global context. But in the last instance, this book is an appeal for theorizing from the (non-Western) particular and taking seriously the possibility that it may hold universal lessons for the world.

To understand the tremendous deployment of violence in Hindu-majoritarian India today, we need to look beyond the Indian fascination with Hitler, seductively bewildering though it is. Wherever books are sold in India, one can find *Mein Kampf.* On mats on the ground, where roadside sellers peddle their wares, in the gift section of bookshops in the glitzy part of cities like New Delhi: Hitler sells. In India, his name is not a stand-in for pure evil. On the contrary, Hitler is well remembered and respected in India today, and there is little historical consciousness of the Holocaust (Shoah). Hitler is remembered as a political strongman, a leader with an iron will who took on great foes in the interest of nationalism: foes like the British empire, India's enemy. There is a postcolonial, vernacular Hitler in India, and there are doubtlessly parallels in other former colonies. Today, the strongman appeals especially to middle-class, educated Indians, who believe a power of this type is needed to surmount the immensity of India's problems in the twenty-first century and command international respect. In India, Hitler is "cool." There is a history to be told here, but it did not impress itself on Indian thought, and it cannot explain the nature of Indian political violence past or present. What follows presents a truer approach to fascism in India.

In summary, theorizing "fascism" through Indian eyewitnesses, *Fascism in India* examines ideas of popular sovereignty beyond democracy and connections between fascism and communism (Chapter 1). Centering India reveals new ways of thinking about race in the context of Hindutva, an ideology that eschewed purity and embraced race mixing in a way unimaginable to Nazis or White supremacists and yet equaled both in the potential for eradicative violence (Chapter 2). Recognizing the global malleability of ideas of "race" allows for a far-reaching revision of our understanding of race in Nazi Germany itself, where, as the first conceptual history of "caste" in German-language use shows, caste signposted a racial conflict that obstructed the deep integration of the nation and the emergence of the general will, as it did in India (Chapter 3). The book further develops ideas of Hindu sovereignty and examines why these were anchored in territory beyond India, jettisoning the geography of the nation-state as well as "blood and soil" (Chapter 4). Stretching into the postindependence era, the book finally considers how Hindutva was reinvented after the creation of Pakistan, retracing how breaking with the tradition of parsing "Hinduness" (the literal translation of "Hindutva") from the Hindu religion allowed Hindutva to finally became synonymous with aggressive Hinduism, as it remains today (Chapter 5). *Fascism in India* thus offers a major interpretation of Hindutva, the founding theory of Hindu nationalism, in its initial formulation by Savarkar and its reinvention by Upadhyaya after Indian independence and Partition, exploring how Hindutva generated ideas of race and religion that had the potential to erase Muslims by violent absorption. By rethinking race, caste, popular sovereignty, and sovereign territory from the perspective of India, *Fascism in India* explores how political grammar was radically remade in the global fascist moment.

CHAPTER ONE

AN INDIAN THEORY OF FASCISM

Fascism and imperialism did not necessarily seem much different when viewed from the colonies. Indeed, their similarities were highlighted from the Caribbean to Latin America and from Africa to Asia, where anti-fascism, anticolonialism, and anti-racism cross-pollinated.[1] Yet this connection did not strengthen a principled opposition to fascism everywhere. In India, only the unwavering Jawaharlal Nehru (1889–1964) and the socialist M. N. Roy (1887–1954) seemed adequately appalled by German National Socialism and Italian Fascism. Other Indian nationalists, including Gandhi, precisely because they failed (if that is the word for it) to view these movements as essentially different from Allied imperialism, also failed to regard World War II as a fight between good and evil.[2]

Communism, whose appeal across the colonies was abiding, had something to do with anticolonial attitudes toward fascism. Vladimir Ilyich Lenin had supported anti-imperialism and cooperation with (at the behest of Roy, only the revolutionary elements of) bourgeois nationalist movements in the colonies early on.[3] And later under Joseph Stalin, the Communist International, or Comintern, after making war on Social Democrats as "social fascists," had espoused the formation of a "Popular Front" with nonrevolutionaries against Hitler and fascism.[4] Lenin had famously explained imperialism as "the highest," "parasitic or decaying" "stage of capitalism," but the famous quote that "fascism is capitalism in decay" is misattributed to him.[5] Instead, it was the British communist of Swedish-Indian descent Rajani Palme Dutt (1896–1974) who transferred Lenin's observations on imperialism to fascism as the latest stage of decaying capitalism.[6] Moreover, not the term "fascism" itself but its generic use originated with its enemies on the Marxist Left.[7]

Fascism and communism were presented as opposing propositions: Nehru certainly viewed them as such, and for this reason, Roy's camp in the Indian National Congress supported the British war effort in World War II, prioritizing the defeat of fascism over Indian independence.[8] Yet curiously, neither India's greatest theorist of fascism, Benoy Sarkar, nor its greatest practitioner, Subhas Bose, viewed the relationship between fascism and communism as hostile and exclusive. Instead, they viewed them as comparable or combinable. Most importantly, for Sarkar, and to some extent for Bose, fascism curbed the defining threat of the interwar years. This was the threat to nationalism and the nation-state posed by Russia's October Revolution.

The following discussion explores three points: first, Bose, Sarkar, and Roy—thinkers with a Hindu background—accessed fascism and its place in their world through vying with the philosophy of their own religion, Hinduism. In doing so, they shackled fascism to a discussion of Hindu monism. Second, Sarkar and Bose (though not Roy) refused to view fascism, and even the Nazi state, as exceptional. They regarded fascism as an extreme form of nationalism, which they supported against the onslaughts of internationalism, especially in its Soviet Communist form. But at the same time, and this is my third point, Bose and Sarkar recognized that with fascism, something new had entered the world of political ideas, which offered new possibilities for India.

Benoy Sarkar and the Problem of Monism

Benoy Sarkar was one of India's foremost social scientists, and he had a global reputation in the interwar years. Subsequently all but forgotten outside India, Sarkar has recently enjoyed a renaissance. His works are today called upon to decolonize sociology or bring about a "global" turn in international relations.[9] His recent rediscovery as a thinker of interest to global intellectual historians owes itself to two related academic interests: the search for antecedents of postcolonial theory—the critique of orientalism—and examples of interwar internationalism, presented as a "past future" of a hopeful moment subsequently spoiled by violent nationalism and racism.[10] Sarkar figures as a liberal cosmopolitan and interwar internationalist but also, in intriguing contrast, as a prime suspect in recent academic discussions of Indian fascism.[11] His close engagement with the intellectual productions of Italian Fascism and German National Socialism has been used to expose the dark underbelly of Indian nationalism or trivialized as a "weakness," an Indian's fatal seduction by a political strongman and a fast track to freedom and development.[12] Ultimately unable to cross the fascist threshold, Sarkar emerges from these discussions a compromised liberal: a not-altogether-satisfactory conclusion.[13] After all, we learn little from "catching" a Sarkar or a Bose at being, or failing to be, a European-style fascist and everything from reconstructing what they viewed as the defining political and ideological possibilities, or dangers, of their time.

I hope to show that what structured Sarkar's thought and conditioned his engagement with fascism was his problematizing the ideology and politics of "internationalism." Rather than fascism or totalitarianism, Sarkar identified internationalism and humanitarianism in their liberal and socialist guises as the main antagonist against which a politics of anticolonial liberation needed to constitute itself. In this fundamental critique, the Bengali poster child for interwar internationalism finds his equal in his German contemporary, Carl Schmitt—unlike Sarkar still considered a relevant theorist today—who is associated with this line of defending "the political" against its eradication by internationalism and humanitarianism.[14]

Sarkar was born in Malda in Bengal in 1887; was educated at the University of Calcutta's prestigious Presidency College, which he entered at the tender age of thirteen in 1901; and came of age intellectually and politically with the Swadeshi (Home Rule) movement.[15] Swadeshi, the first mass protest in India against British rule, was sparked by the first partition of Bengal in 1905: a momentous year for Asian anticolonial nationalism that also saw the first victory of an Eastern nation (Japan) over a Western one (Russia) in modern times. Sarkar departed for England in 1914 and did not return to India for eleven years. During this time, he traveled extensively through Europe, East Asia, North Africa, and the United States.[16] Abroad, he threw himself into cosmopolitan intellectual and Indian expatriate nationalist networks; pushed the case for "Young India"—Indian independence and a deorientalist view of India as modern—in academic and public discussions; and picked up fluent German, French, and Italian in the process.[17] Sarkar socialized with the Labour leader Ramsay MacDonald and the Fabians Beatrice and Sidney Webb in London, inserted himself into the modernist avant-garde in New York, and read Machiavelli in Berlin.[18] Returning to India in 1925 with his Austrian wife, Ida Stieler (1892–1962), and their newborn daughter, Indira, Sarkar was appointed professor of economics at the University of Calcutta.[19] Yet the latest development in social and political "energism" or "dynamism" that he devoted his career to tracing—fascism—drew him back to Italy and Germany in 1929–1931. He spent a semester teaching at Munich's polytechnic university (Technologische Hochschule) at the invitation of his long-term admirer, the geopolitician Karl Haushofer (1869–1946).[20] Sarkar even unsuccessfully tried to secure a permanent position at a German university before finally settling in Bengal, where he taught at the University of Calcutta until his retirement in 1948.[21] He died shortly after on a lecture tour of the United States.

Sarkar defies disciplinary categorization. Though an economist by title, he strikingly injected all his writings with an almost obsessive engagement with comparative political thought. What Sarkar called his "ideological histories" were a strange genre by anyone's standard.[22] His 1928 publication *The Political Philosophies since 1905* was a chronicle of innovations in intellectual, social, economic, and political thought, put into a linear timeline of book publication dates and interspersed with political events that Sarkar crucially understood as "political philosophy embodied." For Sarkar, the political world was a product of the intellectual will and, like it, animated by dialectic "wars and revolutions."[23] Ideas had primacy over matter; they constituted the sociological "milieu" (a favorite Sarkarism) in which people acted and drove history. Sarkar's works seem to aspire to a total representation of modern political and social thought for the benefit of India's students—its future leaders, who lacked up-to-date library facilities—and to break through the red tape of an Anglocentric education.[24] A sense of urgency compressed a staggering amount of political thought into thousands of tightly written pages. These showcase a talent for digesting and reproducing thought in enormous quantity while their author rendered himself invisible: a cacophonous record player, not a unitary voice. But Sarkar's selections, summaries, and masked commentaries make for highly subjective chronicles of his agenda. To equal the scales with Europe, Sarkar's early works forage in India's and Asia's past political thought in order to reclaim the "rightful place of the Asians in a scientific study of comparative politics."[25] This early antiquarian research was, however, soon outweighed by an overwhelming concern with modern and contemporary innovations in political thought. It was in theorizing the new in political thought that Sarkar came into his own. In appraising the political experiments of his own time, Sarkar was truly innovative.

Sarkar's book *The Futurism of Young Asia*, published in 1922, is sometimes cited as an *Orientalism* before that of Edward W. Said.[26] In the title essay, Sarkar rejected not only the superiority of the West over the East but the assumption of any essential difference between them in the first place.[27] He was a "futurist" who believed that with what he called the "ideas of 1905" (the Swadeshi movement primarily), Indians had burst out of the "waiting room" of history (Dipesh Chakrabarty's evocative phrase) to which colonialism and historicism had confined them.[28] Sarkar believed Indians to have been catapulted to a global now-time, which the Great War had further accelerated.[29] His *Futurism* was testimony to this belief. It is my contention that the book for which he is best known today also contains the key to his future treatment of fascism—in its discussion of socialism and communism. Sarkar was not immune to the charms of communism—how could he be?—given that the experiment with communism in Europe's most backward country, Russia, showed a way for "backward" colonies to skip over hundreds of years of development as it had happened in the West—a way of cheating history and drawing even.[30] Moreover, Lenin was the first Western leader to commit himself to the right to self-determination of subject peoples.[31] Sarkar was optimistic about Indian independence at the time of writing *Futurism*, as India had its first taste of mass struggle. But he knew that independence would not come easy; it would not be gifted from colonial powers who were no more willing to give up their colonies after the war than they had been before.[32]

Famously, the British empire was at its greatest extent after the Great War, and Sarkar knew it. In his view, the world had never been more firmly colonial yet never more surely moving toward freedom from colonialism through the seeds of future unrest long ripe in Asia and now sown in Europe by the Treaty of Versailles. Nothing was therefore more foolish than for colonized Young Asia (as he called it) to listen to the "vague dreams of a millennial utopia" propounded by "Communists, Syndicalists, Anti-militarists and 'International Workers of the World'" and give up their nationalism.[33] It was a "misunderstanding of recent events in Russia" and a "counterfeit Bolshevism, manufactured in England, 'not for internal use,' however, but 'for external application'" to demand that Young India do so. For, wherever there was foreign rule, "*swaraj* (sovereignty)" was the first desideratum.[34] Just as "no amount of argument in the name of international humanitarianism could convince an American of the wisdom of placing the United States under, say, French domination, because, for sooth, the interests of the American masses would be better handled by the countrymen of St. Simon," so "internationalist Eur-America," if it be a true friend, would not ask "nationalist Asia" to relinquish its nationalism.[35] Sarkar made this argument with a nod to the Third International's position on the colonial question. Rather, "Eur-American" well-wishers would cooperate with anticolonial nationalism "until foreign domination is overthrown."

Sarkar treated internationalism, pacifism, and humanitarianism as forms of deception: a "hallucination" relying on "Western good-will" that colonized Asia could not afford to indulge in, though free and contented "Eur-America" may.[36] Thus, in the high moment of "interwar internationalism," Sarkar actually anticipated the Nazi-friendly political thinker Carl Schmitt's diatribes against "humanity" talk in his *The Concept of the Political*.[37]

Much later, in the midst of World War II, Sarkar would write that the early interwar years had been "the epoch *par excellence* of Lenin and Lenin alone." But "the dose administered by Lenin to the suppressed races and classes . . . was too strong." Was it therefore any wonder, he asked, that the antidote had been developed in the three countries most affected by Lenin's siren call: Russia, Germany, and Italy?[38] Long rendered untouchable by its association with Ernst Nolte, on the losing side of the *Historikerstreit* ("historians' dispute") in the late 1980s about German memory culture and the Holocaust, the proposition that the October Revolution might be connected to the success of fascism in interwar Europe has recently received new attention. The challenge is to avoid repeating Nolte's mistake of blaming the Left for the crimes of the Right.[39] Unlike Sarkar, Subhas Bose was a self-identifying socialist. But what attracted both men to fascism was its counter to Lenin's call to world revolution. Fascism—and, for Sarkar, not only Stalinism but mature Leninism—established the nation as the proper subject of revolution.

Sarkar called this "Leninism No. II." Though discrediting the term "totalitarian" as ideological, he classed Italian Fascism, German National Socialism, and Soviet Communism together.[40] Yet unlike totalitarianism's Cold War critics, he did so because all three had successfully restrained the geographically untethered aim of international socialism—"the Utopian communistic state of all nations and classes."[41] For, where colonialism only denied national sovereignty in practice and temporarily, international socialism (at its worst) denied it in principle. Consequently, Italy, Germany, and Russia had each neutralized the communist threat by inventing their own brand of "anti-communistic socialism," Sarkar expounded in a 1938 article with the colorful title "Stalin as the Manager of Leninism No. II." Each had adopted nationalism after an initial infatuation and subsequent break with Marxist communism. Mussolini came from the revolutionary socialist tradition, but Sarkar misjudged the "Marxist origins" of Hitler's coming-of age story.[42] Sarkar left no doubt that he sided with Hitler in "the tug-of-war . . . between nationalism and Marxism" in Germany in the first of his famous series of articles on the nature of fascism and the fascist state that he began in 1933, the year of the *Machtergreifung* ("seizure of power").[43]

There is further ideological weight to the fact that Sarkar's presentation hinges on an unfaithful treatment of the communist tradition.[44] He had the peculiar notion that Lenin had converted from Marxist ideologist and world revolutionary (what Sarkar called "Leninism No. I") to nationalist statesman and *realpolitiker* ("Leninism No. II") with the New Economic Policy of 1921, which abolished war communism, reintroduced money, and returned some nationalized industries to private ownership.[45] There were "two Lenins," argued Sarkar: the first, "the prophet and the metaphysician of the communistic Utopia," and the second, who adopted nationalism, retreated from Marxist economics, and paved the way for class solidarity to replace class struggle.[46] Thus, according to Sarkar, Lenin himself revised the relation between the national and the international in communist practice that is usually attributed to Stalin and his dictum of "socialism in one country."[47] Leninism No. II had nationalized the revolution. To Sarkar, it was naive and dangerous if the colonies still viewed Lenin as the architect of a "new Utopian world order."[48] Sarkar's interpretation stood for the most part by 1928, and he reaffirmed it in 1941, the year of Hitler's attack on the Soviet Union.[49]

In *Mein Kampf,* Hitler had opposed his theory of the *völkisch* ("folkish," "people's") state to the state of Marxism, which, as was popularly known in *völkisch* circles, "negates the state as such."[50] As a veteran of Weimar *Geopolitik* and a theorist of international relations, Sarkar had given much thought to the significance of national borders, and he would have agreed with Hitler.[51] After all, "utopia," which Sarkar identified with Leninism No. I, literally means "no place." Utopia is borderless; it annuls the territorial principle on which Sarkar staked his conception of national sovereignty. Second, and relatedly, being everywhere and nowhere at once, utopia permits no outside and no antagonism.[52] Marxist utopianism neutered geopolitical antagonism, which Sarkar viewed as a creative force. Translated into a pivotal concept in Sarkar's thought, Marxism and its utopianism was monism par excellence.

By identifying Marxism with monism, Sarkar operated within the arena of Indian religion. Monism, traditionally called *advaita* or "nondualism," had emerged as the central philosophy of Hinduism through the combined efforts of colonial knowledge production, "native" informants, and nineteenth-century Hindu reformers. Together, they elevated one of the Upanishad commentaries, Adi Shankara's eighth-century Advaita Vedanta (lit. "the end of the Veda of nondualism"), to the essence of Hinduism. This school—traditionally favored but by no means the only one—taught the identity of the *brahman* and the *atman*, the Absolute and the "soul" of the individual self. Schools that propagated *dvaita*, or nonidentity, were marginalized. Through Shankara's Vedanta, Europe first glimpsed Hindu philosophy.[53] Hinduism defined this way captured the imagination of European romantics but came to pose a fundamental problem for projects of national remaking in India and beyond.

Through its traction in German idealism, neo-Vedanta, as it is called, also assumed the status of an inner "problem" in Germany. Notably, Nazi ideologist Alfred Rosenberg felt called upon to extensively vie with Indian religion in his famous book of 1930, *The Myth of the Twentieth Century*, where he complained of contemporary Germany that "one preaches Buddhism and Hinduism today to nauseating extremes."[54] The shortfall of Buddhism in a political sense was its *ahimsa*, or "nonviolence." Characteristically collapsed into one, Hinduism-Buddhism embodied the unpatriotic utopias of pacifism, world peace, and "humanity" to Rosenberg; to the pioneer of "Paneuropa" in Germany, the Austrian Japanese Count Richard von Coudenhove-Kalergi (1894–1972); to race ideologist Houston Stewart Chamberlain (1855–1927); and to Hitler himself.[55] In 1942, Hitler told Bose in their only meeting that his deprecatory remarks about Indians in *Mein Kampf* sprang from his fear that Germans, like Indians, would use passive resistance to fight the oppression of the Treaty of Versailles.[56] German "Aryanists" regarded Indian "quietism" and asceticism as a deep fall from their original Aryan religion of action and believed that Hindu-Buddhist pacifism paralyzed the "wrestling match with nature," with dysgenic consequences.[57] And so the Nazis held spiritualism accountable for the degeneration of India, a once-great civilization that could now no longer produce a hero but only a Mahatma.[58]

Criticizing as Hindu philosophy what was, in fact, Advaita Vedanta, Rosenberg blamed the *brahman-atman* identification for eliminating the very concept of action. He argued that, in Germany, the much-celebrated doctrine of monistic identity—*tat tvam asi*, "thou art that"—denied all difference and dismissed all phenomena as "deception and illusion" (*maya*), to the conclusion that only the ignorant will and act.[59] Thus, Rosenberg reversed the value judgments of Arthur Schopenhauer's idealism.[60] But this was not all. India's history also demonstrated what the erasure of the distinction between self and other, or, with Carl Schmitt, friend and enemy, led to.[61] According to Rosenberg, the Indian Aryan conqueror started to "also worship in the Shudra the divine soul that he feels lives in himself." Racial degeneration ensued. Thus, "the idea of All-oneness [*Alleins*], put into practice, led to the catastrophe of a people [*Volk*]."[62] The twentieth century has been described as the "Nietzschean century," requiring a new philosophy of action and enmity,[63] and India's Vedanta marked its opposite. Sarkar operated in this arena of the "problem" of the Hindu religion when he redesignated "monism."

Sarkar stood for action, dynamism, and energism and against the orientalist identification of India with an otherworldly, self-sacrificing religion. Yet he also recognized that religion was what India's energism had historically turned to and where it had won many *digvijayas*, or "world conquests." Thus, Buddhism, whose nonviolence Sarkar recognized as India's historical deficiency, also stood for a history of power. It had given India one of its greatest emperors, Ashoka, and the conquest of a "Greater India" beyond its shores.[64] In his next move, however, Sarkar reinscribed the contents of Indian idealism itself by claiming that a new Vedanta had been consummated with the "ideas of 1905," which had caused a revolution in Indian life that broke with the Vedanta of orientalism. Nineteenth-century India had admittedly been "a land of vegetating animalcules" withdrawn to their quietist religion, and proud of it, too. But, he wrote,

> The Young India of the twentieth century does not pride itself in the imbecility forced into the intellectual consciousness of the last three generations by adverse circumstances. The philosophy of ***Vedânta*** is not now the gospel of dreamy inaction and invertebrate mysticism that it was alleged to be. The genuine idealism of the ***Upanishads***, ***Gîtâ***, ***Vedânta***, etc., viz., transcendentalism based on (and in and through) the positive, i.e., energistic romanticism, has now been inspiring the life and activity of Indians. The age of pseudo-Vedantism is gone; the spirit of the originators, creators, and pioneers of India's greatness has "come back." There has thus been initiated a ***real*** renaissance in modern India.[65]

This new Vedanta of pure energism had resurfaced in Ramakrishna (1836–1886) but even more in his great disciple, Swami Vivekananda.

Vivekananda, who is uniquely credited with propagating Hinduism to the world (and in some accounts Hindu nationalism) on a neo-Vedantic basis, was not a "monist" in Sarkar's view.[66] He was not a man of the Vedanta or even primarily a Hindu but rather a pluralist, an energiser, above all a creator, a "Carlyle of Young India," who "realise[d] and exploit[ed] the dynamic possibilities of a philosophy undreamt of by Shankarâchârya."[67] Indeed, Vivekananda had replaced the world-shunning pursuit of liberation (*moksha*) with "practical Vedanta." He had toned down the signification of *maya* as illusion or deception and turned it into something more palatable—the apparent contradictions that the "divine play" of life necessarily entailed.[68] To Sarkar, he was a man animated by and attuned to the forces of life, which functioned plurally, dialectically, even antagonistically. Here, Sarkar shared ground with the poet Rabindranath Tagore (1861–1941), who likewise accentuated the Vedantic *brahman-atman* relationship, traditionally designating the subject's deep unity with the Divine, to describe the play of immanent forces in the world.[69] However, while Tagore's neo-Vedantic emphasis on a unifying harmony underlying the play of the Divine minimized friction, Sarkar exaggerated it.[70] Tilting the balance between the diversity of phenomena and the underlying oneness of the *brahman,* Sarkar contended that unlike Marx's pure monism, Vivekananda's neo-Vedanta was plenary enough to let the forces of *dvaita,* dualism, play.[71] Vivekananda's "practical Vedanta" proved more than serviceable for Indian nationalism. In a historical sense, for Sarkar, it also marked a return to the "Monism in Pluralism" shared across Asia's ancient religions, which forged a "synthesis between the one and the many, the spirit and the matter, the transcendental and the positive, the infinite and the finite, the universal and the particular."[72] It was a return to action—to the world and to politics—after a long interregnum in which Hindus had stagnated, grown indifferent to questions of power, and allowed India to fall to foreign rule.

In Sarkar's view, monism alone, rather than force, could suppress freedom. Crucially, freedom to Sarkar meant both political freedom (sovereignty) and social freedom (development). Monism, being unipolar, was opposed to dualism, or what Sarkar referred to as *dvandva* ("pair"). Dualism was the force of "conflict" that animated life itself.[73] For Sarkar, this took the form of Hegelian dialectics. However, as its parts (thesis and antithesis) remained in a state of tension, the final synthesis was converted into an infinite provisional status that liberated the telos of history, the progress of freedom, from all limitation.[74] History issued into radical openness. Sarkar called this fundamental motor of life the "creative disequilibrium." It approximated the Vaishnavite idea of divine play (*lila*), which Subhas Bose, after a tortured rejection of

Shankara's Vedanta, which he had espoused in his youth, explained thus in his unfinished autobiography:

> The world is a manifestation of Spirit and just as Spirit is eternal so also is the world of creation. Creation does not and cannot end at any point of time. This view is similar to the Vaishnavic conception of Eternal Play (Nitya Leela). Creation is not the offspring of sin; nor is it the result of "avidya" or "ignorance" as the Shankarites would say.[75]

Looking back on his youth, Bose reflected that "Shankara's doctrine of Maya," which he then regarded as the "quintessence of Hindu philosophy," had been "like a thorn in my flesh."[76] But British acts of racism against Indians were hard to shrug off as an "illusion" and had shaken his belief in the doctrine. Then, he was expelled from Presidency College for agitating against a British professor accused of mistreating Indian students, and "Shankaracharya's Maya lay dead as a door nail."[77] Bose's contemporary Vinayak Savarkar, the noted atheist among Hindu nationalist leaders, in turn rejected Vedanta for rendering action and enmity unthinkable, writing that Vedanta philosophy "relaxed every fibre and nerve of my mind. . . . It destroyed my will and my power to act."[78] For Bose and his generation of Indian and, crucially though at first sight paradoxically, Hindu nationalists, only the denunciation of the doctrine of illusion and inaction defined as the essence of Hinduism allowed the recovery of the political: "what we badly need today is a double dose of the activist serum, *rajas*."[79]

For Bose, as for Sarkar, reality was "not static, but dynamic." Hegelian dialectics, which was forever "unfolding," approximated it better than Herbert Spencer's evolutionism or Henri Bergson's *élan vital* and certainly better than Shankara's denial of reality.[80] It followed from similar observations for Sarkar that "Leninism II," which was the antithesis of "Leninism I," was no final state, nor was any other.[81] There could be no static end before the progress of humanity, which tended toward what was good, or *sat*, only contingently on the basis of the foregoing problem.[82] From the viewpoint of this dialectic without final resolution, all "monistic" convictions were to be rejected as "cults" that were irreducible to human nature and life itself, let alone unworkable for pragmatism. Beyond orientalism, Sarkar, who complained of his Bengali compatriots that they "sw[ore] by Marx in everything from fried potato to futuristic paintings," fought Marxism—as political ideology and theory of history—as the main "monism" of his day.[83] Whatever else his sins, Hitler had combatted "monistic materialism" and "injected" a vital dose of energetic "spirituality" into Germany and the world, as had Johann Gottfried von Herder, Johann Wolfgang von Goethe, and Immanuel Kant before him.[84]

Though today lauded as a cosmopolitan, Sarkar was in fact exceptional for the intellectual rigor with which he sustained his partisanship with politics over idealism and with nationalism over internationalism. Insofar as fascism stands for the "reaction of the particular against the universal, the national against the international," it seemed to Sarkar a more attractive proposition than "millennial" utopias.[85] Understood in the quotidian sense of the term as a (positive) future expectation, of course, the futurist Sarkar was emphatically a utopian thinker. In this sense of the term, scholars following Reinhart Koselleck have credited modernity with an accelerated sense of utopianism.[86] But, for Sarkar, perpetual peace was unbelievable, unthinkable, and insufferable. His rejection of finality and confident embrace of energism ensured constant social evolution and national revitalization, such as the utopias of a peaceful "one world" and "one humanity" forestalled, though attracting others from his side of the colonial divide. Sarkar's rejection of Marxist monism and his defense of the national is the first step toward understanding his theory of fascism, to which we return at the end of the chapter.

M. N. Roy's Theory of Fascism

Though anti-Marxist himself, Sarkar counted the famous Indian communist M. N. Roy among his former students.[87] Roy had founded the Communist Party of India in 1920 and traveled the world in support of the Communist International before incurring Stalin's displeasure and being expelled from the Comintern in 1929. He had opposed Lenin's New Economic Policy, calling it "a retreat over the whole front," in which Sarkar (and much for the same reason) saw the salvation of Leninism that was Leninism No. II.[88] In 1939, Roy's steadfast refusal to join the Forward Bloc foiled Bose's plans for left-wing hegemony within the Congress and his replacement of Gandhi as its leader. Unlike Bose, whom he suspected of being a fascist sympathizer, Roy called a halt to the Indian nationalist struggle while Britain was at war with fascism.[89] To Roy, World War II presented a civil war between fascism and its enemies fought at a global scale and for the future of all humanity.[90] He did not share the belief that fascism was devoid of anything meriting the name of theory or political thought. Rather, fascism had a philosophy of its own, which he explored in his 1938 treatise, *Fascism: Its Philosophy, Professions and Practice.*[91] Fascism's aim, as expounded by Roy, was reactionary: preserving capitalist society from communist onslaughts and undoing the tradition of the French Revolution and liberalism. But above all, fascism in its Italian and German varieties was deeply continuous with Hindu philosophy.

Fascism proclaimed with the Italian philosopher Giovanni Gentile (1875–1944) that "Man is nothing." That was its first postulate. But fascism was a faith, wrote Roy, that allowed the one professing it to "vicariously drow[n] himself in the all-embracing being of the divinity only to resurrect as an instrument of the Almighty, his will and action free from all the laws of this world." Thus, fascism combined contempt for humanity with a "cult of all-mightiness" that allowed fascist man to become one with God.[92] Unlike for Sarkar, for Roy, the fascist was a Vedantist. The union of *atman* and *brahman* was achieved by becoming the Superman, an idea that was traceable from Nietzsche to Schopenhauer, who took it from "the divine philosophy of the *Gita,* according to which all powers (*Bibhutis*) on earth are powers of God." In other words, "the roots of the philosophy of Fascism" that currently rolled back centuries of human-affirming philosophy and emancipation from religious superstition in Europe led to India.[93]

But how had so "combative" a "creed" as Nietzsche's developed out of the "pessimism" of Schopenhauer?[94] The key was that like the Brahmin, the fascist lived in the Kaliyuga, the dark age, in which "the high ideal of pure spiritualism can not [*sic*] be realized." Their spiritual ideal of renunciation and release from this world thus unattainable, the Brahmin and the fascist were encouraged to lead a worldly life—as long as they did so with detachment.[95] Thus, Nietzsche had made European philosophy safe for capitalism, Roy claimed, in an argument similar to that of historian Brian Hatcher that nineteenth-century "bourgeois Vedantins" made India safe for capitalism by reorienting spiritual attainment to worldly success.[96] A cynical life affirmation and will to power had also been born: as long as one mastered one's will and remained unattached, one could indulge not only in the essential "crime" that, to the pessimistic worldview, is life but in any excesses of cruelty and oppression, without "polluting" one's "essential being."[97] Hitler himself said, "'Let it be written on our epitaph: We have been hard; we have been ruthless, but we have been good Germans.'"[98] The will to power that asserted its sovereignty on earth so brutally bore "a striking resemblance to the Indian spiritualism of the Vedanta school as well as the dualist systems which visualize the world as the *leela* of the Almighty," wrote Roy, smoothing over significant doctrinal differences.[99]

The will to power was met by the "human herd" over which it claimed "the right to rule and subjugate" with a doctrine of meek submission and self-sacrifice whose modern prophet was Gandhi, but its age-old buttress was the sovereign dispensation of caste.[100] Bhimrao Ramji Ambedkar (1891–1956), the Dalit leader and author of the Indian Constitution, had found the Nietzschean Superman come to life in the Indian Brahmin, from whose subjugation of the Shudras the Nazis "had a great deal to learn."[101] Roy expressed a similar intuition when he wrote that by preaching the acceptance of suffering as a virtue, "Gandhism as a philosophical tradition has led to Hitlerism."[102] Roy rejected, as ideological justification of exploitation and oppression, the theory of desireless action (*nishkama karma*) that Bal Gangadhar Tilak (1856–1920) had inscribed into Indian political life as the solution to the central conflict of the epic Bhagavad Gita: whether Arjuna should or should not kill the kinsmen he faces in battle.[103] Do your duty and never care for the results or your gain? Accept your lot in life? For Roy, the doctrine of desireless action and the school of Vedanta, which taught that abject material suffering was only an illusion (*maya*), was opium for the people.[104] "Spiritualism" now enslaved fascist Europe, as it had India since time immemorial, blinding it to the materialist explanation of its contradictions and forestalling the socialist revolution.

In the last instance, however, "while Schopenhauer was the grandsire of Fascism" and Nietzsche "its prophetic herald, the credit for formulating the fundamental principles of the philosophy of Fascism [went] to Bergson."[105] Henri Bergson (1859–1941) had carved out a place for mysticism outside the reach of the scientific, experiential paradigm of the day and reasserted the preeminence of the spiritual over the material. He had thus thrown European philosophy back into "the vicious cycle of dualism" that placed God above creation and supported monarchical absolutism as well as fascism, wrote Roy, who also rejected Vedantic monism. Moreover, according to Roy, Bergson had fathered fascism in a philosophical sense by "pervert[ing] Hegelian dialectics."[106] Georg Wilhelm Friedrich Hegel had not invented dialectics, which for Roy was an ancient philosophical position and a scientifically proven fact of life. Dialectics was, in essence, the natural "dynamic process of becoming" by which a new "factor" arose through the destruction of a prior factor, whose contradictions had inspired their own negation.[107] Roy stated, "Real synthesis, therefore, [wa]s not a compromise between the contradicting factors; that would mean not progress but reaction."[108] Rather than meeting halfway, in a synthesis, the antithesis annihilated the thesis. Thereby, the antithesis "lost its negative character" and became the "new positive."[109] That is what Hegel had meant when he called real synthesis "the negation of negation."[110]

Dialectics in the hands of historical materialists was a theory of revolution. Roy gave Bergson the credit for reinventing the antithesis for the anti-revolutionary bourgeoisie. He recognized earlier than Gilles Deleuze that Bergson's remarks on negation in his famous book, *Creative Evolution* (1907), which explains development over time, could have significant implications for Hegelian dialectics.[111] Negation, nonexistence, or "the nought," wrote Bergson, was misunderstood where it figured as "*less* than [. . .] something."[112] Instead, it was *more* than something, since it contained the identity of the "object 'existing,'" plus the mathematical command "not."[113] Negation consequently lacked the power of creating ideas, for "it ha[d] no other content" than the affirmation of the (non)existence of a given object.[114] Deleuze would later build on Bergson's insights into negation in his own concept of *difference* and "differentiation," which was "never negative but essentially positive and creative."[115] For Roy, as a consequence of the dismissal of the positive, constructive aspect of the antithesis, evolution according to Bergson degraded into an "endless chain of negations." The result was fascism, for which "there are no principles, no laws."[116] Bergson's splendid vista of the vital urge to life that attracted not only Bose but Sarkar in his reflections on the creative disequilibrium and that giant of energism, Vivekananda, was to Roy nothing but directionless change and sterile negation.[117] One could not prove the inevitable historical defeat of capitalism with Bergson. Nor, ultimately for Roy, could one understand, let alone combat, fascism in Europe and indeed India equipped only with Marxist materialism, which disregarded religion and the role of ideas in history.[118] Thus, Roy increasingly lost his "faith in the liberating significance of the Russian Revolution," and by the mid-1940s, he reinvented himself as a "Radical Humanist" committed to Enlightenment values and secular modernity, against the danger of Gandhi's anti-modernism and spiritualism plunging India into fascism.[119]

Subhas Chandra Bose and *Samyavada*

While German National Socialism and Italian Fascism memorialized their power capture as a victory over communism, and Soviet Communism reinvented itself through the creation of a "Popular Front" against fascism, to Bose, fascism and communism were compatible and productive models for a colonized country like India. Indeed, both Bose and Sarkar viewed fascism as a reaction to communism, yet neither viewed their relationship as irreconcilably hostile (in the sense of a "European civil war," Nolte's controversial phrase).[120] This flies in the face of the many alliances among anti-fascism, anticolonialism, and anti-racism observed across the colonial and racial divide.[121] Regarding Bose, the fundamental and never conclusively answered question is this: how could the self-declared socialist and "Leftist" Bose throw in his lot with fascism?[122] The following is an attempt to answer this question.

Unlike Sarkar the theoretician, Bose was a politician, and one of the highest caliber. A Bengali like Sarkar (though born ten years later, in 1897), Bose chose nationalism over a career in the Indian Civil Service as a young man, and, after getting his start in municipal politics in Calcutta under the tutelage of Chittaranjan Das (1870–1925), known as Deshbandhu, he rose to the highest positions within the Indian National Congress.[123] He was rounded up and imprisoned with other Congress leaders to stop civil disobedience in 1932, but, always of delicate health, he was set free by the British on the condition that he leave India to seek medical treatment in Europe. Bose set up base in Vienna, where he met his future wife—his Austrian secretary, Emilie Schenkl (1910–1996).[124] He also took advantage of his European exile by traveling throughout the continent to canvas support for India and make important European contacts. In Italy, he met Mussolini and was fascinated by, though he remained ambiguous to, the success of the National Fascist Party in creating a "new nation" in which no individual stood apart from the state.[125] But Nazi Germany, whose national reawakening came coupled with racial chauvinism, disappointed him.[126] Bose himself suffered racist abuse in Munich. He protested Hitler's anti-Indian utterances in *Mein Kampf* as well as the proposed racial laws, though characteristically only where they touched on Indians: "I do not demand that you give up your race theory, no matter how many scientific reasons we might offer against it. We only want it to be modified so that it wittingly or unwittingly, does not provoke any bad opinion about Indians." He did not mention the Jews.[127] Nor would he later, when he consigned them to a German domestic matter that, along with other ideological differences, would not prevent his forming a pact with the tripartite powers.[128]

Bose was elected Congress president upon his return to India in 1938 and again in 1939, but this time he resigned over a struggle with Gandhi for control of the Congress. Gandhi had nominated his own candidate, whose defeat he took as his own and as the defeat of the principles for which he stood. Bose, in his presidential address at the Tripuri Congress in March 1939, called for exploiting Britain's weakness in the face of looming war to offer it an ultimatum on Indian independence, rejecting which Indians should resume civil disobedience.[129] Gandhi was against this ultimatum because he "smell[ed]" too much "violence in the air" for him to trust the Indian people to carry on *satyagraha*. Congress as it stood "cannot deliver the goods, cannot offer civil disobedience worth the name."[130]

Yet Gandhi knew that Bose stood for a different program. Gandhi refused to cooperate with Bose's plans for a "composite" Congress Working Committee representing the "2 main parties or 'blocs'" within the Congress that Bose judged to be equally matched: his own "Leftist" bloc and the "Rightist" bloc represented by Gandhi.[131] But Gandhi did not want to blend proposals. He instead suggested that Bose draw up his own working committee and proposal and put it to a vote before the All India Congress Committee. If Bose's proposal lost, he should resign from the presidentship.[132] Shackled to Gandhi's vote of confidence in the Congress Working Committee by the Pant Resolution, Bose finally offered it to Gandhi to form in an act of desperation.[133] When Gandhi refused, Bose saw no option but to resign.[134] Soon afterward, in May 1939, he formed the Forward Bloc to consolidate the Left within the Congress and try to gain ascendency over it that way. As the "antithesis" to the Gandhian "thesis" of right-wing consolidation within the Congress, the Forward Bloc was, to Bose, the "product of historical and dialectical necessity."[135] But this project also failed.

Bose and Gandhi had never seen eye to eye. Out of the many antagonists the Mahatma has been paired with—recently, Savarkar and Ambedkar—Bose was the most sustained critic of Gandhian tactics for bringing about freedom (while others had objections about aims). Bose resented the way Gandhi had made himself the "virtual dictator" of the Congress but was willing to go along with his leadership as long as it yielded results.[136] The problem was that Gandhi's leadership since 1920 had failed to win India *swaraj* ("self-rule"). Bose echoed the words of his mentor, Chittaranjan Das: "The Mahatma opens a campaign in a brilliant fashion; he works it up with unerring skill; he moves from success to success till he reaches the zenith of his campaign—but after that he loses his nerve and begins to falter."[137] Again and again, according to Bose, the Mahatma bungled imperial negotiations because he tried to play two incompatible roles: "the role of a political leader and that of a world-teacher [. . .] who had come to preach a new faith—that of non-violence and world-peace."[138] Certainly, Bose's own commitment to nonviolence was only skin-deep. He put before the public as early as 1934 that in any country but India, Gandhi's "doctrine of non-violence would have led him to the cross or to the mental hospital."[139] In India, too, Gandhi had been able to erupt on the scene the way he did in 1920 only because of the double failure of constitutionalism and armed revolution.[140] But Gandhi had long since become a spent force. Once a historically necessary antithesis that had swung the Congress left and thus saved it from stagnation, he now represented "Rightism," while Bose represented the new "Leftism."[141]

"I do not know who you consider a Leftist and who a Rightist," observed the astute Jawaharlal Nehru in a letter to Bose over the Congress Working Committee crisis, except that Bose seemed to consider all Gandhi's opponents "Leftists." Yet it seemed to Nehru "that many of the so-called Leftists are more Right than the so-called Rightists."[142] He continued,

> The association of vague Leftist slogans with no clear Leftist ideology or principles has in recent years been much in evidence in Europe. It has led to Fascist development and a straying away of large sections of the public. [. . .] I did not at all fancy the direction in which apparently you wanted us to go.[143]

Nehru was right. Bose had a highly problematic conception of Leftism simply as an increase in radicality over yesterday's radicalism. Thus, yesterday's Left became today's Right, just as youth, which was to Bose an inherently revolutionary force, grew old. India needed a new leader—himself—not "the lone figure of the ex-revolutionary, ex-Leftist leader of India," Gandhi, whose revolutionary potential—his nonviolence—was exhausted by the late 1920s.[144] "May be [*sic*], it is the effect of age," he wrote.[145] Since nonviolence could not deliver the goods of independence, Gandhi now stood for the drift back into constitutionalism and compromise with Britain.[146] "Gandhiism has ceased to be revolutionary," wrote Bose in his famous "Kabul Thesis" en route to Nazi Germany in May 1941, as justification for actions yet to come.[147]

Bose was aware that his use of the word "Leftist" was idiosyncratic and required explanation. Propounding a two-phase theory of Indian revolution, he held that "in the present phase," Leftism was synonymous with the "uncompromising fight with Imperialism." "In the next phase of the movement, Leftism will be synonymous with Socialism." For Bose, the revolution was always on the Left, the generative side and the side of action. "It may be," he continued, "that in the ordeal that is ahead of us, some of those that are branded as Rightists today, will prove to be the genuine Leftists—Leftists in action, I mean."[148] The Indian Left had fractured at the outbreak of World War II. There were those—"pseudo-Leftists"—who, forgetting that it was an imperialist war, regarded Winston Churchill as "the greatest revolutionary going," just because he fought fascism.[149] Not shirking a fight with imperialism or with the "Frankenstein" of constitutionalism and talk of federation in the Indian Congress, that was the true test of Leftism, explained Bose in his "Kabul Thesis."[150] The issue with the Communist Party of India, he wrote in his additions to *The Indian Struggle since 1920* while on board the submarine that took him to Japan in 1943, was that "it talked too much about Socialism, which was after all a thing of the future."[151] A true Leftist, a true revolutionary in the colonies, was in the first instance a nationalist, according to Bose, who reportedly greeted Hitler in their single, much-anticipated meeting as "an old and experienced revolutionary" and asked his advice on how to conduct a national revolution.[152]

To Bose, World War II represented a "crisis" and a "grave emergency" that held the possibility of revolutionary rupture.[153] Irreducible to popular representations of him as a *realpolitiker* and Axis collaborator acting on the dictum of "my enemy's enemy is my friend,"[154] Bose fundamentally believed that the war represented an "event" in the sense of a rupture in time and an "opening" for radically new possibilities.[155] It enabled Indians to capitalize on the "explosive force" in the world previously represented by Soviet Russia but now by Fascist Italy and Nazi Germany.[156] World War II also presented a shortcut, as "even a child" should understand that Indian independence would come easier while Britain was handicapped by war. Indians had missed their chance in the previous world war, argued Bose, who had found empowerment through military training in that war.[157] He was not going to let that chance slip again.

Plainly though conspicuously unacknowledged, Bose's actions during World War II took inspiration from the Ghadr movement of (mainly US-based) Indian revolutionaries who received help from the Germans during World War I to oust British rule in India, dubbed the Hindu-German Conspiracy. It is no coincidence that Bose's competitor for the role of India's spokesman and for Indian POWs in Italian captivity with whom to man a Free India Battalion during World War II, Mohammad Iqbal Shedai (1888–1974), was an ex-*ghadri* (though a supporter of Pakistan).[158] The Ghadr itself referenced the Indian Rebellion, called the Sepoy Mutiny by the British, which was incredibly successfully reinterpreted as the first Indian War of Independence by Vinayak Savarkar and treated by Bose as such.[159] The rebellion posed the greatest challenge to the British empire in the nineteenth century. Had Indians not submitted to disarmament following the events of 1857, Bose believed the British would not have been able to hold India.[160] Given its significance and the obvious echo in his own military actions, Bose rarely cited the rebellion, preferring foreign examples of freedom struggles that had organized from abroad, like Lenin's famous sealed-train journey through Germany to make revolution in Russia.[161] Thus hiding in plain sight, Bose's actions between 1941 and 1945 connected to two previous high moments of imperial insurrection.

For Bose, Gandhi's limitation as a leader, his uncompromising nonviolence, was never greater than in this moment of rupture and possibility, whose stakes Bose explained thus at the All-India Anti-Compromise Conference, in Ramgarh, on March 19, 1940:

> The crisis that has overtaken us may be rare in Indian history, but it is nothing new in the history of the world. Such crises generally appear in periods of transition. In India we are now ringing down the curtain on an age that is passing away, while we are at the same time ushering in the dawn of a new era. The age of Imperialism is drawing to a close and the era of freedom, democracy and Socialism looms ahead of us. India, therefore, stands today at one of the crossroads of history. It is for us to share, if we so will, the heritage that awaits the world.[162]

A similar crisis was the October Revolution in Russia, when Lenin had denounced all compromise of Bolshevik ideals. Italy, too, had been "ripe for Socialism" in 1922, but the socialists had hesitated, and so, instead of an "Italian Lenin," Italy got a Mussolini. Because of this failure in socialist leadership, "Italian history took an altogether different turn and Italy ultimately went Fascist instead of going Socialist."[163] At the outbreak of war, India was likewise at a crossroads: between compromise with and fight against imperialism, between Right and Left. Which way would "she swing"? Lacking this fight with empire, Bose, never squeamish about violence, prognosticated that violence would turn inward and divide the country, as it had in Ireland: "A compromise with

Imperialism will mean that an anti-imperialist national struggle will soon be converted into a civil war among the people themselves."[164] Of course, this was exactly what happened. Violence that Bose incited against the foreigner in the end turned against the neighbor. Anticolonial war became civil war, fratricide, as pioneering work by Shruti Kapila shows.[165] In the 1940s, Bose stood increasingly alone in regarding India as locked in a "life-and-death struggle" with the British empire, the British as India's only enemy, and freedom from British rule as the only goal.[166] He remained a pure anticolonial nationalist in this sense, as unseduced by Hindutva as he was dismissive of the two-nation theory and the idea of a Pakistan for India's Muslims.

World War II, which Britain had unilaterally entered India into, was for Bose the appointed time for a final, concerted fight for Indian independence: "Gird up your loins and prepare for the impending struggle."[167] The Congress adopted a position of neutrality toward the war, but Bose called for civil disobedience. He was arrested on sedition charges in July 1940. After going on hunger strike, he was released from prison and put under house arrest at his family home at 38/2 Elgin Road, Calcutta. Early in the new year in 1941, Bose made his legendary "great escape," which involved him hoodwinking his own mother about his flight to deceive the British.[168] Sometime after midnight on January 17, 1941, Bose, bearded and disguised as a Muslim named Mohammad Ziauddin, had his young nephew Sisir Kumar Bose, later the editor of his uncle's collected works and letters, drive him out of the front gate of his home, right under the watchful eye of the police. Bose drove, rode, and trekked all the way to Afghanistan, arriving in Kabul on January 31, 1941. There, he marched into the German embassy and obtained permission to travel to Germany via Soviet Russia. Though some—Soviet-friendly—collaborators of his in Kabul and Berlin have since claimed that Bose initially was aiming to reach the Soviet Union, it is more likely that, as his biographer and great-nephew Sugata Bose suggests, Bose's destination was Germany all along, as Germany, not the Soviet Union, was at war with Britain and had Indian prisoners of war.[169] However, it is plausible that Bose may never have turned to Berlin had Germany then been at war with the Soviet Union.[170] He was reportedly devasted when news reached him of the German attack on the Soviet Union later that year.[171]

Now using the Italian alias Orlando Mazzotta, Bose arrived in Berlin on April 2, 1941, to beg Hitler to back an Indian government in exile and help invade India to oust British rule. He met with high Nazi officials and was reunited with Emilie Schenkl. Their only child, a daughter, Anita, was born in November 1942.

Bose was recognized as an asset—"in the Indian question the best horse in our stable," Joseph Goebbels (1897–1945) commented in his diary—and allowed to do propaganda work for the Germans, speaking to his Indian compatriots via radio broadcast.[172] All the while, the German public was kept abreast of Bose's endeavors for India and his denunciations of British rule, as confirmed by copious Nazi collections of newspaper clippings on Bose in German archives. Eventually, Bose was given command of a troop of British Indian POWs, who were given the choice between remaining POWs in German captivity or forming a Free India Legion (Indische Legion), poised not to fight for Britain in Europe and North Africa but against the British in India. But Hitler, still hoping for a settlement with Britain, was hesitant to give Bose and Indian independence his official backing. Hitler admired the British empire in India, which he viewed as a model for Germany's "living space" (*Lebensraum*) in the East, and Bose was deceiving himself when he thought Hitler was out to destroy it.[173] His stay in Germany laced with disappointment, Bose consequently jumped at the chance to transfer to Germany's ally, Japan, via a secret submarine passage.

Bose reached Tokyo in May 1943 and, with Japanese help, revived the Indian National Army (INA), which under him grew to approximately forty thousand troops composed of Indian POWs and Indian expatriate volunteers. The latter were an untapped resource that demonstrated the expansiveness of Bose's notion of the Indian "people." As the nation in miniature, the INA further included an all-female Rani of Jhansi Regiment, named after the warrior queen and heroine of 1857, in another nod across time. Bose claimed for himself the introduction of a third way into the Indian national struggle: the regularization of violence in a formal army, which overcame the failed methods of both individual revolutionary violence (bombs and assassinations) and nonviolence. He was apparently unaware, when building out the Free India Legion in Germany, of Mohan Singh's (1909–1989) creation of a first INA in Japanese-occupied Malaysia, which drew inspiration from Bose and cast him in the role of future leader.[174] In Japanese-occupied Singapore on October 21, 1943, Bose proclaimed a provisional government of India, which he called Azad Hind ("Free India"). Establishing a free Indian government had been one of his core, yet unfulfilled, demands in Germany, built on a long history of him urging Indians to "storm" the "citadels of power" by "set[ting] up parallel institutions" in British India.[175] In 1930, Bose had unsuccessfully moved an amendment as part of the Congress's historic *purna swaraj* ("full independence") resolution for a parallel government to be immediately established in India.[176] And again, at the outbreak of war in 1939, he demanded that a responsible provisional national government "should be set up at once."[177] For Bose, the way to sovereignty was to mimic and usurp it.

World War II allowed Bose to reframe British rule in India. Gandhi had insisted that "the English have not taken India; we have given it to them. They are not in India because of their strength, but because we keep them."[178] Bose disagreed. He used Europeans' own experience of occupation in World War II to make India's situation comprehensible to them as one of conquest and occupation. Rendering the conquest transparent, he framed India as occupied by the British and the Indian army as an "army of occupation."[179] With limited success seeking international recognition, he construed India in parallel with the European countries that had been overrun by the Germans and formed governments-in-exile in London, like de Gaulle's France Libre. In granting Azad Hind, Japan finally recognized Bose's desire for reframing and usurping British power in India—though this disqualified him in the eyes of many of his compatriots. However, after his failure and death, in mounting a case for the defense of the INA soldiers by "compar[ing] Bose's Government to the Governments of the Occupied European countries in the U.K. during the war, and the I.N.A. to de Gaulle's Free French," as the Indian viceroy Archibald Wavell (1883–1950) unsympathetically noted, the Congress would come around to his view.[180] Naturally, Bose himself acted as head both of the government and the army of Azad Hind.

Bose made his two expatriate armies a microcosm of Hindu-Muslim union, set against growing communal antagonism.[181] In this, he again mimicked the events of 1857 that had seen sepoys, Hindus and Muslims, take up arms "in defense of [each other's] religious prejudice."[182] Bose imagined the "front-fighters," who would be cleansed of communal feeling in shoulder-to-shoulder combat, as a "vanguard" for the nation: a trope to which the third chapter returns. Naively, he assumed that the vanguard of the army would thus figure out and "announce" the solution to the communal problem "to the whole country." Revolution itself would work a profound change on the Indian people, who, led by this vanguard, would consequently find it "easy" to solve questions like communalism "which to-day appear difficult to solve."[183] Bose, who rejected federation as much as Pakistan, was adamant that Hindu-Muslim compromise must not be a precondition for independence. Instead, communal feeling would wither away as a result of the new revolutionary national mentality. Bose was no anti-Muslim chauvinist. But beyond the merger into the stream of Indian nationalism in common violence and self-sacrifice, he had no offer to make to India's Muslims.

Though its fate was tied to Japanese military success, the Azad Hind government is, at least as far as Bose was concerned, wrongly branded a Japanese puppet government. Bose asserted his government's independence and again and again rejected the idea of Indian freedom coming as a gift of the Axis victors of the war. Instead, Indians must do the fighting—and the dying—themselves. Nehru misunderstood him on this point when he objected to Bose that it would be "psychologically" bad for Indians to be liberated by an outsider.[184] Bose naively believed that an invading force, if spearheaded by Indians, would be met in India by a popular uprising; the Indian army would mutiny, as it had in 1857. The Quit India movement, launched by Gandhi in August 1942, was appropriated by Bose as his own victory and served to reiterate his calls for total mobilization. Indians should transition to guerrilla warfare, with two aims: "to destroy Britain's war-production in India and to paralyse the British administration of India."[185] Indians should sabotage the British in India (the suggestion to cut down telegraph lines was another unacknowledged nod to the events of 1857) to the point of even sabotaging their food: Indian domestic workers in British service were to cook "bad food or to mix undesirable things with food and drink—so that living in India will be impossible for Englishmen."[186]

British power in India rested on force, so Bose would use force to unseat it. British power rested on the army, so he would steal it away from the British. To this end, Bose was liberal with the shedding of Indian blood. His INA speeches are full of the trope of "blood," which to Bose was the "price" of freedom.[187] Drawing deeply on the sacrificial idiom of Indian nationalism, he fixated on the arbitrary, though symbolic, number of one hundred thousand Indian troops that would have to be sacrificed for freedom—"if you can do that and I can do that"—as if passion and the readiness to sacrifice oneself alone could secure India's freedom.[188] Though undoubtedly brave, Bose was no military strategist. Sri Aurobindo Ghose (1872–1950), the revolutionary nationalist whom Bose admired turned yogi of Pondicherry, had written of him, "All this insistence upon action is absurd if one has not the light by which to act. [. . .] The advocates of action think that by human intellect and energy making an always new rush everything can be put right."[189] Bose's entire wartime project, in its mind-boggling audacity, was shot through with utopianism.

On December 29, 1943, the Japanese handed over the Andaman and Nicobar Islands to the Azad Hind government, allowing Bose to make good on his promise to stand on Indian soil before year's end.[190] Promising to march on Delhi (*Dilli chalo!* was Bose's slogan), the INA was deployed in Burma and Northeast India in a disastrous military miscalculation that decimated its troops. Then, on August 14, 1945, after the nuclear bombing of Hiroshima and Nagasaki, Japan's capitulation ended the war. Germany had already surrendered on May 7, 1945. Bose, still the head of the Azad Hind government, was flown to safety with the aim of reaching the Soviet Union, but his plane crashed, and he died of his injuries in Taipei, Taiwan, on August 18, 1945. Many did not want to believe he was dead (the British had pronounced him dead before, yet he had turned up triumphantly in Berlin). Some still believe he lives, like Elvis. The surviving INA leaders were court-martialed at Delhi's iconic Red Ford, bringing Nehru himself out of retirement as a lawyer in their defense. Nehru afterward described how little was known about the INA in India during the war. Knowledge of their activities only erupted with the INA trials, but then spread into even the remotest villages.[191] There have been several parliamentary inquiries into Bose's disappearance (there is no body, only ashes), and recently, the whole secret archive was declassified, digitized, and made available to the public to dispel the many conspiracy theories surrounding his death.[192] It is undeniably these events—from Bose's "great escape" to his sudden and mysterious disappearance four years later—that make him a folk hero in India, and especially his native Bengal, to this day. It is for his incarnation as a warrior prince who collaborated with fascism that Bose is still revered today.

In his 1935 book, *The Indian Struggle,* Bose infamously suggested a "synthesis between fascism and communism," which he called *samyavada.*[193] He retracted this statement in a well-known 1938 interview with the communist Rajani Dutt (the same who originated thinking about fascism as capitalism in decay), in which Bose explained that his thinking on the matter had since evolved. What he had meant to say was that India wanted both national freedom and a socialist foundation. As Indian communism had appeared to him "anti-national" and fascism only an "aggressive form of nationalism" (before it had embarked on imperialism), their "synthesis" had suggested itself to him, though admittedly the expression "was not a happy one."[194] Though this excuses him in the opinion of some scholars, Bose's public retraction was likely a concession to his position as Congress president at the time and an attempt not to alienate the left wing of Congress, let alone his interviewer.[195] Bose certainly knew his position was unpopular. It was not the first time that he had suggested a synthesis of fascism and communism, however. In his address to the Calcutta Corporation shortly after becoming mayor of Calcutta, in September 1930, Bose called the vision of his great mentor and political idol, Chittaranjan Das, for their city "a synthesis of what Modern Europe would call Socialism and Fascism." To be sure, Bose here deployed a fuzzy and conceptually anemic definition of fascism, which stood in for "efficiency and discipline," while socialism stood for an orientation toward the poor.[196] After all, "fascism" figured as a metaphor in India and beyond.

But Bose subsequently reiterated his thesis of a synthesis between fascism and communism in Tokyo in 1944.[197] He, as an Axis collaborator professing socialist commitments, also lived this synthesis. We must therefore conclude that his conviction held. Bose's original remarks in *The Indian Struggle* had aimed at Nehru, who had unequivocally stated in December 1933 that "fundamentally the choice before the world today is one between some form of Communism and some form of Fascism, and I am all for the former, that is Communism. [. . .] There is no middle road between Communism and Fascism." But Bose radically dissented, writing that

> unless we are at the end of the process of evolution or unless we deny evolution altogether, there is no reason to hold that our choice is restricted to two alternatives. Whether one believes in the Hegelian or in the Bergsonian or any other theory of evolution—in no case need we think that creation is at an end. Considering everything, one is inclined to hold that the next phase in world-history will produce a synthesis between Communism and Fascism. And will it be any surprise if that synthesis is produced in India?[198]

Bose's synthesis of the unsynthesizable has been interpreted as an anticolonial move, and his "rather mechanistic" Hegelianism was noted.[199] Certainly, Bose rejected the dumb application in India of whatever new "-ism" came from the West. In clashes with Indian communists in his trade union work in the early 1930s, Bose elaborated that the rejection of Western blueprints emphatically included Moscow-style communism. As the idiosyncrasy of Russian conditions had produced Bolshevism, so India would develop its own brand of socialism.[200] Envisioning such an act of creative adaptation as a "synthesis" suggested itself to Bose from the first. Yet Bose's was no general defense of the particular against the universal. He studied world history for lessons on how national freedom was won and progress secured, as did Sarkar. England, he found, had made the greatest contribution to global political thought in the seventeenth century (constitutionalism and democracy); in the eighteenth century, it was France ("liberty, equality and fraternity"); in the nineteenth century, it was Germany (Marxism); and in the beginning of the twentieth century, it was Russia (proletarian revolution).[201] Yet both men shared the belief that European blueprints had exhausted themselves as the twentieth century progressed. They believed in India's potential for universality, which would produce a new political "object lesson to the world."[202] Bose's ambition for India's synthesis of fascism and communism was of this order.

Communism would not be adopted in India, Bose wrote in his 1935 book, because "Communism today has no sympathy with Nationalism in any form and the Indian movement is a Nationalist movement—a movement for the national liberation of the Indian people."[203] Fascism, in turn, was the antithesis of communism, demanding by the law of progress a new synthesis: a synthesis of nationalism and socialism such as German National Socialism had failed to achieve.[204] In "My Personal Testament," written before he went on hunger strike in jail in 1940, Bose reaffirmed his conviction that neither communism nor Nazism, nor indeed Gandhism, could be the last word on political philosophy or the final political system: "The next stage of world-evolution demands a new Philosophy, a new ethical conception and a new economic & political system."[205] Though Bose cleaved to Hegel's account of evolution, he now decided that Hegelian dialectics was too "monotonous." It did not account for "something explosive, accidental, inexplicable in actual evolution," which was better captured by Bergson's *élan vital*.[206] In a speech on the day observed by Congress as Independence Day, January 26, in 1943, and printed in *Āzād Hind*, the English-German bilingual monthly newspaper he had founded in Berlin, Bose explained that to Indians, "life is one long unending wave. It is God manifesting himself in the infinite variety of creation. It is 'Leela'—an eternal play of forces."[207] Setting aside the shock value of Bose's suggestion of a "synthesis" of fascism and communism, and without trivializing it either, it becomes apparent that such a "synthesis" was just what Bose would expect given his conception of reality as continuously and dialectically evolving. In other words, Bose's *samyavada* was precisely the consequence of the "perversion" of Hegelian dialectics, forged under the unwholesome influence of Hindu philosophy, that Roy feared.

One could argue, as did a contributor to Bose's *Āzād Hind*, that Lenin had already forged, if not a synthesis, then a "common front" of nationalism and socialism in the fight against imperialism.[208] Yet, according to Bose, "Lenin's thesis [. . .] seem[ed] to have been given the go-by since the failure of the last Chinese Revolution." In China, nationalists and communists had split and were embroiled in a bloody civil war by 1927; Moscow-trained Chinese revolutionaries had defected over to the nationalists. At the Sixth International in 1928, it was therefore decided to depart from Lenin's colonial thesis. The new thesis was that imperialism only survived *because* of bourgeois nationalism. Left nationalists like Bose were consequently criticized and thrown in with the likes of Gandhi by the Communist Party of India.[209] In "The Fundamental Problems of India," his famous address to students and faculty at Tokyo University in November 1944 in which he repeated his aim of a "synthesis" of nationalism and socialism, Bose insisted that Chinese mistakes must not be repeated in India. A split between nationalists and communists, as in China between the Kuomintang and the Chinese Communist Party, was both unnecessary and avoidable in his country, where the nationalist movement championed the cause of the poor and toiling masses: "because we have their interests at heart, there is no *raison d'être* for a separate party like the Communist Party."[210]

"The Indian movement will have two phases," Bose had declared in "The Anti-Imperialist Struggle and Samyavada," his presidential address read in absentia at the Third Indian Political Conference in June 1933 in London, in which he first mentioned *samyavada*. The first phase would be a "'national' fight against Great Britain," the second the achievement of "perfect equality (social, economic and political)."[211] Crucially, the two steps of the revolution would take place under the same leadership because it would represent Indian labor from the beginning. Thus, Bose emancipated India from fealty to the historical sequence of events as they had occurred in Russia, where October had succeeded February. In an interview with Romain Rolland in Geneva in 1935, Bose abandoned any semblance of a two-step process, opining that "the fight for political freedom will have to be conducted simultaneously with the fight for socio-economic revolution."[212] The impetus is clear: merging the nationalist with the socialist revolution. Again and again, Bose reiterated that the party that had captured the British "fortress" in India and won independence should stay in power to bring about the country's reconstruction on socialist lines. Thus, the chaos of the French Revolution would be avoided, along with Chinese conditions.[213] In ridding himself of the historical necessity of "two successive revolutions—a national-democratic and a socialist revolution," Bose, of course, ran afoul of Leninism.[214] But this was just the point: India's contribution to global political grammar would be the fusion of the national with the socialist revolution—against Russian blueprints.

Samyavada, in Bose's bare-boned description of it in 1933, was about equality and the "party of dedicated men and women" prepared to sacrifice their all to achieve it—the Samyavadi Sangh.[215] "'Samya,'" he explained in a letter of 1934 to his Czech Jewish friend Kitty Kurti living precariously in Berlin, "means 'equality.' 'Samyavadi' means 'one who believes in equality.' 'Sangha' means 'Society' or 'Association.'" *Samyavada*—literally "the doctrine of equality" but in Bose's diction "the doctrine of synthesis or equality"—was the Indian name for the ideal now brandished in Europe as socialism but in India going back millennia to the time of the Buddha.[216] However, though pegged to equality, another concept in the tripartite slogan of the French Revolution encapsulates the full meaning of *samyavada* as synthesis: freedom. "The Samyavadi Sangh will stand for all round freedom for the Indian people—that is for social, economic and political freedom."[217] It was the party envisioned by Bose to bring about the twofold revolution in India, which combined national freedom with social freedom (or equality).

This entailed a discussion of means: first, Bose proposed a "radical" alternative to Gandhism.[218] As well as moving from passive resistance to active fighting, Bose subscribed to vanguardism, by which a numerically small but radical and organized following of "'Freedom-intoxicated' missionaries"—full-timers, ready to undergo "maximum sacrifice and suffering"—could achieve what an unwieldy, unarmed mass movement could not.[219] A vanguard was, by definition, undemocratic, as was its identification with the army—unless one regarded the army as the true nation—though the hope was that it would incite a general uprising. Indeed, all of Bose's actions following the "great escape," when he arrogated for himself the right to act for and represent India on the international stage to the point of declaring Indian independence and war on Britain and the United States, were formally undemocratic. Bose came as close as any of the larger-than-life men of the mid-century catastrophe to realizing the ideal of the Superman (an oft-mentioned figure in Bose's writings) and the latent divinity of man expressed in bending the world to their idea.

"We want not reform—but radical transformation. The whole of our life—both individual and collective—has to be recreated," he stated. Creation required a prior act of destruction, a revaluation of values.[220] Therefore, as elaborated by Bose in 1944 as both supreme commander of the INA and sole leader of the Provisional Government of India—two roles outside democratic sanction—the socialist reconstruction of India could not work within "a so-called democratic system."[221] Bose, who had always rejected "democracy in the mid-Victorian sense of the word," concluded that "we must have a political system—a State—of an authoritarian character."[222] Yet authoritarianism was not what defined *samyavada* because authoritarianism—the rejection of parliamentary democracy and belief in party rule and the supremacy of the state—as discussed approvingly by Bose, was already the common basis of fascism and communism.[223] "Totalitarianism" was the word Bose's contemporaries invented for it. What Bose suggested as a synthesis was, in his eyes, novel and not already shared by fascism and communism as a common denominator. National Socialism had been able to create "national unity and solidarity," but it had not abolished capitalism. Communism had replaced the capitalist system with a planned economy, but it had no appreciation for "the value of national sentiment."[224] What *samyavada* in action would look like remained underarticulated, just as Bose's earlier vision of a "Socialist Republic" in India centered on equality and nondiscrimination had remained conspicuously vague.[225] Crucially, however, India's break from Russian blueprints in the interest of nationalism entailed the rejection of class war.[226] Bose's *samyavada* presented the synthesis of nationalism and socialism that was sought between 1917 and 1945.

Though undemocratic, *samyavada* stood firmly on popular foundations, since both the vanguard that won India freedom and the state it subsequently founded would work "as the servant of the masses."[227] Elaborating on the idea of the leader in the context of fascism and communism and his own struggles for leadership of the Congress, in 1939, Bose noted the "mystical" aspect that underpinned it. As a leader, "one should try to merge one's individual consciousness in mass-consciousness." Being tuned in to the "mass-mind," this process of induction and transfer between the leader and the masses that Bose likened to the merging of the self in the stream of Bergson's *élan vital,* had to be met by the scientific study of historical events for patterns and of current global affairs for possibilities and the moment to pounce. Only this combination of the intuitive and the objective allowed leaders to discharge their tremendous responsibility. Leaders made history. Bose's example was Russia, whose history would have been different had Lenin embarked on a different course of action in 1917.[228] Bose, not lacking self-esteem though suffering from a feeling of utter insignificance as a child growing up in a big family, saw himself in the same category as Lenin.[229] In his religious practice, Bose would vary between two exercises: "self-assertion," by which he sought to overcome his weaknesses, and "self-surrender," by which he visualized the flow of divine energy and himself as "an instrument of the Divine."[230] Bose was alive to his own historical mission and perhaps imbued with a feeling of being chosen when he made his "great escape" and so flamboyantly acted on India's behalf.

That Bose's view of leaders has little to do with liberal representation may come as a surprise. But under colonialism, it was by necessity the turnout of crowds and the ability to incite mass action, rather than elections, that made national leaders. (Gandhi stands as a case in point.) But Bose went further in his lone-wolf actions between 1941 and 1945 when he acted on what Benoy Sarkar called the objective "world forces" (*vishwashakti*)—global political, social, and cultural currents through which India could achieve freedom—and sidestepped what Bose up until then considered the only legitimate forum for Indian political aspiration, the Congress.[231] His calling as India's leader resulted from his ability to read these objective forces in history, as he had already correctly predicted the war (though deceiving himself about Britain's inevitable defeat). Objective qualification and being on the right side of history outstripped even popularity in making a leader. Bose worked hard to gain recognition as India's best spokesman abroad because he was expatriate and thus free. He expected India's people to joyously rise to greet his invading army, but he refused to channel the general will into a liberal-democratic mold. In this, he exemplifies the fate of many postcolonial states. Bose cannot be reclaimed as a democrat, as he believed that parliamentary democracy's revolutionary potential and ability to shape a better future was spent. Nevertheless, his posthumous legend and the postwar appropriation of the INA by the Indian masses and those Congress heavyweights who quarreled with him in life, Gandhi and Nehru, proves that he was not wrong about his claim to speak and act for India.[232] Today, Bose enjoys the status of an Indian Founding Father. In his thinking popular sovereignty outside of democracy, as well as seeking a nationalist solution for the social question, Bose again shared ground with Benoy Sarkar.

The Epoch of "Demo-Despotocracy"

Bose sought the synthesis of fascism (understood as ultranationalism) and socialism. But for Benoy Sarkar, that synthesis had already occurred: in Germany, in

Italy, and in Russia. For Sarkar, Soviet Communism, Italian Fascism, and Nazism were essentially similar attempts to fuse the national with the socialist idea. Thus, he insisted that Mussolini, though combating communism, had "not come as the enemy of the masses." Likewise, the "socialism of national-socialism [*sic*] [wa]s a genuine commodity." However, the beneficiary of this socialism was the nation and most emphatically not humanity. In this sense, like Lenin's late offering, Italian Fascism and Nazism were Leninisms No. II.[233] Not only that, but in their departure from classic democracy as well as despotism, the three regimes represented something new in the history of political ideas. All three were "neo-democracies" or "neo-despotisms," what Sarkar called "demo-despotocracies."

For Sarkar, the project of the French Revolution, the political emancipation of the people, had not reached its pinnacle in nineteenth-century liberalism. Characteristically making his argument through deep intertextuality, in 1936, Sarkar summarized the Nazi jurist and theorist of the state Otto Koellreutter (1883–1972) to convince Indian audiences that National Socialism deepened this project as it democratized participation in the state.[234] Koellreutter argued that only the *tiers état,* the victorious bourgeoisie, had occupied the space of the nation and declared itself sovereign with the French Revolution as "an embodiment of Rousseau's volonté générale."[235] This class maintained its antagonistic orientation toward other classes; the exclusion of the *Volk,* or "the people" proper, had continued.[236] Only with the Great War had the moral political universe of the middle class (*Bürgertum*) collapsed and a search for new state forms on the Right and the Left begun, Koellreutter concluded.[237] According to François Furet, liberal and Marxist accounts of fascism fail to account for the fact that, with the Great War, European politics "had escaped from the bourgeoisie."[238] The masses had burst onto the scene, eulogized as a classless fraternity of the trenches and a crucible of the nation by Nazis and Italian Fascists, a point to which I return in Chapter 3. In this sense, although National Socialism declared war on the "ideas of 1789," Sarkar was right when he viewed fascism as a deepening of the revolutionary idea of "the people" as sovereign.

Sarkar had an unmatched talent for reading and an effortless command of the German language. Few Indians had consumed more of the intellectual output of National Socialism or were more seduced by it. And so, Sarkar walked Indians through Koellreutter's position in the totalitarianism debate raging among Nazi-era jurists. Rejecting the characterization of the Nazi state as either "totalitarian" or "total," which another camp of Nazi jurists espoused,

Koellreutter redeemed the Nazi state as a *Rechtsstaat* (a state operating under the rule of law).[239] This was a state in which popular sovereignty and the "leader principle" (*Führerprinzip*) were commensurate, as the existence of a *völkisch* totality permitted their "total representation" (*Gesamtrepresentation*). As Sarkar paraphrased Koellreutter, the "totality of the people" under National Socialism was not to be conflated with the "totality of the state" in Italian Fascism, which based its authority on force.[240] Instead, *völkisch* equalization within the Nazi state bound "conflicting life forces to a healthy union."[241] Individual liberty need not guard against the overreach of sovereign power given the deep democratic channeling in the *Führer* state.

Sarkar confirmed the founding myth of the *völkisch* state, and he did so with great continuity. In 1933, he insisted on the constitutional rise and popular foundations of the Hitler state, which he celebrated as the first "'real' revolution in Germany."[242] The article in which he did so, titled "The Hitler-State," was proscribed in Bengal in 1946.[243] In 1939, Sarkar unambiguously put liberal democracy—Neville Chamberlain's license to ignore the British Parliament—in direct contrast with nonliberal popular sovereignty—the "vox populi" that spoke through Hitler—and sided with the latter, writing that "in spite of his traditional British ideology Chamberlain is a despotocrat. In spite of his Nazi philosophy Hitler is a democrat."[244] Observing the mismatch between the theory of liberal democracy and its reality, Sarkar co-opted the British commentator and Labour politician G. T. Garratt's (1888–1942) stance that Britain under Chamberlain was "something essentially plutocratic" and that French democracy amounted to the "despotocracy of the 'two hundred families.'"[245] Mussolini used the word "plutodemocracy," drawing on Vilfredo Pareto (1848–1923), to defame the monied parliamentary systems of England and France.[246] Garratt had witnessed how, in the atmosphere of the Great War, "the old European Liberal tradition just faded away," and he asked: what if "the two ideas of liberty and democracy [we]re not always inseparable"?[247] Their separation was exactly what intrigued Sarkar.

Sarkar's logically consistent assumption of a democratic habit as operative in all peoples at all times and in all places disarticulated the "historic compromise," as it has been called, between liberalism (or republicanism) and democracy (or popular sovereignty), theorized by Schmitt as a "crisis" of parliamentary democracy.[248] What of it if Germany, Italy, and Russia were "proud to call themselves the destroyers of democracy?"[249] They were better representatives of democracy than the liberal democracies that safeguarded monied interests, intercepted the general will, and kept the people at a remove from politics.[250] Sarkar's thought has been read as a failure to "think" terror and totalitarianism and scrutinized for its implications for postcolonial liberalism.[251] However, liberalism was not what was at stake for Sarkar: Emma Hunter, a historian of twentieth-century Africa, is right to critique "methodological liberalism."[252] If Sarkar drew material from critics who responded to a sense of crisis from within the liberal tradition and harbored anxiety about the future of democracy and civilization, this only demonstrates that Sarkar did not share their predicament.[253] If Sarkar did not jump to the defense of liberty and democracy against "totalitarian" onslaughts, this was because, for him, liberal democracy's emancipatory potential was already exhausted. Instead, he was interested in tracing the interwar emergence of postliberal states and new types of nondemocratic yet popular sovereignty.

In 1928, Sarkar anticipated his conception of demo-despotocracy in such a way that it would later allow him to accept the popular foundations of National Socialism. This was in a long discussion of the Dutch juridical thinker Hugo Krabbe (1857–1936), whom Sarkar considered the best exponent of the "state of law" thesis.[254] Krabbe resolved the question over which had primacy, sovereignty or law, by declaring the "sovereignty of law." Sarkar, by contrast, fundamentally viewed this antithesis as a false one, which he (mis)represented as the polarity between absolutism (sovereignty) and democracy (law). He argued,

> Instead of concluding that law is encroaching upon or replacing sovereignty, as Krabbe does, one should rather argue that the demos is getting used or rehabilitated to the enjoyment of both sovereignty *as well as* law-making. It is the people, the people's control, the people's interests and voices in legislation, the sovereignty of the people that, in spite of Krabbe's terminology, constitute the chief element in the "modern idea" of the state as explained by himself. Thus . . . what is really established by him is "popular sovereignty" or democracy as the fundamental feature of "modern states."[255]

Sarkar's unfaithful treatment of Krabbe contrasted with those who criticized legal thinkers like Krabbe for eliminating the concept of sovereignty—among them, Carl Schmitt.[256] For Sarkar, the modern rapprochement between sovereignty and the law pointed to the popular moorings of sovereignty. Modernity, then, did not spell the end of personal sovereignty, whose "content" had merely undergone change. In Sarkar's own time, sovereignty and law, which were of equal antiquity, had been transferred to the "masses."[257] It follows that Sarkar did not celebrate "statism" but, on the contrary, something rather like "populism."[258] Sarkar celebrated the epoch-making arrival of sovereignty with the people in his own time, even or especially in the new dictatorships.

In 1928, Sarkar published a chronicle of the intellectual and political developments that made the modern age, with a pivot in the interwar years: *The Political Philosophies since 1905*. The publication of a successor volume published in three book-length parts between 1941 and 1942 intimated that, for him, another pivot of global socio-intellectual "ideals" had come with German Nazism, Italian Fascism, and Soviet Communism.[259] Sarkar was convinced that what had happened in these three countries could not be captured by traditional projections of democracy versus tyranny but rather that they constituted new types of illiberal though not undemocratic polities. Bolstering the University of Calcutta's prestigious *Calcutta Review* with a "Miscellany" section that veiled private opinion behind snippets of "facts," for example, he hosted a discussion on the nature of the Italian Fascist state in the sole form of quotes from Mussolini's *The Doctrine of Fascism* (1932).[260] With Sarkar as ventriloquist (and the philosopher Giovanni Gentile as coauthor), Il Duce enlightened Indian readers that unlike the "negativism" of the "'lazy'" liberal state defined by the absence of coercion, the "positive" totalitarian state organized the nation in all aspects of its existence.[261] This was no revival of older forms of absolutism and tyranny, for "Mussolini is a futurist" who knew that "'history does not travel backwards. . . . A party holding 'totalitarian' rule over a nation is a new departure in history. There are no points of reference nor of comparison.'"[262] Presenting report, not opinion, Sarkar put himself beyond reproach.

Mussolini further elaborated in *The Doctrine of Fascism* (though in a section not quoted by Sarkar) that Italian Fascism did not "desire to drive the world back to positions occupied prior to 1789."[263] The Italian Fascist state was "not the tyrannical State of a medieval lordling. It ha[d] nothing in common with the despotic State existing prior to 1789."[264] Fascism's curious claim to inherit the French Revolution served to reject liberalism, which had arisen as a reaction against absolutism and, Mussolini claimed, "exhausted its historical function" when the state had come under the control of the people.[265] In 1939, Sarkar wrote of the three Leninisms No. II that before them, "there was no such interpenetration of dictator or despot and the masses in any previous epoch of absolutism, rule without parliament, 'new monarchy,' enlightened despotism, etc., in East or West."[266] Two years later, he added that the new "dictators are not equivalent to the Pharaohs of ancient Egypt, the Emperors of Rome, the *Padshahs* of Asia or the enlightened despots of Europe." Instead, their "alphabet" was "derived from the language of 'government of the people, for the people and by the people.' It is the people—the folk, the *Volksgemeinschaft*."[267]

Throughout World War II, Sarkar chronicled and celebrated the advent of the new "political philosophies of to-day," in the face of which "the conventional categories of the eighteenth century, the French Revolution, nineteenth century liberalism, nay, of pre-war politics will have to be abandoned."[268] He thus anticipated what liberal thinkers like Hannah Arendt and Jacob Talmon (both Jewish émigrés) would come to argue at mid-century: that totalitarianism may be not the antithesis of democracy at all but its extension.[269] Talmon indicted Jean-Jacques Rousseau and the Enlightenment for birthing the fatal urge to freedom that culminated in totalitarianism. The problem with fascism and communism as so construed was therefore less the top-down, nonconsensual workings of terror but democracy's tragic flaw: its foundation in popular support. Sarkar's great flaw is that he refused to be appalled by the limitlessness of the idea of the sovereign "people." Posterity does not take kindly to it.

Indicating "the people's side"—"the demos, the *vox populi,* general will, democracy"—for Sarkar, Jean-Jacques Rousseau stood at one end of the polarity of sovereignty; on the far side and marking a relationship of force or a pure state stood Thomas Hobbes's *Leviathan*.[270] Between them spanned the world of modern politics as Sarkar saw it. "Demo-Despotocracy and Freedom" was Sarkar's mature pronouncement on the nature of the state, notably published in the *Calcutta Review* in 1939. The Leviathan, as Sarkar here elaborated, was built on the purity of force and fear of punishment, corresponding to the principle of *danda* (punishment, lit. "stick") in ancient Hindu statecraft.[271] For Sarkar, a state of "hundred-per-cent. Leviathanic *Gestalt* [form]" was a state without popular consent.[272] However, as the state was a form of human association, and no human association could exist without a contract, which, for Sarkar, implied consent, consent to even the most "Leviathanic" of states was "inevitable."[273] He contended that the British Indian state was of this order—an unpopular argument and a curious move for a twentieth-century Indian nationalist. By signing their powers over to the British, the Indian princes—and by their lack of rebellion, their subjects, the Indian people—had submitted to the "exigencies" of the international order, where, as Sarkar had long maintained, a state of nature prevailed.[274] That their consent had come via surrender to superior force did not invalidate the contract. This was pure Hobbes, who magicked factual (de facto) into legitimate (de jure) sovereignty.[275] Yet in referencing Hobbes, Sarkar turned to the same political thinker whom he had accused of teaching a "doctrine of non-resistance" in 1918, when he himself had required a political theory of revolution.[276] Then mobilizing for Indian independence in America, Sarkar had argued that British rule in India rested on force and was maintained through the disarmament of Indians.[277] At the time, he had welcomed a show of violence, which would force the international community to recognize that Indians had been at "war" with Britain since the eruption of Swadeshi in 1905.[278] In Sarkar's later thought, the relationship between Indian subjects and British rule lost the purity of force. In the end, conquest itself became implicated in his remodeling of consent.

In the view of one modern scholar, who argues that Hobbes actually agrees with Rousseau on the general will, Sarkar might have had enough in Hobbes.[279] But because Sarkar required dualism in everything, while Hobbes taken alone appeared "monistic," Sarkar formulated the modern convergence of authoritarianism and populism as a hybrid.[280] He brought this down to the seemingly nonsensical formula "Every polity = democracy^x × despotocracy^y."[281] It was a peculiar mixture of Hobbes, who holds that conquest does not make the covenant but rather it is the conquered's choice to submit to the conqueror, and Rousseau, who stood in for ideas of social contract and popular sovereignty, that allowed Sarkar to sublate conquest into consent.[282] Where the liberal tradition regards the state as inherently coercive and bases its authority on convention, Sarkar countered with the purity of Rousseau's social contract, which grounds the authority of the state in subjective consciousness. A real conflict between individual freedom and subjugation under the state was unthinkable in this view, as consent was assured by the general will. The state's violent foundation could therefore not repress *swaraj,* liberty, and democracy because it did not exist in an antagonistic relation to them. The inner world of sovereignty, as complex as the human psyche, gave the lie to the absolute dichotomy between the "eternal" and "ubiquitous" facts of Hobbes and Rousseau: despotism and democracy.[283] Hobbes's primacy of power and Rousseau's primacy of the people fused into the political reality of "demo-despotocracy." In other words, for Sarkar, all modern states were founded on popular sovereignty—even, and in some ways especially, those called "authoritarian," "despotic," and "totalitarian" by contemporaries.[284]

In the last instance, there could be no fundamental difference between modern democracy and dictatorship because Sarkar believed the dictum that the state must serve the welfare of the people to have become a global standard with Otto von Bismarck's social legislation (1883–1889), devised to weaken the attraction of socialism.[285] For Sarkar, the prospect of a healthy, educated, improved, and socially equalized nation trumped classical liberal freedoms. Therefore, though dislike of compulsion was universal in man, exigency dictated it. Similarly to Bose, Sarkar hoisted his political flag in 1941:

> Nothing short of a totalitarian socialism such as has been found effective in Eur-America and Japan should have to be placed before the Indian public administration as the goal of social mobility to be attained within the shortest possible time.[286]

Instead of joining the liberals' lament, the irrepressible Sarkar declared a new era of social demo-despotocracy: "In spite of all *digvijayas* (world conquests) of dictatorships the expansion of democracy is the most outstanding fact of societal organizations and theories throughout the world."[287] The nation, in Sarkar's view, had captured the state by orienting it toward its own principle: the furtherance of its life.[288] For Sarkar, the modern raison d'état was the social.

Benoy Sarkar was India's greatest theorist of fascism, and he diagnosed the proximity of fascism and communism as nondemocratic forms of popular sovereignty and vehicles of national emancipation. He formulated one of the most comprehensive theories of sovereignty and raison d'état in the twentieth century, provocatively arguing on this basis that the Nazi state marks the ultimate development of modern doctrines of popular sovereignty and statecraft. With rhetorical flourish and inimitable wordplays, Sarkar's insights into fascism are as original as they are politically uncomfortable. And yet, when taken seriously as theory, they can shed new light on aspects of Nazi thought, as demonstrated in Chapter 3. Subhas Bose was the Indian practitioner of fascism, and he lived the proximity between fascism and communism. Both men viewed fascism as an affirmation of national sovereignty against socialist internationalism, from which neither expected India's liberation. They did not subscribe to ideas of race, to which we now turn. Instead, it was Hindutva's founding theorist, Vinayak Savarkar, who made the idea of race serviceable for India, though it was maximally divergent from the Nazi conception of "race."

CHAPTER TWO

SAVARKAR'S MISCEGENOUS RACE

On July 26, 1940, Prem Datta Sharma, a branch postmaster in Jammu Province, brought the matrimonial eccentricities of a "certain friend" before Vinayak Savarkar, then president of the Akhil Bharat Hindu Mahasabha (All-India Hindu Great Assembly), for his counsel. Sharma's friend belonged to "a respectable Brahman family" but wished to marry a Muslim girl. The girl was of age, "ha[d] no objection and [was] willing to be converted in the way our Hindu Dharma allows or permits." But therein lay the problem. "Kindly," the man asked, would Savarkar "say if our Dharma allows such marriages?"[1] Dropping the "certain friend" as an alias straight away, Savarkar's office advised that Sharma "immediately" marry the Muslim girl, for "he [Savarkar] thinks that marrying with other girls from other religions and getting them converted into Hindu religion is not a sin but a bounden duty of every Hindu youth." Other religions did so freely. They increased their numbers while the Hindus "have lost and are loosing [*sic*] their population strength day by day." Should Sharma find it "impossible" to celebrate his marriage at home (alluding to family and community opposition), the couple should go to Amritsar or Bombay, where the Hindu reformist Arya Samaj or the local Hindu Sabha would "willingly" assist them. "Anyhow you will not loose this opportunity in marrying the Moslem girl and getting her converted into our Hindu religion." Remarkably, Savarkar inserted a handwritten and, given his usually clear and attractive handwriting, urgently scribbled note into the typewritten letter. It was full of unbridled first-person emotion. "The Hindu," it charged, "had been silly enough to [. . .] loose their girls to the Moslem fold over [*illegible*] arguing their religion but to add a girl to Hindudom was a sin! Think of a man who allows [*illegible*] work him as a meriticious act but to earn is a sin! We must give up [this] absurdity!"[2]

The following themes emerge: intercommunal marriage and conversion (*shuddhi*) into the Hindu fold were Hindu duties. Savarkar strikingly and at every juncture asked "the Hindus" to remodel themselves after his enemy, with whom he intensely identified: the Muslim man. Muslims, his reasoning went, were successful: they would trump Hindus because they did not put miscegenation beyond the pale of sin. Moreover, women were at the crux of Savarkar's project, which was based on consanguinity. Intermarriage (consensual where possible, forced if need be) was the primary means for Savarkar to consolidate and increase the Hindus. His Hindutva was consequently at war with orthodox Hinduism. This is a puzzling intellectual inventory to be taken of the chief theorist of Hindutva and the main antagonizer of India's Muslims, but it strikes at the heart of "Veer" Savarkar's thought.

As the author of *Essentials of Hindutva,* the leader of the Hindu nationalist movement before independence, and a co-accused in the murder of Gandhi, Savarkar needs no introduction.[3] Indeed, he is currently being canonized as the most controversial of India's Founding Fathers. Savarkar was famous even before he wrote *Hindutva.* Born to a Brahmin family near Nasik, Maharashtra, in 1883, Savarkar was attracted to revolutionary nationalism from boyhood. He founded a secret revolutionary society in 1900 and later made a name for himself as a student radical in London, where he had come to study for the bar in 1906.[4] Savarkar was enamored of Tilak's brand of sacrificial nationalism.[5] In London, he was drawn to the history of the Italian Risorgimento with its Catholic idioms of martyrdom and duty, the contemporary Irish independence movement, and Russian terrorism.[6] His activism for Indian independence, headquartered at Shyamji Krishnavarma's (1857–1930) famous India House, and his implication in yet another political assassination in which he did not pull the trigger earned Savarkar transportation for life to the Andamans in 1910.[7] On the ship, he attempted a spectacular escape at Marseilles. He jumped overboard and swam ashore to claim asylum. Savarkar was recaptured, but his adventure became a case in international law and made him an international celebrity. So Savarkar was already famous as a freedom fighter when, thirteen years later and by now repatriated to India though under house arrest and banned from politics, he published *Essentials of Hindutva* (better known by its title from 1928 onward as *Hindutva: Who Is a Hindu?*). It was immediately recognized as the pioneering theoretical foundation of Hindu nationalism. The foundation of the Hindu nationalist volunteer and paramilitary organization RSS in 1925 was inspired by it, and *Hindutva*'s author was catapulted to the highest office of president of the Hindu nationalist party, the Hindu Mahasabha, immediately upon his release from all legal restraints in 1937.

In the year of Indian independence in 1947, the British anarchist turned humanist Guy Aldred (1886–1963), Savarkar's "comrade" from his London years, likened Savarkar's breakthrough in *Essentials of Hindutva* to overcoming the religious determination of "the Jew." He wrote, "The word Jew is not distinct from Christianity but from Gentile. And the word Hindu has a parallel meaning to Gentile not to Christian."[8] He had a point. In *Essentials of Hindutva*, Savarkar fixed and asserted "the Hindu" as an identity. He did not do so through conventional definition, for the problem was that "the Hindu" was both over- and underdetermined. Prior attempts at definition (of which there were many) had failed to cohere the Hindus' religious (as adherents of Hinduism, but what was Hinduism?), ethnographic (as inhabitants of the land below the Indus), and legal dimensions (as subjects of Hindu law).[9] Instead, Savarkar *named*.[10] He defined "the Hindu" as one who possesses Hindutva (lit. "Hinduness") and "Hindutva" as what the Hindu possesses—a circular argument, brilliant in its simplicity.[11] In other words, rather than defining *what* the Hindu is, Savarkar asserted *that* the Hindu is. The name—Hindutva—designated a pure lack of meaning that had the corresponding ability to incarnate the fullness of incoherent meanings attached to the name "Hindu."[12]

Savarkar's immediately recognized achievement lay in emancipating the Hindu from the notoriously undefinable Hinduism, which was a religion characterized by its failure to resemble a "proper" religion with a sacred book, a finite pantheon, central beliefs, shared rites, and identifiable adherents. So Savarkar rejected that "Hinduism" should define the Hindu. Instead, "Hinduism" should designate all that a Hindu may practice and believe or be jettisoned as a concept: "Hinduism means the 'ism' of the Hindus," no more.[13] In *Essentials of Hindutva*, Savarkar managed to constitute the Hindu as a plausible political subject for the first time by making "the Hindu" and "his" essence, Hindutva, absolute.

Savarkar's fixing of Hindu identity was in many ways set against the other defining political question of the time: the question of Indian Muslim political identity. Muslims, as countless scholars have remarked, straddle an ambiguous position between inclusion and exclusion in *Essentials of Hindutva*.[14] They are included as indigenous converts, having what Savarkar calls their "fatherland," *pitribhu*, in India. But they are excluded by India's jealous requirement of being one's only *punyabhu*, or "holyland"; Muslims, according to Savarkar, have their holy sites in Palestine, Mecca, and Medina.[15] Most scholars, and even some of Savarkar's contemporaries, have explained this ambiguous belonging by a reversal of Savarkar's position on the Muslim question from inclusion to exclusion in the fourteen years that elapsed between *The Indian War of Independence of 1857*, Savarkar's youthful work of his London years that is a story of Hindu-Muslim cooperation against the common British enemy, and the publication of *Essentials of Hindutva*.[16] But this is misleading insofar as Savarkar never contemplated Hindu-Muslim unity in a Nehruvian or Gandhian frame.

For Savarkar, both at the time of writing *The Indian War of Independence* and restated throughout his career, the prerequisite for Hindu-Muslim unity in 1857 was the rebirth of Hindu sovereignty and the prior destruction of Muslim sovereignty in India.[17] The Mughals' defeat at the hands of the Hindu Marathas in the eighteenth century was key here. Note that Savarkar used the pseudonym "An Indian Nationalist" in 1909 but substituted it for "A Maratha" in *Essentials of Hindutva*, whose publication he promptly followed up with a history of the Maratha empire, *Hindu-Pad-Padashahi*.[18] This certainly seems to underscore Vinayak Chaturvedi's recent suggestion that "Hindutva *is* history," and a violent one.[19] For Shruti Kapila, it is the name and history of a war.[20] Through the Maratha episode, Hindu-Muslim relations had been set right and Hindu ownership of "Hindusthan" (as Savarkar called it) reasserted—crucially, as a direct dyadic confrontation between Muslim and Hindu power before the British and not triangulated by them.[21] Hindu victory had made Hindu-Muslim alliance possible in the uprising against the British in 1857, in Savarkar's 1909 account. The following decade and a half had revealed to Savarkar that the Indian Muslim potentiality for sovereignty was not dead. Separate electorates for Muslims, the Moplah Rebellion, and, more than anything, the Khilafat movement and pan-Islamism convinced him of this. In Janaki Bakhle's words, Savarkar "never really got over it [the Khilafat]."[22] Subsequently, for Savarkar, only once Muslim power was defeated and Muslims had sacrificed their separate ambition could Hindus "join hands" with them as the "brothers by blood" he had always known them to be.[23]

"The Hindu" so boldly asserted by Savarkar as master of the house was, in reality, far from it. Colonial governmentality and, above all, the census had turned Indians into a majority (the Hindus) and a minority (the Muslims), ensuring that this idea, rather than liberalism's individuals or democracy's "the people," defined the political imagination in India.[24] But the ostensible majority struggled to keep the margins from breaking away—the Sikhs, the

Dalits (then called Untouchables), the Adivasis (tribals), and the millions following popular, syncretic religions.[25] At a fundamental level, Hindus were only ever a theoretical majority as long as they were riddled by caste. Muslims, in turn, might constitute a minority at the all-India level but found themselves in the majority in some regions.[26] Crucially, the superior power of Hindus over Muslims in India was tied to their population strength, and this could flip, fueling a numbers game and fears over relative demographic decline among Hindus.[27] Savarkar responded by pulling the Hindu into an integral union that mimicked and replaced the "nation" of Indian nationalism, capable of not only consolidating the Hindus but—and this is my point—imbibing Muslims, too.[28]

Savarkar forged Hindus into a national race from sexual and reproductive unions across caste and religion. This was socially transgressive in India and would have been considered "miscegenation" by the race ideologists of the time. The issue, for Hindutva's architect, was not that Muslims were a foreign race that polluted Hindu blood, nor was his aim to exclude the Muslim "other." Nevertheless, Savarkar's project was emphatically about race, as most recently explored by Vinayak Chaturvedi.[29] Aryanism, purity, and eugenics, however, had nothing to do with it; the template of Nazi racism applied by many scholars to Hindu nationalism is seductive but misleading, as are ubiquitous conflations of race with color.[30] Instead of purity or pedigree, Hindutva's "race-ism" was about kinship and biological relation. Savarkar projected "the Hindu" as a future consummation, to be achieved through social and biological amalgamation. The Muslim, this chapter seeks of demonstrate, signposted its frontier rather than its border.

Savarkar's miscegenous politics contrasted sharply with Gandhi's known anxiety about racial and religious miscegenation and the "lust" that founded them. This anxiety was especially evident in the African context but also in Gandhi's private life.[31] Writing to advise his son Manilal against marrying a Muslim girl, Fatima—and in a typical maneuver seeking his son's consent to what was essentially a paternal dictate—Gandhi declared interreligious marriages to be against *dharma* (religious duty), whether they were accompanied by conversion or not. The girl's conversion (the boy's was not considered) would concede faith to lust. For Gandhi, uniting two religions in one household (and bed) was like "'putting two swords in one sheath,'" exposing each partner to the risk of losing their religion.[32] But Savarkar, unlike the Mahatma, could not allow communities to run parallel like railway tracks.

Savarkar championed intermarriage to glue together the Hindu race. Not social or metaphorical but *reproductive* intermixing was his solution—not only to caste but to the "Muslim problem." India's Muslims originally sprang from the Hindu race; mixing with them was, for Savarkar, the means to reclaim and erase them. Hindu racism, it is usually understood, must mean casteism.[33] This chapter offers a fundamental critique of this view. Savarkar's thought pushes us to consider caste thinking outside of a binary of good and bad and complicates the meaning of "race" in the global fascist moment. Hindutva's genocidal logic functioned through life rather than only death, as conventionally argued.[34] The metabolism of conversion, marriage, and reproduction would break down a particular kind of life, the Muslim woman, and reassemble her as a Hindu. This reproductive conquest mirrored, reversed, and avenged Islam's historical conquest of India.

The Miscegenous Origins of the Hindu "Race"

The Hindus, wrote Savarkar in *Essentials of Hindutva,* were "not only a rashtra [nation] but also a jati," meaning "a common blood," a "race."[35] He could draw on nineteenth-century conceptions of the manufactured, self-willing nature of national races, which combined "acquired" and "inherited" aspects of race.[36] Savarkar had assimilated orientalism and the classics of evolutionary and race theory—Charles Darwin, Herbert Spencer, Thomas Henry Huxley, John Tyndall, and Ernst Heinrich Haeckel.[37] He was also conversant with newer research into "heredity and race," which showed him a way to offset the lasting ill effects of criminal transportation when in Cellular Jail in the Andamans.[38] Criminal transportation had then appeared to him as a form of enforced celibacy bringing reproductive loss to the motherland. He countered it by harnessing the erotic and reproductive capacities of Hindu ex-convicts, convinced that the procreation of Hindu criminals, and their intermarriage with Indigenous women in the Andamans, posed no congenital risks.[39] Savarkar took his overwhelming focus on kinship and reproduction from nineteenth-century anthropology. He particularly shared anthropology's paradoxical approach to reproduction through the lens of paternity, which overwrote heredity in the female line but ultimately reaffirmed women as reproductive "biocapital."[40] His keen understanding of the crucial importance of women to a consanguine political order ultimately motivated his grotesque violence toward them. Savarkar secured "the Hindu" through reproduction somewhere between biology and metaphor. His thought, in a nontrivial sense, anticipates the genetic turn of the second half of the twentieth century, with its diffusion of racial purity into natural variation within national populations. But ultimately, Savarkar's was a fictional project of kinship. The consolidated "Hindu" was a future consummation, established through Hindu *sangathan* (organization), *shuddhi* ("purification," or (re)conversion to Hinduism), and miscegenation.[41]

For Savarkar, the Hindus were a race not because they were uniform in phenotype or origin but because they were all related. What connected them as a race was all-around miscegenation, as the racists would call it, or "intermarriage" in India. But how could *all* Hindus be biologically related given their division into castes? The answer Savarkar offered in *Essentials of Hindutva* was that the caste system was not what it was made out to be. Colonial anthropologists and orientalists agreed that caste reflected a racial divide stemming from the ancient conquest by (White) Aryans of (dark) Indigenous Dravidians. Yet for Indian nationalists, there were definite drawbacks to simply restating the kind of Aryanism according to which Aryan invaders became Brahmins to preserve their race from miscegenation in India.[42] For one thing, the supposed foreign extraction of the bringers of civilization humiliated Indians' national pride, contemporaneously with Savarkar eliciting a number of repatriations of the Aryans to an original Indian homeland, among them the second RSS *saranghchalak*, or leader, M. S. Golwalkar.[43] Moreover, as much as the Aryan invasion theory extended an offer of Brahmin hegemony and kinship with the White colonizer, it also fanned anti-Brahmin struggles.[44] In Maharashtra and Tamil Nadu, where lower-caste movements had been particularly strong since the nineteenth century, the Aryan conquest theory was ingeniously upended and Shudras and Dalits identified as India's original and rightful inhabitants, who were subjugated by foreign invaders and their Brahmin descendants.[45]

But Savarkar could afford to uphold the Aryan invasion theory because, for him, the Aryan conquest did not impart the race that mattered. He transferred that agency to Hindusthan. Locked into the concentric circles of the Sapta Sindhu, the seven rivers of the Indus River delta, the Aryan newcomers had been welded into a nation and taken on the name and identity of Sindhu/Hindu.[46] But the name "Hindu" itself hailed from a "time so immemorial" that it pushed even further back, before the Rig Veda and the Avesta found at the "twilight of History," to a time so remote that "even mythology fails to penetrate to—trace it to its source."[47] Hindus and Hindusthan were pushed into an antiquity bordering on autogenesis as Hindusthan thickened into a subcontinental empire through amalgamation rather than displacement.

Hindus and Hindusthan grew as they pushed the frontier of miscegenation to the shores of the Indian Ocean, welding the Hindu race from Aryan-Dravidian fusion. Hindu making, in this sense, was a reproductive conquest reminiscent of settler-colonization.

Hindusthan functioned as an imperial space, which forged race by transforming all who lived within it into blood relations. The mechanism by which it did so was caste, which Savarkar conceptualized away from endogamy (marriage within *jati* subcastes) to the assumption of general exogamy across castes. For colonial anthropology, as we have seen, caste indexed racial division, which had prevented Indians from fusing into a nation and thus disqualified Indian nationhood.[48] For Savarkar, by contrast, caste was fusion itself. Restating the Brahmanic theory of the origin of *jatis* from (il)licit unions across the four divisions of *varna* (lit. "color") and the fifth division of outcastes, Savarkar came to a radical conclusion. Rather than division or degeneration, the proliferation of castes gave "testimony to a common flow of blood from a Brahman to a Chandal."[49] In other words, Savarkar turned the multiplication of subcastes into a historical index of biological relation. Different castes were not different races. Instead, the totality of the caste system constituted a single, if heterogeneous, race (also, *jati*). The caste system, for Savarkar, thus gained the cohesion of what I call a "reproductive network," as ubiquitous exogamy (despite Brahmanic injunctions) produced a common bond of blood.[50] I use this term deliberately rather than familiar ones like "sexual economy" because the latter connotes contractual exchange whereas the "reproductive network" gains cohesion through myriad sexual connectivities. "Sexual attraction," for Savarkar, had assured the triumph of "nature" over religious prohibition, causing blood to flow to foreign blood with such force that there really was "but a single race—the Human race."[51] Arguing "nature" enabled Savarkar to defend the Hindus against disqualification as a "race" on account of the many foreign incursions into their "blood," an accusation that Savarkar returned to all nations, especially the conquest-ridden British. And like the British, whom he, with a sly stab at their sensitive point in history, asked whether "they care[d] to change the name of their land or their nation and call it Normandy instead of England," he founded his national myth of origin on general admixture after the conquest.[52] Yet Savarkar did not throw the baby out with the bathwater: he acknowledged mixture across all humankind, but not to deconstruct "the Hindu." Instead, he argued that from the crucible of ancient race mixing, the Hindu had risen as an alloy so deeply bonded that its only equal in a world of lesser-fused mongrel nations was the Jewish race.[53] Miscegenation (intermarriage) had established genetic union.

In 1945, the African American scholar Oliver Cromwell Cox (1901–1974) perceptively teased out the implications arising from a caste-based conception of national race. Drawing on the colonial anthropology of India's castes and tribes, Cox argued that caste distinction was not the same as racial distinction: "The world view of the caste is turned in-ward, and its force is centripetal; that of Negroes is turned outward, and its force is centrifugal."[54] Mixed-race unions in America consequently blended the racial divide, according to Cox eventually leading to the complete disappearance of "Negroes." In India, however, female hypergamy (*anuloma* marriage) only produced more castes without breaking the caste system itself.[55] No fusion took place; difference merely proliferated.

In the proliferation of castes, where Cox saw proliferating separation, Savarkar saw mixture *deepening*. His crucial maneuver was to counter the dominant theory deriving the caste system from the Aryan conquerors' self-imposed endogamy in India with his own theory of caste as a centripetal force of incorporation, which forced exogamy onto all within Hindusthan. For Savarkar, the anthropological record of Sanskrit scripture exposed Brahmanic injunctions against intercaste marriage as legal fiction. Savarkar had awoken early to a reevaluation of the biology of caste that was new in scholarship in the first half of the twentieth century. Orientalist philology and physical and social anthropology were by no means disambiguated but habitually converged on the Sanskrit record when *Essentials of Hindutva* appeared. And theorizations of caste made on this basis were beginning to show the breakdown of caste endogamy, from the Aryan conquest onward.[56] Away from Brahmanic idealization, ethnography revealed the complex interplay of exogamous and endogamous rules that structured lived marriage custom.[57] It was in Savarkar's own Maharashtra that examples of a "vernacular sociology" refuting the purity of castes and alleging their inextricable mixture had emerged at the close of the nineteenth century.[58] Finally, in Calcutta, coming out of the Zoological and Anthropological Survey of India, the assumption of caste purity would eventually give way to the discovery of a ubiquitous, graded mixture between castes. The raw material was Herbert Risley's (1851–1911) anthropometric data on the castes and tribes of Bengal.[59] Risley's research had reframed race in India as a graded mixture that diminished in purity along an "ethnic frontier" left by the Aryan invasion.[60] But under the survey's first director, Nelson Annandale (1876–1924), and its statistician, the famed mathematician (and

Brahmo Samaji) P. C. Mahalanobis (1893–1972), caste mixture transmuted into a statistically measurable variable. The Mahalanobis distance, or D^2, of 1936, which measures the degree of semblance between castes (as standard deviations from the mean) along geographical and social parameters (i.e., caste status), crowns the survey's decade-long engagement with caste and race mixture in India.[61] In this sense, Indian science not only kept step with but advanced modern population genetics, which developed from the "Modern Synthesis" of Darwin's theory of evolution and Mendel's laws of inheritance in the 1920s and 1930s.[62]

While eugenics still dominated discussion in India's leading anthropological journal, *Man in India,* Savarkar anticipated the new, statistical concept of "race" that would convert race and caste in India from anthropological ideal types into statistically related variables.[63] The conviction that caste meant endogamous, race-making isolation would prove recalcitrant in Indian science well past independence.[64] Nevertheless, for those (few) prepared to do so, caste could be increasingly viewed as adaptive and even miscegenous, to the point that finally, in 1940, Benoy Sarkar would invite "investigations with the naked eye" to see that all around was and had always been *varna-sankara* ("fusion of colours"), or caste mixture, making racial kin of the social high and low.[65] Savarkar founded his national myth of origin on general admixture.[66] Mixing the conqueror with the conquered, the Aryan with the Dravidian, Brahmin with Dalit, he created his "pan-Hindu" by blunting the lower-caste critique of caste.

It should not have taken Vikram Sampath's panegyric to remind the larger public that Savarkar was anticaste and vehemently opposed to untouchability.[67] He preached against casteism and publicly interdined with Dalits. Savarkar is misunderstood when he is treated as an orthodox Brahmin invested in the preservation of Brahmin hierarchy and purity, rather than as the revolutionary and deliberate defiler of Brahmanic mores that he really was. But the new danger today is that Savarkar's anti-untouchability activism should be used to exonerate him. Caste was identified as the major impediment to Hindu consolidation, forged against perceived Muslim unity by an earlier generation of Hindu nationalists. But Savarkar was more radical than his forerunners. When the Hindu Mahasabha's conservative founder, Madan Mohan Malaviya (1861–1946), appealed for the removal of untouchability in his 1923 presidential address, "of course he did not force the high class Hindus to eat with them or to inter marry [*sic*]."[68] Not so Savarkar, who prided himself on having led an "'Anti-caste Society' movement" since 1924 in a letter sent to a regional Mahasabha functionary in 1943 written explicitly in his personal capacity as the leader of this movement, rather than in his "official capacity as President of the Hindu Mahasabha which takes neither side in such matters."[69] His correspondent, a Brahmin, had previously intercepted Savarkar at a railway station and asked his blessing for his son's marriage to a girl from the Scheduled Castes. Their marriage was not a matter of love but of principle, wrote the proud father, whose twenty-three-year-old son had fully consented to the marriage, for "he is more your devotee than me."[70] Savarkar had given his blessing, and the father had been encouraged to write to him. In his reply, Savarkar recommended "intercaste marriages" as "most helpful to consolidate the Hindu race and inculcate the Pan-Hindu spirit throughout Hindudom."[71] For Savarkar, caste was the womb and frontier of the pan-Hindu.

Savarkar aligned his position on caste with that of B. R. Ambedkar, Gandhi's famous adversary on the issue of the annihilation of caste. In a note congratulating Ambedkar on his birthday on April 14, 1942, Savarkar praised the Dalit leader's "Herculean efforts" in raising the Depressed Classes. But he dismissed Ambedkar's "occasional anti-Hindu utterances and attitude." Predicting that caste would be inevitably "swept away within a couple of decades," Savarkar imagined a future in which only the "Pan-Hindu cause" prevailed.[72] Savarkar was serious about the removal of untouchability. But, representing the stickiness of the Hindu fold that Ambedkar had come to resent, he derailed and appropriated the Dalit movement for his own cause of Hindu making.

Savarkar almost uniquely viewed the solution to caste in sex and reproduction, rather than in the social digestion of prejudice.[73] This distinguishes him from other (predominantly upper-caste) Hindu reformers and nationalists. Marriage was a key social alliance, and sex was central to ritual purity or pollution; as such, Savarkar deliberately stabbed at sanctity. Hindutva required the destruction of (lived) Hinduism, which Savarkar defined by its obsession with purity. To this end, as Vikram Visana has recently demonstrated, Savarkar embraced "shamelessness" as an attack on Brahmanic injunctions against pollution, especially of bodily functions. Hindu political community, Visana argues, was forged through such transgression.[74] Naturally, Savarkar alienated orthodox Hindus. His sizable incoming correspondence, which is kept at the Nehru Memorial Museum and Library in New Delhi, forms an archive of the resistance to his pan-Hindu idea from across its constituents: Jains, Arya Samajis, Buddhists, Sikhs, and others whom Savarkar petitioned to register, for example, as "Jain Hindu" in the census to bulk up Hindu numbers.[75] But the main opposition to Hindutva came from "sanatanist" or orthodox Hindus, who opposed Savarkar's abolition of caste. In the words of the general secretary of the appropriately named All India Varnashrama Swarajya Sangh (*varnashrama* designating the fourfold caste order), "Mr Savarkar usually gives out that our agreement is 95 p.c. and disagreement is only 5 p.c. This percentage is fixed by giving Vaidic Dharma & Culture very small Value."[76]

The Female-Specific Mode of Absorption

It is no coincidence that for Savarkar, at the time of writing *Essentials of Hindutva,* the only non-Indians who had managed to transform themselves into Hindus were women. Sister Nivedita, born in Ireland as Margaret Noble (1867–1911) and inspired by Swami Vivekananda himself to dedicate her life to India, was a Hindu celibate (*brahmacharini*). So was the British-born Theosophist Annie Besant (1847–1933), who had separated from her husband and lost custody of her children (ironically, over her promotion of contraception).[77] For Savarkar, they were the "exception" to the "rule" of Hindutva's consanguine foundations.[78] Savarkar could accept these White women as Hindus because they were celibates without family ties who had come to India as new brides entering the Hindu joint family. No foreign man or couple could convert to Hinduism as a closed-off reproductive unit. Hindudom could, however, accept and be replenished by progeny naturalized into it by a Hindu father. They would be racial Hindus and their status, unlike Nivedita's, hereditary. A Hindu husband made up for the lack of Hindu racial patrimony in the female convert, for "the sacrament of marriage with a Hindu which really fuses and is universally admitted to do so, two beings into one" made a woman's race.[79]

Savarkar's later showcase of a non-Indian Hindu was Savitri Devi (1905–1982) of Calcutta, the "distinguished, learned, patriotic Hindu sister" whom he invited to the 1941 Tilak celebration in Pune, all expenses covered.[80] Born in France as Maximiani Portas, Devi's desire for intimacy with the "Aryan" earned her a PhD in philosophy. It brought her to adopt first Greece and then, from 1932 onward, India as her "second motherland"—"my motherland," as she wrote in a crossed-out Freudian slip in a letter to Savarkar dated December 1, 1944.[81] Devi believed India to have preserved the original Aryan civilization that would be rebuilt in Nazi Germany by the *avatar* of Rama and Krishna and savior of the race, Adolf Hitler.[82] This peculiar brand of Nazi esotericism owed much to Asit Krishna Mukherji, who became her husband—for ideological comradeship, not for love, as she insisted.[83] Rhapsodizing about Savarkar's recent reception of a blood transfusion in the same letter, Devi confessed that she "env[ied]" the "noble young man who gladly gave his blood to prevent the Hindu Nation from losing such a valuable soldier as you."[84] The mingling of Devi's blood with Savarkar's own would have made for a metaphorical supplement to the comingling of blood through marriage. It is entirely in line with Savarkar's ideology to have accepted this defilement by non-Brahmin blood.

We are thus dealing with two distinct forms of incorporation into the Hindu body politic in the female mode: one is compacted by marriage, based on heterosexual sex and, at least potentially, fertility. This form is applicable on a large scale. The other is the "exception" of a single female individual, upon whom infertility is imposed. Both are simultaneously metaphorical, legal, and highly somatic events constituting what I purposefully call an "adoption." Adoption voided existing patriarchal power. Traditionally, and codified as "legitimate" marriage into Anglo-Hindu law, the bride, upon taking the seventh step (*saptapadi*) around the sacred fire in the Brahmanic marriage ceremony, fuses with her husband's body and is absorbed into his lineage (*gotra*).[85] As a form of adoption, marriage stripped a woman of her native kin and appropriated her for a different set, as was not possible for men. So did slavery, which was feminized in India.[86] I will return to this point. While the social contract was dissoluble, Hindus were compounded through kinship bonds and gendered adoptions that totally committed their sexed bodies and reproductive futures.

The powerful metaphor of "adoption" into the Hindu race draws on the historical practice of adoption in precolonial India, which became legalized in Anglo-Hindu personal law with the Guardians and Wards Act of 1890. British perceptions of succession law had narrowed Roman understandings of agnatic succession (of children and dependents united under the power of a common *paterfamilias* and traceable through the male line) to where *agnatio* arose from *cognatio* (natural blood relation) and not from adoption, as was possible for the Romans. Thus, the British were able to annex Indian kingdoms by the doctrine of lapse. Countering this in *The Indian War of Independence of 1857*, Savarkar recognized the succession of two adopted sons to the titles of their nonbiological fathers, which the British did not: Nana Sahib's succession to Bhaji Rao II, the last peshwa of the Maratha empire, and Appa Sahib's succession to the throne of the last nominal emperor of the Maratha empire, Pratap Singh Bhosle, raja of Satara.[87] There is still more offense to British conceptions of agnatic kinship (and also upper-caste sense of propriety) in Savarkar, to whom the epic Mahabharata revealed that even the mythic king Pandu himself resorted to *niyoga,* a practice by which an impotent or deceased husband may receive a legitimate child by having another man—or, in this case, a god—father a child with his wife.[88] It follows that Pandu's sons, the Pandavas, heroes of the epic, were bastards when viewed through another lens. Of Chandragupta, the founder of the Maurya empire (reigned ca. 321–297 BCE), Savarkar could write after the catastrophe of India's Partition, when this emperor assumed to him the significance of a first Hindu emperor, that he was the bastard son of a concubine to the detestable last Nanda emperor of Magadha. Savarkar rejected all later fables that Chandragupta's mother was the emperor's wife or that she was the legitimate wife of a fellow clansman and in no way connected to any emperor.[89] He asked, "Was Chandragupta a concubine's son? Was he not a Kshatriya? What matters though!"[90] Her name was "Mura (Mayura)," and her son, who was "proud of his maternal extraction," was the founder of the Mauryan empire and a peerless, self-made Kshatriya.[91]

Savarkar regarded the ability to absorb as an index of national strength. Finding contemporary Hindus lacking in this regard, he had shown himself "deadly opposed" to (male) Hindus marrying European women "at this stage in our national life," in a letter from the Andamans to his brother Narayan, dubbed "Bal."[92] Further incorporations still threatened the kind of consummation that Savarkar was trying to achieve in 1923. This was in stark contrast to the virile absorption (combining Aryan masculine virility with what Ronald Inden has called Hinduism's "feminised ability to absorb and include") shown in the Hindu past.[93] Just days from the beginning of World War II, Savarkar reiterated his long-held belief that Hindus had historically always "welcomed even non-Hindus" into their fold. Again and again, he cited as proof the mass conversion of Greeks under Chandragupta and the emperor's own marriage to a "Greek" princess.[94] The creation of a new subcaste (*jati*) had allowed especially large groups of outsiders to be assimilated "en masse," as they were "slowly incorporated into the gigantic pan-Hindu structure" of the caste system.[95] Yet both mechanisms were defunct in the modern age of caste rigidity. Hindu history had gone wrong, Savarkar held, when Hindus had lost the ability to expunge the enemy by absorbing them. The leader of the Arya Samaj, Swami Shraddhanand (1856–1926), came to a similar conclusion in his aptly titled book *Hindu Sangathan: Saviour of a Dying Race*, written shortly after *Essentials of Hindutva* in 1926. In ancient times, Shraddhanand wrote, no foreigner had been able to leave an imprint on India, as they were "absorbed" and became "part and parcel of the Indian nation," just as Greek princesses "became good Hindus as those born of Indo-Aryan parents."[96] For Shraddhanand, the trouble began when Hindus began converting away from Hinduism, contracting foreignness from within. But for Savarkar, the development of a Brahmanic worldview sounded the death knell for intermarriage. Thinking with Chaturvedi's postulation of Hindutva as "a history in full" constitutive of Hindu Being, Savarkar saw the history of gendered incorporation into the Hindu race as the history of a power lost.[97] *Shuddhi*, for Savarkar, was the means to reestablish this lost power.

For Savarkar, writing in 1939, the conversion of the Greeks in happier times found an echo in the *shuddhi* ceremony undergone ten years earlier by an American from Seattle, Nancy Ann Miller, who "was afterwards married to [the former] Maharaja Holkar of Indore."[98] Joined by the conjunction "and" (rather than "afterwards") in *Essentials of Hindutva*, conversion and marriage were defined by a necessary relation.[99] The *shuddhi* ceremony for the maharani-to-be on March 13, 1928, in Gangapur, Maharashtra, filled some, and especially her initiator, the Jagadguru Shankaracharya of Karvirpitham, Dr. Kurtkoti, with hopes for a new era of regenerate, competitive Hinduism destined for global victory as the universal religion.[100] A Sanskritist with an American doctorate and a friend of the Hindu Mahasabha (he presided over its 1924 and 1938 All-India sessions), the Shankaracharya treated the crowd of ten thousand who had gathered to witness the unprecedented spectacle of a White future maharani's conversion to an anecdote of his visit from the eminent German religious scholar Rudolf Otto (1869–1937).[101] On this occasion, Otto had stressed the need to create a universal religion "acceptable to all, embracing the essentials of all religions in the world" but stripped of dogmatism, intolerance, and other such familiar targets of religious criticism.[102] "But," his Indian interlocutor recalled, "I pointed out that there was already such a religion."[103] To her initiator, the *shuddhi* of Nancy Miller (or Devi Sharmishta, as she was henceforth known) proved that Hinduism was destined for world conquest.[104] Generations of Hindus would look back on May 13 as a day of "achievement," when an American, a native of the pivot of modernity, had converted to Hinduism, the "true religion" of the future of all humanity.[105]

The seeming orthodoxy of hours of ritual chanting of Vedic hymns, the Shankaracharya placing a red *tikka* on Miller's forehead, her eating coconut flesh at his hands, and her touching his feet and subsequently performing *puja* and ritual bathing could not hide the fact that this *shuddhi* was a ritual invention of the first order. Arousing great interest in India and America alike, Miller's conversion had almost been thwarted by "a dispute between rival prelates."[106] It was finally performed amid "demonstrations of sympathy and hostility" in nearby Nasik, overrun with visitors, that tipped "the orthodox . . . against the reformers, the Brahmins against the Non-Brahmins and the depressed classes against the upper classes."[107] Unlike most orthodox or "sanatanist" religious specialists, the Shankaracharya of Karvirpitham had responded to the call for Hindu *sangathan,* the creation of *shuddhi* ceremonies, and a unified theology that had gone out in Maharashtra.[108] For Kurtkoti, *shuddhi* was about global religious idealism. But for the Arya Samaj who misappropriated this crucial rite of purification to turn Hinduism into a proselytizing religion in the 1880s, and for Savarkar, *shuddhi* showed the way to consolidating the Hindu race.[109]

Savarkar was never shy to admit that *shuddhi* was a "new-fangled movement," but he justified it by the need to combat the "ancient" conversion rites of other religions.[110] The invention of a *shuddhi* ritual, he informed a correspondent in 1944, was a "pious fraud," for the scriptures contained no precedent. In Savarkar's own Maharashtra, a "reasonable" ritual convention had formed around the so-called Shuddhi Sanskar, which could be adopted, as could the Arya Samaji conversion ritual inspired by the Devala Smriti, dated to the eighth to tenth centuries. If these rituals would not do, Savarkar's correspondent could always "improvise" one.[111] *Shuddhi* and *sangathan* were Savarkar's major campaigns of Hindu consolidation, complemented during World War II by the Hindu militarization campaign designed to arm and train Hindus for eventual battle with the Muslims for control of India.[112] Jinnah perfectly understood Savarkar's motive for asking Hindus to cooperate with Britain's war effort.[113] But militarization did not replace incorporation. In 1944, even as he stoked civil war, Savarkar still considered one *shuddhi* performed more fruitful than twenty working committee meetings.[114] Its main targets were not White women, however, but those at the margins (oppressed castes) and beyond the pale of Hindu society, in particular Muslim women.

Reproducing Hindus or Muslims?

Savarkar predicated Hindutva on the very thing that masculinist imaginations of the nation and state exclude: consanguinity, women, and the family. None other than Sister Nivedita offered a theorization of the neglected, gendered aspect of nation making that merits exploring here succinctly as scaffolding for Savarkar's own. Speaking at the First Universal Races Congress held at the University of London in 1911, Nivedita delivered a remarkable address on the "Eastern" concept of nationhood. Unlike the Western "civic ideal" that "transcends or ignores the family," she argued, the Eastern concept of nationhood was based on the "family ideal," on consanguinity. Had Eastern thought been left undisturbed by foreign influence, it would have eventually evolved a concept of political community predicated on race instead of nationality. Race, which scaled from family and group up to caste, and from caste to "*ecclesia* or *samaj*" and finally up to race, was a natural extension of the "community of blood and origin" within which marriage was possible. For Nivedita, this racial principle of nationhood was epitomized by Islam, which encouraged intermarriage between all coreligionists.[115] Not only that, but Indian nationality was derivative of Islam, though Hinduism, too, possessed a strong principle of internal organization. It was a "growth," not an organization, "a tree, not a machine."[116] Still, only the arrival of Islam had engendered an all-Indian nationality. This was under Akbar, who fused Hindu and Muslim, thus repeating Mohammed's original "welding" of "warring brothers into a united family" of tribes in Arabia.[117] Nivedita called on India's Muslims to revive this power—not, however, to link up with Arabia, but with India.[118]

Savarkar also considered Muslims particularly gifted race- and nation makers, with the focus of his acute envy and enmity springing from intimate identification.[119] In contrast to Hinduism, Islam was outward facing and imperial.[120] Islam's power of imperial growth had trumped Hindusthan's traditional power of incorporation. For Savarkar, there was something in Islam that imparted nationality by the touch of conversion. He later described this as an instant fanaticism, which made Hindu converts to Islam set themselves apart and turn against their own blood.[121] As a consequence, and vexingly for Savarkar, caste's reproductive network had not been able to reverse the Muslim conquest as it had all earlier invasions. Speaking in 1938, he argued that the leaders of the 1921 Moplah Rebellion had shown the true basis of nationality to lie not in territory but in "religious, cultural and racial unity," namely when they took to forcibly converting Hindus.[122] Appropriating Islam's power to make a national race, Hindutva aimed to reverse the direction of consanguine nation making: from making Muslims to reproducing Hindus.

Yet Savarkar never strayed from his view that Indian Muslims were indigenous converts of Hindu blood. The Mahasabha under his aegis actually used the kinship argument to refute Indian Muslims' claim to separate nationhood after the 1940 Lahore Resolution, insisting that Hindusthan was not a multiracial state like the Soviet Union or the United States.[123] The issue was that Muslims, though of the blood, did not have the *will* to be one with the Hindus. Hence, Muslims were ambiguously situated in Savarkar's thought as racial kin and as the historical enemy, who needed to be reclaimed—or erased. Savarkar, by the late 1930s unhopeful of crushing Muslim political will, formulated his own version of the two-nation theory. Muslims, he now alleged, regarded Hindus as enemies and Hindusthan as *dar-al-harb,* "enemy land."[124] Division was *maya* ("illusion"), but if India's Muslims practiced it, so must the Hindus, who were regrettably always inclined to pursue the Vedantic ideal and relinquish their separate soul, even if their Muslim counterparts were not.[125] Savarkar's stance was seconded by fellow Mahasabha leader B. S. Moonje (1872–1948), who was forced to issue a press statement in 1943 to quell controversy over Savarkar's repeated public assertions that Hindus and Muslims were one race. If Muslims insisted on turning themselves into foreigners and enemies of Hindusthan, though factually untrue, Moonje opined, they deserved to be treated as such.[126]

Likewise for the Hindu Nazi Savitri Devi, writing in 1940, Hindus and Muslims were unambiguously of one blood. Her solution to the Muslim problem was deeper amalgamation, not a Pakistan, which meant war. Like Savarkar's recourse in population genetics, Devi argued that Hindus and Muslims were not one nation yet but were also not two nations. Instead, they were "two huge flocks . . . but undoubtedly two flocks of the *same population.*" Nationality was recast as a matter of choice: "*do they desire to become two nations or one*?"[127] The Lahore Resolution had answered this question. Through political will, India's Muslims had made themselves a pseudo-nation, though not a race, apart. Of course, for Hindu nationalists, such parasitic nationhood did not entitle them to self-determination, nor could they claim dominion in Hindusthan, which belonged to only one nation-race, the Hindus. This was the context in which Savarkar threatened India's Muslims with the fate of the Jews, whom he considered a foreign race and a threat in Germany but not in India.[128] Infamously, RSS chief Golwalkar gave Indian minorities the blunt choice between complete, self-effacing assimilation (improbable) and the Nazi purge of the Jews.[129] But unlike Golwalkar, Savarkar's investment in (female) Muslim incorporation was real. What was at stake for Savarkar was the erasure of the Muslim as a potential site of sovereignty.

Sovereignty, for Savarkar, was gendered male.[130] Muslim *men* were capable of sovereignty. This needed to be crushed out of them; they needed to be defeated, to be absorbed—if they could be absorbed at all. The case of women was different. Savarkar inevitably cast Hindu-Muslim unions as *anuloma* marriages, in which the woman takes on her husband's social, religious, and, for Savarkar, racial identity. This made Muslim women assimilable; their integration was biological, gendered, and reproductive. At the same time, Muslim women were not a true subject for Savarkar. Muslim men were, though converts of Hindu blood. But the Muslim woman could never be an original identity because the signification of *shuddhi* is that of a *reconversion* to Hinduism, which takes the Indian Muslim as a convert and the Hindu as the zero or starting point. For Savarkar, women differ from men in their boundless capacity for reinscription. Woman, unraced, without *gotra* (lineage) and having neither religion nor race or nation in the state of nature, is free for male inscription (by the father at conception) and reinscription (by the husband or abductor) through conversion and marriage. The reinscription process can theoretically be repeated ad infinitum as, in Savarkar's imagination, women were abducted back and forth across community lines.

That the Muslim woman was only ever a transitory state for Savarkar is illustrated by his attempt to influence Muslim personal law. In the debates preceding the passage of the 1939 Dissolution of Muslim Marriage Act, Savarkar advocated that a Muslim woman's conversion to Hinduism should suffice to dissolve her marriage to a Muslim husband. He failed. The act that was passed in 1939 no longer treated apostasy as grounds for divorce. Instead, it forced the apostate wife to reconvert and rejoin her Muslim husband, known as restitution of conjugal rights.[131] Yet amazingly, Savarkar did not actually speak of Muslim women in this context. In a striking slippage, the Muslim women at issue in this bill became for Savarkar "Hindu widows, or virgins, or married women having their husbands alive [. . . but] enticed away by Muslims and often married to some Muslims."[132] The Muslim woman's conversion became a "rescue," as if from a prior misappropriation. The convert became a *revert*: behind her always lurked the Hindu woman she had been, could have been, or should by rights be.

Rakshasa Marriage by Capture

The figure of the abducted woman, both fictional and real, has received close scholarly attention. Her emergence as a literary figure in historical romances of the 1920s defines the site of Hindu-Muslim transgression as one where conquest vied with an underlying desire for intimacy.[133] The term "abduction" itself loses its salience in a discourse that categorically denied consent in intercommunal relationships and tended to frame all love marriages as abductions and all conversions as predatory.[134] It is significant that Savarkar risked violating the major condition of his early release from jail—that he abstain from politics—over his deliberate spreading of rumors of forced, illicit, and predatory conversions in a 1925 article.[135] The offending piece, titled "The 'Suffering' Muslims of Kohat" and published in the *Mahratta* on March 1, 1925, was designed to escalate violence in Kohat, in the Muslim-majority North-West Frontier Province, where communal conflict on a new scale had broken out.[136] It alleged that in Kohat, "Hindu wives" had been taken from their "Hindu husbands," converted, and made "Moslem mistress[es]." This outrage had the sanction of "Mahomedan Law," which regarded a convert's marriage with a "kafir" "null and void." Who could then blame Hindus if they launched a *shuddhi* campaign to reclaim their women?[137] Savarkar had no compunction about spelling out that the real perpetrator behind Muslim abductors was their religion. Pleading his knowledge of Islamic scripture and traditional exegesis in a letter justifying his actions to the government, Savarkar alleged that religious leaders had incited Kohat's Muslim men "to capture any woman, married to a non-believer, whether Christian or Jew or Hindu, and not only marr[y] her but in virtue of that conversion or capture or marriage with her 'unbelieving' husband."[138] This they had drawn straight from the Quran. Savarkar failed to convince but was let off with a warning.[139] Later, in 1943, and by now president of the Hindu Mahasabha, Savarkar alleged that Muslim proselytization campaigns preyed on starving Hindus in famine-stricken Bengal.[140]

Savarkar could work from a Hindu common sense since the 1920s accusing the Prophet, Muslim rulers, and even ordinary Indian Muslims of sexual depravity and abductions.[141] A 1924 publication titled *Rangila Rasul*, or "The Colorful Prophet," which mockingly praised the Prophet Mohammad as an ideal Hindu householder, albeit one compromised by sexual excess and serial polygamy, is infamous to this day.[142] The Hindu Mahasabha engaged in restoring (reabducting?), reconverting, and remarrying "abducted" Hindu women from the 1920s onward. When violence escalated into civil war in 1946, the Mahasabha formally launched its own rescue and defense mission under Syama Prasad Mukherjee (1901–1953), Savarkar's competitor for control of the party.[143] But for Savarkar, recovering "abducted" Hindu women was coupled with teaching Hindu men how to "kick in return."[144]

Savarkar unleashed the full, gendered, and genocidal violence of his Hindutva in the context of the civil war of Partition. Not only did he justify Partition rapes after the fact and in a literary form in his last and bloodiest book, *Six Glorious Epochs of Indian History,* written in sickness and old age in 1963, but he also actively recommended the rape of Muslim women to Hindu Rashtra Dal volunteers (the Mahasabha's youth and military wing) in May 1947, just months away from Partition.[145] Savarkar recommended a war strategy of out-deviling the "devils." To beat the Muslim "Rakshasas" (or demons), Hindus had to become fully like them. Savarkar classed the Hindus' perennial war against the Muslims as "religious warfare," distinguished from normal warfare in that it required a strategy of superlative "hyper-barbarity."[146] Both Visana and Jyotirmaya Sharma have convincingly linked Hindutva to the collective recovery of *rajas* ("passion") as capable of generating Hindu political community. This involved cruelty as a form of justified, vengeful excess against perceived victimization by Muslims.[147] After the ancient "religious wars" with the demonic rakshasas, Savarkar wrote, there followed entirely "political wars" that did not require the most barbarous of war tactics, causing this tactic to be subsequently forgotten. When "religious war" commenced anew with the Muslim conquest, the Hindus were consequently unequipped to face it. The "perverted" idea of "chivalry towards enemy women" had rendered the Hindus' armed wing, the Kshatriyas, incapable of vanquishing their Muslim foe—by raping like him.[148] Savarkar drew additional fodder for this idée fixe from a book called *Hindu Superiority* (1906), written by the high-ranking Arya Samaji Har Bilas Sarda (1865–1955).[149] Where Sarda extolled the chivalry of the Rajputs—"descendants of the ancient Kshatriyas"—toward their enemies' womenfolk, and emphatically toward Muslim women, Savarkar ridiculed and condemned it.[150] Incited by Savarkar to become Kshatriyas in the war against Muslims, Hindus had to relearn what I have elsewhere described as "*rakshasa* marriage."[151]

Rakshasa marriage by capture was an Anglo-Indian legal construct and an obsession for nineteenth-century anthropologists, whose archetype was taken straight from the ancient Manusmriti. *Rakshasa* marriage, according to Manu, is the "marriage by seizure of a maiden by force from her house, while she weeps and calls for assistance, after her kinsmen and friends have been slain in battle or wounded, and their houses broken open."[152] In the nineteenth century, the God-given naturalness of patriarchal monogamy had come into question as anthropology and sociology had come into their own. In Darwin's wake emerged a new theory of the evolution of patriarchal marriage (marriage's highest form) from a primitive stage of tribal wife capture, first tamed at the dawn of civilization by polyandry (female polygamy) and matriarchy and only later superseded by patriarchy.[153] Following Scottish anthropologist John Ferguson McLennan's (1827–1881) *Primitive Marriage* of 1865, the bride captures that preceded matriarchy in the state of nature were called *rakshasa* marriage.[154] Crucially, Manu permitted *rakshasa* marriage for the warrior caste alone. Savarkar may have encountered the anthropology of *rakshasa* marriage in Herbert Spencer (1820–1903), whose ideas he soaked up through his mentor in London, Krishnavarma.[155] A straight reception history of "*rakshasa* marriage" leading from Spencer to Savarkar cannot be proved, but perhaps this is not necessary. *Rakshasa* marriage in the state of nature was, like evolution and the progress of human society from primitivism to civilization, simply in the air at the time. But the connection with Spencer is suggestive since it was Spencer who, in the *Principles of Sociology* (1874), unequivocally made war the cause of bride capture and exogamy, as discussed in a long section on the evolution of state and society from "primitive" "domestic relations" that no reader could miss.[156] By contrast, McLennan had ascribed bride capture to the practice of female infanticide that the Victorians widely assumed to be the state of nature, which resulted in a shortage of women who had to be captured from other tribes.[157] Crucially, for Savarkar, Spencer associated exogamy with victorious tribes who stole women from the enemy to diminish their numbers.[158] Ritu Menon and Kamla Bhasin, Urvashi Butalia, and Veena Das have taught us to view women as the chief victims and battleground of Partition.[159] In Savarkar, we have a theorist who made overt how women's sexed and reproductive bodies became the stakes, objects, and battleground of civil war. He made women the basis of sovereign violence by robbing Muslim men of their sovereignty as patriarchal powers.

Ambedkar, too, engaged with *rakshasa* marriage—in the context of caste.[160] For a young Ambedkar formulating a first theory of caste as a student at Columbia University in 1916, caste was, above all, endogamous. This endogamous system had evolved from the pioneering matrimonial self-enclosure of the Brahmins.[161] Ambedkar's central intervention, which destroyed the very premise of all previous theorizations, was that there was no "caste": "*Caste in the singular number is an unreality. Castes exist only in the plural number.*"[162] Savarkar would agree that caste was a system but not with its endogamous nature. But even for Ambedkar, endogamy was not the original order. Caste originated only with the "superimposition" of endogamy on a "primitive" order of exogamy between *gotras*.[163] The second and, in this context, decisive difference between Savarkar and Ambedkar is that for Ambedkar, caste was based on "maternity," *Matrasavarna* in Sanskrit. For Savarkar, it was ideally based on what Ambedkar called "paternity," or *Pitrasavarna*.[164] As Ambedkar explained, drawing on the Brahmanic origin story of the proliferation of castes, a child of an upper-caste father and a lower-caste mother loses the father's *varna*. Yet this had not always been the case. Originally, the mother's *varna* would have been "of no account," and she did not need to be of equal birth. Manu had later effected the "most revolutionary change" in family law, which Ambedkar, in the 1950s, turned into the pointed nineteenth of the "Riddles in Hinduism": "The Change from Paternity to Maternity: What Did the Brahmins Wish to Gain by It?"[165] Arguing that the patriarchal Hindu family should have operated under *patria potestas*, as it did in Rome, Ambedkar insinuated that it must have been in the Brahmins' interest to make a woman's heredity outweigh a man's, in blatant contradiction to the patriarchal laws otherwise governing Hindu society and an obvious detriment to the father.[166]

Crucially, for McLennan, the archtheorist of this idea, *rakshasa* marriage was the opposite of "caste," which he identified with "endogamy" based on friendly patriarchal consent.[167] For McLennan, endogamy's "opposite"—"exogamy," or marriage outside the group—was indexed by *rakshasa* marriage.[168] Yet for Savarkar, jilting anthropological definitions, caste as originally practiced meant exogamy. *Rakshasa* marriage's contribution to modern Indian political thought and the source of its particular appeal to Savarkar was that it expropriated other patriarchs (enemies) of their women, thus toppling the existing patriarchal order and establishing new sovereigns.[169]

Indeed, Savarkar regarded Muslims as converts of Hindu blood, but this took on a different framing that would gain ground over time. Namely, he put an intriguing spin on the idealized Muslim hierarchy in the subcontinent between *ashraf* and *ajlaf*, purported descendants of India's foreign Islamic conquerors and indigenous converts. In 1938, Savarkar raised alarm over "systematic Muslim proselytization" in Burma, where Muslim men fraudulently married Burmese Buddhist (read: Hindu) women to spawn Muslim "progeny."

If unstopped, Muslim proselytization would "break up the Racial, Religious and Cultural homogeneity in the Burmees [*sic*] Nation and divide it as happened in India and mainly through the same process."[170] Elsewhere, Savarkar described India's Muslims as hybrids who had "forgotten" their Hindu mothers, taking instead after their Muslim fathers and swearing enmity on their Hindu half brothers.[171] In *Six Glorious Epochs,* the only book he wrote after independence and Partition, Savarkar finally scaled Partition-era abductions up into a new origin story of Muslims in India. He now argued that a small band of male Muslim invaders had grown into a community many millions strong by capturing, converting, raping, and marrying Hindu women.[172] Savarkar's late theorization of gender difference in ancestry made Indian Muslim men foreign by patrilineal descent. And Indian Muslim women were Hindu women who had been captured by Muslim invaders. Muslims in India had, in short, followed the law of Ravana, who abducted Sita, as victors always had, by *rakshasa* marriage: "To carry away the women of others and to ravish them is itself the supreme religious duty of the Rakshasas."[173] McLennan himself had puzzled over the fact that a Hindu form of marriage should have been named after the enemy tribe of the Ramayana and concluded that this group must have preserved the original exogamous practice of marriage by capture perfectly while the Aryan Kshatriyas only followed it imperfectly.[174] For Savarkar, Hindus had to become the abductor, Ravan, the rakshasa ("demon") or Muslim, in his fight against the hero of tradition, the Hindu husband Rama.[175]

In *Six Glorious Epochs,* Savarkar explained how "primitive" African tribes and Indian Nagas killed enemy men in war, "but not the females, who are eventually distributed by the victor tribes amongst themselves." Alternatively, killings specifically targeted enemy women, since "to kill one woman who cannot be captured alive is to kill five men," for the purpose of decimating enemy populations. To Savarkar, the "excess of cows over the oxen" in the animal kingdom enabled maximum reproductive gain.[176] Hindus and Muslims, for Savarkar, had become mere animal populations. By the same token, ventriloquizing a fictional royal edict issued by the council of the Marathas under Shivaji (1630–1680) in their fight against the Muslim ruler Tipu Sultan, Savarkar demanded that the Hindu warriors be rewarded with "'young and beautiful Muslim girls'" who had been captured and converted to Hinduism.[177] Through war and animal breeding, Savarkar had arrived at polygyny (male polygamy).

Operating in full war mode by 1945, Savarkar sought to enshrine polygyny, which he considered a widely practiced caste custom, as a legal right for all

Hindus with the Hindu Code Bill that meandered into law only after independence.[178] Savarkar knew women to be the decisive factor in population size: polygyny could bring no absolute increase of children. But this was not the point. What mattered was a *relative* increase vis-à-vis the Muslims. Polygyny could only increase Hindu numbers if it was assumed that these women would not be snatched from reproductively capable Hindu men, leaving some with harems and others as bachelors, but from Muslims. Crucially, with polygyny, Savarkar appropriated the major mechanism that "saffron demography" holds accountable for Muslims outpopulating Hindus.[179] He was fully backed by Moonje as well as regional Hindu Mahasabha branches.[180] One of the loudest and most candid petitions sent to the Hindu Law Committee in 1945 on the rights of Hindus to polygyny came from the party's Madras Branch:

> With Muslims multiplying through polygamy and through conversions of polygamous minded Hindus, the population of India will be predominantly Muslim in a couple of generations *and the New Hindu Code based on monogamy may get the credit of having converted the whole of India into a vast Pakistan where the surviving Hindus will be treated as strangers in their own Fatherland.* Suicidal folly cannot go further. *You cannot enforce monogamy on Hindus so long as there is a rival society like that of the Moslems which permits polygamy.*[181]

The petition continued with the threat that female infanticide and the murder of barren wives were unavoidable should Hindu men's right to procreation be curbed by monogamy.[182] Demanding, in his inimitable fashion, that Hindus drop their "goody goody attitude" and "mealy-mouthed and spineless gentility," Savarkar endorsed marriage's crudest forms, *rakshasa* marriage and polygamy, which he identified with the Muslim.[183]

After Partition, the failure to restore abducted Hindu women to a society suffering from a pollution complex confirmed Savarkar's loathing of traditional, "suicidal" Hinduism.[184] A nation that rejected women as impure for no other reason than for exhibiting their reproductive capability would destroy itself.[185] In this context, Savarkar finally revised his position on the origin of caste. In *Six Glorious Epochs,* caste no longer appeared as the great centripetal force that had assimilated India's ancient conquerors but as a conservative reaction *to* these conquests.[186] Caste's "parentage" system and weapon of social "ostracism," he now claimed, had answered the need to preserve the Hindus' "racial seed and blood" and restored order after the ancient conquests.[187] But only the later Muslim invasions had caused caste to become entirely rigid, a permanent barrier in Hindu society against Islam's race making. In the process, the "charmed amulets" of caste had become debilitating "native fetters": "Lotibandi," "Rotibandi," "Betibandi," "Sparshbandi," "Shuddhibandi," "Sindhubandi"—bans on drinking, dining, and marrying across caste, as well as on reconversion and sea voyage, but enjoining untouchability.[188] Caste, now indexing "fear of pollution," had become Islam's foothold in India.[189] Proselytization had been as simple as dropping "half-eaten loaves of bread . . . or the meat of cows" into village wells, causing the drinkers' loss of caste and exclusion from Hindu society, wrote Savarkar, clearly recalling forced conversion ceremonies during Partition.[190] Caste subsequently ensured that conversion stuck because converts were permanently beyond the pale of Hindu society. Muslim rule did not need force of arms to uphold it where native society worked as marvelously in its favor as in India.[191]

Reintegrating abducted Hindu women thus required a profound restructuring of Hindu society and religion. Seeking to accomplish this with the fig leaf of religious tradition, Savarkar turned to the Devala Smriti on which the Arya Samaj dubiously based their *shuddhi* ritual. Its "liberal attitude" toward women appeared to Savarkar as "specially laudable":

> It enjoined that the women forcibly converted to Islam, or those who served in the Muslim households as menial servants or slaves be considered pure after their next menses, and should be completely absorbed in the Hindu community. Even a pregnant Hindu woman, freed from the Muslim bondage, was to be considered as pure as a bar of gold after being heated in the goldsmith's chafing dish, once her foetus came out after delivery.[192]

Savarkar did not believe that sex with a Muslim spoiled a Hindu woman's reproductive future. Under Malaviya, the Hindu Mahasabha would not even "touch the question" of widow remarriage, as Lala Lajpat Rai (1865–1928) complained in *Stri Dharma*, the Women's Indian Association's magazine, in 1928.[193] Savarkar again sided with Arya Samaji radicalism: Swami Shraddhanand's *Hindu Sangathan* not only noted a "consensus" in the Smritis (excepting the Vedas) "sanctioning the remarriage of unconsummated child widows" but further stated that "the Smritis also hold that if a virgin is forcibly carried away and violated she does not lose her position as a virgin if she has not willingly gone through marriage rites with her ravisher."[194] (This was certainly no ancient legal "consensus," but it was supported by two of the four authors of the Dharmasutras: Vasishta and Baudhayana.)[195] Savarkar sought to recuperate reproductively capable women, yet he did not concede the heredity of race to the womb even in this critical instance where numbers mattered.

Denying dual descent (*cognatio* in Roman law), which makes all humans the biological hybrids of two parents that we are, for Savarkar, it was descent down the male line—the father's right—that mattered. He therefore regretted that the Smritis "should have failed" to consider the children born of a Hindu man and a Muslim woman as pure. Going beyond the Devala Smriti, Savarkar's "revolutionary redemption of the 'fallen'" included Muslim women and their progeny only if fathered by a Hindu, in which case they would all be completely "absorbed."[196] Savarkar here went significantly beyond the official state line on the recovery mission that, as Constituent Assembly of India debates show, also considered recaptured Hindu and Sikh women as reproductive assets.[197] Still, the recovery scheme's overwhelming tenor was that India must rid itself of Muslim women, whose presence in non-Muslim families in India compromised India's sexual morality, national honor, and purity.[198] Here, Veena Das detects a mismatch between "practical kinship" and the official state line on pure kinship: the state's project of abstract honor rendered abducted women visible and extractable from families and communities that had already solved the problem they posed by silently absorbing the women.[199] Savarkar alone endorsed as policy the practices of quiet absorption that were already underway at a family level and contributed to women's experiences of violence in the Indian Partition.

The appropriation of women into the families of their captors had strong connotations of slavery, made overt in the discourse on *rakshasa* marriage and by Savarkar himself.[200] Suzanne Miers and Igor Kopytoff famously concluded that African slavery, once divested of Western conceptions of the slave as chattel, represents a transaction in kinship relations, which Indrani Chatterjee suggests likewise holds true in the Indian context.[201] Slavery, like marriage, solves the bonded woman's initial state of "kinlessness" with an exacting expectation of her swift submission to complex and hierarchical household and kinship relations.[202] Merging the registers of marriage and slavery in a distinct way, Savarkar's idiosyncratic notion of the Hindu race turned women into valuable and eventually fiercely fought-over assets.

Savarkar viewed Hindu-Muslim relations as war, ensuring the large-scale killing of Muslim men. With "enemy men" decimated and their sovereign potential crushed, and with "enemy women" apportioned to Hindu warriors, Muslim reproduction would be destroyed. I know of only two instances where "enemy men" are included as objects of large-scale absorption in the same way as women. One was in Savarkar's 1963 account of the "glorious epoch" of Chandragupta Maurya, when "the nation [had been] valiant enough to absorb not only the progeny of those enemy-women but the whole enemy communities in [*sic*] their own and leave no trace of their origin behind!"[203] The other instance is truly remarkable and not literary. On May 25, 1947, Savarkar sent a note congratulating a fellow member of the Mahasabha for converting eight hundred Muslim families to Hinduism. Savarkar declared that at the touch of conversion, these families had been "assimilated into Hindudom beyond recognition" and deserved "loving and equal treatment."[204] That Savarkar could applaud the absorption, by conversion, of Muslim families inclusive of their menfolk into the Hindu body politic on the eve of Partition, when he preached war and rape, starkly shows that his war on Muslims aimed at their erasure through imbibition. He would likely have recommended that the second generation of converts marry outside their group, the better to fuse into the larger Hindu body politic.

Reproducing Hindutva

In India, conversion mended the Hindu race. Unlike genetics, with its slow temporal order of mutation, gene expression, and reproduction, for Savarkar, conversion-cum-marriage was an instantaneous somatic event. The tremendous violence of his project of race was staked on the demand for complete consanguinity within "Hindusthan," as he unerringly termed it, meaning "the land of the Hindus," not the nationalists' "India." The key to consolidating Hindudom, for Savarkar, was intermixture. Before his death in 1966, he even set aside money in his will for a "*shuddhi* fund."[205] What was *shuddhi* in Savarkar's time has become *ghar wapsi* ("homecoming"); the alleged Muslim campaign to abduct, convert, and marry Hindu women has been rebaptized a "love-jihad." Always seeking to emulate his enemy, Savarkar's genocidal project of incorporation was predicated on women being without race in the state of nature and ready for (re)inscription by the male agent. As hijacking their fertility erased the Muslimness of women, Muslim men were erased by forced infertility and war. Hindutva, as elaborated by Savarkar in his prolific writings, speeches, and personal papers, thus posited a particular vision of the Hindu race that bridged the gap between the opposite registers of *rakshasa* marriage (as exogamy in intergroup conflict) and caste (traditionally understood as endogamy and patriarchal consent). Here, in relation to gender and race, Hindutva's violence came into its own.

Instead of purity, *miscegenation* founded Hindutva's myth of blood. In so arguing, this chapter has gone beyond radically revising our picture of Hindutva. It also mounts a challenge to the identification of race with purity and color and miscegenation with deviancy or resistance. The idea that national races needed to be forged (through war, history, cultural assimilation, or even biological fusion) was integral to nationalism in the eugenic age. Usually, the breeding vision reproduced the exclusion of the unassimilable, such as African Americans in the United States and Jews, among others, in Germany.[206] But Savarkar did not put the relevant "other" beyond the pale. His thought therefore needs to be disambiguated from the postcolonial, anti-racist commitments to biological and cultural creolization that it, intriguingly, resembles. As Marilyn Strathern has suggested, the artificial boundary separating "culture" from "nature" runs between the "cosmopolitan" and the "creole," who is a "genetic hybri[d] by nature."[207] As Mendelian hybridity disproved (to those who would listen) that biological fusion led to deracination, inferences were drawn about the potential of racial fusion to ameliorate humans and unite humanity. Benoy Sarkar and Cedric Dover (1901–1961), the Anglo-Indian crusader and self-declared first Indian nationalist among Calcutta's mixed-race Anglophiles, shared such eugenic enthusiasm with the British German race ideologue Houston Stewart Chamberlain.[208] In Brazil, Oswald de Andrade (1890–1954) sounded a triumphantly cosmopolitan "mestizo" "cannibalism," while a Mexican, José Vasconcelos (1882–1959), harbored hopes for the Mexican "race," which had fused Black, White, and Indigenous, to become the "matrix race" that in the future would unite all of humanity.[209] Where we appeal to diversity today, Savarkar's colonial contemporaries built utopian futures on the promise of biological fusion to combat racism and bring unity and peace to humankind, though some, like Dover, were soon cured of such hopes.[210]

Yet race mixing could also be integral to colonial projects of race making or take the form of whitening projects in settler-colonial contexts.[211] Nationalism in settler-colonies was forced to address the history of large-scale miscegenation. Responses could be violent repression, as in the well-known cases of the United States and South Africa, but also accommodation. Brazil's fascist movement, the Brazilian Integralist Action (Ação Integralista Brasileira), for example, valorized the blending of races that had forged the Brazilian nation. The movement welcomed Black and Indigenous Brazilians without, however, giving up White hegemony.[212] The search for a national race in settler-colonial Ibero-America thus furnishes the closest parallel to Savarkar's miscegenous Hindu race. Likewise, race mixing in Ibero-America had constituted an initial tool of conquest, which functioned through the reproductive body of the *indigena*.[213] National Socialism, too, at its late stage of imperial expansion, developed ideas of absorbing racially allied (i.e., blue eyed, blond haired) parts of the populations of the conquered European East, thus turning enemies into kin.[214] As Heinrich Himmler (1900–1945) proclaimed, "Polish nationality and the Polish people [*Volk*] has to be dissolved in two directions": through this so-called Germanization (*Germanisierung*)—or extermination and enslavement.[215] Nevertheless, Nazism's significant other, the Jew, remained firmly beyond the pale of absorption. Hindutva, by contrast, developed its extraordinary violence primarily through a particular vision of the gendered incorporation of its enemy. The annihilation it envisaged came as incorporation, assimilation, and imbibing—biological metaphors that are more than rhetorical ornament. To characterize Savarkar's project as seeking dominion over Muslims, who would be relegated to second-class citizens, still underestimates its scope and capacity for violence. The Hindusthan that Savarkar envisioned was no apartheid state. I do not believe Savarkar's Hindutva would have recognized the limit of even a completely subjugated "minority."

Hindutva has produced two distinct yet complementary biological foundations. One is the foundation Savarkar posited in relation to the Muslims, which was based on sexual reproduction and violently founded on women. Hindutva's other biological buttress, the one particularly resonant with the RSS, is the *brahmacharya* ideal, which was built on fraternity and grounded in celibacy and the exclusion of women from reproduction in metaphorical if not biological terms.[216] For the RSS and its affiliates, the role of women was and is to reproduce Hindutva ideology at home.[217] Savarkar's Hindutva, by contrast, propagated by enacting itself upon Muslim women. The frame for this was always war, rather than the Hindu family. In this way, Savarkar's conception of the Hindu race combined fraternal and consanguine foundations, as the fraternity of male Kshatriyas forged reproductive bonds with women looted from the enemy community.

Race as conceived in Nazi Germany, by contrast, oscillated between genealogy, eugenics, and biology (the genotype), on the one hand, and the myth of the "Aryan" phenotype, on the other—"racial science" and "race mysticism" in one characterization.[218] Crucially, race could not be expunged by conversion. It was on this grounds that shortly after the onset of Nazi rule, in 1934, Bombay's theosophical monthly, *The Aryan Path,* exposed the Nazi "race" as a fiction. The contributor, Cecil Roth, argued that antisemitism, by historically forcing Jews to convert to Christianity, had caused the Jewish "race" to disintegrate and blend into the German population, in which it now represented no more than a thin genealogical trace. If the "inquisitional precedent"—the nomenclature of "New Christians" updated into the "Half-" and "Quarter-Jew"—were to be followed rigorously, "it is doubtful whether there would be enough pure-blooded Germans left to man even the S.A."[219] As the *Reconquista* of Moorish Iberia had decreed the purge of Jews and Moors, forcing their conversion or expulsion, the new converts acquired the taint of suspected "crypto-Judaism."[220] The suspicion of a "taint" in New Christians in turn induced the production of Old Christian lineages of purity, or *limpieza de sangre* ("purity of blood"). Diametrically opposed to the purity ascribed to Old Christians or Germanics, the reconquest of Hindusthan imagined by Savarkar countered pedigree with the directive to blend blood. Yet the early modern world of "purity of blood" is implicated in the modern development of the concept of "race" and racism, to which the Nazis made a curious return with the genealogical fixing of the "Jew."[221] It is likewise implicated in the concept of "caste," whose German iteration is the focus of the next chapter. The Nazi case of "caste" showcases the potential for the universality of Indian concepts. It also puts to the test Sarkar's convictions about the popular foundations of Nazi rule.

CHAPTER THREE

THE NAZI *VOLK* AGAINST *KASTE*

Democracy and National Socialism should not go together. Indeed, they do not. And yet Benoy Sarkar observed that though National Socialism was democracy's declared enemy, it did not lack popular foundations. There was popular support: free, manufactured, and violently coerced. And there were attempts at justification in political thought. Nazism did not like to think of itself as a dictatorship that imposed the will of the one or the few on the German nation. The ideal of *Volksgemeinschaft* ("people's community") announced the equality and fraternity of its fellow members.[1] The *Führerstaat* ("leader state") ideal proclaimed that the interests of the ruler and ruled were not opposed. Brushing this aside as "ideology" or "propaganda" to deprive Nazism of the status of political thought (well-meaning though this may be) simply will not do. Nazis and Nazi sympathizers propagated national consolidation as an alternative to class war. And they promised a kind of popular sovereignty without democracy.

Democracy in the tradition of John Stuart Mill, as scholarship on the global color line has demonstrated, required racial homogeneity as its basis.[2] As theorized by Carl Schmitt in the interwar crisis of parliamentary democracy, democracy needed sameness and extended equality only to those considered equal.[3] Democracy's formal denial but implicit assumption of biological foundations is no doubt one of the reasons our current global anti-racism discourse has appropriated a loaded Indian concept to designate the persistence of inequality and disenfranchisement in formally equal and democratic societies, especially in the United States. This concept is "caste," in the US context designating the enslaved, racialized African American as a counterpart to the Indian Dalit.[4] The metaphorical identification of the Untouchable with the Black slave has history in both the African American and Dalit struggles tracing back to the nineteenth century.[5] But as a cipher for oppression, it misses the mark of the political signification in which "caste" was originally generalized into modern political grammar.

The "caste" view of politics, as Mill well knew, hailed from the ancient view that rulers were antithetical to the people they ruled by inherited rights or conquest.[6] "Caste"—*Kaste* in German—designated and denounced the illegitimate rule of illegitimate elites, not the experience of the slave or Dalit. From the time of the French Revolution, as diligent genealogical tracing of the term shows, "caste" designated those safeguarding their power at the top, rather than those chained to the bottom of society. There was only one caste, the aristocratic caste, which derived its privilege from its genesis as a foreign race that had conquered the "nation." The revolutionary idea of "the people" demanded that this "caste" must go. German retained this usage to the point that under National Socialism, *Kaste* was fashioned into the major antithesis of the valorized *Volk* ("nation").

My aim in this chapter, therefore, is to disentangle "caste" from the Indian "social" and reveal it in its global political signification, beyond and contrary to its generalization as a system of racialized oppression. I characterize caste's framing simultaneously as an Indian particular and a universal. This is no contradiction. Both, in fact, make up the concept of caste as we know it. The common orientalist story is how Europe othered India by framing its social system as different and exceptional. Colonial governmentality then proceeded to reify or "construct" caste.[7] At the same time, caste has long been generalized into the sociology tool kit, not least out of a desire to understand Black-White relations in the segregated American South.[8] The "caste school of race relations," as African American sociologist Oliver Cox dubbed it, fell from favor in America after its heyday in the 1930 and 1940s. South Asianists briefly revived it in the 1960s. The classic researchers of caste theory, Louis Dumont, André Beteille, Gerald Berreman, and so on, all made statements about caste's comparability with race elsewhere.[9] So while not conceptually new, the recent comeback of the equation of caste(ism) with race(ism) is suggestive. Not ten years ago, Indian scholars could complain that caste oppression in India had to be translated into the hegemonic language of "race" to be understood internationally, thus elevating the product of a particular European and transatlantic history to a universal concept while shearing "caste" and untouchability off their potential universalism.[10] Isabel Wilkerson's Oprah-recommended instant bestseller, *Caste: The Origins of Our Discontents* (2020), now a major motion picture, reversed the problem.[11] Now, scholars of South Asia struggle to defend the particularity of India's caste in view of its reduction to a metaphor for America's problem with race.[12] Seemingly (but only seemingly) free from the biological trappings of "race," "caste" is again called upon to give a social explanation of the house that racism built.[13]

In the Nazi German context that is inevitably drawn into these discussions, "caste" consequently serves as little more than a metaphor for the racist oppression of Jews.[14] Beyond that, it points to the cliché of Heinrich Himmler's Kshatriya-inspired Schutzstaffel (SS), as explored later.[15] Conventional accounts frame the Indian "lawgiver" Manu, to whose authority the fourfold division of "caste" (*varna*) into Brahmins (priests), Kshatriyas (warriors), Vaishyas, (merchants and agriculturists), and Shudras at the bottom is traced, as a model for Nazi visions of inequality, Aryan world rule, and eugenic breeding, with precedents in Nietzsche and the trailblazer for esoteric Nazism, Jörg Lanz von Liebenfels (1874–1954).[16] Incidentally, it was the Viennese psychoanalyst Wilfried Daim (1923–2016), who discovered Liebenfels as *The Man Who Supplied Hitler's Ideas,* who provided one of the most original and insightful treatments of the Nazi case of "caste."[17] This was in a remarkable, undeservedly forgotten book of 1960 titled *The Casteless Society,* in a subtle deviation from the "classless society" of socialism.[18] Drawing on Manu and defining caste by its concern with purity, Daim contended that the Nazi ideology of *Volksgemeinschaft* rhetorically performed and in some ways actually achieved rendering Germans into a "caste."[19] Consolidation on the inside and exclusion of the outside functioned through what Daim calls a "caste-making border" (*Verkastungsgrenze*).[20] Within caste's borders, he argued, lay the *Volksgemeinschaft* as the sanctified "center of caste," which must be shielded from pollution and polluters.[21]

Yet the issue with either metaphor of the Nazi variety of "caste" is this: Nazi language does not support it. The Nazis never identified the *Volk* with *Kaste,* as Daim did. Nor could they imagine such a thing as an oppressed "caste," as do those who equate caste with race and racism. Instead, the Nazis promised to free the *Volk* from the "caste" that split and oppressed it. That the semantic opposition of *Kaste* and *Volk* should have anything to teach us about the ideological content of Nazism may seem a tall claim, but it builds on, and contributes to, crucial historiographical debates. Through tracing the signifier *Kaste,* I demonstrate a fundamental conceptual contradiction between *Rasse* ("race") and *Volk* in Nazi German thought, thus reinforcing the need to revise the "Nazi racial state paradigm" in view of the malleability of Nazi ideas of *Volk* and race.[22] Second, and contributing to discussions about the consensual, popular, or "populist" rather than repressive dimensions of National Socialism, I show how an alternative notion of popular sovereignty and meritocracy developed in Germany, which was compatible with hierarchy but not with "caste."[23] The challenge was to keep Nazi racism and eugenics from driving the wedge of caste right back into the *Volk* by sorting the "valuable" race from chaff.

This is not a history of an elective affinity between India and Germany.[24] Nor is it about Nazi views of India, the occult, or German Indology and the question of its implication in Nazi crimes.[25] It is not even primarily concerned with that famous instance of Germany borrowing from India: the Aryan.[26] Instead, as well as showcasing a separate, revolutionary genealogy of "caste" as *Kaste* that only later fused with the Aryan one, this chapter argues that the quest for political modernity in Germany and India made them problematize "caste." Owing to the deep domestication of Indian themes in German thought—no doubt a consequence of German orientalism and idealism but highly abstracted from its one-time Indian reference point—caste came to designate a domestic problem in Germany, as it did in India.

In India, since the establishment of the Arya Samaj in 1875, the idea had not been simply to preserve or abolish but to redefine the caste order: in the words of Arya Samaj founder Dayananda Saraswati (1824–1883), to spiritualize caste values and affiliation away from "the substance of the ova and sperms." Caste hierarchy was to be made flexible to accommodate the rise of new, spiritual elites.[27] More radically, for Hindutva's architect, Savarkar, the Hindu subject could only emerge through the breakdown of caste barriers, as shown in the previous chapter. Finally, in Shruti Kapila's formulation of Ambedkar's thought, caste emerges as the "crucible" of "the people" in India.[28] For the beloved Dalit leader and "father" of the Indian Constitution, as Kapila reads him, the caste system anchored Brahmin sovereignty, which is traditionally immanent in society as a "dispersed monarchy" rather than the "singularized" monarch of European tradition—and not as easily decapitated.[29] It follows that popular sovereignty and a republican order in India could only emerge through breaking that power by converting caste antagonism into peaceful agonism. Yet considering caste an Indian singularity, Ambedkar would have been surprised to find that Germans after the defeat of 1918 likewise drew the battle lines between "the people"—*Volk*—and *Kaste*.[30] Two latecomer nations, India and Germany, uniquely articulated their push for political modernity through the problem of caste. Significantly, both rejected the path that was blueprinted by the French Revolution.

Of Conquerors and the Conquered

This section brings a novel twist to the familiar history of "caste." It is generally acknowledged that the term "caste" derives from the Portuguese *casta,* which is usually traced to the Latin *castus,* meaning "chaste" or "pure" but acquiring the connotation of "purity of blood" and "race."[31] None of the Indian descriptors of hereditary, ritual, and occupational communities, such as *gotra, varna,* and *jati,* have the concerted meaning of "caste." The term owes its existence to a complicated transatlantic history that transferred Iberian anxieties over "purity of blood" (*limpieza de sangre*) following the *Reconquista* of Moorish Iberia to the regulation of sexuality and heredity under conditions of colonialism and slavery in early modern Ibero-America. In the New World, a grid emerged for classifying degrees of mixed heredity that linked status, lineage, religion, and "race" (*raza*) in an unprecedented way, the "system of castes" (*sistema de castas*).[32] Transposed to Indian society in the early modern period and soon afterward losing its Iberian reference point along with initially positive assessments of Indian society, the usual viewpoint is that "caste" henceforth served to negatively contrast Indian with European civil society, thus denying the subcontinent's equality and "coevalness" with Europe and confirming its place in the colonial hierarchy of civilizations.[33] German usage marked this shift by nativizing the term as *Kaste.*[34]

Kaste entered German via the French.[35] As doctoral work by Blake Smith has shown, prerevolutionary French thinkers going back to Montesquieu (1689–1755) defended France's estate-based society by contrasting it with the oriental despotism of India's caste system, with Brahmins at the top. Yet with the French Revolution, both aristocratic self-defense and revolutionary critique identified "caste," away from the Indian reference point, with the French aristocracy.[36] Caste thus identified was contrasted with the Third Estate, which alone was identified with the "nation." Instead of four, there was only one, the aristocratic "caste." I differ from Smith in insisting on the logic and significance of this shift.[37] It suggests that at the hour of birth of the idea of "the people," the aristocratic caste was framed as its opposite and negation.

It was in this signification that *Kaste* entered German. Its first appearance in 1772, in Christoph Martin Wieland's orientalizing *The Golden Mirror or the Kings of Sheshian,* already invokes *Kaste* in a political argument about good government.[38] Wieland employed *Kaste* to designate a group of aristocratic and priestly profiteers who usurped kingly prerogatives and were to blame for the king's growing estrangement from his people.[39] Wieland remained opposed to republicanism and democracy.[40] But the French Revolution unambiguously announced the solution to the problem of *Kaste* to be the sovereign nation—the *demos* or *Volk.*

German dictionaries preserve some of the significance and polemical punch that *Kaste* possessed in the nineteenth century. A political term contrasting with vernacular markers of social differentiation, *Kaste* was an indictment of the aristocratic dispensation of power: the insularity of aristocrats, the way they protected their power and privilege. It was only fitting that a new term, "caste spirit" (*Kastengeist*), denoting "conceit" (*Dünkel*), described the aristocratic mentality to its critics.[41] Superlatives like "the evil spirit of caste" (*Kasten-Ungeist*) exaggerated this critique and were countered by defenses of aristocratic "caste honour" (*Kastenehre*).[42] At the Frankfurt Parliament (Germany's first) in 1848, therefore, while the term *Volk* appealed across the ideological divide (though its content differed), *Kaste* was exclusive to the vocabulary of the republicans, liberals, and socialists seated on the left at the Paulskirche.[43] *Kaste* constituted what linguist Horst Grünert calls a "definite N[egative]-sign" that marked the aristocratic adversary but never the nonprivileged groups championed by the "left," which were labeled "class" (*Klasse*), "estates" (*Stände*), and so on.[44] To invoke *Kaste* was to mount a profound challenge to the entire political and social order. Its original and, as metaphor, abiding foe was the aristocracy.

Caste also possessed the enduring connotation of "race." As *Kaste* was fully generalized into German political grammar in the nineteenth century, it was amalgamated with the myth of the Aryan race of conquerors that arose from the discovery of the Indo-European language family: Tacitus fused with Manu.[45] Dictionaries in Weimar and Nazi Germany unsurprisingly favored the "racial" derivation of the Indian caste system from the Aryan invasion, rather than from social differentiation. Few dictionaries directly defined the generic term *Kaste* along with the Portuguese original as "race," although a dictionary that went through no less than eight editions from its first publication in 1930 to 1941 did so.[46] But many expressed the sense that where such a system had developed, it spoke of a past invasion that had dispossessed the conquered and reproduced their dispossession through the separation of the conquering and conquered races into endogamous "castes."[47]

Scholars have criticized how European thinkers, prominently including Henry Maine, Émile Durkheim, Max Weber, and Herbert Risley, envisioned the evolution from kinship to state and civil society in such a way that India's caste signposted its failure.[48] Caste appeared to them as an excess of the social that curtailed the development of modern political and social organization. The controversial political theorist Francis Fukuyama more recently restated the predicament of the Indian political thus: "India had a strong society that prevented a strong state from emerging in the first place."[49] But in the German trajectory, we find that "caste" points directly to the foundations of sovereignty. *Kaste* implied the norm of the warrior state, with its origin in conquest rather than social contract or organic growth. This thesis had become established to such a degree by the end of the nineteenth century that the influential *Meyer's Lexicon* took the supremacy of the warrior "caste" (the aristocracy, to which the monarch belonged) as the "natural" dispensation of power arising from conquest.[50]

India presented the society that must be the outcome of conquest, structured by inequality and binary power relations.[51] In his 1897 discussion of the problem of *Inbreeding and Mixing in Humans,* the Austrian medical doctor Albert Reibmayr (1848–1918) posited two different origins of "caste." One was conquest by a foreign race, the other an internal division of labor. The political consequences were staggering. Where a ruling caste had evolved from internal differentiation, rule and even abuses of power were generally countenanced. But where rulers and subjects belonged to different "inbreeding peoples" (*Inzuchtvölkern*), political conflict never ceased. In such cases, rule could only be upheld by violence, until such a time as the conquerors had biologically fused with the conquered.[52] If prominent sociological theorizations have subsequently defined caste as a system of inequality based on implicit consent, this strategy was clearly not followed here.[53] It follows that *Kaste* did not (principally) index the fourfold hierarchy of *varna.*[54] Instead, it signposted the dyadic political and social order that emerged from conquest, which, with Nietzsche, naturalized the aristocracy of the conquerors.[55] The challenge was how to put a state birthed by conquest on a popular foundation. This is the key to understanding the term *Kaste* in the context of Nazism.

In his lectures at the Collège de France in 1975–1976, titled "Society Must Be Defended," Michel Foucault made the extraordinary claim (similar to Léon Poliakov in *The Aryan Myth*) that modern European nationalism originated in a new historiographical practice that emerged in the sixteenth and seventeenth centuries. Historians in France and England were the first to speak of an ethnic divide between the rulers and the ruled.[56] Foucault claims that "racism" originated with this new genre of national history writing that offered a "counterhistory" to the Western juridical tradition based on Roman legal universalism and the sovereign right of kings.[57] Unlike the Hobbesian abstraction, this history spoke of a real war—what Foucault calls "race war"—through which one group or "race" established its rule over another.[58] Foucault strips "race" of everything we associate with it, namely *racism*.[59] However, the Foucauldian account misses the mark in denying the specificity of Nazi racism and antisemitism. Yet, as we shall see, political thought under the swastika actually combined the racist and the social and political "race war" that Foucault describes.

For Foucault, the Abbé Sieyès's (1784–1836) famous tractate of 1789, *What Is the Third Estate?*, typifies how the French Revolution reworked the "counterhistory" of race war into the modern imaginary of "the people."[60] That Sieyès frequently substituted "caste" for the noble "class" struck at the heart of the revolutionary intervention.[61] "Caste" telegraphed the idea that the origin and purpose of the nobility were "foreign" to the nation. It did not owe its powers to the people, onto which it was parasitically grafted.[62] In Sieyès's parody of aristocratic self-description, it owed its power and privilege to the "rights of conquest." If the aristocracy traced its privilege back to the Frankish conquest, Sieyès pointed "to the year that preceded the conquest."[63] The people had a prior claim to the land, an original right to rule. Revolutionary conflict, it would thus appear, broke open the social and political order that resulted from ancient conquest. In this way, "caste," the racism of the privileged class, has designated the enemy of the "nation" since the French Revolution.[64] Yet unlike Poliakov, Foucault viewed England—not France, in which Henri de Boulainvilliers (1658–1722) had famously identified "two nations" or races—as the nation that had fractured along the lines of race, one common and one noble.[65]

Arthur Comte de Gobineau's (1816–1882) *Essay on the Inequality of the Human Races* (1853–1855) pontificates at length about "caste," a term applicable to both India and Europe since Aryan conquerors formed the precious racial strata—the aristocratic caste—in both cases.[66] In other words, "caste" conjoined ideas of "class" and "race." Hannah Arendt was characteristically alive to this possibility when she wrote that Gobineau "'must be regarded as the last heir of Boulainvilliers and the French exiled nobility which . . . feared for the fate of the aristocracy as a 'caste.'"[67] Gobineau was little known in Germany before *Völkische* of the Bayreuth Circle popularized him at the turn of the twentieth century. But even the *Völkischen* felt the contradiction of an increasingly biological conception of a race that could no longer be identified with the German *Volk*.[68]

As Wagner's son-in-law and author of the *völkisch* classic *Foundations of the Nineteenth Century* (1899), Houston Stewart Chamberlain was a Bayreuth fixture.[69] When war erupted in 1914, the ex-Briton and elective German penned a remarkable "war essay" that indicted English society and government for being nothing but the rule of one race over another.[70] This was a popular nineteenth-century trope invoked by both Benoy Sarkar and Vinayak Savarkar, though they argued that all nations were once conquered and now racially mixed.[71] Chamberlain spun it to mean that the English aristocracy, which was Norman by race and had segregated itself from the Anglo-Saxon people it ruled, was an immediately recognizable "caste." It possessed a distinct physiognomy, voice, and manner, even its own language—"to be exact, its own accent." Titles mattered little to it; what mattered was "caste."[72] In its fundamental aspect, therefore, the English aristocracy differed from all other aristocracies, emphatically including the French of the ancien régime.

While a numerous tribe had conquered and settled Gaul, reasoned Chamberlain, only a small group had set out to conquer and rule England.[73] Unlike the Franks in Gaul, England's conquerors had not "amalgamate[d]" with the native population but reproduced by "incest." Ventriloquizing Thomas Hobbes, Chamberlain complained that "'Silence! Thou art but an Englishman!'" was the only response an "English" (meaning Anglo-Saxon) critic of Norman "tyranny" could expect from noble tyrants.[74] The English language was born of the same refusal to assimilate, which existed on both sides, Norman and Anglo-Saxon. English, though long regarded as a paragon of successful fusion, marked for Chamberlain the failure of fusion by perpetuating "two warring idioms," each aiming for supremacy over the other: "one above and one below, one noble and one common."[75] Chamberlain concluded that like their language, the "English" (British) were marked by an irreconcilable "split" (*Zwiespaltung*).[76] For Chamberlain, unlike for Gobineau, nationality overdetermined race, which was not originally pure but forged from successful amalgamation.[77] In the *Foundations of the Nineteenth Century,* he had praised the English as the ideal national race whose purity was forged from historical and racial admixture.[78] In the crucible of war fifteen years later, the Germans replaced them.

Racial mixing famously explained the degeneration of the French aristocracy to Gobineau. But that mixture was what redeemed them in Chamberlain's eyes as nationalism won over racism and equality over inequality in the enthusiasm of war in 1914—referred to as the "ideas of 1914."[79] Chamberlain's essay, named after the "England" that it derides, is introduced by an abstract commentary on the making of national character. If certain historical moments revealed glimpses of the constitution of a nation's character, he argued that the Great War exposed the hopeless division of the English—to the shock and embarrassment of their cousins, the Germans.[80] The Germans, though of less unadulterated Germanic stock than the English and more liberally interspersed with Jews, had proven themselves one united nation in the "enormous uprising" of 1914.[81] The call of duty to war was given so general an answer that it "swept away" even the distinctiveness of the Jews, who were "no longer detectable as 'Jews'" but performed "their duty as Germans." This concession is striking coming from so notorious an antisemite as Chamberlain. He explained, "When a nation rises, the Jew follows, he does not lead."[82] In this case, "the Jew" had followed German patriotism and cut their ties to foreign coreligionists. Boundless enthusiasm over the final delivery of German unity in the crucible of war made possible Chamberlain's (temporary) revision of his position on the Jewish question.[83]

An English-language version of Chamberlain's essay simultaneously appeared in an American journal.[84] What earned Chamberlain ire in America, along with advice that he should relocate to Berlin since his opinions were "of the Wilhelmstrasse variety," was the claim that the treasure and pride of the English, their liberty, was but the "liberty of a caste."[85] England's political truth was "tyranny," its parliament a "machine" given a "democratic coating."[86] By defining liberalism as a surface-level production masking violent antagonism, Chamberlain shot British condemnations of Germany's failure to evolve political liberty back at the accusers. Liberal imperialism in India was likewise built on the "disavowal of conquest."[87] To expose this conquest became the first task of Indian nationalists. Chamberlain's exposé was different in that it transposed the conquest that had produced the abnormality of the "'virtually despotic government of a dependency by a free people,'" in Henry Maine's words, from the colony to the "liberal" metropole itself.[88]

According to its myth, the German "ideas of 1914" annihilated factionalism and caste in the "crucible of the idea of the people" that Ambedkar similarly envisaged for India.[89] In the crucible of war, the ideal of popular sovereignty seemed reconciled with German realities for the first time, and the German *Volk* was finally forged—in frontline fraternity. Such was its appeal that, in 1927, Artur Mahraun (1890–1950), a Freikorps leader after the war but an enemy of Nazism, immortalized the mission of the "front generation" as *The Young German Manifesto: Nation against Caste and Money.*[90] Mahraun argued that "frontline camaraderie has proven the injustice of caste to the front generation. It demands its continuation in the spirit of the *Volksgemeinschaft* with elemental force."[91] Yet the appeal of the *Volksgemeinschaft* transcended political ideologies during the Weimar Republic.[92] Among those who experienced the war as a form of "kinship of the entire nation" was the first ordinary professor of journalism in Germany, a Social Democrat and later opponent of Nazism, Erich Everth (1887–1934). Writing in 1916, Everth had no compunction about praising the Social Democrats for finally espousing the "national comrades" (*Volksgenossen*) as their political object. Moreover, he identified its opposite, significantly dubbed "caste spirit" (*Kastengeist*), as that which "prevents healthy blood circulation in the body of the *Volk*."[93] Yet, as if preempting Schmitt's conclusions about "the political," for Everth, it was not "enmity" but "love" that grounded national feeling.[94] Everth was explicit: nationalism required internal unification rather than exclusion. It was heir to the French revolutionary abolition of the system of estates rather than the European backlash against Napoleon. The familiar expression was true, he concluded: what had become a state in 1871 had only become a nation in 1914.[95] The fraternity of soldiers forged and purged of *Kaste* in the trenches of war became the first building bloc of the Nazi idea of *Volksgemeinschaft.*[96]

Race, Class, Caste: Adolf Hitler's War

In the Weimar Republic's fourteen turbulent years of existence, *Kaste* became a staple denouncement of the political establishment from antidemocratic ultranationalist, *völkisch,* and National Socialist quarters. At the same time, the term remained a self-description in aristocratic laments over the "collapse" of 1918 that had deprived aristocrats of "caste" status. Ultraelitists like the "Conservative Revolutionary" Edgar Julius Jung (1894–1934) did not seek to abolish "caste."[97] In fact, Jung attributed the degeneracy of his time to the absence of a real, duty-bound aristocratic "'Kaste.'"[98] This he understood as connected to an aristocratic tradition that "relentlessly imposes laws upon itself, which are also relentlessly executed." He now found it replaced by its opposite, the self-contradictory "'honor code' of the rabble."[99] Jung sought a return to the hierarchical society of the Middle Ages, but even he did not desire the return of the old Junkers.[100] His influential 1927 indictment of the Weimar Republic as the *Rule of the Inferior* stated paradigmatically, "Every caste, also that of the civil servants, needs fresh blood and outsiders."[101] "Superior quality" (*Hochwertigkeit*) rather than property alone should be the qualification for rule.[102] The ruling caste needed reconstituting from below. This was close to Nazism, but not close enough: Jung was murdered by the Nazis in 1934.[103]

If the Conservative Revolution, which shared considerable ground with Nazism, could endorse *Kaste*, the question adapted from Quentin Skinner's famous dictum is this: what did *Kaste* "do" for the Nazis?[104] Precisely because its use was not inflated (unlike *Rasse* and *Volk*), *Kaste* remained conceptually sharply articulated and provides a window into Nazi thought. It was both a critique of power and a name for extreme social division. Though for the most part abstracted from India, sometimes a particular association with the "priestly" or "warrior caste" recalled India's Brahmins and Kshatriyas as well as European feudal society. The crucial point is that rather than being celebrated as a paragon of inequality and racial rule, as one might expect, *Kaste* overwhelmingly retained its derogatory sense in Nazi usage. During their rise to power, it buttressed the Nazis' demand to forge state and society anew. In power, it continued to designate the opposite of *Volk*, thus becoming central to arguments about *völkisch* consolidation and the aim of *Volksgemeinschaft*.

Take, for example, Leni Riefenstahl's 1935 film, *Triumph of the Will*, that immortalized the 1934 Nuremberg rally.[105] In it, Reich youth leader Baldur von Schirach (1907–1974) salutes the assembled Hitler Youth as those who would "know no class and no caste." In the youth, the future consolidated German *Volk* was already manifest. Like the old dream of the *Volk*, the Nazi *Volksgemeinschaft* was a future concept.[106] Reinhart Koselleck has described the term *Volk* as historically "undermined" by three terms approaching it from two sides: "first, by the term 'race' from the Right, second by the term 'class' from the Left, third by the term 'masses' from the Left and Right."[107] I suggest adding a fourth term: "caste." The *Volksgenossen* would have no caste to divide them and everything to unite them.

Hitler publicly employed the term *Kaste* about two dozen times between his rise from obscurity in the belligerent scene of postwar Munich and the "seizure of power" (*Machtergreifung*) in 1933.[108] While this may not be impressive statistically (compared to, say, mentions of *Volk* or *Rasse*), *Kaste* served a key purpose for Hitler. It was a fighting word of the "fighting time" (*Kampfzeit*), a tirade against the status quo, which thereafter receded from Hitler's vocabulary.[109] Interviewed in January 1934, Hitler declared that it was the "prewar viewpoint" that politics stood apart from everyday life and was the domain of a "predestined caste." His movement, by contrast, concerned the entire *Volk*, and there was no more "room for the unpolitical human."[110] *Kaste* belonged to the old "bourgeois" or "middle-class" (*bürgerlich*) world order that the Nazis claimed to have toppled.[111] It may be at least of poetic significance that the political signification of *Kastengeist* did not enter German dictionaries until the Nazi years.[112] Hitler thus stylized his movement as the long-awaited triumph of the *Volk*—not only over elite power and its *Kastengeist* but over the "class madness" (*Klassenirrsinn*) that, during the Weimar Republic, threatened to break it.[113]

With great consistency, Hitler maintained that only the complete loss of traction between the rulers and the ruled had allowed two antagonistic movements to develop in Germany: the proletariat and the bourgeoisie. In 1918, the German nation had fractured over them. Crucially, Hitler blamed the 1918 revolution on "middle class" politics that had ignored the development of a "fourth estate" within the nation.[114] Thus, the failure of the "caste" in power had allowed a "new power in the state" to grow unchecked and become antithetical to the state. The *Volk* was collapsing, sandwiched between the complacent bourgeoisie (*Bürgertum*) as a "caste in itself" and the Jewish "destroyer" who preached class struggle to prize apart the German "workers of the fist and of the forehead."[115] Only a political movement that forged a "*united front*" between nationalism and socialism but smashed their partisan parties could still reconcile the working masses to the state—if it could show them that "*the fatherland [wa]s not [there] for a caste*" but for the "*millions*."[116]

The strategy of appropriating socialist rhetoric while battling communism and socialism as its greatest enemies dates to the earliest days of National Socialism. Rudolf Jung (1882–1945), who was instrumental in inserting the term "National Socialist" into the German Workers' Party (Deutsche Arbeiterpartei, DAP) that Hitler joined in 1919, advanced a similar argument in his programmatic text of early National Socialism.[117] In *National Socialism*,

Jung condemned what he framed as socialist attempts to "tear" the "fourth estate" from the "body of the nation" (*Volkskörper*) and turn it into a "caste," as had happened with the aristocracy and clergy in the Middle Ages, when each had attempted to turn the state into an instrument of their "caste" alone. The "proletariat" must not be allowed a repeat.[118] During Weimar Germany, the communist class struggle posed the greatest threat to the unity of the *Volk*—the unity of the German race.

Hitler's use of the term *Kaste* was not always systematic. For example, summoning the memory of the front generation in a 1930 speech, he spoke of "insurmountable barriers" of "class and caste" as an infestation of the body politic and of the "duty" to prevent them.[119] Though here Hitler expunged the difference between caste and class, he did not consider *Kaste* as reducible to social class for the most part. In one signification, it was a class backed up by power: the ruling class. In another, it was social division grown deep and intransient and made divergent from and antagonistic to other parts of the *Volk*: the aggravated, Marxist understanding of class requiring class war. It was in this context that Hitler restored the Indian flavor of caste that was lost elsewhere.

In a paradigmatic speech of 1922 setting up the Nazi alternative to the bogey of communism, Hitler stated the first postulate of his movement to be the identity of the "national" and "social." Then proceeding to the second, he continued,

> There are and there can be no classes. *Class means caste and caste means race*. If there are castes in India—yes, indeed—it is possible there, there [in India] were once Aryans and dark natives. Among us in Germany where everyone carries the same blood who is at all German, and has the same eyes and speaks the same language, there can be no class, there is only a nation [*Volk*] and nothing else.[120]

What he stated here as fact was actually a political maneuver. Resurrecting the Aryan conquest in India allowed Hitler to disqualify inner-German class struggle as the sort of racial antagonism that he reserved for Jews. He thus made the most of the conjunction of "class" and "race" (as the caste of power) that the term "caste" had projected since the ancien régime. Hitler knew that Indian society's division into castes prevented its fusion into a nation that could present a united "front" against the British.[121] In his prior pivotal quote, which a *Lexicon of National Socialism* of 1934 even went so far as to use to define the crucial entry on "race," *Kaste* functioned to identify class politics with the catastrophe of race war.[122] Hitler required "caste" in the signification of race/class to be purged from the *Volksgemeinschaft,* along with its communist advocates and any antagonistic or agonistic politics based on the recognition of difference. Some occupational division of the nation—into "estates" (*Stände*) if one so wished—had to exist. But categorically, "the struggle [*Kampf*] and the partition wall [between them] must never become so great that the bonds of race break over it," as had happened in France.[123]

In 1932, Hitler announced that only once the "caste of masters" (*Herrenkaste*) was finally defeated could the two classes be reconciled, an otherwise inevitable proletarian revolution avoided, and the "brokenness [*Zerrissenheit*] of the past" mended.[124] The negative use of the Nietzschean term *Herrenkaste* here is significant. Who, then, succeeded the aristocracy as the new enemy of the people? Communists, finance capital, *Politikaster* (as Hitler scornfully called politicians), the Weimar establishment, and, behind them, "the Jew." For a major, perverse Nazi tenet held that "the Jew" undermined national foundations and usurped power simultaneously from above and below, from right and left, as a "capitalist tyrant driv[ing] the masses to desperation" and as a socialist agitator whipping them up. Because the bourgeoisie had failed the masses and was ultimately overpowered by them, "the Jew" had been able to seize the chance.[125] "The Jew as dictator" in Weimar Germany preached "class against class / instead of / Germans against Jews," wrote Hitler in notes to a speech of 1920, and he suggested a reversal.[126] There had been occasional calls to eradicate the *Judenkaste* even in the nineteenth century.[127] Definitively under Weimar Germany, the figure of the Jew fused analytically, if not explicitly, with the old enemy that split the people: the aristocratic *Kaste* of power. Like the *Volk,* "the Jew" projected a kind of sovereignty—in Nazi eyes, an international enemy power that negated German and all national sovereignty. Only once the shape-shifting enemy was defeated would the dead state give way to a "living" *Volk,* neither riddled nor ruled by caste.[128]

The NSDAP emerged as the strongest party in parliament with the general election of July 1932. But short of an overall majority and opposed by President Paul von Hindenburg, the Nazi "seizure of power" could yet be prevented. A precarious government without parliamentary support and relying exclusively on emergency decrees was formed under Franz von Papen. Preempting a vote of no confidence, on September 12, 1932, Papen dissolved parliament. He now operated completely outside the constitutional frame; Weimar democracy had run out of defenders.[129] The NSDAP telescoped its take on these critical events into one caption: "Caste against the People: The People against Caste." This appeared as a special title—a unique distinction, to my knowledge—on the front page of the October 1932 issue of the *National Socialist Monthly,* the Nazi party's "theory-organ" edited by Alfred Rosenberg and, until 1934, Hitler himself.[130] The title had been adapted from Rosenberg's own article published in the same issue, "The Conflict between Caste and the People."[131] A very similarly titled "People's Right against the Power-Hungry Caste!," almost certainly also penned by Rosenberg, appeared in the Nazi press in Chile.[132] Both articles shaped the events of September 12 into a fierce critique of a *Kaste* of aristocratic reactionaries that had outraged the general will by forestalling the legitimate assumption of power of its appointee, Adolf Hitler. With Papen, the charge went, Hindenburg had appointed a man who "had no right whatsoever to rule Germany," but he did so by relying on "the social strata related to him, without consideration of the avowed will of the nation." In other words, both men represented a "caste," which, relying on the army to "secure" its "usurped leadership," "presented [itself] to the nation as its 'ruling class [*Führerschicht*].'"[133] It would not last. Crucially at this point, and in keeping with the Nazis' fig-leaf approach to legality, Rosenberg located the general will in the ballot box.

Speaking at an NSDAP convention in Munich a few days prior, Hitler had explained the political stakes of the moment as the final capture of the German state by the sovereign people. The German state, he argued, had never been a "people's state" (*Volksstaat*). It had only ever been a "party state" and a "pure class state" ruled by a "caste," namely of aristocrats and Jews.[134] This sentiment was not new: it echoed disillusionment with the achievements of the Second Reich and German unification in 1871.[135] In Paul de Lagarde's memorable words that Rosenberg transferred to the Weimar Republic, "'There has never been a German state.' 'The (present) state is a caste, political life a farce, public opinion a cowardly harlot.'"[136] The breakthrough came when Hitler "seized power," as Nazi propagandists termed it, on January 30, 1933. After the misguided French example of 1789 and the short-lived German "ideas of 1914," the Nazi "revolution" of 1933 finally defeated *Kaste* and delivered the German *Volk*.[137]

Democracy was an early casualty of the new regime. Hitler ridiculed the idea that the "people [had been] sovereign" during the Weimar Republic, when "international capital" was the only "sovereign" and parliament an ineffectual tool of the victors of Versailles.[138] The Nazis stood for repatriating sovereignty by defeating the "international Jew," and they made a point to present themselves as popularly elected. But the Nazis used democratic language and methods only where it suited them. Their reality was contempt for democracy. Hitler spurned the "Jewish" "majority" principle, which offended his social Darwinist tastes. His heart beat for the gifted "minority," the small band of stormtroopers ready to break socialist skulls, whom he considered as worth more than millions of "vote cattle" (*Stimmvieh*).[139] It beat for the great "personality," the driver of history. Such a man could speak for the *Volk*—not because the majority elected him, not because he was "popular" or represented them, but because he was "fanatically" committed to the objective requirements of its life. Nazi rule ensured its popular foundations by manufacturing them as the *Volk*. The *Volk*, in this view, was not cut off from sovereignty because it was in a perfect, hierarchical organization connected from the smallest individual up to the highest leader. The brotherhood arrayed around the leader at the top was meritocratically recruited from the best of the blood that theoretically flowed in every German's veins. This was a peculiar kind of popular sovereignty; it was nondemocratic, but in the eyes of its advocates, it was a superior form of popular sovereignty that functioned—better than French and English examples and infinitely more German—through a *Führer*.[140]

The lesson was easily brought home to Indians that a "veritably national community" could only be established once the nation was no longer "artificially divided into classes" and "hypnotized by caste prejudices" and when the "singing of songs of hatred" had ended. The Indian presenter of Nazi Germany's wartime radio propaganda for Indians—Bose's show—asked, "Can there ever be a better appeal formulated for the existing conditions of India today?"[141] The episode on February 3, 1941, in their series on "The Social Policy in New Germany," recalled the spectacle of German workers marching in unison on May Day in 1933, the first under Nazi rule, which the Nazis had carefully choreographed to celebrate the end of class struggle through the union of labor and capital. The war that inhered in society had to be redirected.

Modeled on myth making around the dissolution of caste in 1914, the *Volksgemeinschaft* coexisted uneasily with ideas of nobility that simultaneously resurged. Showing himself confident of victory in September 1932, Hitler mocked the "inherited nobility!" (the Papens and Hindenburgs) that conspired with an "international clique of Jews" and thereby hoped to deprive the nation of the victory brought to it by "this young nobility that has fought for it[s title]."[142] This "nobility" was the Sturmabteilung (SA) and SS, which had won or, in the case of its aristocratic members, renewed its title in the fight against communists, Jews, and the Weimar state.[143] After all, political taste decided whether the whole *Volk* was allowed to share in the casteless fraternity of the veterans. With enormous repercussions for Italian and German fascism, the brotherhood of the trenches marked the dawn of a new elite: the "trenchocracy [*trincerocrazia*] is the aristocracy of the trenches," Mussolini wrote, even before the Great War was out.[144] Nationalism repressed it. But in the end, Nazi racism and elitism resurrected the old aristocratic trope of the merit of "caste." With this final puzzle piece in place, we now explore how, for Nazis and Nazi sympathizers, "orders of inequality" (Stefan Breuer) may satisfy the desire for popular rule and, paradoxically, both equality and hierarchy.[145]

Noblesse de Race

The scholarly convention of alleging Nazi sympathy for the caste system as India's monument to inequality rests on the actualization of nineteenth-century visions of a "new aristocracy" (*Neuadel*) in the field of Nazism.[146] This nexus of ideas of blood and rule reemphasized older understandings of "race" as an aristocratic, not a national, quality—a *noblesse de race*. Breeding noble blood lineages of hunting dogs, falcons, and aristocratic humans in the Middle Ages is one origin story of the concept of "race."[147] Ideas of *noblesse de race* developed in eighteenth-century France as a defense of the "aristocracy of the sword" against its demotion by the upstart "nobility of the robe" recruited from the Third Estate.[148] The revival of these ideas in German expectations of a "twilight of the aristocracy" (*Adelsdämmerung*) was a reassertion of Nietzsche and Gobineau against the nationalist democratization of "race."[149] Propagators of a "new aristocracy" demanded that the aristocracy absorb "'elite-elements'" from below and conversely "'discharge'" those that were no longer elite.[150] Those who had liberally intermarried with Jews were especially to be cast out, as theirs was a racist concept of meritocracy, which revived but repopulated "caste."

The ability of Europe's class to condition social mobility was exactly why, for Sister Nivedita, it was the "exact opposite" of India's caste. Namely, as enterprising individuals in India were unable to rise above their caste, as one could with class, they had to raise their caste instead.[151] Drawing on French aristocratic conceptions in her 1901 essay "Noblesse Oblige: A Study of Indian Caste," Nivedita argued that "caste" should be translated as "honour" to avoid the confusion that other translations had caused.[152] The "ugliest" root of caste was "the sense of race, the caste of blood." It had withered away with Aryan-Dravidian admixture. Nevertheless, every caste, whether high or low, continued to proudly guard its "treasure of birth." Ethical in nature, caste was nothing to be "thrown off lightly."[153] It followed, for Nivedita, that caste, denoting (caste-specific) "honour" rather than (hierarchical) "rank," could not be the opposite of democracy that it was made out to be.[154]

Nivedita's caution notwithstanding, neo-aristocratic conceptions of *Kaste* in Nazi Germany combined precisely the two elements that Nivedita insisted were not caste: "blood" and social mobility. The curious result was a racist conception of meritocracy. Hitler himself arguably championed something like "equality of opportunity," crediting his movement with tearing down the old "diseased social order" that had prevented a "new selection" (*Auslese*) of talent rising from the working class.[155] Nordic blood replaced blue blood's right to rule for those whose inspiration came from the Germanic warrior aristocracy of the Middle Ages that had formed after the *Völkerwanderung,* or "migration period," that captivated the Nazi imagination.[156] In the eyes of Richard Darré, chief "blood and soil" ideologue, agriculture minister, and head of the SS Race and Settlement Main Office, the old "Germanic" aristocracy had been unique in that it was a breeding community of excellence sourced from the body of the *Volk.*[157] The "Reich Peasant Leader" expounded on this theme in his book of 1930, *New Aristocracy of Blood and Soil,* where he contrasted the ancient "Germanic" ideal of aristocracy based on the eugenic merit of blood with the later German aristocracy defined by privilege.[158] Yet Darré categorically rejected what some eugenicists or "racial hygienists" (*Rassenhygieniker*) proposed: breeding a new aristocratic *Kaste* according to the old aristocratic principle of "equality of birth" (*Ebenbürtigkeit*), discussions already entangling India and Europe in the nineteenth century.[159] After all, the strict regulation of the *connubium* was the distinguishing feature in both cases of "caste."[160] A review of racial theories published in 1915 even telescoped this breeding model into a suggestive chapter heading: "Castes, Nobility."[161]

In rejecting eugenicist fantasies of "caste" breeding, Darré likely had one of his major influences in mind: Hans Günther.[162] "Race-Günther" (*Rassengünther*) followed Gobineau in regarding the Brahmin caste as an inbreeding unit through which the Aryan race had preserved itself in India. The famous eugenicist was incensed by what he saw as the degeneration of the racially sensible system of "'equality of birth [*Ebenburt*]'" that had once distinguished "caste" in India and medieval Europe into a racially senseless system of purchasable nobility.[163] It is significant that Günther, who found Germans short on Nordic blood, used the term *Volk* contemptuously.[164] Günther supported breeding as per *Ebenburt* but thought that race should replace class considerations: Nordic aristocrats should wed Nordic peasant girls, not degenerate princesses or Jewish bankers' daughters.[165] By contrast, Darré objected to "equality of birth" precisely on the grounds that it would reintroduce an insurmountable barrier into the "body of the *Volk*" (*Volkskörper*), again barring the "ruling caste" from constantly renewing itself through good racial stock rising from below. Complete reproductive isolation as per "equality of birth" only made sense where substantially different races existed. Even there, it would inevitably lead to ossification and decay—as in India.[166] Therefore, Darré concluded, "We generally reject everything that is connected to the term caste."[167]

Günther and Darré's disagreement over "caste" was not always noted. Herbert Meyer (1875–1941), an influential "Germanist" jurist desiring a return to Germanic law, concluded that both Darré in *New Aristocracy* and Günther in *Führer-Aristocracy through Clan Cultivation* endorsed a class of rulers deeply rooted in, instead of imposed upon, the *Volk*.[168] Meyer's own 1937 publication, *Race and Law among the Teutons and Indo-Europeans*, noted Günther's colorful characterization of the Teutons' "double face" (*Doppelgesicht*) as "peasant-nobles [*Adelbauern*] or warrior-peasants [*Bauernkrieger*]."[169] Violent subjugation of a prehistoric peasant tribe by a "warrior caste" could not explain this hybrid character, Meyer insisted, tracing it instead to the peaceful amalgamation of two separate tribes of the same Germanic family.[170] The lessons of history charted the future course. Where conquerors had never ruled peasants, the present task could not be to breed a "Nordic master strata" (*Nordische Herrenschicht*) to rule the *Volk*. This would mean "death" to the German nation, while "eternal life" required constant rejuvenation sourced from the biological reservoir of the *Volk*.[171]

In short, Nazi ideologies and policies of *Rasse* and *Volk* clashed spectacularly and on several counts. The majority view was that Germans were not a race.[172] "Aryan" was used mainly synonymously with "German" to disenfranchise Jews and "gypsies," not for hard scientific classification. Germans were a mixture of five or six European racial types, of which the Nordic was the highest and the leading part. It was the creator of German culture and the "glue" that held Germans together; if Nordic blood collapsed, so would Germany.[173] The issue was that Nazi Nordicism, if pushed to the extreme, collapsed into a blue-eyed, blond-haired imperialism that was no longer coextensive with German nationalism. This would again produce a *Kaste* as separate from and ruling over the German *Volk*. *Volk* and race clashed over *Kaste*, and minds clashed over Nietzsche.

Nazi court philosopher Heinrich Härtle (1909–1986) recognized, even if contemporary scholarship does not, that Nietzsche's ultimate concern was not to breed three or four castes—the priestly, warrior, and peasant castes in parallel with the European estates.[174] There was only one distinction that mattered to Nietzsche, Härtle explained in his "popular handbook," *Nietzsche and National Socialism*, published by the Nazi party's official publisher in 1937 and variously reprinted during the war: the distinction between the aristocracy and the rest.[175] Even during his lifetime, Nietzsche had been criticized for "dwell[ing] exclusively on the contrast between the ruling and the subjugated caste."[176] Härtle agreed with Darré that caste was conditioned on serious racial difference that was not found in Europe.[177] He also agreed that the Indian caste system was based on race. Yet, as major Nazi theorist Alfred Rosenberg explained, India's Aryan conquerors had originally occupied the first three castes and aboriginal Indians the lowest caste of Shudras. This meant that the "last division," the one between the third and fourth castes, "[wa]s the most important." It alone was racial.[178] *Kaste* paralleled the Nietzschean distinction between master and slave.

Rosenberg regretted that the original system separating Aryan and Shudra had subsequently degenerated. Miscegenation was usually considered the cause but was only a secondary effect for Rosenberg, who identified the primary cause in a development in Indian religion. With the *brahman-atman* identification (*All-Eins*, Rosenberg called it) designating the deep unity of the individual soul with the Absolute, the Aryans had adopted a monistic religious philosophy that denied the very principle of distinction, let alone division or enmity. Originally, the *atman* doctrine had expressed the "aristocratic self-recognition" (*Selbstbesinnung*) of the Aryan soul, which felt itself to be as colossal and awe-inspiring as the universe.[179] But now the result was the perilous identification of the Aryan self with the Shudra other. It led the Indian to "also worship in the Shudra the divine soul that he feels lives in himself."[180] Miscegenation, ossification, and the degeneration of "the original concept of caste as race" into an occupational system must ensue where race was viewed as "illusion," *maya*.[181]

Drawing on Gobineau, Günther similarly believed the creation of the Brahmin caste and Brahmanism, its religion, to be degenerations of the Aryan "spirit" of race. The previous Rig Vedic age had known only two castes: conquerors and natives.[182] The former were called Arya, the "nobles" (*die Edlen*), who were blond; the latter were called *dāsa,* initially meaning "enemy" and then, "significantly" for Günther, taking on the connotation of "slave."[183] Likewise, one may argue that there were also only two castes in America: White masters and Black slaves.[184] The ancient Indian distinction between freeman and slave (twice-born castes and Shudras) had been pointed out from the earliest days of orientalism, including by Henry Thomas Colebrooke in his seminal *Digest of Hindu Law* (1797). Colebrooke had aspirations of becoming a slave-plantation owner himself, showcasing how the colonial formalization of caste in India was already inflected by the transatlantic context of slavery.[185] The forced labor aspect of caste was viewed as central early on, but in the nineteenth century, British administrators denied it to erase the similarity between untouchability and slavery that they were no longer supposed to endorse once Britain had lost its profitable American colonies.[186] The Indian Marxist M. N. Roy came down on the side of the slavery-caste equation, giving it pride of place in his 1938 book on the anatomy of fascism. He blamed Gandhi making a virtue of suffering, every bit as much as Nietzsche's cult of power, for paving the way to fascism.[187]

Nietzsche was a widely popular, though by no means homogenous, entity under National Socialism.[188] Härtle nevertheless spoke as an astute Nietzsche interpreter and a nationalist Nazi when he concluded that Nietzsche and Nazism had to part ways on the point of caste. Härtle understood that such a thing as an organically grown community was inconceivable to Nietzsche because proximity between ruler and ruled was unthinkable.[189] But the Nazis had succeeded where Nietzsche failed. Instead of aristocracy, they had arrived at an organic conception of the state based on "family, clan [*Sippe*] and tribe [*Stamm*]."[190] The democracy Nietzsche categorically rejected was again in the picture: as a "synthetic" democracy, equidistant from liberal democracy's first postulates of equality and elections and Italian Fascism's foundations in "'violence and consent,'" or from "aristocratic Caesarism" and the "collectivist madness of the masses."[191] National Socialism, in Härtle's view, was "true" "people's rule" (*Volksherrschaft*), where the *Volk* crowned a *Führer* who in turn was duty-bound to the *Volk.*[192] Nazism, to Härtle, was an alternative democracy. Instead of bridging the gap between people and "the people" through abstraction, as in the French Revolution, Härtle went the opposite way of securing the *Volk* through consanguinity—what Savarkar did for "the Hindus" through *shuddhi*, sex, and *sangathan*.[193]

Härtle's antipode was Alfred Baeumler (1887–1968), perhaps the most famous Nietzsche interpreter in and for Nazi Germany and a follower of Rosenberg. Baeumler's thinking was aristocratic, anti–French Revolution, and anti-*Volk*. Like Nietzsche's sister, Elisabeth Förster-Nietzsche (1846–1935), Baeumler lifted selected passages from Nietzsche's *Nachlass* and pasted them into an overarching narrative of his own making, creating a nazified Nietzsche whom he popularized through paperback editions.[194] Baeumler's influential Nietzsche endorsed "hierarchy" (*Rangordnung*) and the breeding of a new ruling caste that Härtle eschewed. *The Will to Power*, Förster-Nietzsche's redacted Nietzsche, was to Baeumler the master's magnum opus and a guiding catchphrase. He republished and furnished it with an introduction in 1930. In this collection of aphorisms, Nietzsche ruminated on the resentment against the "caste" of power that spanned from Christianity, the "Tschandala" religion par excellence (*chandala* being an "untouchable" caste), to the French Revolution.[195] It was here that he suggested "breed[ing] a ruling caste—the future masters of the earth."[196]

Baeumler's own compilation of Nietzsche aphorisms, *The Innocence of Becoming*, included generous discussions of Manu and, time and again, caste. Baeumler concluded with Nietzsche that democracy was the rule of the rabble, which he contrasted with the principle of aristocracy that he endorsed as that of noble humans, of breeding, of "caste." Power rather than gentility was the origin of the noble caste, which was in the beginning always the "caste of barbarians"—pointing toward blond beasts who ruled by right of conquest, rather than to Jewish world power.[197] Under the chapter heading "Europe / The Germans" and repeated as the finale of the book, Baeumler summarized Nietzsche to mean that "Germans should breed a ruling caste" to rule Europe and beyond. Baeumler focused only on the German ingredient, to be sure, but he curiously did not cut Nietzsche's suggestion that Jews (bringing financial talent) and Slavs (vitality) would be key ingredients of this new global ruling caste.[198]

Härtle, in turn, considered Nietzsche's cardinal mistake his thinking that Germans and Europeans were hopelessly bastardized, wherefore he saw no other solution but to rake together what was left of good race in Europe and start breeding.[199] But Germans were not so bastardized as all that. The problem with aristocratic castes was that they lacked "roots," making any architecture built on them liable to come crashing down, as in antiquity. But the Nazis had learned the lessons of history and biology. They had realized that breeding needed to start from "natural" community and serve the *Volk*.[200] Rather than aiming to breed a trans-European elite caste—"superm[e]n" and "masters of the earth"—and doing away with the principle of nationality altogether, Härtle argued that Nietzsche should have trusted in the racial amelioration of Germans through "Nordicization" (*Aufnordung*)—that is, the increase of Nordic blood in the German population.[201]

Racial purity was neither starting point nor aim for Härtle, nor did he forget other, nonracial bonds and the forging force of history. Only the Jews were beyond the pale. The *Volk* was held together by bonds of kinship between distinct yet closely related racial strains, led by the Nordic strain. To prove this point, the Nazis revived the outdated idea of *Sippe* ("clan"). Remarkably, Härtle argued that what mattered was kinship, "not racial purity [*Reinrassigkeit*] in the biological sense," again as in Savarkar's Hindutva.[202] Compatible with population genetics up to a point and streamlining ideas of *Rasse* and *Volk*, Nordicization, for Härtle, even transcended the physical. Combining Darwin and Lamarck, "breeding" (*Züchtung*) and "discipline" (*Zucht*), Härtle invited all Germans to model their character on the Nordic component of their mixed blood.[203] Nordicization was the inversion of Nordicist visions that degraded the *Volk* into a well from which the Nordic ruling caste could be replenished.[204] For Härtle, it constituted a *völkisch*-democratic ideal. A kind of compromise between Nazi nationalism and racism, Nordicization recognized the degree of Germans' racial degeneration but countered it with a racial rebirth to serve the whole *Volk*.[205] Nordic supremacist visions of an imperial race and the ideology of *Volksgemeinschaft* could coincide in nationalism.[206] But my point—the subject of endless contention among Nazis and Nazi-friendly thinkers and the rhetorical point of *Kaste*—is their conceptual tension.

Masters and Slaves in the East

In Nazi Germany, slavery appealed. It was assumed that the Aryan (Indo-Germanic or Nordic) race had formed the "ruling class" (*Herrenschicht*) wherever it appeared. "Masterdom," it stood to reason, must be an "inherited" racial quality.[207] One might ask whether this entailed a return to the kind of tyranny with which "caste" was customarily associated. In other words, would Nazi racism and elitism drive the wedge of caste right back into the *Volk*? The trick here was geographic and ethnic displacement: masterdom characterized only outside, not inside, relations. Visions of what German society's internal organization should look like drew on an image of Indo-Aryan or Germanic prehistory as an internally casteless, egalitarian society that developed in two contexts that could not have been more different. In one, anti-Brahmanic reinterpretations of the theory of India's Aryan conquest in nineteenth-century Maharashtra branded the upper castes as foreigners, an interpretation inextricably bound up with the name of Jyotirao Phule (1827–1890).[208] The major evidence for this theory was the absence of a rigid caste order (*varna*) in Rig Vedic times. In the other context, Nazis assumed that ancient Germanic society had been casteless and home to a uniquely Germanic variety of freedom and equality as an alternative to the radical egalitarianism of the French Revolution, a tradition coming out of the nineteenth-century revival of Tacitus's *Germania*.[209] In the twentieth century, these visions allowed the Nazis to confirm slavery as the basis of their empire without, seemingly, undermining *völkisch* equality.

An Indian sadhu named Thanwardas Lilaram Vaswani (1879–1966) plunged into these German discussions in the 1920s. A fairly well-known figure in Germany at the time, Vaswani had followed in Vivekananda's footsteps by launching his career at a congress on religion held in Berlin in 1910.[210] His English and German publications included such tantalizing titles as *The Shapers of the Future and the Aryan Ideal*, a book in which he contended that "Âryavárta," the North Indian home of the ancient Aryans, "knew nothing but freemen." It neither knew an ossified caste nor was conducive to absolutism.[211] Rosenberg recognized the fellow Aryanist as a "more powerful endeavo[r]" than Tagore and Gandhi but rejected his message of *völkisch* Aryan reinvigoration as essentially a copycat Indian fascism.[212] The geopolitician Karl Haushofer, a friend of Benoy Sarkar, accused the sadhu of costing Indian nationalism all foreign sympathy in his attempt to blend the old Indological India with the new India represented by Sarkar.[213] Vaswani was a Gandhian, an admirer of Ramakrishna and Dayananda Saraswati, and an influential, largely overlooked pundit of Hindu Aryanism in interwar Germany.[214]

For the "racial hygienist" Günther, hierarchical orders like the Indian caste system and the European aristocracy were evidence of racial "stratification" (*Schichtung*).[215] Conversely, where racial homogeneity signposted a society of "equals" because racial nobility was shared, only mild social stratification according to merit developed. Merit itself was congenital, of course. No eugenicist would deny it. But the point, for Günther, was that neither hereditary aristocracy nor serfdom could develop where there was only one race.[216] Such had been the case with the predominantly "Nordic" Germans up until the Middle Ages, where "peasant-nobles" (*Adelbauern*) were proud and free and kingship an elective office.[217] Baeumler's conclusions were of a similar nature: "Why has there never been a firmly established German state? Because, according to the Germanic view, the king is not an emperor, just a military leader and protector of law. The Germanic only recognized a leader [*Führer*], not a master [*Herrn*]."[218] For Härtle, too, only vast racial difference warranted steep, hierarchical, aristocratic rule, with slavery as its extreme. Such was the origin of Greece's distinction between freemen and slaves and the organizing principle of European colonialism, which ruled the colonies differently from the metropole: "The greater the racial difference between different strata of society [*Volksschichten*], the steeper the ruling organization; the more related the parts of the people [*Volksteile*], the closer are leadership and following."[219] Freedom, popular sovereignty, and relative equality could only exist among racial equals.[220] Those considered unequal were beyond the ethical demand of equality, thus reproducing the distinction between master and slave.

The one context in which Härtle, too, could reconcile his National Socialism with Nietzsche's idea of creating a transnational ruling caste was beyond Germany.[221] He even suggested that the formation of a "caste ruling over Europe" (in *Beyond Good and Evil*) may counter Europe's racial "mishmash" and restore its greatness. Härtle took pains to demonstrate that Nietzsche assigned Europe's leadership to its Nordic component—that is, to Germany as Europe's most Nordic country in gross numbers, if not in percentage of population.[222] Social Darwinism, "caste," and its relationship to conquest, which were so problematic between Germans, were uncontroversial in the New Order (*Neuordnung*) that the Nazis devised for Europe and particularly the Slavs.[223] And so Darré hoped to make Germans more Nordic by planting farmers into soil where they would take deep root and accrue quality over many generations.[224] This vision may have harmonized better with Hitler's aim of conquering "living space" in the East, thus transplanting German "blood" to foreign "soil," than often assumed.[225] A recent biographer even identifies Darré as the decisive influence behind Himmler's refashioning of the SS into a reproductive order of conqueror-peasants who would found new aristocratic clan lineages in the conquered East.[226] The difference might be one of emphasis: While Darré emphasized peasants, Himmler emphasized warriors.[227] As Darré was outmaneuvered in internal power struggles, it was Himmler's more extreme vision of breeding a Nordic race of "military peasants" (*Wehrbauern*) that shaped Nazi settlement policy at the beginning of the war.[228]

Himmler's SS implies "caste": the warrior caste, especially the Indian Kshatriya and the Japanese samurai. Aged twenty-five in 1925, Hitler's later right-hand man enthusiastically commented in his reading list, "'Kshatriya caste, this is what we have to be. This is salvation!'"[229] Men like the young Himmler seemed to be hailing from the Kaliyuga, the dark age of ancient Indian thought from which the warrior caste had disappeared and the age in which we are currently said to live. Ironically and perhaps not without psychological significance, a Nietzschean aphorism identifies Jews with the loss of the intermediate castes. Included in Förster-Nietzsche's highly tendentious selection in *The Will to Power* was the aphorism that states how all Jews must in consequence be either Brahmins or Shudras.[230] The Kshatriyas and the sovereign power they represented were marked by absence, recalling the Maharashtrian cemetery of the Kshatriyas from which both Dalit politics and Hindutva emerged as claims to Kshatriya identity. In Savarkar's own Maharashtra, according to Brahmin orthodoxy, an epic war had wiped out all intermediate *varnas,* leaving only Brahmins and Shudras. Crucially, the Kshatriya *varna* had disappeared, forcing Maratha rulers—beginning with the Hindu nationalist hero Shivaji in 1673—to try to wrest recognition of their Kshatriya status from Brahmins who regarded them as Shudras.[231] Likewise, in Germany coming out of the crisis of 1918, as Martin Ruehl has argued, there emerged a certain thematization around the empty seat of German sovereignty: emptied, to be precise, by the death of the Holy Roman emperor, Frederick II, in 1250.[232] As Wilhelmine and Weimar-era Germany appeared as a "present Interregnum" and "'this time without emperors,'" expectation grew for the arrival of a new emperor.[233] In this context, Franz Haiser's (1871–1945) curiously titled *Freemasons and Counter-Masons in the Battle for World Rule* inspired the young Himmler to counter this privation of power and rule with a warrior fraternity: the Kshatriya caste.[234]

Haiser's book framed history as a process of the degeneration of rule down the fourfold division of caste.[235] History thus showed how the weak had usurped the natural sovereignty of the strong. Nietzsche; Gobineau; the breeding fantasist of "Mittgart," Willibald Hentschel (1858–1947); Günther; and the influential trio of race scientists, Erwin Baur, Eugen Fischer, and Fritz

Lenz, made up Haiser's intellectual itinerary.[236] More directly than Gobineau, Haiser linked the rise of absolutism to the specific historic defeat of the "caste of warriors" by the Brahmins. Mapping onto Catholic "priestcraft," the Brahmin usurpation of the power of the (Kshatriya) king had drawn extensive commentary from Protestant colonial administrators and indologists and resonated with Nazi critics of Christianity.[237] The defeat of the Kshatriyas set in motion the historical degeneration of rule. Rule first passed from the warriors to the priesthood in the Middle Ages, then to the Vaishyas—the *varna* of traders, the Third Estate that included the Jews—and finally to the present Kaliyuga of Shudra, socialist, and Jewish rule.[238] Against the Shudra religions of Buddhism and Christianity, Haiser envisaged a return of the Kshatriya religions enshrining "the idea of state power," like Brahmanism and Islam.[239] Kshatriyas were not born; they had to be made through war. Dismissed and complaining about it by contemporary German race scientists, especially Baur, Fischer, and Lenz, Haiser announced his Lamarckian belief in amelioration by breeding (*Höherzüchtung*), which assumed the heredity of acquired as well as inherited traits.[240] Haiser wanted to see the "promotion of Kshatriya selection and inhibition of Vaishya selection," meaning that "fresh Kshatriya race from the *Volk*" would replace the "degenerate Kshatriyas in the upper classes."[241]

Haiser projected the "Kshatriya emancipation" as a particular kind of freedom. This was neither the general unfreedom of the Middle Ages where Brahmins ruled nor the present universal, quality-leveling liberty. Instead, it was a "real freedom," a "freedom as difference of value," which depended on a biological "value gradient" (*Wertgefälle*). Taking the distinction between free and enslaved people to have "fertilized culture" in ancient Greece, Haiser insisted that the "pendulum," which in his time had swung too far to the left, "must swing all the more strongly back to the right." He prognosticated, "We are standing before the revolt of the noble race, which will form a new master- and upper class, in other words a Kshatriya-emancipation."[242] The strong were free to rule over, and enslave, the weak. Haiser envisioned nothing less than a "blue International."[243]

By the time of the Nazis, Germans had thoroughly domesticated the Indian epic Bhagavad Gita, in which Arjuna confronts his cousins on the battlefield of Kurukshetra and is faced with the moral conflict of killing his own kinsmen.[244] The conflict is resolved by Krishna, who advises Arjuna that doing his caste-specific duty (*dharma*) as a warrior means fighting, regardless of the results. Germans had found their courage through reading, even translating the Gita in the trenches of World War I.[245] It fit the Nazi warrior worldview that life was struggle and killing justified. Himmler dove deep into Indo-Aryan prehistory through the Ahnenerbe, and his entourage produced a nazified, Aryan Gita.[246] It taught the SS chief, said to have always carried a copy of the Gita on his person, to commit crimes against humanity as a detached duty.[247]

In this context, Himmler's comment about the Kshatriya caste in 1925 is meaningful but nevertheless rare. *Kaste* was not a staple of Himmler's vocabulary, perhaps because he could not shake the negative connotations of the aristocratic caste that his SS resembled. Himmler saw his SS as a Nordic racial vanguard. He used racial criteria to select not only his SS men but also their future wives, though elite racial selection broke down over manpower shortages in the war in the East.[248] Like Savarkar offending conventional sexual morality in pursuit of the "right" kind of racial offspring, the Reichsführer-SS, Himmler, founded homes for unwed mothers-to-be and sanctioned reproductive, extramarital relationships for SS men; Himmler himself had children with his girlfriend as well as his wife. Particularly notorious was the so-called Procreation Order of October 28, 1939, which asked SS men to father children before going to the front so their good racial stock would not be lost to the German *Volk*.[249] Nevertheless, Himmler was at least aware of the divisive potential of the Nordic ideal. As he told secondary school kids in 1938, the Nazis could not allow those with a particular racial physiognomy to consider themselves superior to other Germans, as this would shift the "overcome social class struggle" to a "racial" one. Nordic blood should therefore be viewed "not as the dividing but the all parts of Germany connecting blood share."[250]

Heredity was built into it, yet Himmler stipulated that one third of new SS recruits should come from non-SS families. He cited the cautionary tale of the German aristocracy, which had come to a "standstill" without the invigorating force of "young blood" drawn from the *Volk*. The SS could only stay "forever young" through meritocratic selection (*Auslese* was the oft-used word).[251] Himmler obliquely confronted the overarching problem of caste in other ways, too. By speaking of the Germans collectively as a "master people" (*Herrenvolk*)—like Hitler, he learned from the English, who dominated the much more populous India with only a small group—Himmler democratized and nationalized ruling-class status through colonial expansion.[252] Deporting and exterminating Jews and Slavs, resettling Germans and ethnic Germans (*Volksdeutsche*), and screening the native population for blue-eyed, blond-haired racial traits that qualified them for re-Germanization while enslaving the others, Himmler aimed to turn the occupied East into a vast colony, a *Lebensraum* for the Germans. The racial new order harked back to a vision of early history, in which a "Germanic Nordic master stratum [*Herrenschicht*]" had ruled Europe's East. Miscegenation had set in until, in the medieval period, the Germans had been called in to again colonize the East and the cycle of colonization and miscegenation had begun anew.[253] Thus, instead of turning the SS into a reproductively closed-off "caste" in Germany, Himmler's racial vision amounted to turning the German *Volk* into the ruling "caste" in the East by racially segregating it from the "natives." But for this to work, Germans needed to revert to what they had been: the Nordic race, the best blood in the world, the master caste to rule them all.[254] And so Nazi negative eugenics aimed to weed out the "subhuman" that arose from the "dregs of the [German] race" itself, formed by centuries of miscegenation with peoples East and West.[255]

Rosenberg, an elitist who might similarly be accused of wanting to breed a new "caste," was intimately familiar with Indian ideas that he viewed as a German domestic problem (for he identified them with the nihilistic Vedanta, not the activist Gita). Nevertheless, he juxtaposed "rule by caste" with the Nazi aim of *Volksgemeinschaft* and continued to employ *Kaste* in the sense of a group sequestered from and turned into an illegitimate power ruling over the *Volk*: the church and priesthood in Germany until Luther, the Bolsheviks in the Soviet Union, or the political elite in England, similarly branded a *Kaste* by Goebbels in his diaries and evoking Chamberlain's essay on England.[256] In a speech at the Berlin Sportpalast in October 1933, Rosenberg argued that keeping the people at a remove from politics belonged to the world of the nineteenth century, not to the Nazis; he insisted, "We are not a dictatorship, a tyranny of a small caste."[257]

Unlike Himmler and Hitler, who escaped the hangman's rope by committing suicide, Rosenberg was sentenced to death at the Nuremberg trials. Yet before his execution in 1946, he managed to write his autobiography, in which he returned to the figure of the officer that, like the clergy (the Brahmins), was linked to an ancient Indian *varna*: the Kshatriyas. Rosenberg, the Baltic German from Tallinn (Reval) who emigrated to Germany only after World War I, wrote of his admiration for Prussia and its officer class as the "heir" to the medieval order of knights, whose descent into a "more and more self-segregating caste—in order to preserve its past value"—or utter disappearance into the nouveaux riches he regretted.[258] Rosenberg admired the "officer type" bred by Helmuth von Moltke in the nineteenth century, though by 1914, it had become a caste in, "for Germany[,] unorganic isolation" because it alone was committed to honor when all around was commercial society. This "type" had sacrificed itself on the battlefields of 1914 to 1918, and a new type of soldier had arisen from the casteless fraternity of the trenches that birthed "front socialism" and National Socialism.[259] Rosenberg mused that "soldier" had become a dirty word after 1918 and that the soldier's dignity was only restored in 1933, the great difference being that the soldier of 1933 was "no longer a caste next to or above the *Volk* but a brother of the people [*Volksbruder*]."[260] The Nazi ideal, which Rosenberg preached to the assembled heads of army and navy in March 1935, was that of the "political soldier." In his words, this term and the act of wearing a uniform "today directly connects the Wehrmacht with the German people and prevents the army from again becoming a caste." For in militarizing society, National Socialism blurred the distinction between soldier and civilian.[261]

Rosenberg wanted a new aristocracy, beginning with the fighters for the Third Reich. As he elaborated in *Myth of the Twentieth Century,* titles would be passed down from father to son but, unlike the old and now defunct aristocracy, would be forfeited if one generation should prove unworthy: "Through this regulation, the nobility would no longer be tied to a caste as a horizontal social class but would run vertically through all classes of the *Volk* and would spur all healthy, strong, creative forces to the highest achievement."[262] The new aristocracy would be a "blood- and performance nobility." Selected through deeds rather than "head-index-numbers," its constituents would nevertheless be "80 percent" phenotypic Nordics, for what was demanded coincided with what was in their blood.[263] Rosenberg later spoke of a "value-conditioned hierarchy" (*wertbedingte Randordnung*), which replaced the ideal of the bygone age: that of a hereditary leisure class of "gentlemen," defined by not having to work. Only this performance principle assured that the "tough type of the fighting years" remained dominant in peacetime. He concluded, "Only then will it be possible to prevent a caste from emerging again at some point."[264] *Kaste* was the ossification of life, a dying thing cut off from the blood supply of the eternal *Volk,* even to someone with the aristocratic tastes of Rosenberg.[265]

Where Do We Go from Here?

It is not the case that Nazi Germany's only despotism was an excess of the idea of the people. Collapsing the interplay between coercion and consent into a "consensus" on Nazi rule in Germany is, as one scholar has noted, like "clapping" "with one hand."[266] Certainly, as well as a favorite Nazi propaganda tool, the *Volksgemeinschaft* was a "coercive" category, with the promise of inclusion in a homogenized nation built on the exclusion of Jews and other "community aliens."[267] Violence was a pillar of the regime. More than that, violence and war were essential ideological aims. The "front spirit" (*Frontgeist*), as Hitler made clear in a speech of 1930, was misunderstood as a guiding ideal. It could not be "striven for" in the abstract. Instead, it had to be perpetually "renewed" in "living struggle."[268] Both the casteless *Volk* and the new racial aristocracy required the momentum of unending battle for their emergence and maintenance. This is another parallel with Savarkar's Hindutva, which was entirely couched in the moment of war against its enemy; others had to reinvent Hindutva for post-Partition India. National Socialism is inconceivable in a static state, once it had achieved its goals. In twelve short years, it had consumed itself in a work of enormous destruction.[269]

Still, the popular dimension was real enough. During their rise to power, as this chapter has shown, the Nazis identified the Weimar establishment and Jews as the illegitimate ruling "caste"—the "caste" of power—that they singled out to fight and eradicate. Yet *Kaste* also indexed entrenched social division. The German *Volk*, forged by the Nazi project, would be casteless. The *Volk* so conceived stood on consanguine foundations, and thus, sovereign power could finally be popular. In the Third Reich, no longer usurped by a caste of intermediaries and not needing to be limited as in the liberal tradition, popular sovereignty could speak through a *Führer*. "The people" would no longer be divided against itself, the ruler no longer opposed to the *Volk*, for they were one: "One *Volk*, one *Reich* [empire], one *Führer*," as the Nazi slogan went. At the same time, in pursuing a European New Order, National Socialism raised demands for a truer, homegrown "new aristocracy" as an imperial race linking back to the old aristocratic "race" of the Germanic conquerors. By mitigating its resonance with *Kaste*, Nazi theorists assured that this new aristocracy would never again be shut off from the *Volk*.

The significance of this history beyond Nazi Germany is a striking case of an Indian concept and political problem that was fully incorporated into modern political grammar. "Caste" entered modern political grammar as both aristocrat *and* slave, divergent meanings produced by different political and linguistic histories (slavery in America, aristocracy in Europe). For the most part, they did not interfere with one another. But where the generalized meanings converged, they formed a particularly nasty Nazi common sense: that those who ought to be slaves had made themselves a global ruling aristocracy. They were, of course, talking about the Jews.

Since the story of *Kaste* begins with the French Revolution, there is no getting around the place of National Socialism in the history of European political thought. Did National Socialism manifest the latent dangers of democracy slipping into demagogy that were pointed out throughout this history?[270] Succinctly put, was Rousseau the problem? No, not quite. What is certain is that the Nazis claimed to roll back the hands of time before the French Revolution, back to an idea of the Middle Ages held in timeless perpetuity.[271] So what about the *Volk* and *Kaste,* its enemy, if Nazism launched an assault on the French Revolution? One way to cut through this conundrum is again with Benoy Sarkar, who categorically insisted that fascism was a new departure in the history of political ideas. Nazism was no old-school despotism. Its "alphabet" was "derived from the language of 'government of the people, for the people and by the people.' It is the people—the folk, the *Volksgemeinschaft*."[272] No matter what the Nazis might say, concluded Sarkar, there simply was no stepping back behind the idea of "the people." The early Middle Ages served to ground the fiction of the organic *Volk* that perverted the civic idea of "the people" in Nazi Germany. In the Middle Ages, there had been *Sippe,* kinship, organic association, and kings elected by their racial peers. There had been a consanguine and therefore more socially equitable order as the basis of the new idea of popular sovereignty that, yes, the Nazis rejected in its French revolutionary form. In Nazi Germany, citizenship was tied to the Aryan certificate (*Ariernachweis*). The history of *Kaste* reveals how the Nazis based popular sovereignty on biological foundations. The longer genealogy demonstrates how, at the birth of modern democracy, an Indian social problem became the defining political problem of making "the people" sovereign.

CHAPTER FOUR

THE HINDU CROWN

"Blood and soil" (*Blut und Boden*), the Nazi slogan, is familiar to the point of cliché. If the previous two chapters uncoupled ideas of "blood" from purity in India and Nazi Germany, this chapter aims to change the terms of the debate around "soil." The basic argument is that what mattered to Hindu-minded nationalists was not Hindusthan as territory per se but the idea of a "Hindu Crown." A scholarly consensus assumes the primacy of the geographic salience of India, which nationalists are supposed to have worshipped as their Bharat Mata ("Mother India"). Whether as a product of colonial map making, political economy, or Hindu cosmography, Indian nationalism is thought to have succumbed to the enchantment of land, with Savarkar widely figuring as the primary thinker of India as spiritualized territory.[1] But scholars have too long let the iconography of the map and the identification of *pitribhu(mi)* and *punyabhu(mi)* ("fatherland" and "holy land") in *Essentials of Hindutva* do their conceptual heavy lifting for them. The territorial idea might have taken precedence for all-India nationalists such as Nehru and as the basis for Hindu-Muslim unity, but for Hindu nationalism, the goal was the attainment of Hindu sovereignty. And the integration of territory with this kind of sovereignty was not at all straightforward. Where Savarkar directly addressed the territorial conception of nationhood, he found it deficient. Hindus, he wrote, may dupe themselves into thinking that the "Indian nation was but a territorial appellation of the Hindu nation," but this was not so.[2] Hindu selfhood was wrapped up with their territory, to be sure, but not as its primary determinant. Always looking to inherit his enemy, Savarkar claimed that Muslims knew territory was no basis for nationality, even if Hindus of the Congress type did not.[3] Territorial nationalism encompassing all those who lived in Hindusthan was not equivalent to "Hindu sovereignty."[4] Hindutva was no territorial expression.

India's figuration was important, no doubt, but this chapter demonstrates a much more tenuous relationship between sovereignty and space in the Hindu nationalist imagination. Only its detractors called India a "geographical expression." If India was to be more than a "collection" of raids and conquests, wrote the future British prime minister Ramsay MacDonald in his introduction to Radhakumud Mookerji's (1884–1963) groundbreaking *The Fundamental Unity of India* of 1914, then it must be a "political unit naturally the subject of one sovereignty—whoever holds that sovereignty, whether British, Mohammedan, or Hindu."[5] India must have an innate tendency to form an imperial center—the "paramount sovereignty," as Mookerji called it—which the British claimed in India.[6] The primary addressees here, however, were not the British. The exercise was not simply about stealing Britain's Indian empire away from them.[7] Rather, for Hindu nationalists and sympathetic Indian nationalists, the issue was that India's imperial center could not come as a gift of British or Muslim imperialism. It needed to be embedded in a deeper Hindu past.

In a series of seminal interventions, Sheldon Pollock hypothesized how the language of the gods, Sanskrit, became the language of political power across South and Southeast Asia in the first millennium.[8] As we shall see, this was a "Brahmin hypothesis" of the "Indianization" of Southeast Asia.[9] And he marked the "Death of Sanskrit" when Sanskrit became incapable of articulating new ideas and, repulsed by politics, retreated to repetition and religion.[10] Pollock is adamant: it was not the coming of Muslim power that killed Sanskrit but the fact that its world shrank, preferring the local and the vernacular.[11] By the time of the British, Hindus were believed to have no history of power, unlike the Muslims. Allegedly, Hindus were focused on religion and retreat from the world. While Muslim powers had dominated the subcontinent before the British, anticolonialism and the prospect of expelling the British presented a chance for Hindus to finally make a play for sovereignty.

The discovery of "Greater India," the first focus of this chapter, was one such attempt at grasping sovereignty. For the most part, it was not intended to renew India's claim to a past aquatic empire in Southeast Asia. Rather, it expanded the shrunken political horizon of the Hindus and allowed for the rediscovery of Hindu sovereignty. Greater India was also an excess of the imperial force behind the idea of Indian unity. When the Hindu Crown, as I characterize it in this chapter, disappeared from India, it took refuge in other, "strange" spaces. Savarkar's Hindu Crown, the second focus of this chapter, was the capacity for Hindu sovereignty to reconquer India from whatever space it emerged: historically, from the Maratha Confederacy, but in Savarkar's own time, from the Kingdom of Nepal. Insofar as it was spatialized, Savarkar's Hindu Crown projected a kind of radical dispersal of the idea of sovereign territory, as explored—the third focus of this chapter—in the context of Partition. Hindu sovereignty could fleetingly anchor in, and emerge from, territory much larger or smaller—and, moreover, outside the India that became independent in 1947.

Greater India and the Recovery of Hindu Statecraft

Since Susan Bayly's groundbreaking essay of 2004, the term "Greater India" has designated the interwar discovery, mainly by Indian intellectuals, of ancient civilizational links between South Asia and East and Southeast Asia—links recently revived in the popular imagination by William Dalrymple's *The Golden Road*.[12] Though celebrated as an Indian form of colonialism, the Greater India discourse is understood to have provided Indians with a "superior moral geography" to European empire.[13] Where European colonialism was territorial and coercive, Greater India was allegedly seen as benevolent and civilizational, even spiritual in nature. Through Greater India, Indians managed to combine their nationalism with a "pan-Asian," internationalist, and cosmopolitan ethos.[14] Unsurprisingly, this vision was suspect to Southeast Asians, who sought emancipation from the status of a receptacle of either of the great civilizations between which they were sandwiched, India and China.[15] Recent work by Jolita Zabarskaitė challenges the benevolent substance of Greater India along with its timeline, pushing it back to the last quarter of the nineteenth century and the watershed of the Swadeshi movement in 1905.[16] Crucially, Zabarskaitė argues that Hindu nationalism cannot be evacuated from the Greater India vision, though she continues to privilege its civilizational orientation.[17] Greater India was certainly no uniform discourse. Some contributors doubtlessly seized on the potential of antique links across the Indian Ocean for more disembodied and benevolent formulations of a Greater India. Others are reminiscent of Mr. Everything Comes from India from the BBC skit show *Goodness Gracious Me,* who, as the name entails, believes that everything comes from India. Contrasting with former interpretations, my reading approaches Greater India through the political problem it was called upon to answer at the time. This was the problem of producing a history of Hindu sovereignty for India.

Rather than the founding of the Greater India Society in 1926 (in Bayly's account) or the Swadeshi (homegrown; lit. "one's one country") national arts and education movement (in Zabarskaitė's), another event in 1905 grounds this story: the rediscovery of the ancient *Arthashastra* of Kautilya.[18] Its rediscovery by Rudrapatna Shamasastry (1868–1944) "vindicate[d] the Indian tradition" that the treatise was a genuine ancient work on statecraft authored by none other than Chanakya, the minister to the Maurya emperor Chandragupta and, in Benoy Sarkar's words, the "Indian Bismarck."[19] A "Calcutta School" of Hindu political thought, to which Sarkar belonged, was formed immediately in response to Shamasastry's rediscovery.[20] Inspired to undertake a translation of an ancient treatise of statecraft himself, the *Sukraniti*,[21] Sarkar's life's work followed the trajectory opened up by the discovery that ancient India had a deep political history and an ocean-wide political imagination.[22] Another member of the Calcutta School, the celebrated historian and lawyer Kashi Prasad Jayaswal (1881–1937), drew out the unprecedented scope of both Hindu imperialism and constitutional advancement as laid out in the *Arthashastra*.[23] The Hindu polity, according to his instant classic on the Indian university syllabus, was unsurpassed anywhere in the world until the seventeenth century.[24] Savarkar later identified Jayaswal as a member of the revolutionary Abhinav Bharat society of his youth.[25] To Shamasastry and Jayaswal, according to a 1963 publication by the Hindu supremacist Bharatiya Vidya Bhavan, went the credit for recovering Hindu political theory: "to the first for discovering and editing Kautalya [*sic*] and to the other for the rediscovery of the science itself."[26]

As is characteristic of ancient Indian political thought, the *Arthashastra* has a weak notion of territorial sovereignty.[27] The king is viewed as the guarantor of cosmic order in his realm, and, through the identification of the political realm and the cosmos, he assumes universal kingship as the *chakravartin*.[28] This king, who becomes a universal sovereign through the conquest of the quarters of the world bounded by the seas, always remained on Benoy Sarkar's horizon. The aim of Hindu statecraft, as Sarkar saw it, was not to sacralize a king but to help realize the pure potentiality that marked the ruler—any Hindu ruler—as a "would-be *dominus omnium* or *sarva-bhauma*, i.e. the imperialist nation builder."[29] Indeed, Sanskrit was so persuasive as a language of power during its heyday due to the characteristic fuzziness of its epic geography, the cosmos, which could be identified with any concrete space of power, or polis.[30] The concept of Greater India took off because of the *Arthashastra*'s rediscovery, though the text's significance was sometimes downplayed and Hindu cosmology foregrounded. For example, the Puranic Yavabhumi was generally agreed upon to be Java; Suvarnabhumi was Malaysia, perhaps including Burma; and Suvarnadvipa, the "gold-island," was Sumatra and other islands in the Malay Archipelago.[31] The inference was that the geographic horizon of the ancient Indians must have been exceptionally wide, as well as seafaring.[32] Kautilya's modern discoverer and translator, Shamasastry, made it thinkable. Mookerji brought the proof.

The key text in the history of Greater India is Mookerji's *Indian Shipping*, published in 1912.[33] Mookerji was Sarkar's friend and, like him, a member of the Calcutta School.[34] What distinguished the book in Mookerji's own account was its novel use of manuscript sources, especially the *Arthashastra*, whose rediscovery coincided with Japan's victory over Russia. Mookerji was buoyed by this conjunction of the present and past of Asian statecraft.[35] *Indian Shipping* represents India as England's twin, from splendid isolation to empire by way of commerce: during the supremacy of the South Indian Chola empire ("from the middle of the 7th century up to the Mohamedan conquests"), India had become a land of shipbuilders; through ships, an empire of commerce and war; and, through both, a world power.[36] As British rule had come to India, so sword accompanied trade in this blend of the Vaishya (through trade) and Kshatriya (through war) hypotheses of the Indianization of Southeast Asia. Through titles like R. C. Majumdar's (1881–1980) "The Decline and Fall of the Śailendra Empire," an obvious allusion to Gibbon's famous *The History of the Decline and Fall of the Roman Empire*, proponents of Greater India claimed India's successorship of Rome, disinheriting Britain itself.[37] But uncovering India's maritime past did more than patch a colonial minority complex.[38]

Though little known in the historiography on oceans, India marks a crucial location in Carl Schmitt's geopolitics. It demonstrates England's aquatic nature, thereby structuring Schmitt's fundamental distinction between land and sea.[39] This alone should discredit the view that there is something inherently benevolent, emancipatory, and decolonizing about water as the supposed antidote to the terrestrial (and partitioned) state produced by colonialism and anticolonial nationalism. In the Greater India imaginary, India succeeded the British empire in mooring its sovereignty to the sea, in the words of Schmitt, in becoming a "'fish.'"[40] No longer a dividing *kala pani* ("black water"), the sea became the connecting tissue of India's body politic. Contrasting with Schmitt, the *Nomos of the Earth* did not lose itself to the sea.[41] Indeed, in the view of Greater India, it seemed that India had achieved what England, according to Schmitt, never could, and had developed lion as fully as fish, terrestrial state as well as sea power, Behemoth as well as Leviathan.[42]

The *Arthashastra*'s early Western commentators drew attention to what appeared to be a "kingly obligation" to colonization, to which they dated the commencement of the Indianization of Southeast Asia or, as art historian and particularly enthusiastic proponent of Greater India O. C. Gangoly (1881–1947) phrased it, of "vomiting out inhabitants."[43] Gangoly rejected this dating, pushing Indian colonization into even deeper antiquity.[44] In Puranic times, "before" the *Arthashastra,* Southeast Asian islands had already appeared "sanctified as *karmabhūmis* or appropriate areas of Indian cultural activity."[45] For Gangoly, *karmabhumi* was wherever Indians "lived, fought, traded and performed their religious duties (*yajña, tapas,* etc.)," and what was *karmabhumi* was Bharatvarsha (India).[46] None other than Benoy Sarkar, writing in the *Calcutta Review,* explicated what Gangoly meant: "*That* is India, where Indians have lived and developed Indian culture!"[47] India had become mobile: a Behemoth "expanding" by growing "limbs" across the sea and in the process morphing into Leviathan, the fish.[48] India's "Mediterranean" was, potentially, the globe.[49]

Greater India opened up a "vision of Indian history and culture not circumscribed by the *modern political delimitation of India,*" wrote the Greater India Society's founder, Kalidas Nag (1892–1966).[50] It was also a fugitive or ersatz sovereignty. In 1918, and constituting what Nag called "a new chapter in Greater Indian Studies," the French orientalist George Cœdès (1886–1969) had been able to prove the existence of a powerful ancient kingdom in Indonesia that dominated sea trade and commanded suzerainty over a dozen vassal states in the Malay Peninsula: "The Kingdom of Çrīvijaya" (Srivijaya, eighth to twelfth century CE).[51] The same kingdom was known as Zabag to the Arabs and San-fo-ts'i to the Chinese. Its ruler commanded the title of maharaja, and in 1025, it was conquered by the Tamil Chola dynasty under Rajendra Chola I.[52] Indian scholars claimed that even Srivijaya's previous Shailendra rulers had been "new arrivals from India" whose dynasty was identical with the Shailodbhavas of Kalinga.[53] Philology, archeology, and anthropology were drawn upon to furnish proofs that took the form of an identification of *this* with *that*—*this* dynasty in Greater India with *that* origin in India: the Shailendras with the Shailodbhavas, or the Malays of Malaysia with the

Indian Malava tribe of ancient Sanskrit literature. In 1936, Himansu Bhushan Sarkar, one of the *Journal of the Greater India Society*'s most prolific contributors, was accused of "turn[ing] Java into a miniature replica of Bhāratvarṣa," an ancient name for India.[54] Indo-European linguistics patterned the familiar slippage from language to "parent stock" and from cultural contact and morphological similarity to the assumption of identity.[55] Theorists of Greater India proved the migratory expansion of Indian sovereignty before the Muslim conquest, where it could be designated "Hindu." Exceeding mere *cultural* supremacism, it was the past and future potentiality of Hindu sovereignty renewed in and projected onto Greater India that formed the point of convergence with Hindu nationalism.[56] In Greater India, there remained Hindu kingdoms, while in mainland India, they had fallen.

One of the most striking features of the *Journal of the Greater India Society*, launched in 1934, is its concern with dynasticism itself. Focused on lineage but not "race," participants in this discussion revealed an older imagination of royal blood. Contributors spoke of empires, armies, and kings. Recurring themes were the Indian origins and seaborne expansion of dynasties, whose Greater Indian conquests sometimes "took the crown and the crowned head," too.[57] Where Indian "Aryan" princesses married into Sri Lankan dynasties, their sons traced their descent through the maternal line, as this carried royal blood.[58] In Greater India, "the heroic types of Indian Princes" were "justly deified as Devarājas or 'Divine Kings' after their death."[59] For the historian and notable Hindu nationalist R. C. Majumdar, "Hindu rule" in Bali only ended and Dutch colonialism began in 1908, when the last king, the Deva Agung of Klungkung, "remembering the proud examples of his Kṣatriya [*sic*] forefathers, . . . seized the sacred sword, and rushed out with his nobles, wives, and children to meet with an end worthy of his race."[60] The cultural influence endured even after "the political supremacy of the Indians in those far-off lands [wa]s merely a dream of the past."[61] Even Subhas Bose, in exile in prison in Burma in the mid-1920s, mused that "there is no doubt that many Kshatriya tribes migrated to Burma from India."[62]

Coronation rituals and the extraordinary power of Sanskrit kingship likewise emerge from the *Journal*. Southeast Asian rulers anointed as Hindu kings claimed a universal empire as a *chakravartin* or "seal[ed] the mystical union of the empire and the universe" as a *devaraja*.[63] A Sri Lankan ruler of the third century BCE, Devanampiya Tissa, became king by importing the *abhisheka* consecration ritual from the emperor Ashoka himself, along with the required ritual specialists and their instruments.[64] According to Gangoly, "successive chains of Brahmin minsters"—dynasties in their turn—"advised the Cambodian kings."[65] This is known as the Brahmin hypothesis of Indianization, and it worked through Sanskritization. Given the Greater India project's central concern, it may be less distinct from and no more soft than the Kshatriya theory than it would initially appear. While the Kshatriya hypothesis obviously claimed political power, the Brahmin hypothesis proved Indians were creators and exporters not only of sovereignty but of sovereign languages.

Nevertheless, Buddhism, more so than Hinduism, had won India its aquatic empire, but Buddhism's legacy in India was ambiguous, to say the least. Its extreme *ahimsa* made it capable of incarnating India's moral superiority to Europe, but it eroded the political. In Kalidas Nag's view, which launched the Greater India Society's publication of a *Bulletin* in 1926, Buddhism had made India internationalism itself.[66] Nag's manifesto asked why India had failed to produce a national history and drove its entire argument toward one conclusion: because India was internationalism personified. Lack was converted into fullness. India had demonstrated that "political nomenclatures like the *Victor* or the *Vanquished* are misnomers" and revealed the need "to sacrifice the *Ego* for the *All*."[67] This Buddhist internationalism that Indians spread was termed "monism" by Sarkar. Nag did not deny that conquest had accompanied India's "penetration" of Southeast Asia, in contrast to East Asia, where penetration (as Buddhism) had been entirely peaceful.[68] But for him, the antique "*dream of world empire*" of Persia, Greece, and Rome that Europe had inherited was countered by Ashoka, the Indian emperor who converted to Buddhism and replaced military conquest with a "new philosophy of conquest by Righteousness (Dharma-vijaya)."[69]

Yet Mookerji made overt and reinforced the links between Buddhism and universal monarchy that Nag tried to prize apart. The eminent historian, who later sat on the Bengal Legislative Council and became vice president of the Hindu Mahasabha, dismissed outright the claim that Ashoka's grandfather Chandragupta, "founder of the Mauryan Empire," "was only imitating the models and methods set by the Achæmenian Empire of Persia."[70] Instead, wrote Mookerji, Buddhism inherited the imperial idea from "Hindu *political* thought as distinguished from Hindu religious thought."[71] The Buddha, in his own time, was rightly understood as a *chakravartin*, a world conqueror, who turned the "royal chariot-wheel" representing the ideal of Hindu universal sovereignty into the "wheel" that kept on rolling, the wheel of *dharma*.[72]

The ninth-century Mahayana Buddhist temple of Borobudur on Java, whose relief panels showed Mookerji "ships in full sail" from India, was, to a European contributor to the *Journal,* an""imperial construction" rather than an ordinary stupa.[73] It was a "reduction" of Mount Meru, the cosmic mountain of the Hindu universal monarch, the *chakravartin.*[74] Negating Buddhism's traditional sense of distinction from Hinduism, theorists of Greater India appropriated Buddhism's world conquest.

Excess and India's Fundamental Unity

Mookerji, the man of Indian shipping himself, can also be credited with coining "the fundamental unity of India" in his 1914 book of that title. The "fundamental unity of India" was the basis on which Savarkar and his Hindu Mahasabha protested the Cripps proposal for loose federation or Pakistan.[75] When Bose gave an account of the Indian independence movement in his immediately banned *The Indian Struggle* of 1935, he too based its backstory on Mookerji's persuasive argument about the fundamental geographic and political unity of India.[76] The book wedged itself between the eminent historian Vincent A. Smith's famous *The Early History of India* of 1904, where India figured as "indisputably a geographic unit" but its political unity as a British invention, and his *Oxford History of India* of 1919, where India was seen to possess a "deep underlying fundamental unity" and where paramount power (the *chakravartin*) represented an ancient indigenous ideal that the British had finally realized in India.[77] Smith now even contended that the long-cherished ideal of Indian political unity went "a long way to explain the acquiescence of India in British rule."[78]

If India possessed fundamental unity, why did Mookerji go oceanic? The answer is that the two were connected. Greater India was an excess of the kind of expansionist drive that sought to conquer and unify India from shore to shore. Mookerji explained, "Indeed, there can hardly be a more convincing proof of the reality and strength of Indian unity than the story of Indian colonizing activity and the gradual development of a Greater India across the seas."[79] Greater India was a spillage and excess of sovereign claims that Mookerji would later weaponize against Pakistan.[80] By then, he had added another fighting term to his vocabulary: the "integral unity" of India, which is the subject of the next chapter.[81]

The furthest point of India's spillage was, pointedly, America.[82] Proponents of the theory that ancient Hindus had discovered and civilized America include the seminal names of Hindu nationalism: the pioneering Dayananda Saraswati, founder of the Arya Samaj, in the nineteenth century; Golwalkar; Hindu Mahasabha founder Malaviya; and even Savarkar, who noted in *Essentials of Hindutva* that Buddhism had made India the holy land "from Misar to Mexico."[83] In an obvious appropriation of Aryanism, (Hindu) Indians appeared as the world-conquering race that carried the torch of civilization to the entire globe, including the New World. Hindu America is Hindu nationalist common sense to this day. For instance, interviewed by Martha Nussbaum in 2004, the centenarian cofounder of the Vishva Hindu Parishad, K. K. Shastri (1905–2006), voiced his belief that American "Indians" really are Indians.[84]

Plots pivoted around the episode of the twelve-year exile of the five Pandava brothers in the Mahabharata, preceding the victory over their cousins in the Kurukshetra War in the main part of the epic. In the Arya Samaji Har Bilas Sarda's rendering, the Pandavas' exile became "a conquering expedition to foreign countries."[85] Patala, the netherworld of Hindu scripture, was America. Arjuna, contended Sarda, had conquered Patala and married Alopi (Ulupi), daughter of the king Kuroo (Kauravya), of America.[86] Aztec serpent worship bore the imprint of Hindu influence, and modern Mexicans looked and dressed typically Indian.[87] Speculation about the peopling of the Americas is, of course, as old as its European "discovery." At the birth of Indo-European comparative linguistics and Aryanism, Sir William Jones (1746–1794) himself had classified the people of Mexico and Peru (Aztecs and Incas) as offshoots of the Hindus.[88] Theosophists and their informants did their part.[89] The theory of Indian diffusion, though never the most popular, was still more than pulp fiction in twentieth-century Mexico, and it became folklore in India, influencing even Roy's desire to visit Mexico during World War I, at a time when his "socialist conversion was not yet deep enough to counter the patriotic belief that in the prehistoric days Indians had somehow managed to cross the ocean and colonize Mexico."[90] A copy of the journalist Chaman Lal's popular book *Hindu America* (1940) can even be found in Nehru's personal library.[91]

From this extreme of geographic excess, we return to the theme of India's unity. In *Essentials of Hindutva,* Savarkar drew heavily on Mookerji.[92] Mookerji did not coin the name that mattered, and he did not appreciate that the essence of things lay in their names: "Hindu" and "Hindustan" were, for him, exonyms.[93] Still, the similarities are striking. Both men started their argument about the unity of India/Hindusthan with the geography of the Vedic river hymn. Both men also knew that the earliest cradle of the seven rivers, worshipped and loved though it was, was not India/Hindusthan. In both accounts, consolidation came about through imperial expansion and the conquest of South India.[94] Bharat, the conqueror, became the first all-India emperor.[95] Mookerji later wrote that the "India of the Indus or Sindhu" had grown to its full subcontinental extent in "ever-widening circles" that reflected but pushed the frontiers of that first riverine cradle, now in turn echoing the watery circularity that characterizes Savarkar's prose in *Essentials of Hindutva.*[96]

In the fight against Partition, Mookerji would come to judge the "deification of the motherland" to be the contribution of "the Hindu" to global political thought.[97] In *The Fundamental Unity of India,* he set out how India became salient as an object of devotion through its circumambulation by pilgrims traveling to holy sites, the holiest of which lay in the four corners of India, claiming the vast expanse that lay between.[98] In *Nationalism in Hindu Culture,* published just before *Essentials of Hindutva* and when the Khilafat movement was still in full swing, Mookerji noted how "remarkable" it was that "not a single one of these numerous holy places [. . .] has been situated outside the borders of the mother country." "The Hindu" did not have to "traverse beyond the sacred precincts of his native land to some far-off Palestine to pay homage" to his gods and saints. Why should he want to? "He is too much in love with his own country to think of establishing any tie of allegiance with any foreign country," Mookerji concluded.[99] In *Essentials of Hindutva,* famously, the Muslim's "Holyland [wa]s far off in Arabia or Palestine," and he could not accept Hindusthan as the "land of his love" and "worship."[100]

Yet all-India sovereignty required more than sacred geography: it required a paramount sovereign.[101] The Hindu ideal of kingship, Mookerji wrote, was universal sovereignty, which only necessity had "reduced" to "the whole of India" up to the seas. "Adhiraja" (overlord), "Rajadhiraja" (king of kings), "Samraj" (supreme ruler), "Ekaraj" (sole ruler): the Vedas in the earliest of times documented the conception of a paramount king.[102] Mookerji wrote books about the major, historically documented "Hindu" emperors—Chandragupta, Ashoka, and Harsha—who had achieved the "traditional Kṣatriya [*sic*] ideal" of bringing the whole subcontinent "under the 'umbrella' of one authority" and become "king[s] of kings."[103] But Sanskrit literature contained lists of kings who preceded "the so-called *first* paramount sovereign of India," Chandragupta Maurya.[104] Among them was Yudhishtira, the eldest Pandava brother in the Mahabharata epic.[105]

In his classic of colonial historiography, *The History of British India* (1817), James Mill accused the orientalists and their chief, William Jones, for being taken in by the "pretensions of the Brahmens [*sic*] who spoke of an antecedent period, when the sovereigns of Hindustan were masters of great power and great magnificence."[106] The Brahmin fables spoke of a monarch who had "universal sovereignship of India" before the Mughals or the British, threatening imperial justifications based on the claim that there was no such thing as the natural political unity of India.[107] Mill consequently debunked the Hindu chroniclers who shuffled whole dynasties around, erased them from the record, or invented them.[108] Mookerji knew these lists of kings could not be historically verified, but he took them as illustrative of the ancient ideal of paramount rule.[109]

Crucially, all-India sovereignty required an act of scaling up, rather than the scaling down and isolation that village republics represented. Benoy Sarkar, for one, explicitly pitted "Empire vs. Village." In the light of history, he wrote, the "self-sufficiency and genuine autonomy or rural *sva-râjes* must have been prominent by their absence during the ascendancy of *sârva-bhaumas* [world-emperors] like Chandra-gupta Maurya." Sarkar did not "wail over the disappearance of the 'little republics,'" as both British and Indian writers had. The loss of the village assemblies, which these writers had taken as ruling precolonial India, constituted no loss of "independence" or "freedom" but an "occasional" interregnum in which a supreme power was absent. "Local self-government and national imperialism militate against each other," he averred.[110] Village republics may have proven Indians' capacity for self-rule, but they could not buttress Indian nationalism's claim to all-India sovereignty. For this, the centripetal force of an emperor was needed.

Savarkar's Hindu Crown

Vinayak Savarkar was not indifferent to the historical spectacle of Indian "sea-faring monarch[s]" in Greater India.[111] In *Essentials of Hindutva,* he claimed that the bond of nationality was not broken when Hindus settled abroad—the modern version of Greater India. All who descended from Hindus and looked upon Hindusthan as their holy land were Hindus.[112] Greater India certainly appealed to Hindu nationalists within and beyond the Mahasabha, and as its president, Savarkar developed organizational links with Southeast and East Asia.[113] Yet the inference that Savarkar aimed to "appropriate Asia as a Hindu-Buddhist continent" is wrong.[114] This was because Buddhism was Hindutva's negation. Hindutva was crafted to curb the universalism or globalism inherent in the Indian tradition through which India had exceeded itself—in other words, failed to achieve identity with itself. It was against Buddhism's global spillage, no less, that Savarkar erected the "frontier line" of the Indus River.[115]

Savarkar evaluated the world historical role of Buddhism in India in much the same way as Kalidas Nag: as internationalism. But although the religion had made India "the very heart—the very soul" of the world, "Buddhism had its geographical centre of gravity nowhere."[116] Buddhism was the world's "greatest attempt" at "a universal religion," but its "opiates" of universal brotherhood and nonviolence had disarmed India and made it porous.[117] In adopting Buddhism, India had "tr[ied] to kill killing by getting killed."[118] Hindutva, as Shruti Kapila reminds us, was crafted in opposition to the *ahimsa* that Buddhism stood for as much as Gandhi.[119] India's fall to foreign rule was in this way prefigured by the Buddha, the prince by birth who had eradicated the principle of national sovereignty itself. In *Essentials of Hindutva,* Savarkar narrated how, as he was setting up his "Buddhistic Church," news was brought to the Buddha of the vanquishment of his native Shakya republic. But it "left the Enlightened unconcerned."[120] The "Prince of the Shakyas had grown into the Prince of Princes—the Lokjit—the great conqueror of worlds."[121] What was the fall of a terrestrial kingdom to the universal lord? If Greater Indianism functioned through Buddhism's world conquest, for Savarkar, it eroded the political. That which is "common in us with our enemies weakens our power of opposing them." Buddhism had left India defenseless against Buddhist enemies. What was needed was a "national" "Church."[122] And so the Brahmanic reaction against Buddhism's universalism began with the revival of boundaries, namely caste and the prohibition against crossing the sea. For Savarkar, these were politically necessary overreactions.[123] The Hindu was reaffirmed in the iron clasp between the "Sindhu and Sindhu, from the Indus to the Seas."[124] The word "Sindhu" meant either the riverine land of the Indus or the "frontier," the same as the sea. For *Hindutva*'s author, it meant both, as he played on the supreme self-referentiality of Hindusthan.[125]

Savarkar was suspicious that pan-movements like pan-Asianism erased national sovereignty. Therefore, Hindutva could not be synonymous with Hinduism when outside India, and the two should be no more confused than "a Hindu with an Indian" inside India's borders. In the summer of 1938, Savarkar made this case before Rash Behari Bose (1886–1945), an Indian expatriate revolutionary nationalist, a pan-Asianist, and a Japanese citizen from 1923, who would prove crucial in the INA and the Azad Hind movement before "Netaji" Subhas Chandra Bose (no relation) stepped in.[126] As Savarkar explained in a follow-up letter to Rash Behari, the Japanese and Chinese, though "co-religionists," could never be "Hindus" in the sense Savarkar had crafted. Inverting the famous exclusion of Muslims in *Essentials of Hindutva* in a logically consistent way, Savarkar explained how the Japanese and Chinese regarded India as their "holyland" but not as their "fatherland."[127] As Buddhists adherents to a religion within the Hindu fold, they could form part of a "Hindu Dharma Parishad" but not a "Hindu Rashtra Parishad," a religious but not a Hindu national council.[128] Ending his letter by requesting that Bose open a Hindu Mahasabha in Japan "as soon as possible," Savarkar made it sufficiently clear that its members could only be Indian expatriates like Bose himself.[129] Savarkar sent a copy of *Essentials of Hindutva* along with his letter, putting his full persuasive power behind the pan-concept of his own making, the Hindu.

Hindu sovereignty, for Savarkar, did not lie in Greater Indian kingdoms. Nor was it evenly distributed across the expanse of Hindusthan. Instead, Savarkar located sovereignty in what I call the Hindu Crown, which could withdraw to and emanate out of small, strange spaces from which to (re)conquer Hindusthan. To define what I mean by the Hindu Crown, I first need to clear a few preconceptions and state what it is *not*. Savarkar's projection of Hindu sovereignty did not place the Brahmin above the king, as Louis Dumont famously did.[130] Savarkar's intent was to resurrect Hindu sovereignty, not make the king subservient to *dharma*. Nor was Savarkar concerned with sacral kingship or representing the body politic. We must therefore dispense with "the king's two bodies," pirated from European political thought and reverberating through recent scholarship on Indian monarchism.[131] "There is no extra sacredness in the person of the king" in Indian thought, according to Benoy Sarkar.[132] Milinda Banerjee has recently argued that undetected by historians looking for republicanism, monarchical conceptions of sovereignty issued into the era of twentieth-century Indian nationalism.[133] For Banerjee, nationalist India attempted but ultimately failed to produce a "national monarch."[134] But Savarkar was not ideologically attached to monarchism.[135] His was no confrontation with republicanism. What mattered to Savarkar was precisely what his enemies said: Hindu Raj. Savarkar was not looking to construct a European-style sovereign who ruled over a homogenous realm. He needed an emperor, who could stand at the center of a web of smaller rulers who vowed "loving allegiance" to him.[136] Hindusthan was an empire in need of an emperor.

To fashion one, Savarkar's writings turned to history and the kings of Hindu scripture. This gesture to origins was loose, however, as *Essentials of Hindutva* alone offers a choice between two mythical kings—Ramchandra and Bharat—as metonyms of the original Hindu emperor from whom Hindu sovereignty subsequently flowed.[137] Savarkar's multiple accounts of the forging of the Hindu Crown inevitably require an act of imperial consolidation, whose creative violence he explored. After its wreckage, in each case, the crown is forged again in the crucible of war against a common enemy. As is always the case for Savarkar, self becomes known to itself through a confrontation with nonself. His last book, *Six Glorious Epochs,* underscores the negative origin of the Hindu Crown by ascribing its original forging to a foreign invader, Alexander the Great, who "put all the crowns and coronets of Kings, and kings of kings and of all the small Rav's and Raval's, into a melting pot and forged a single crown to proclaim himself the Emperor of India."[138] Once forged, the kingmaker and author of the *Arthashastra,* Kautilya/Chanakya, appropriated the crown of Hindusthan for Chandragupta.[139]

Savarkar never imagined a tabula rasa of sovereignty in the subcontinent. Totality of rule neither characterized the colonial present nor India's recent precolonial or deep past. The existence of petty rulers could not invalidate all-India sovereignty, as long as there existed an imperial center. Creating this center, however, required borrowing from the enemy: Mughal constructions of imperial suzerainty and the British notion of paramountcy.[140] The British had established the doctrine of "paramount power" after the Indian Rebellion, thereby allowing the Indian princely states to retain some sovereign attributes while reserving higher-level sovereignty for themselves. The test of paramountcy was allegiance to the British Crown.[141] With paramount power, the British claimed to have inherited a native institution and set themselves up as successors to the Mughals.[142] They also appropriated the ritual of Mughal overlordship to this end: the imperial *darbar* (court), to which all Indian princes were summoned, as Bernard Cohn points out in a lesser-known chapter in Eric Hobsbawm's *The Invention of Tradition.*[143] Mookerji, to prove India's fundamental unity, also appropriated the *darbar* for Hindus when he wrote that the eldest Pandava brother, Yudhishtira, proclaimed his paramountcy at the "Imperial Durbar at Indraprashta."[144] The trope of a *darbar* to mark Hindusthan's consolidation under a Hindu emperor at various historical points runs through

Savarkar's most iconic writings.[145] Savarkar was invested in reconstructing India's imperial center as a Hindu one. For this purpose, the last Mughal emperor himself needed to be reinscribed.

In his tremendously successful recoinage of the events of 1857 as the first Indian War of Independence, Savarkar paints a striking picture of the common uprising of "sepoy and civilian, king and pauper, Hindu and Muslim," "Brahmin and Sudra, Kshatrya [*sic*] and Vaisya."[146] The "ideas of 1857," as one might call them, did for Indians what the "ideas of 1914" did for the Germans: war reconciled a divided nation that became sovereign without needing to sever the heads of kings. In Savarkar's rendering, the great bonfire that the British had made of India's premodern dispensation of power had brought about this momentous event. Symbols from the Battle of Plassey to the Koh-i-Noor, representing conquests and annexations of Indian kingdoms, were thrown into this sacrificial fire, which Savarkar modeled on Indrajit's famous sacrifice in the Puranas that earned him the celestial boon of an unconquerable war chariot. Out of the pyre of premodern sovereignty rose the "deity of National Anger," the singularized nation, the sovereign people.[147] For Savarkar, 1857 marked "the first indication in modern India of the omnipotence of the *vox populi*, the power of the people."[148] From that time on, rulers had to derive their legitimacy from the people. And, most perplexingly, "the people" appointed the Mughal emperor.

Savarkar's narrative follows the mutinous sepoys to Delhi, where, on May 11, 1857, they conferred the "Emperorship of Hindusthan" on the deposed Mughal emperor, Bahadur Shah Zafar (1775–1862). Savarkar could not deny that this had happened, but he could reinterpret it. Though it could superficially be viewed as a restoration, Savarkar insisted it "was no restoration at all."[149] Rather, this Bahadur Shah whom the mutineers crowned was "not the old Mughal succeeding to the throne of Akbar or Aurangzeb" but a powerless man placed on a new and unfamiliar throne, as the old Mughal throne had already "been smashed to pieces by the hammer of the Mahrattas."[150] Marking the only difference to the Savarkar of 1923, the Savarkar of 1909 regarded the thousand-year war against Muslim rule that had begun when Mahmud of Ghazni crossed the Indus as won.[151] The relation of rulers and the ruled that divided them struck down by the Maratha, Sikh, and Rajput sword prior to the confrontation with the British, Hindus and Muslims had finally been able to unite as "brothers," as touched on in Chapter 2.[152] The "raising of Bahadur Shah to the throne of India" in 1857 thus signified that the "conquerer was conquered," Hindu "honour" vindicated, and Hindus again "masters of the land of the Hindus."[153] Marked by almost complete passivity on the part of the emperor, Bahadur Shah's ascension to the throne of Hindusthan erased Muslim sovereignty from the subcontinent by erasing the emperor's own dynastic identity. Reemerging in the most unlikely of places, the Hindu Crown adopted the last Mughal emperor as heir to the Marathas' fight against the "Feringhi" (foreign) Raj of his own predecessors.[154]

Savarkar dwelled on the reemergence of "Hindu power," a spectacle that played out in recent precolonial history, rather than a mythic "golden age."[155] Therefore, though his writings invoke numerous symbols and emblems of royal power, Savarkar mainly drew from the Maratha empire: the "Jaripatka" flag, also known as the "Geruwa [Gerua]" or "Bhagava banner" for its saffron color; the Peshwa ministers' "drum"; and the "great white Umbrella of Sovereignty" called "chatra"—and his wielder, the "Chatrapati," Shivaji's self-given title.[156] What had happened in Maharashtra in the seventeenth century was special. "Never [s]ince the fall of Vijayanagar," the medieval South Indian empire, wrote Savarkar, "had a Hindu Prince dared to have himself crowned as an independent ruler, a Chatrapati." The crowning of Shivaji broke "the spell." "Never again" had the Muslims been able to beat the Hindus in battle.[157] Hindu sovereignty projected out from the Maratha empire to all of Hindusthan so much so that for Savarkar, the revolutionaries of 1857 had only to follow the dictum that Ramdas, the guru, had given to Shivaji: to fight for *swadharma* and *swaraj*.[158] The Maratha empire was the defining historical space of Savarkar's Hindu Crown.

In 1935, Benoy Sarkar—a Bengali, not a Marathi—made explicit, in ten short pages, how modern, all-Indian nationality and sovereignty could grow from the cell of the Maratha empire. For this, he too turned to Ramdas, the teacher, over Shivaji himself. Sarkar's article in the *Calcutta Review* was a response to widespread contestation over the legacy of the Maratha empire in the 1920s and 1930s. Particularly controversial was the declared mission of the Marathas to "propagate the dharma of Maharashtra," as was guru Ramdas's council to the heroes Shivaji and Sambhaji, his son.[159] The controversy revolved around historian and Bombay High Court judge M. G. Ranade's pioneering work in English on the *Rise of the Maratha Power*, published decades earlier in 1900. This work had pulled seventeenth-century Maharashtra *dharma* into modern times.[160] Scholars have interpreted Ranade's intervention as a watershed in the formulation of a Marathi regional identity as distinct from, but uniquely destined to lead, Hindu India.[161] Maharashtra *dharma* has been described as a "regionalism" and a precolonial "patriotism."[162] Sarkar recognized it as the cradle of all-India nationalism.

Ranade, as Sarkar read him, offered two distinct definitions of Maharashtra *dharma*: one where it is simply the *dharma* of the *maha rashtra,* the big state, and another where it is the Maratha territory itself that acquires a religious (*dharmic*) dimension.[163] With Maharashtra *dharma,* Ramdas had pioneered a purely territorial conception of nationalism in Indian thought. Most remarkably, this was a territorial nationalism to which any particular territory was merely coincidental.[164] Ramdas had not addressed himself to all of India, explained Sarkar, because there was no such thing as India before the Maratha state began its imperial spread. Instead, Ramdas had addressed himself to the "regional category" that was "normal and natural" to him and "which ha[d] already shown the way to *Hindwi Swarajya*" (Hindu/Indian self-rule).[165] Maharashtra *dharma* was not provincial; it was imperial. It commanded expansion into a great state and laid the grounds for national consolidation, as Johann Gottlieb Fichte had for German unification.[166] Put bluntly, "Maharastradharma = Hindurastradharma" (the *dharma* of the Maratha state equals the *dharma* of the Hindu state).[167]

Savarkar likewise acknowledged Ranade as an inspiration for his work on Maratha history, *Hindu-Pad-Padashahi.*[168] Naturally, its orientation was different from that of Sarkar. Aiming to preempt communalism, Sarkar insisted that Ramdas's struggle against Aurangzeb's Mughal tyranny was "secular" and "territorial" and Muslims were free to join.[169] But for Savarkar, the Maratha episode served to anchor Hindutva in history. He wrote, "The Maharashtra Dharma was a new force animating the dying spirit of the national life of the Hindu race."[170] Hindu *dharma* could not triumph, nor "Hindavi Rajya flourish," unless the Muslim power was completely defeated and *Hindu-pad-padashahi,* the Hindu empire, was established in all of India.[171] To this end, "all the scattered centres of Hindu strength" had to be consolidated and "the frontiers of the Maharashtra kingdom [expanded], to get it ultimately identified with the Indian Empire itself."[172] Thus, the Marathas managed to "'dethrone the Moslem'" and make a Hindu power "'the paramount power of Hindustan.'"[173] Savarkar was aware of the problem of tying national integration to the violent expansion of a warrior state. The Marathas had not been devoid of "selfishness" and lust for "self-aggrandisement," even as a greater patriotism acted through them. It would have been "immensely more patriotic," he admitted, had the

Maratha Confederacy expanded through persuasion rather than conquest. But this would have required unity among Hindus, which was precisely what they lacked, or else the Muslims would have never have "been able to cross the Indus at all." [174] Savarkar was particularly careful to avoid all semblance of dynasticism. As with Bahadur Shah's throne at Delhi, the Hindu Crown was no personal property.

To drive his point home, Savarkar argued that the Marathas themselves were incidental to their empire or confederacy. He stated, "From a Pan-Hindu point of view every one of [the Hindu rulers] had equal right, nay, owed even a duty to strike the Moslem as best as he could and, failing to found a powerful, one, and invincible Hindu Empire, at least try to carve out as many Hindu kingdoms, small or great, as possible."[175] However, only the Marathas had been strong enough to consolidate Hindu power. For this reason, the pan-Hindu empire, "Hindu-pad-padashahi," had to be, by default, "a Maharashtra-padashahi too," but theoretically it could just as well have been a "Rajput-padashahi or a Sikh or a Tamil or a Bengali or even a Kolarian one."[176] As with Sarkar's Maharashtra *dharma* as a territorially agnostic principle of territorial nationalism, for Savarkar, the identity of the cell was incidental to the Hindu Crown that grew from it.

The Marathas had broken Muslim power in India. By the mid-eighteenth century, they were the "*de facto* emperor[s]," though by the grace of "the descendant of Shivaji," the descendant of Aurangzeb retained "the luxury of the name," the imperial title.[177] Eschewing this title and refraining from disassembling the Mughal empire, the Marathas had exhibited the same political expediency as the later British, who pretended to be "agents" of the Mughals until the events of 1857 revealed their true nature.[178] Hindu power, unaided by the British, had irretrievably broken Muslim rule, and Hindu paramountcy in Hindusthan had been reasserted. But in 1818, under a new generation of incapable rulers, the Marathas lost to the formidable new British foe, "and with them fell the last great Hindu Empire—the last great *Indian* Empire." The Sikhs in the Punjab kept a flicker of "Hindu independence" alive for a little longer, but soon this died down, too.[179] Had the Hindu Crown died with them? It had not. "When the banner of Hinduism dropped from the hands of the Mahrattas in 1817," commented a Britisher in Kathmandu in the year of the Indian Rebellion, 1857, "they solemnly conjured the Nepalese to take it up and wave it proudly till it could be again unfurled in the plains by the expulsion of the vile Feringis [the British], and the subjection of the insolent followers of Islam."[180] And indeed, simultaneously with his coinage of Hindutva, Savarkar placed the crown (*chhatra*—umbrella, *danda*—stick) of Hindusthan before the king of Nepal.

Nepal, the Last Hindu Kingdom

Hindutva's famous formula, "from Sindhu to Sindhu," cuts to the west of Nepal; the lines drawn "from Sindh to Bengal," and "from Kashmere to the Cape [Comorin] and from Attock to Cuttack," leave Nepal to the north and west.[181] Yet Nepal was squarely on the map of Savarkar's Hindusthan.[182] The reason was not simply that the Nepalese were coreligionists, because so were the Japanese and Chinese whom Savarkar excluded. What made Nepal integral to Hindutva was that it was a Hindu sovereign space—the "only independent Hindu Kingdom."[183] Writing eloquently on this subject in his books and in articles in the vernacular press, Savarkar explained that from Vedic to historical times, Nepal had been as much a "part" (*hissa*) and "province" (*pranth*) of Hindusthan "as Punjab, Bengal, Maharashtra and Madras." If today it appeared otherwise, this was because the subcontinental "map" was flecked with the "red ink" of British rule, from which Nepal alone remained free. It alone still had a king. And because it remained color coded in the "yellow-golden color of freedom," people took it as "foreign country [*videshi*]!"[184] Nepal did not figure in the calculations of the Indian freedom movement.[185] Savarkar concluded this was "because Nepal is still free, in Nepal there is Hindu power [*satta*], in Nepal the statues in Hindu temples were not destroyed by the sword of [Mahmud of] Ghaznavi," the Muslim conqueror.[186]

Legal historian Lauren Benton alerted us to the discrepancy between the "iconic" "pink shading" of British possessions on the world map and the predominantly uneven and fragmented nature of British imperial territory.[187] Savarkar was keenly alive to this discrepancy. After Partition, he still described the Himalayan kingdom as "the best part of Hindu India," though he stated that "our frivolous history books" represent it as distinct and severed because it remained free from Muslim and European domination.[188] The point was clearly not about inheriting the British empire in India. Instead, Savarkar located Hindu sovereignty off the map of British India. His vision of the non-dynastic succession of Hindu imperial power could grow from and retreat to the smallest "nucleus": the Maratha and Sikh empires in the seventeenth and eighteenth centuries and Bahadur Shah, the emperor of Hindusthan, in

1857.[189] But in Savarkar's own time, the "nucleus" of Hindu sovereignty was Nepal.[190] Nepal came closest to an imperial center from which Savarkar's dispersed Hindu Crown could issue.

Savarkar had shown interest in Nepal from a young age. According to the eldest Savarkar brother, Ganesh Damodar, the Abhinav Bharat of their Maharashtrian youth already envisioned a "specific goal" regarding the revolutionary organization of Nepal. When Savarkar was in London, the arrival (around 1908) of Maharaja Chandra Shamsher Jung Bahadur Rana produced quite a stir in the India House chapter of the secret society. Allegedly, none other than Madanlal Dhingra, who shot Curzon Wyllie, triggering a police clampdown on India House that ended in Savarkar's criminal transportation to the Andamans, delivered the letter inviting the Nepalese ruler to accept the "crown" of the "Indian empire."[191] It would not be the last time that Savarkar offered the crown of Hindusthan to the king of Nepal.

Savarkar began to seriously write about Nepal in the early 1920s, crucially around the same time as *Essentials of Hindutva*.[192] He explicitly contextualized what Nepal did for the Hindus through the Khilafat. India's Muslims had pan-Islam, but Hindus were also consolidating and organizing around Nepal.[193] If, according to Gandhi, Hindus owed allegiance to the Muslim caliph in Turkey, Savarkar claimed their allegiance to the king of Nepal.[194] (By this he meant Nepal's de facto rulers, the hereditary Rana prime ministers, and not the symbolic Shah monarchs. Savarkar's project was not about symbolic power.) "Nepal is ours," he stated, even if it never became an official province of Hindusthan.[195] Nepal was like an Indian princely state, wrote Savarkar, but even better, because it was not "dependent." He viewed India's Nepali brothers as "free" (*swatantra*).[196] Not even Heinrich von Treitschke, who was hired to invent the theory that Alsace-Lorraine was part of Germany, rather than France, could claim that Nepal was not part of Hindusthan.[197] "The Hindus have a place which is their own, but very few know of it, and know that the place goes by the name of Nepal," Savarkar wrote in his memoir of that microcosm of India and displaced battleground for Hindus and Muslims, the penal colony of the Andamans.[198] The Muslims had Hyderabad; the Hindus had Nepal. In 1919, the nizam of Hyderabad threw a dinner to celebrate Britain's recognition of Afghan independence. Then why, Savarkar questioned, did the Hindus not celebrate the British recognition of Nepal's sovereignty and independence in 1923?[199] Savarkar concluded, "Nepal is our Afghanistan."[200]

Nepal was "one" with the Hindus of Hindusthan: culturally, historically, religiously, and—naturally, for Savarkar—in terms of "blood" (*rakt*).[201] And yet, in 1857, the Nepalese, like the Sikhs, had turned "loyal traitors."[202] Their failure to join the rebels had doomed the Indian War of Independence.[203] Significantly, Savarkar wrote two further books in Marathi, both of which are lost: *History of the Sikhs* (1909) and *History of the Nepalese Nationalist Movement* (1931), the latter apparently coauthored by his older brother, Ganesh.[204] For Vinayak, the Sikhs of the Punjab had risen to front the Hindu fight for sovereignty under their tenth guru, Guru Govind Singh (1666–1708), who founded the Sikh militant order, the Khalsa, against Mughal persecution.[205] Sikh militancy was central to Savarkar's history of "Hindu sovereignty," and the Sikhs, of course, were "Hindus" in the sense of Hindutva.[206] The Sikhs and Nepalese had kept the Hindu Crown alive, and they could not be let go. Savarkar refused to confront the irreducibility of Sikh and Nepali demands of sovereignty to his Hindu empire.[207] This time, the traitors of 1857 had to fight on the side of the Hindus. If Ramdas lived now, wrote Savarkar in the 1920s, he would vest his hopes in Nepal, not Maharashtra.[208]

"Amidst this general wreck of Hindu crowns and coronets," only Nepal remained standing. "Can it be," asked Savarkar in 1926, that the "emblem and insignia that once authorised the Marathas to lead the cause of the Hindu race and religion have now been handed over to thee, Oh Nepal [. . .]?"[209] In the nineteenth century, the relation between India and Nepal had been inverted. Nepal, the traditional *pradesha*—the imperial periphery—had become the center (*desha*) of the Hindu sovereign cosmos of Bharatvarsha.[210] In stylizing Nepal as the last Hindu kingdom, Savarkar followed Nepal's careful curation of this image in the nineteenth century, as enshrined in the National Code of Nepal, the Muluki Ain, of 1854: "In the Kaliyuga this Kingdom is the only kingdom in the world where cows, women and Brahmans are not killed."[211] Nepal's self-fashioning as a Hindu kingdom met the immense need for legitimation after the Gorkha Kingdom's aggressive "unification" of the Kathmandu Valley in the second half of the eighteenth century.[212] Nepal became a patrimonial state, buttressed on its claim to succeed India as the protector of Hindu *dharma* in a subcontinent otherwise polluted by Muslim and British rule. In indologist Axel Michaels's words, Nepal became "more Catholic than the Pope, more Hindu than India."[213] Paradoxically, Hinduism, which linked Nepal to a subcontinental pan-civilization in the first place, allowed Nepal to found national sovereignty.[214] Nepal actively promoted its reputation as the land of pure Hinduism in India, and this propaganda strategy may have been rather too successful for its own good.[215]

British intelligence was keenly aware of Savarkar's interest in Nepal, and they tracked his party's courtship of the Nepalese ruler. For instance, when Maharaja Bhim Shumsher Jung Bahadur Rana and his family paid a visit to Calcutta in 1932, the Hindu Mahasabha praised his shining example of "Hindu Kingship" and underlined Nepal's role in "shaping the destiny of the Hindu Nation." The Mahasabha begged "the Ruler of the only Independent Hindu Kingdom" for "guidance," "patronage," and "assistance."[216] In the winter of 1939, when his successor, Juddha Shamsher Jang Bahadur Rana, visited Calcutta, the Mahasabha had made more elaborate preparations. Crowds greeted the maharaja at Howrah station with shouts of "Hindu Maharaj ki jai!" (Long live the Hindu king!).[217] The party historian and secretary of the Maharashtra Hindu Mahasabha, Indra Prakash, wrote in the Hindu press of the Nepalese ruler's "'true spirit' of 'Hindutva'" and concluded that "'Nepal is Hinduism and Hinduism is Nepal.'" Under this dynast, Nepal could never "'become a Pakistan.'"[218] Syama Prasad Mukherjee and a fellow member of the Mahasabha (inconsistently identified as Nirmal Chandra Chatterjee, the distinguished judge) even secured an audience with the maharaja. According to government sources, they used it to complain that Nepal risked its reputation as the "only Hindu State" by allowing the British army to deploy Gurkha troops meant for the Allied war effort to suppress Indians. Nepal was losing its "fame abroad as the only Hindu State." The maharaja assured his visitors that he would allow no such thing. On this occasion, plans were allegedly made to dispatch a Hindu Mahasabha envoy to Nepal.[219]

A three-man deputation left Calcutta for Nepal on May 20, 1944, with "detailed instructions" from Mukherjee and Chatterjee. The three men left in secret and were advised not to risk making openly anti-British statements in Nepal.[220] They were given no special welcome, and it is uncertain whether the maharaja knew of their arrival. Prior to their departure, there had been talk of forming a Hindu Mahasabha in Nepal. This plan was abandoned not only because the maharaja was unlikely to allow an Indian political organization to take root in Nepal, as British officials mused, but also because the delegation found "'that everything [in Nepal] was typically Hindu and consequently was not certain about the necessity of starting a Hindu Mahasabha organization there.'"[221] Nepal was simply too Hindu to require the work of Hindu organization.

The Nepalese ruler's well-advised unwillingness to be drawn into the "vortex of Indian politics" and risk Britain's wrath stood as a bulwark against the Hindu Mahasabha's courtship of Nepal.[222] The British told themselves that the Mahasabha's "overtures" to Nepal's ruler were met by "polite evasions."[223] Shows of indifference were certainly made to the British, but it was impossible to know the "real mind of the Maharaja."[224] Leading Nepalese figures were repeatedly invited to preside at Hindu Mahasabha sessions.[225] Apparently, the maharaja himself was offered the party presidentship in the 1920s.[226] Indeed, his successor had confessed at a party in Delhi in 1935, thrown in his honor by the Mahasabha, that "he was one of them."[227] In the 1940s, "it [wa]s believed the Hindu Mahasabha were angling for Nepal's moral and financial support," though without obvious success other than, "possibly, a modest donation from the Maharaja."[228] Nevertheless, when the Wavell Plan was declared on July 14, 1945, the maharaja of Nepal immediately sent a cipher telegram to the Government of India in which he "expressed some surprise that leaders of Hindu Mahasabha would not be summoned by Viceroy."[229] Assessments of the traction of the Hindu Mahasabha with Nepal's ruling elite, therefore, varied. From an intercepted letter to Ashutosh Lahiry (1892–1976), the Hindu Mahasabha general secretary, in 1945, colonial intelligence learned that a certain Pandit R. C. Sharma "had been to Kathmandu (Nepal) and found that his friends and princes were admirers of the Mahasabha and looked to it for guidance."[230] British intelligence further believed that the Hindu Mahasabha fed stories of Muslim atrocities to the Nepalese ruler "to rope in Nepal in aid of the Bengal Hindus."[231] None of this was conclusive, but it was more than enough to keep British suspicion alive.

On the question of Pakistan, certainly, Nepal's natural sympathy was thought to lie with India's Hindus. The British envoy to Nepal, Geoffrey L. Betham, reported as much regarding his conversation one summer evening in 1942 with General Baber Shumsher Jung Bahadur Rana, commanding general of the Nepalese army and a high-ranking royal. Betham was told that Nepal wanted no part in Indian politics, but he concluded that if the Government of India supported the Pakistan demand and left, "who did I [Betham] expect the Nepalese to side with?"

> He [the General] said "We have got to side with either Hindu India or with Pakistan. How can we side with Pakistan? Therefore we will obviously have to side with Hindu India or what is virtually the Mahasabha?

> [*sic*]" In Delhi, said he, I do all I can to avoid Mahasabhites but I can't always do it. When I do they invariably turn to the subject of what Nepal is going to get out of this war, hinting that they should have land in India.[232]

Most worrying for Britain in the Mahasabha-Nepal connection was that it confirmed their suspicions about Nepalese territorial designs on eastern India, though the maharaja denied them.[233]

Things came to a head at the twenty-third session of the Hindu Mahasabha in 1942. Savarkar had deliberately chosen the location—Bhagalpur in Bihar, close to the Nepalese border—and the date—January—to clash with Bakr-Id celebrations and create a communal situation that he hoped would arouse "pan-Hindu consciousness" among the Nepalese.[234] In an intercepted letter, he wrote that winning the Nepalese for the cause would "'secur[e]'" "'the future of Hindudom [. . .] to such an extent as no other single factor in our programme can do. Hindu power, Hindu strength, Hindu organization is at present a living thing throbbing with vital energy in Nepal alone.'"[235] The session was banned.[236] In defiance of the government ban, Savarkar launched a *satyagraha*, or civil disobedience campaign, and was arrested alongside other Mahasabha leaders. They were released on January 5, 1942.[237] The campaign was nevertheless a publicity win for the Mahasabha. Savarkar's repressed presidential address, titled "Loyal Homage to His Majesty the King of Nepal," was leaked to the press and widely circulated.[238] Its most explosive demand was that the British compensate Nepal for lending its Gurkha troops to defend India's borders "by restoring to Nepal at least those districts of Bihar and on the borders of Punjab which were a part of the Kingdom of Nepal only a century ago and were then annexed by the British."[239] The British perfectly understood that Bhagalpur had been chosen for its proximity to the Nepalese border.[240] And they realized the full significance of Savarkar's address—namely, "for the first time [. . .] the demand is made for the restoration to Nepal of the border districts [. . .] which originally formed part of the Nepalese territory" and were ceded to British India as part of the treaty of 1816 that ended the Anglo-Nepalese War.[241] For Savarkar, coming under Nepalese rule meant that these districts would be the first in British India to be freed—that is, put under Hindu rule.

In his Bhagalpur address, Savarkar also made threats against Afghanistan that caused diplomatic embarrassment to the Government of India and caught the attention of Muhammad Ali Jinnah. The Quaid-e-Azam took Savarkar's address to mean that "they do not want three-fourth; they want the whole" of India—and for good measure want to annex Afghanistan up to the Hindu Khush.[242] Hindusthan's annexation of Afghanistan was an aggressive excess and territorial spillover from the fight for sovereign control of India between two ideologies uniquely characterized by their surplus of claims—to nationhood (the two-nation theory, the Hindu race), land, and sovereignty: Hindusthan and Pakistan. This extreme antagonism between Hindu and Muslim power created a forcefield that strikingly eschewed the map of British India.

The "Pakisthan Millennium" and the Battle for Akhand Bharat

> "Before they vivisect India, let us vivisect their Pakistan first."
> SAVARKAR, May 23, 1947

> "The choice therefore is not between two sets of personalities but between two ideologies, not Indian Raj or Hindu Raj but Moslem Raj or Hindu Raj, Akhand Hindusthan or Akhand Pakistan."
> SAVARKAR, September 25, 1947

Due to the excessive nature of his antagonism to Muslim power, Savarkar's fight for control of India finally spilled into a Greater India in a statement issued in early summer 1942 that survives among Jinnah's personal papers.[243] The context was the 1942 visit of a Chinese Muslim delegation to India that called on Jinnah and the nizam of Hyderabad. In his statement, Savarkar claimed that the Muslim League counted on the Muslim world "from Afghanistan to Turkey" to help them "carve out a Western Pakisthan" in India's northwest. Now, China's Muslims were likewise "get[ting] themselves initiated into Pan-Islamic mysteries" as latecomers to the Islamic globalism that burgeoned after the Great War. Savarkar accused the Muslim League of trying to orchestrate a united Chinese-Burmese Muslim front to force a "Pakisthan" in India's east. But here, the Hindus had "some trump cards" of their own. Against a united Muslim front, the Hindus could mobilize a "United Hindu-Buddhist front from Jammu to Japan." Savarkar closed,

> Just as a frog cannot but remain a frog even if she jumps in the sea, so also the hopeless Indian Moslem minority can never grow into a

dominating majority even if Mr. Woo woos them with all the Chinese Moslems and the Pakisthan can never fail to share the fate of a Papi-sthan whether it raises its head in India or China.[244]

"Papi-sthan" means "land of wrongdoers." This is pure Savarkar. He could never resist a good pun. In fact, Savarkar liked his "Jammu to Japan" and "Woo woos" puns so much that he repeated them and the gist of this statement in a simultaneously published article in the *Mahratta*.[245] During the war, Savarkar heaped scorn on the Muslim League for allegedly signaling to other Muslim nations for help to "realise the Pakisthan Millennium" when these same Muslim nations themselves thrashed around for help against any combination of foes, from Britain to Germany to Russia.[246] The Khilafat cast a long shadow. Islam's inherent globalism, which Savarkar in equal measure understood, feared, and deeply envied, colored the meaning of Pakistan and pulled Hindusthan out of its iconic triangular shape to match and meet Pakistan at every scale, both smaller and bigger than itself.

It was a widely held belief at the time that Pakistan meant more than a state carved out of India's Muslim-majority provinces. According to K. M. Munshi, the former Congress man and Gandhian who broke with nonviolence and turned leader in the fight for Akhand Bharat ("Undivided India")—Akhand Hindusthan, for Savarkar—the "sinister" meaning of Pakistan was to link up with Muslim countries abroad to conquer all of India for the Muslims.[247] Reportedly, even the king of Nepal regarded "'Pakistan' as a possible and plausible octopus" spreading from India's northwest "with tentacles stretching South and East in India to strangle Hinduism."[248] As India's agent-general to Hyderabad, Munshi tellingly went on to oversee independent India's annexation of the huge Muslim princely state that at independence cut a hole the size of France into India's middle as well as the "third front of Partition" in 1947–1948.[249] Jinnah was right to observe that Savarkar's Hindusthan left no space for Pakistan. Yet for Savarkar and his followers, Pakistan signified no territorial compromise either. It was a gambit to take all of India. The nizam's Hyderabad was the major nuclear cell from which Muslim Raj in India could grow.[250]

Writing in *Harijan* in October 1940, Gandhi had hesitantly proposed that the nizam of Hyderabad could be made emperor of India.[251] The princely states represented a sovereign order not based on a demographic logic.[252] Hyderabad, for instance, though ruled by a Muslim prince, was overwhelmingly Hindu in population. But it also had fighting power, and this, more than anything, would matter if the independence movement abandoned nonviolence, as Gandhi thought likely in 1940. He continued,

> If independence is taken by force of arms, then the strongest power will hold sway over all India. And this may be Hyderabad for aught I know. All the big and the petty States will be free willynilly [*sic*] from the British yoke. They will each fight for their existence and succumb to the strongest who will be the Emperor of India."[253]

Under nonviolence, in turn, the nizam could rise to the same position, but this time as the "chosen servant of the people," asserting not his sovereign rights but fulfilling his duty to Indians.[254] In response to Gandhi, Savarkar, strikingly and significantly (and not for anonymity's sake), took up his old nom de plume of Mahratta, under which he had published *Essentials of Hindutva*. As elucidated by Mahratta/Savarkar in the *Khyber Mail*, Gandhi's proposal of handing India over to Muslim rule meant declaring the battle for India lost before it had begun. Savarkar's "virile antidote" to Gandhi's defeatism was for the king of Nepal and India's Hindu princes to join forces to launch an offensive, the same as the Muslims from Muslim princely states, to establish Hindu rule in India.[255] Savarkar regarded Hyderabad and Afghanistan, the proverbial gateway through which India's Muslim conquerors had come, as the major force behind Muslim rule, or "Pakistan." Nepal and the Hindu princes stood as a bastion against them.

On May 15, 1947, exactly three months away from independence and Partition, the party's general secretary, Ashutosh Lahiry, assured the maharaja of Alwar, Tej Singh, that the "Hindu Mahasabha has always stood by the cause of Princely India."[256] Lahiry's letter contrasted sharply with Nehru's letter to Singh written just a few days earlier, in which Nehru warned that he could "not conceive [of] any State continuing to have an authoritarian government" in union with "free and democratic" Indian states.[257] Nehru's uncompromising republicanism certainly was the beginning of the end for princely India. Hindu princes viewed themselves as rulers by divine right; the notorious maharaja of Alwar had called an All-India Kshatriya Conference in Delhi at the close of April 1947, where he allegedly trumpeted, "'Only those races have the right to rule India who can save Hindu *Dharma* by the might of their swords. India's salvation lies in a Kshatriya Kingdom alone and time has now come to establish such a kingdom.'"[258] The Hindu princes were known financiers of the Mahasabha as the closed ranks of princely India fractured along communal lines in the 1940s.[259] Less than a fortnight from the famous stroke of midnight on August 15, 1947, Alwar hosted the All-India Hindu Mahasabha Working Committee at his Delhi residence, in which a resolution was reportedly passed "'declaring a Hindu State as its aim in India and dubbing the Congress leaders as traitors to the country and called upon the people to replace them by a new leadership.'"[260] The Hindu maharajas were widely believed to have armed the RSS to hunt Muslims in their states. Some, including Tej Singh, joined Golwalkar at an RSS mass function in the first December of Indian rule in 1947 and were rumored to be implicated in the murder conspiracy against Gandhi.[261]

Nevertheless, the princes' appeal to Mahasabha traditionalism has been overstated, at least where Savarkar is concerned.[262] Questions of whether "hollow crowns" and "pensioners" of empire could convincingly claim traditional Hindu kingship aside, Hindutva was not a conservative project.[263] As well as inheriting the luster of "Hindu power" that had vanquished the Muslims prior to the advent of British rule, as also elaborated by Moonje, in Savarkar's time, the princes incarnated the Mahasabha's aims to "Hinduize politics and militarize Hindudom."[264] The Hindu princes' motivation in cooperating with the Mahasabha was to salvage what sovereignty they could in the transition to democracy. Doubtlessly, some, like Tej Singh, were also confirmed Hindu chauvinists. But for Savarkar, the princes would be crucial should independence come through fighting and the strongest become emperor of India, as Gandhi had feared. Real military capabilities were crucial here, beyond the metaphorical Kshatriya.[265] Nepal had a famous land force and a fledgling air force that, Savarkar hoped, would soon be "up-to-date and powerful enough to protect not only herself but even Hindudom as a whole."[266] The princes and Nepal anchored Hindu sovereign potentiality, which was deterritorialized due to a lack of organization. Nepal and the Hindu princely states were at the vanguard of Hindutva's project in the endgame of empire—not because they were pure Hindu realms where *dharma* reigned supreme and unspoiled by *feringhi* rule but because they were Hindu sovereign territories from which Hindu Raj could issue.[267]

If Savarkar had been simply the friend of princely India, as he is often viewed, he would have sided with their claim to absolute sovereignty in their states. But in deliberations over the constitutional arrangement of independent India, Savarkar, as head of the Hindu Mahasabha Working Committee, insisted that the princes were not sovereign. There could be no question of their accession, nonaccession, or secession from an Indian union to which they essentially belonged.[268] The Mahasabha's proposal for an Indian constitution entailed a direct reversal of the Muslim League's stance on every point, starting with the naming of the political entity, Akhand Hindusthan. Its main principles were "'the integrity and indivisibility of India; secondly, a strong Central Indian Union; thirdly, one Constituent Assembly to frame the political constitution of such Union; and its federating units; fourthly, adult franchise with one man one vote and fifthly, joint electorate.'"[269] Sixthly, and in direct contrast to Jinnah, as Viceroy Wavell observed to the secretary of state for India, Leo Amery, in 1945, the Mahasabha constitution gave considerable autonomy—even the "utmost greatest measure of autonomy"—to the provinces but only residual powers to the center.[270] The stumbling block was therefore not federation, and on this the Mahasabha leaders, Savarkar, Mukherjee, Moonje, and L. B. Bhopatkar, whatever their differences, all agreed.[271] Federation, now viewed as a past future of Indian independence without Partition and a remedy to the melancholy of the nation-state, was viewed as necessary by members of the Mahasabha to ensure the "integrity" of India, however paradoxical this may appear.[272] Crucially, the federal constitution should have no place for the "new-fangled idea" of the right to self-determination, which was more dangerous than Pakistan itself.[273]

Presiding at the Akhand Hindustan Conference organized at Savarkar's behest in 1944 and in his definitive books on the Muslim question, *Akhand Bharat* (1945) and *A New Approach to the Communal Problem* (1943), Mookerji brandished Abraham Lincoln's victory over states' rights, the Soviet Union's "centripetal" integration of national minorities, and the simile of "divorce before marriage" as intellectual refutations of the demand for Pakistan's creation.[274] Also speaking at the Akhand Hindustan Conference, the acting president of the Hindu Mahasabha, Bhopatkar, marshaled another metaphor. "It was strange," he remarked, that while the former "advocates of the right of self-determination in Europe" were federating, Indian "Muslims were aiming at Balkanization."[275] The princely states' right to nonascension to the "Indian Federation," as granted by the Government of India Act of 1935, set out the possibility of a "rival Pakistan Federation." As a consequence, who was to stop Pakistan from joining with Afghanistan and other Muslim countries to threaten India's security?[276] The Muslim League's demand for "two federations" was to the Mahasabha a "clear indication on the part of Muslims to establish a Muslim Raj in certain parts of the country, leaving the door open for the future domination of the whole of Hindustan."[277] Self-determination had the potential to pluralize the Pakistan threat: India might be shot through with any number of Pakistans. To take self-determination off the table, the party claiming to represent Hindus rejected Cripps in 1942 and the Cabinet Mission Plan in 1946.

According to Ayesha Jalal, only the less astute could conclude that the Cripps mission amounted to conceding Pakistan, since Punjab and Bengal could only achieve independent dominion status if they came to an agreement with their sizeable Hindu minorities, though admittedly the situation was different in the overwhelmingly Muslim North-West Frontier Province.[278] But Hindu nationalists were not contractualists, and a power-sharing agreement was not their Hindusthan. The Mahasabha viewed Pakistan first and foremost as the potential for Muslim sovereignty, rather than a geographically defined space. In this sense, the Hindu party was not mistaken in believing that self-determination meant introducing Pakistan through the back door. Nor was Nehru's reasoning wrong in accepting Pakistan to prevent the further disintegration of India into self-determined princely states.[279] In her work, Jalal has done more than anyone to separate Jinnah's original idea of Pakistan from the "moth-eaten" sovereign state in India's west and east that he got and to split the (lowercase) partitions of the Punjab and Bengal from the (uppercase) Partition of the subcontinent.[280] Jalal's famously counterintuitive argument is that Jinnah never wanted a separate state but a "'Pakistan' at the centre," which would enter into an Indian union based on the principle of parity (rather than numerical representation) with Hindusthan.[281] The aim was to protect Muslims where they constituted a minority, rather than give autonomy to the Muslim majority provinces that had little to fear from Hindus. To this end, Jinnah rejected both loose federation, as a strong center was needed to reign in the provinces in their treatment of minorities, and the division of Punjab and Bengal, whose unpartitioned bulk would take the huge Hindu minority population there hostage to deter Hindu majoritarianism elsewhere. Key to this scheme was the "grouping" of provinces into Hindu and Muslim legislatures, Hindusthan and Pakistan, at the center.[282] Jinnah wanted his dispersed Pakistan centralized, and the Cabinet Mission Plan for a three-tiered federation of India would have given him that center. Yet the mushrooming of plural Pakistans in India that Hindu nationalists feared corresponded to Choudhry Rahmat Ali's (1897–1951) "Dinia," rather than to Jinnah's "grouping."

The Cambridge student remembered for giving Pakistan its name in 1935, Ali also used his playfulness with language to create "Dinia" from an anagram of "India." The changed position of the *d* signified that India was a continent, not a country: "'Indianism'" was a myth.[283] It comprised not one nation—nor two, as Jinnah claimed—but a whole number of non-Hindu nations, including Muslim nations (note the plural). The evocative maps that Ali produced through the years, with slight variations, show "Dinia and its Dependencies" as a Swiss cheese. He claimed for "our" (Muslim) "nations" "at least ten countries, six seas, and four island groups; namely, Pakistan, Bangistan, Osmanistan, Siddigistan, Faruqistan, Haidaristan, Muinistan, and Maplistan in the Continent of Dinia; Safiistan and Nasaristan in Ceylon; the Alam Islands in the Maplian Sea, the Ameen Islands in the Safiian Sea, and the Ashar and Balus Islands in the Bangian Sea."[284] Rather than contiguous landmasses, the unequal distribution of Muslims in the subcontinent produced a littering of Muslim sovereign states. Majorities could form states wherever they lived, without migrating. The creation of Pakistan with an eastern and western wing in 1947 came as a blow to Ali.

Rather than an effect of drawing a line, Shruti Kapila has brilliantly conceptualized the mass violence that left a million dead between Direct Action Day in the summer of 1946 and Gandhi's assassination at winter's close in 1948 as a "lethal hiatus" between the sovereign order of empire (on its way out and no longer able to police, let alone control, the situation by 1946) and the emerging nation-state.[285] Kapila cites the Congress leader and formidable Indian statesman Vallabhbhai "Sardar" Patel (1875–1950) as a cold observer of the real situation in 1946, in which Pakistan could not come about as a British parting kick but only through civil war: "'If Pakistan is going to be achieved, Hindus and Muslims will have to fight.'"[286] In Kapila's view, India had to adopt a republican order in light of the colossal emergence of the sovereign "people" in its most terrifying aspect as a crowd or mob.[287] Violence ended after the assassination of Gandhi and the break between Hindus and Muslims was sutured with the emergence of Indian and Pakistani statecraft. However, the princes as well as Savarkar and his Mahasabha resisted exactly the kind of enfolding into the republican new order that Kapila describes. For those like Savarkar, "Partition violence," or civil war, was an interregnum in which Hindus and Muslims battled for control of India.

No sooner were all restrictions on his political activity finally lifted in 1937 than Savarkar publicly demanded the repeal of the Arms Act that had disarmed Indians after the Indian Rebellion.[288] In the 1940s, the Mahasabha petitioned the government to make arms licenses "liberally" available to Hindus and

Sikhs in places of communal unrest.[289] Sikhs, for Savarkar, were reemerged Kshatriyas and the armed wing of the Hindus. This made them central to the Hindu "militarization" campaign, the code name for the Mahasabha's notorious cooperation with Britain's war effort during World War II. As well as filling the seats of power in ministries and at the negotiating table left vacant by Congress politicians, who had resigned in protest of Britain's unilateral decision to enter India into the war, the Mahasabha encouraged Hindus to enroll in the army to prepare for eventual battle with Muslims.[290] Savarkar's faction within the Mahasabha treated the empire at war as a military training ground and armory for Hindus that would otherwise have benefitted Muslims, who were, like the Sikhs, natural Kshatriyas. A police informant reported that at a Mahasabha rally in Bengal in 1941, Savarkar encouraged Hindu "youths" to join the army in their "thousands" to learn "up-to date warfare," as the Muslims allegedly did in the Punjab.[291] Moonje tried selling the preferential military recruitment of Hindus to the Government of India by swearing that only Hindus could be entrusted with the defense of India, "having no country beyond the frontiers of India to look to for help," whereas the "inherent loyalty" of Muslims lay with Muslim countries outside India's precinct.[292] The obstacle to Hindu militarization was, as ever, the Gandhian "non-sense" of nonviolence.[293] There was truth to the claim of the colonial intelligence officer who warned in 1943 that the Hindu Mahasabha policy of "Hindu Sanghatan and enlistment of Hindus in the armed and civil services [served] as a means of capturing power."[294] Savarkar and his supporters later appropriated Bose's INA as Savarkar's idea, thus revealing his much-criticized collaboration with the British war effort as a secret revolutionary plot.[295]

The Hindu Mahasabha fought the "vivisection" of India until it looked unavoidable, when they changed tactics. Now, they demanded the partitions of Punjab, Sindh, and Bengal. Much has been made of this move by the Mahasabha and especially by Mukherjee, the undisputed Mahasabha leader in Bengal.[296] The blame for Partition is no longer solely attributed to the Muslim League. Partitioning Bengal was no one's first choice, however. It was grudgingly adopted when other strategies (not including compromise with the Muslims) had failed. To flip the demographic balance in Bengal and counteract "'the sinister implication of the Pakistan scheme,'" Mukherjee had even supported "an ingenious, though hardly practicable, suggestion" to amalgamate Orissa with Bengal in 1942.[297] But by 1947, United Bengal seemed to Mukherjee nothing but a "'surrender to Pakistan.'"[298]

On February 20, 1947, the British Labour prime minister, Clement Attlee, made his historic announcement that Britain would quit India by June 1948. Unless the Muslim League could be enticed to join the Constituent Assembly for communal representation at the center, he declared, power would be transferred to whichever entity seemed to best represent the interest of the people, be that a central Government of India or provincial governments. If the Muslim-majority provinces were not partitioned, the Hindus there would risk becoming trapped minorities.[299] However, Joya Chatterji, in her definitive study of the partition of Bengal, has shown that the propaganda machines of the Bengal provincial chapters of the Congress and Hindu Mahasabha had swung in favor of partitioning Bengal even before Attlee's announcement. In fact, the Bengal Congress and Hindu Mahasabha cooperated in a vigorous campaign for partition. They mobilized violence against the Muslim League's Direct Action Day on August 16, 1946, which resulted in the Great Calcutta Killing and ramped up their campaign from March 1947.[300]

At the all-India level, the Mahasabha wavered a little longer on the issue of the "lowercase" partition of the Muslim-majority provinces. But by the time Lord Mountbatten's June 3 Plan of 1947 brought independence—at the price of Partition—forward by a year, partitioning Bengal and Punjab seemed the only way to "rescue" "millions of Hindus and Sikhs from the clutches of the Muslim League."[301] Savarkar privately telegraphed his consent to Mukherjee in late March 1947 and shortly after publicly stated his reasons:[302]

> Pakistan or no Pakistan we must have now a Hindu province in Bengal, Punjab and Sindh in the interest of Akhand Bharat itself. For even if the impossible happens and Britain concedes integrity of India under a strong Central Government then new Hindu majority province in Bengal can openly serve as a faithful sentry checkmating any further treacherous attempt on the part of Moslem majority there. On the other hand in case Pakistan is thrust on us by Britain the creation of these provinces shall form an unbroken link of Hindu majority provinces from east Punjab to West Bengal and with the Hindu kingdom of Nepal and Kashmir in the North and Hindu Assam in the east would consolidate and enable Hindus to reannex the revolting Pakistani areas provided of course we "Hinduise all politics and militarise Hindudom."[303]

If the partition of Bengal and Punjab was the partition that Jinnah did not want, Savarkar and the Mahasabha wanted it for the same reason: because it "vivisect[ed] their Pakistan."[304] If Savarkar had a straightforwardly territorial notion of Hindusthan and regarded its soil as sacred, he could not have proceeded in this way. But Savarkar's concern in 1947 was the spatialization of sovereign potentiality. The partitions of the Muslim-majority provinces would allow the formation of a continuous battlefront stretching across India's entire northern frontier.[305] On this front, Nepal marked a strategic location.[306]

India fractured at midnight on August 15, 1947. In that moment, rather than inhabiting the center left by the British to India, the Hindu Crown dispersed to the Hindu sovereign spaces dotted throughout the subcontinent. Nepal, the Hindu princely states, the Hindu majority provinces, and arms-bearing Hindus in towns and villages across the country merged into a battlefront for Akhand Bharat. Their aim, as Savarkar saw it, was to wipe away the possibility of "Pakistan." This was not the sovereign Pakistani state that emerged after the civil war's end, its threat to India potent yet geopolitically contained. Rather, for Savarkar, Pakistan was an itinerant possibility of Muslim Raj in all of India that, in 1947, formed "two extensive fronts in the main," "one from Kashmir to Junagad" in Gujarat, which was "perhaps under the lead of the Amir of Afghanistan" and helped by the frontier Pathans and Baluchis, and "the other in the South under the command of the Nizam," which threatened the western and eastern coastlines and the Indian heartland.[307] From these two locations, Pakistan strove to envelop the whole subcontinent—unless Hindus fought it, inch by inch. For Savarkar, it was "Akhand Hindusthan or Akhand Pakistan."[308]

"Hanske liya Pakistan, larke lenge Hindusthan" (We got Pakistan by laughing, we are going to take Hindustan by fighting) was the Muslim slogan often heard on and after Direct Action Day: Savarkar distorted it to read "marke" (killing): Muslims will get Hindusthan by killing.[309] Partition and the departure of the British had clearly not settled the issue of Pakistan. Realities were being fought out on the ground. Amid the fighting, the Mahasabha newspaper, *Hindu Outlook*, stoked "'the Muslim rebellion' theory," according to which Muslims aimed to overthrow India's government and "'annex Delhi to Pakistan.'"[310] Again, Savarkar's party projected into and mirrored its enemy, having made it perfectly clear that it did not consider itself "bound" by any agreement on Pakistan entered into by the Congress, which, by conceding Pakistan, had committed treason against Hindus.[311] In that August of independence, the

Mahasabha openly called for the overthrow of the Nehruvian government.[312] It called for the "'men of straw'" of the Nehru cabinet to be replaced by a host of Hindu maharajas, including Alwar, next to Savarkar, Mookerji, Bhopatkar, and Ambedkar, and, at the helm, "'H. H. the Rana of Nepal (Defence Minister).'"[313]

Savarkar never wanted Partition with a capital *P*. The "lowercase" partition of Bengal was not meant to be permanent either; in fact, the Mahasabha was already campaigning to "redress [. . .] the wrong of the partition of BENGAL" before it had even happened.[314] "'There will never be peace unless the separated areas are brought back into the Indian Union and made its integral parts,'" the Mahasabha declared following Mountbatten's June 3 announcement.[315] To be sure, the party also tried to influence the boundary lines in favor of the Hindus and India. In its suggestions to the Radcliffe Commission, it made "much greater inroads into what is admittedly Muslim territory" than even Congress had.[316] But the issue in 1947 was more than a land grab. Recall that Savarkar rejected the territorial idea of nationhood and citizenship. In 1947, the Mahasabha party leadership was quick to claim the Hindus of East Pakistan as "nationals" of India.[317] After Partition, they demanded the transfer of the Hindu population of East Pakistan to India.[318] Savarkar also demanded the expulsion of "at least an equal number of Moslems from West Bengal"—"if necessary, per force."[319] Hindutva refused to conform to the territorial settlement of enmity.

In a suppressed statement issued to the Indian press on September 29, 1947, and reprinted in a sympathetic journal in Glasgow, Savarkar finally posited the Hindu nation as antagonistic to the newly independent Indian state.[320] Then he attacked the state's monopoly of violence, for in the midst of "literally fasting and fiddling to celebrate their bloodless revolution," the Indian state shut its eyes to "realities"—namely that Muslims had declared war on Hindusthan and were already preparing militarily to achieve their objective of making it a "Moslem-srhan [*sic*]." This war needed to be incorporated into India's raison d'état, as Pakistan had done for the Muslims. But instead, the Nehruvian state recognized Pakistani sovereignty without admitting "that there existed any enmity at all between the two states." Savarkar called for the Indian government to be sacked and handed over to a "Sikh-Hindu Sanghatanist Coalition."[321] The Hindu Crown did not come to rest on Nehru's head.

This much is blatantly obvious today: the nonacceptance of Pakistan is an essential part of Hindu nationalism. Savarkar repeated this refusal when standing in the dock at the Gandhi murder trial.[322] Again, in January 1950, when India became a republic, he issued this statement: "True the Partition today is a 'settled fact.' But so had Alexander thought of his conquests in India as 'settled fact.' Verily we have our own ways to resettle settled facts. Let us first consolidate what we have already got and follow courageously the policy of tit for tat."[323] Golwalkar echoed him almost verbatim in speaking of "unsettl[ing]" the "settled fact" of Partition in a speech reprinted in *Bunch of Thoughts*.[324] Twelve years on, when India was at war with China, Savarkar had this to say about Pakistan:

> About Pakistan I must say that the two nations will not become one nation and they should not become one nation. Pakistan which is based on Islam can never become a true friend of India. Ayub Khan says the same thing. For hundreds of years the Moslem kings have said the same thing. On the other hand our nation is based on Hinduism.[325]

Starting from the end of the state of exception and entrenchment of two new sovereign orders, India and Pakistan, Hindu nationalists straddled an ambiguity. On the one hand, they aggressively espoused Indian statecraft and nuclearization against Pakistan. On the other hand, the nonacceptance of the settlement that produced Pakistan as well as India put Hindutva into lasting opposition to the Indian state.

This chapter has argued that Hindutva has a distinctive theory of sovereignty, which I call the Hindu Crown. Though monarchical in expression, the Hindu Crown was not a refutation of republicanism as much as an assertion of Hindu sovereignty in the only form Savarkar found it territorialized in his day: in the Hindu princely states and the kingdom of Nepal. Hindu nationalism thus presents a story of the loss and recovery of Hindu sovereignty, always pitted against the Muslim capacity for sovereignty in the subcontinent. The longer history told in this chapter, which stretches from Greater India to Savarkar's overtures to the king of Nepal, demonstrates that Hindu nationalism developed its theory of sovereignty independently of and preceding the territorial threat to India's unity. By proving that Hindu nationalist assertions of sovereignty were not merely knee-jerk reactions to the threatened "vivisection" of their motherland, the history of the Hindu Crown serves to extricate Hindu nationalist visions of sovereignty from the teleology of territory as well as the history of Partition. But Pakistan *was* created and thus enmity territorially fixed. This finally necessitated a departure from Savarkar's maxims and a full reorientation in Hindu nationalist thought. It necessitated a turn away from the dualism of enmity that is Savarkar's indisputable legacy. After Partition, Hindu nationalism made a dramatic conversion to monism, the theory of nondualism regarded as the "essence" of Hinduism and once identified as the major obstacle to the emergence of Hindu political identity by Savarkar. The next chapter traces how Hindutva finally came to be near indistinguishable from Hinduism.

CHAPTER FIVE

AFTER THE DUALISM OF PAKISTAN

Ekam sat vipra, bahudha vadanti
("Truth is One, though the Vedantins call it by different names")
RIG VEDA

Tat tvam asi ("You are that")
CHANDOGYA UPANISHAD

Had Benoy Sarkar outlived the American lecture tour that suddenly and unexpectedly struck him down, aged sixty-one, in 1949, we might have had the pleasure of a fourth tome of *The Political Philosophies since 1905*. Indian independence—which came at the price of Partition and the twin birth at midnight, as it is famously rendered, of instant enemies India and Pakistan; the incorporation of the princely states; and two republican constitutions—no doubt merited the full attention of the theorist of the new in political ideas. India and Pakistan soon clashed over territory, wars and border skirmishes followed, and Kashmir remains a red-hot issue. The Radcliffe Line—which was lovelessly, many say artlessly, and certainly most speedily drawn across Punjab and became the international border between India and Pakistan—has acquired iconic salience as an immediately recognizable, gashing wound. The jagged line represents artificial division, concocted by the particularly divisive nationalisms of Indian elites and the divide-and-conquer scheming of empire, whose tortured compromise behind the closed doors of power extracted a hideous cost of mass death, displacement, rape, trauma, and suffering from ordinary people. Sarkar recognized, more keenly than most, that borders were foundational for states as the territorial manifestation of the political. Borders functioned less between neighbor countries as enemies and more as dividing lines between the national repository of sovereignty and the temptations of the international that supported no sovereignty and brought no freedom to conquered people. Yet Sarkar knew that "secular" territorial sovereignty was not India's gift to the world (it dated only to Ramdas in the Indian context). Radhakumud Mookerji had identified the Hindus' contribution to global political thought as the deification of the motherland. The astute Sarkar may have singled out something else: the concept of integrality itself. Integrality found application as a territorial idea, certainly, but its proper ambit was the Hindu religion.

"Integral" rose as an ideological matrix just as India lost its territorial and political integrity—with Partition. Before 1947, India's "integral unity" had been marshaled to fix the country as one and indivisible. This strategy failed; India was broken up. If Pakistan could only come about by fighting, as Sardar Patel prognosticated, it might be said that the Hindus had lost that fight.[1] Of course, fighting turned neighbors into enemies, and in this sense, those fighting to avoid Pakistan or Muslim rule were complicit in fixing enmity and the impossibility of Muslims and Hindus living together—namely, as Pakistan. However, as a new sovereign order was established in India under Nehru, Patel, and Ambedkar, Hindu nationalism became opposed to the state. Nehru's republic was not their Hindu Raj. This chapter tracks Hindu nationalism's movement away from Savarkar's conception of gendered warfare to a profound remaking of Indian society into an "integral" unity indistinguishable from the Hindu religion. Though habitually associated with enmity toward Muslims, Hindutva currently claims the transcendent ground of unity above divisions, the universal above the particular, and unitary religious truth subsuming lesser-order religious "sects" like Islam. Appropriating the Nehruvian slogan but evacuating its nonassimilationist pluralism, postindependence Hindutva has made itself the "unity in diversity" that India is supposed to be.[2]

The ability to synthesize, absorb, assimilate, and form unity out of itself had emerged as ubiquitous descriptors in the early days of colonial Sanskrit scholarship. They described, first, the power through which Indic civilization had withstood innumerable foreign conquests without dying, and, second, the theological essence of Hinduism-Brahmanism, fixed as the soteriological aim of the absorption of the self (*atman*) into the Supreme Being or Absolute (*brahman*).[3] As already discussed, Advaita Vedanta was distilled as the "essence" of Hinduism in colonial times. Some scholars even speak of the "colonial construction" of Hinduism as a religion in the nineteenth century, when the notion of "world religions" was also "invented."[4] To summarize their argument: the exclusively Christian *vera religio* ("true religion"), a singular pitted against heathenism, pluralized, leading to the watershed of a sui generis concept of "religion" and "religions" in the last decades of the nineteenth century.[5] It threw open the view to the fundamental equivalence—though not equality—of all so-designated religions. Within this pluralism nevertheless remained a universalist assumption: that one historical religion must best embody the transcendent essence of all religions, called the "universal religion."[6] Christianity was, of course, fixed as the winner of this competition, but there are good reasons for making Hinduism similarly well placed to make a bid for universality at that moment. As universalism was recoined as pluralism, polytheism, which recognized the unity underlying plural appearances, gained favor over the three Abrahamic monotheisms accused of exclusivism and, in the case of Islam, fanaticism.[7] Hinduism's sheer scriptural antiquity placed it at the origin of recorded civilization. Its proverbial lack of form approximated the structure of "spiritualism," which was valorized in the contemporaneous pushback against dogma and organized religion.[8] Finally, Hinduism was an "Aryan" religion promising Europe emancipation from Hebrew patrimony.[9] But the Hinduism that was offered as the world's "universal religion" was a conspicuously new synthesis.

Burgeoning within a larger "global idealist moment" in the nineteenth century, religious and social reform movements in India formed in answer to colonial pressures on society.[10] Benoy Sarkar's talented daughter Indira, interpolating in Indian discussion in the *Calcutta Review* from her studies in Paris in 1948, discoursed on the humanistic philosophy of religion that had taken ground in nineteenth-century Bengal, which she named "Comtism" after Auguste Comte's positivist religion of humanity and "Renanism" after Ernest Renan's *Life of Jesus* (1863), which had made God a man and man divine.[11] The "milieu of Comte and Renan," Indira argued, had produced notables like the poet Nabin Chandra Sen, the novelist Bankim Chandra Chattopadhyay, and the great Hindu reformer Swami Vivekananda, who between them historicized Krishna, rationalized Hindu religion, endorsed an ethic of philanthropic service (*seva*), and entrenched religious universalism so deeply that they posited the fundamental identity of all founders of religions ("Krishna, Buddha, Christ, Mohammad, and Chaitanya") as "*avataras*," or manifestations, of the same God.[12] These men, who were Hindus "in their own way" and "in name only," as Indira Sarkar noted, became the architects of what is variously known as neo-Hinduism, neo-Advaita, or neo-Vedanta.[13] The hyphenation marks the presumed radical novelty of this offering of "Hinduism," which took the shape of Shankara's Advaita Vedanta. The spectacular success of the saffron-robed and turbaned Vivekananda at the World's Parliament of Religions in Chicago in 1893 conventionally marks the watershed of neo-Vedantic Hinduism, which announced itself to the world as the "universal religion."

Tat tvam asi, or "You are that," are three short words of profound philosophical depth that sum up Shankara's Upanishadic lesson on the total identity of the personal soul with the Absolute. Much has been made of South Asian religions becoming protestantized in the process of becoming "world religions": of how Hinduism was shorn off ritualism, based on a sacred book (the Vedas and their Upanishadic commentary), rationalized, and interiorized. More could be said about how Hindu religion was restored to the purity of its presumed monistic origins, its idols not so much smashed but subsumed under divine oneness. Thus, Hinduism became the strangest of monotheisms, an idolator's temple of fantastic proportions housing myriad gods, goddesses, and their mounts yet manifesting profound divine unity. Orientalism, colonialism, Christian missionaries, and nineteenth-century Hindu reformers are usually blamed for the colonial "construction" of Hinduism. My issue with the story of the nineteenth-century discovery of the universalism of "world religions" is that it ties exclusively back to the European tradition. Yet within India, the Mughal era of religious "syncretism" already saw attempts, notably by the seventeenth-century Mughal prince Dara Shukoh, to identify the monotheistic essence of all religions in Vedantic Hinduism.[14] The revival of *bhakti* devotionalism in the fifteenth to seventeenth centuries preached the transcendence of all religious division by centering the loving adoration of and merging with God as the only path to liberation. The Muslim weaver-turned-mystic-poet Kabir and the founder of the Sikh order, Guru Nanak, worshipped an attribute-less Divine that equated Ram with Allah and the Vedas with the Quran. Though annexed to the Hindu tradition as we understand it today, the *bhakti* and *sant* traditions sprang up in opposition to Brahmanic orthodoxy, Vedanta, Sanskrit, the Vedas, and caste; their radical message of social and religious dissent was dismantled by appropriation into the Advaita Vedanta tradition, from Ramanuja in the twelfth century to Raja Rammohan Roy and Rabindranath in the nineteenth and twentieth.[15] The dyad of lover (devotee) and beloved (God, the object of devotion) in the *bhakti* tradition, which suggests a measure of separate identity that deep devotion bridged and merged, could thus be folded into the unqualified monism of Advaita Vedanta. Whether in popular religion or advanced philosophy, it appeared that the Hindus knew no higher goal than to extinguish the self in the stream of the universal.

Hindutva, when it was coined, confronted head-on Hinduism's historical inability to stabilize an other as "other" and enemy, rather than absorb them as inner difference and variation—that is, monistically. Political action itself was predicated on overcoming the impulse of overidentification that stunned Hindus into passivity and pessimism. Keeping within the Indic tradition, one might say that Savarkar sought to cultivate and instill into Hindus a sense of *dvaita*, dualism, which he gave the stronger sense of antagonism, at its extreme meaning the self-enemy distinction that Nazi legal theorist Carl Schmitt defines as the quintessential political distinction that initiates the exception of war.[16] Savarkar's Hindutva was made for and consumed in the moment of "exception."[17] Others had to reinvent Hindutva for independent, republican India after enmity was territorially fixed as Pakistan.

The larger truth in which the Hindu self was allegedly always ready to lose itself (its self, *atman*) was dubbed "humanity" in Savarkar's time. *Hindutva*'s author explicitly held Vedantic monism, *bhakti* devotionalism, and Buddhist nonviolence in abeyance as the loftiest heights of Hindu philosophy that were the deadliest poison to Hindus in their current state—recall also Benoy Sarkar, the theorist of the joys of dynamism, on the opiates of monism, internationalism, and humanism. The Nazis, too, opposed their political philosophy to Vedantic Hinduism, which had seeped deeply into the German mind over the past century and a half. Becoming fascist in the German configuration, and becoming an acolyte of Savarkar's Hindutva, meant overcoming Hinduism's monist temptations. But the fall of Nazism in 1945 and India's independence and Partition in 1947 brought about a profound reorientation. This chapter argues that what distinguishes pre- and postindependence Hindutva above all is their stance on Hinduism. It explores how it was that after 1947, Hindutva came to endorse Vedantic monism as "Integral Humanism." The argument is that Hindutva, under a new set of leaders with Deendayal Upadhyaya at the helm, came to endorse Hindu philosophy (Advaita Vedanta) and lived religion (*bhakti*) to the point that it is almost indistinguishable from Hinduism today.

Savarkar's Humanism

Simultaneously with his full return to militancy in 1947, Savarkar rekindled the international revolutionary networks of his youth—critically, his association with Guy Aldred (1886–1963), the British anarchist, communist, and by this time Christian "humanist." Though the two had never personally met during Savarkar's time in London, there was an old bond of solidarity between them owing to Aldred's conviction for crimes relating to Indian nationalism in 1909 and advocacy for Savarkar in 1910.[18] It was Aldred's monthly, *The Word,* that released Savarkar's suppressed statement calling for enmity to be incorporated into India's raison d'état in November 1947. From June 1947 to about 1950, Aldred's Glasgow-based journal became the mouthpiece in exile for "Savarkarites" through independence and Partition and their marginalization within the Hindu Mahasabha after the assassination of Gandhi by Savarkar's known associate, Nathuram Godse (1910–1949). In the prelude to Partition, *The Word* reprinted Aldred's own youthful articles on Savarkar's London conspiracy case in an April 1947 special "Savarkar issue."[19] Soon, it was publishing letters that had begun to flood in not only from Savarkar's closest associates, like the secretary of the Hindu Mahasabha's head office in Delhi, Lala Ganpat Rai, and Savarkar's personal secretary, Gajanan Vishnu Damle, but from Savarkar himself.[20] Bhai Parmanand, a high-ranking member of the Hindu Mahasabha, asked to be supplied with issues of the journal.[21] As Savarkar himself informed Aldred, reprints and vernacular translations of *The Word* articles had started to appear in the Indian bastions of "Savarkarism"—like the *Kesari,* Bombay's *Free Hindustan,* and the *Agrany* of Poona—from which *The Word* reprinted in its turn.[22]

Apparently, Godse himself "conveyed his best compliments to [Aldred] before his execution." Gandhi's murderer reportedly "read all issues of *The Word* with keen interest up to the very end" and "believed that [Aldred] would understand his attitude and conduct and his protest against the terrible division of India."[23] In the endgame of empire, Savarkar and his acolytes availed themselves of the expatriate platform that remained committed to preventing and, when the fight was lost, undoing Partition—or "Britain's scrap of paper," as Aldred called it.[24] After the murder of Gandhi, *The Word* became the last strange space of Savarkar's Hindu Crown: the most unlikely, most microscopic, and most resolutely deterritorialized of all the strange places to which Hindu power withdrew, from which to emanate and reconquer Akhand Hindusthan. Savarkar's Hindu Crown ended up where he began his career: in a militant, expatriate cell.

At first Gandhi's murderer was assumed to be a Muslim, and anti-Muslim vigilantism was quick to follow. Then, the true identity and affiliation of the murderer was made known. It was rumored that members of the Hindu Mahasabha distributed sweets at the news of the patricide that they, many assumed, had awaited and helped plot.[25] In the ensuing violent pushback against the Hindu Mahasabha and the RSS, Savarkar's house in Bombay, "Savarkar Sadan," was mobbed; his books burned; and his brother Narayan beaten up.[26] The RSS was banned, Hindu Mahasabha leaders were rounded up, and Savarkar was arrested and eventually charged with conspiracy to murder India's father, who was killed because his assassin considered him also "the father of Pakistan."[27] Savarkar was acquitted of all charges at Gandhi's murder trial held inside Old Delhi's historic Red Fort, the old Mughal palace steeped with and chosen for its sovereign symbolism. Though suspicion has never left him, Savarkar stepped out a free man into a new India that he saw only as a halfway house to full independence, meaning the end of the Muslim domination that had been reconfigured as Pakistan.

In 1950, *The Word* was the first to publish Godse's and Savarkar's trial testimonies, which had been smuggled out and securely dispatched to Aldred in Glasgow.[28] The special issue was clandestinely received in India, where, according to one of Aldred's new Hindu correspondents, recipients concealed it "as if it were a bombshell," while no bookseller was "prepared to stock it."[29] From Aldred's perspective, the aim seems to have been to internationalize the persecution of Indian political "sufferers" as part of a global struggle against imperialism and oppression, his lifetime commitments. Most curiously, not only Aldred's authoritative framing in *The Word* but Savarkar himself identified "Savarkarism" with humanism. This remarkable coupling disturbed some readers, who noted that Aldred's championing of Savarkar contradicted the journal's pacifist aims.[30] Savarkar addressed the seeming incongruity of associating his name with humanism in a letter to Aldred, dated May 1, 1947, marked "personal & not for publication." He urged his "comrade" (whom he misaddressed as "Mr. Guy") not to be deceived by "my daily and immediate activities and writings," from which it may appear that "I am interested in and devoted to Nationalism alone."[31] On the contrary, Savarkar professed the view that,

> although Mankind must march on through Nationalism and Federalism, through larger and larger statal Incorporations to their ultimate goal—yet the goal is not and cannot be nationalism but Humanism—neither more or less. The Ideal of all Political Science and Art must be a Human State. The Earth is our Motherland, Mankind our Nation.

Savarkar concluded by claiming that "Historical Relativity" alone had made him a fighter for "Nationalism and Hindu Sangathan," which was only his "immediate Mission."[32]

Such protestations were not a novel attempt at exoneration. They copied almost verbatim Savarkar's mercy petition sent to the British government in 1917 (he had sent many).[33] Writing to his brothers from Cellular Jail shortly after, Savarkar had similarly restated the nineteenth-century trope that nationalism was an "artificial though indispensable" division in the service of the "higher patriotism" of humanity. The penultimate instance of the "welding" of the world state to which Savarkar professed to aspire entailed the "fulfilment" of all national "political selves" through "merging" with the "Human state."[34] In these letters, Savarkar presented himself as a reluctant revolutionary who "abhorred violence"; these claims were doubtlessly meant for the eyes of the prison authorities, but Savarkar's humanist confessions are suggestive.[35] Giving them credence, Savarkar's biographer Dhananjay Keer cites the Aldred connection itself as proof of Savarkar's humanism. In this reading, Hindu *sangathan* was just an intermediate step: "survival" before world "unity."[36] Yet Keer was also one of Aldred's correspondents and contributors to *The Word* at the time and disseminated the message of Savarkar's and Hindutva's "humanism" in the Indian press.[37] Savarkar's "humanism" is Hindu nationalist folklore to this day and has some academic adherents.[38]

The final vision in *Essentials of Hindutva* presents the dissolution of the Hindu: "A Hindu is most intensely so, when he ceases to be a Hindu."[39] This loss or erasure of Hindu-ness ("Hindutva") paradoxically marks the fulfillment of Hindu identity, but only once Hindus had become supreme and unopposed to the point of being able to "dictate" to the world. A sequential logic of necessity unfolds whereby Hindus must first nurture an aggressive identity and organize along purely national lines. Yet having thereby gained a state with the ability to dictate to the world, their "terms," Savarkar suggested, would be the content of the (nonviolent) Gita, Buddhism, Shankara, and the *bhakti* poet Tukaram—otherwise all items of Savarkar's contempt. Co-opting nonviolence and monism only at the point of victory, when all need for struggle with nonidentity is extinguished, Savarkar extends the battle lines of "the Hindu" to the frontiers of the universe. The closing lines of *Essentials of Hindutva* quote the words of Tukaram: "'My country? oh brothers, the limits of the Universe:—there the frontiers of my country lie!'"[40] Savarkar was no monist but rather a unique theorist of dualism, *dvaita*. Even where he promised monism as a deferred aim, it justified extreme antagonism in the present. Savarkar could only envision the transcendence of dualism in the same way that he envisioned Muslim integration: as the complete erasure of the dualism that the other represented.

In 1948, Indira Sarkar concluded her discussion: "The religion of fraternity can no further go. It transcends the limitations of the earthly sphere." Universal humanitarianism had stretched the *fraternité* of the French Revolution to "impossible and inaccessible proportions."[41] Her father, Benoy, would have agreed. Savarkar's life's work was to craft the Hindu political subject, which he stood on foundations of *dvaita*. This was within a broad pan-Hindu matrix, to be sure, and sublated internal difference, but as a distinct identity, it had only enmity to offer to the enemy, so long as the enemy insisted on retaining their difference. Savarkar had no hidden monist message to offer. This also meant that he did not pursue supremacy through Hindu universalism, going the way of Vivekananda and those reformers who had made Hinduism "aggressive" and imperial in the nineteenth century. In the words of Sadhu Vaswani, who exemplified this approach and was familiar in interwar Germany: "Imperialism is the world-view of the Chosen Race. The Aryan world-view *is:—humanism*."[42] Arguably, the neo-Vedantic viewpoint that Vaswani espoused was a project of domination from its nineteenth-century origins.[43] What marks its sharp difference from the monism Hindutva appropriated following 1947, however, is the novel reality of geopolitical dualism that Partition created. Savarkar's conspicuous turn to "humanism" at the same time as he declared war on Pakistan illustrates that this was a new assimilationist idiom, which took the shape of Akhand Bharat. Coming out of the fray of 1947, Hindutva was reconfigured as a kind of integrationist matrix that could erase the dualism of Pakistan. In his incarnation as an international humanist in *The Word*, and through a switch in rhetoric necessitated by the fallout from Gandhi's murder, Savarkar, always a proponent of "responsive cooperation" (i.e., opportunism) in politics, became complicit in Hindutva's new birth as Integral Humanism.

Bhakti—the "Last Resort" against Partition

As the 1940s opened, monism's great critic, Benoy Sarkar, returned to his early interest in folk religion. The common devotional idioms of Buddhist and Hindu everyday practice—*tantra*, Vaishnavism, Shaivism, and *bhakti*—had, in the 1910s, shown Sarkar a Greater Indian civilization that swept across Southeast Asia and extended all the way to China.[44] But when the Pakistan demand (vague though it still was) menaced Bengal with a second partition, Sarkar marshaled folk religion to affirm the integral unity of Bengalis in the last rendition of *The Political Philosophies since 1905*, published in 1942. Sharply turning against the Hindu supremacism that would lead his *bhadralok* coreligionists to prefer Partition to Muslim domination in 1947, Sarkar now insisted that Bengalis were not Muslims or Hindus but devotees of "Bengalicism, the original culture and religion of the Bengali pariahs, that has conquered both Hinduism and Islam" by forcing them to acculturate to its own folk ways.[45] Popular devotionalism erased the separation between Islam and Hinduism that theology had drawn. A religion of "'crows and pigeons'"—vernacular, hybrid, and emphatically low caste and anti-Sanskrit—Sarkar's "Bengalicism" designated the self-worship of common Bengalis.[46] Sarkar's Bengalis prayed to gods created by their own creative genius and in which they deified themselves.[47] Durga, Kali, Saraswati, and Bengal's female pantheon were the women of Bengal, while Krishna, Ganesh, and the male gods were the men.[48] With this late homecoming to the unifying ground of popular religion, Benoy Sarkar was indicative of a broader turn to syncretic religion in the 1940s capable of combating the prospect of division.[49]

Sarkar was no bigot. *His* turn to *bhakti* was certainly curious but not shocking. But in 1946, in the wake of the Noakhali riots, none other than Hindu Mahasabha general secretary, Ashutosh Lahiry, turned to religious syncretism as a last, desperate attempt to avoid Partition. Lahiry beseeched Muslims to "today return into the Hindu fold," meaning their conversion (*shuddhi*). But he promised that the conversion would not be to Hinduism proper but to a "rejuvenated and vital religion" that transcended Hinduism itself and that "even Hindu Society must give way to."[50] He argued that the conversion of Muslims to this new Hinduism should not be difficult, doctrinally speaking, as there was "no fundamental difference in the spiritual aspects of one religion and another." Lahiry intriguingly envisioned that the new converts would resurrect the extinct Kshatriyas: "The Muslims will be able to add to the Kshatriya power of Hinduism, which to a certain extent has been dormant in the [*sic*] recent years." This was a major retreat from Savarkar's Hindutva by one of his closest coworkers, an old revolutionary who had been imprisoned with Savarkar and Bhai Parmanand in the Andamans.[51]

Lahiry patterned the assimilation of Muslims into the "new Hindu religion" on India's devotional traditions, which fused Islam and Hinduism as they recognized God in all forms. He listed the big names of *bhakti* devotionalism—Chaitanya, Kabir, and Krishna—as well as Akbar and Shah Jahan's appointed heir, Dara Shukoh, whom Hindus favorably contrast with his brother and usurper, Aurangzeb, in a tradition of softening Muslim rule against which Savarkar most vehemently turned after initial overtures in *Essentials of Hindutva*.[52] Akbar and Dara Shukoh represented not only the possibility of Hinduizing the Mughals through Sufism and *bhakti* but strongly implicated Advaita Vedanta. Dara Shukoh had commissioned the Persian translation of the Upanishads (*Sirr-i Akbar*) in the mid-seventeenth century whose Vedantic reading was so crucial for the identification of modern Hinduism with Advaita Vedanta.[53] The Muslim prince uncovered the Upanishads as the lost first revelation of God's unity. He found that Vedantic Hinduism was, in fact, esoteric Islamic truth. For his interpretation, Dara Shukoh relied entirely on Shankara's monistic exegesis instead of the then-thriving dualistic or qualified nondualistic schools of Vedanta.[54] If religious scholar Michael Bergunder is right, then Dara Shukoh's monotheistic Upanishads may have even been the basis of Rammohan Roy's neo-Vedanta, thus inscribing Mughal religious universalism into the genesis of modern Hinduism itself.[55] Today, the syncretism of Dara Shukoh and his great-grandfather Akbar, often mischaracterized as "liberalism" or "tolerance," stands for the past future of the peaceful coexistence of Hindus and Muslims in the subcontinent.[56] Its appeal at the dawn of geopolitical dualism challenged Savarkar's order. In his political testament, Savarkar wrote how Akbar's syncretistic Din-i-Ilahi—or "religion of God," which drew on both Hinduism and Islam—was, in fact, "quite different from either." At best, it remained irrelevant outside the royal court. At worst, it undermined Hinduism by inevitably promoting Arabic, Allah, and Akbar himself, who, as Savarkar shrewdly judged, wanted to make himself the supreme "spiritual lord" as well as a temporal lord.[57]

To Lahiry, India's traditions that extolled God's oneness appeared as a "last resort" to combat—engulf and enfold—the irreducibility of Muslim difference that was beginning to materialize as Pakistan. "Adoption and not segregation," according to Lahiry, "[wa]s to be the principle cry of this new Hinduism," which could still tie Indians together.[58] In 1948 repeatedly calling for the Mahasabha to decommunalize and joining Syama Mukherjee in demands to open its membership to non-Hindus against resolute opposition from Savarkar, Lahiry personified the inner-party opposition to "Savarkarism" of which *The Word*'s Hindu correspondents complained.[59] For Lahiry, the objective of Akhand Bharat required the Mahasabha to "organise and consolidate all sections of the people of Hindusthan into one organic whole."[60] This entailed rethinking the divisive term "Hindu" in the party's name, which either had to be reinterpreted to include all who regarded Hindusthan as their "motherland"—Lahiry tacitly dropped its twin, "holy land"—or required creating a new "Associate Membership" for non-Hindus.[61] Yet Lahiry's public resolutions belied the ideological continuity of his hostility. Privately, in rallying volunteers at a Hindu Mahasabha training camp at Shajahanpur in the autumn of 1949, he entrusted responsibility for India to Hindus alone, as Muslims had confirmed their betrayal of the "Hindu Rashtra ideal" during India's "police action" in Hyderabad (its annexation) the previous year.[62] Though antagonism had shifted to a conflict between two sovereign states, the position of the Indian Muslim was that of an embryonic Pakistani, whose treason in the case of war was always assumed. Pakistan's existence confirmed that Hindus were the true nationals of India.

Lahiry not only refused to condemn Gandhi's murderer publicly but even expressed his "admiration" for Godse's "sacrifice" in his farewell letter to Godse written after the date of the execution was fixed.[63] Though flagging their difference "on so many issues in the past," Lahiry fondly recalled their "years of political association" that would "ever" fill him with the "greatest pride and profound reverence" for Godse. Then, he turned to the "issue of Akhand Bharat, which has been so near to you." "I clearly foresee," Lahiry wrote, that the issue of Akhand Bharat would be "put to the final decisive test in not [*sic*] very distant future." And just before his farewell to the doomed man, Lahiry wrote,

> I have no doubt that your disembodied soul will, from the other world, exert its invisible influence on those forces in our country which are struggling for the elimination of our artifices: frontiers and restoration of Bharat-Varsha as one single country from the Himalayas to the Seas.[64]

The shot that killed Gandhi ended the civil war and founded Indian statecraft, as Yasmin Khan has shown.[65] But it did not succeed in making division permanent in the eyes of Hindu nationalists, as the shot was fired for their cause of Akhand Bharat.

Akhand Bharat functioned through *bhakti* from its first conception by K. M. Munshi. The Gujarati politician's *Akhand Hindustan* of 1942 referred to the precolonial "Hindu-Muslim synthesis" forged by Akbar, Kabir, Chaitanya, Guru Nanak, the Pirs (Sufi saints), and even the Khojas (Ismaili Muslims), whom Savarkar especially excluded in *Essentials of Hindutva*.[66] Greater intimacy between Islam and Hinduism was not the solution for Hindutva's arch-theorist. Intimacy was already there: that was the problem between Hindus and Muslims, characterized by Shruti Kapila as an "intimate enmity."[67] The Khojas, whom only a court decree could fix as "Muslim" rather than "Hindu," embodied this intimacy, prompting Savarkar to spell out the division that would turn the Hindus into a political subject and give that subject a proprietary claim on India.[68] Still, Savarkar and Munshi were close allies in the cause of Akhand Bharat, and similarities between them run deeper than meets the eye: Munshi predicated religious syncretism on Hindu-Muslim, Aryan-Dravidian, and caste miscegenation, thus ensuring the longevity of the "Hindu" even as this subject pluralized and mongrelized.[69] For Munshi, *bhakti* demonstrated the Hindus' power to resist the Muslim conquest by "resist[ing] non-self with self."[70] Geopolitical unity required a religious ecumene.

The clear emergence of the *bhakti* idiom in the context of the fight for Akhand Bharat allows me to reframe the Muslim problem for Hindu nationalism. From Munshi's viewpoint, the salience of Muslim political identity and the emergence of Pakistani statecraft marked a refusal to syncretize in the way of Kabir, a refusal to dispel their sovereign status. And just as *bhakti* protest was dismantled by incorporation into Vedantic orthodoxy, the demand that Hindu nationalists would make of India's Muslims after the creation of Pakistan was not syncretism (leaving the imprint of Muslim tradition) but complete self-erasure in Hinduism's monism. At the same time, the devotional idiom would allow Hindutva to enter into everyday Hindu religious practice and finally make it indistinguishable from Hinduism.

The telos of "Undivided India" could not be domesticated through Indian nation-building or deterred by its extreme hostility toward Pakistan, Pakistanis, and India's Muslims. Setting Akhand Bharat as its aim, the new Hindutva institutionalized in the BJS blurred the distinction between a war to erase the border to Pakistan and borderless Hindu monism. Lahiry's word choice regarding the "artifice" of frontiers in this context is striking and intelligible. It consigned Pakistan to the world of *maya* that veiled the deep identity constituting monistic reality. Pakistan was the belief in an illusion, evoking

Gandhi's erstwhile rejection of it as "untruth." An RSS-friendly commentator in the early 1950s did not mince matters: "Pakistan," he said, "is a lie."[71] In reality, no matter the appearance of political maps, the true Bharat or Hindusthan remained *akhand,* "undivided." The hope that Partition would not last, that India and Pakistan and families stranded on both sides would be reunited, was by no means exclusive to Hindu nationalists but was widely shared in the early years after Partition, including by sections of the Indian Left. For Hindu nationalists, though, the ideal of reforging what was broken allowed a reassertion of Hindu power in independent India. After 1947, Hindutva's old language of "assimilation," "merging," and "adoption," which Savarkar aimed toward the biological, was drastically reoriented toward monistic Hinduism as the key to erasing the "other" in Indian society and the ever-deferred aim of wiping Pakistan off the subcontinental map.

Integral Humanism

Integral Humanism replaced *Essentials of Hindutva* as the manifesto of Hindu nationalism at the end of the Nehruvian period.[72] It restored Hinduism to Hindutva, thus disproving any narrative that treats Hindutva as the direct outgrowth of neo-Vedanta or blames Savarkar on Vivekananda.[73] The author of the manifesto was Deendayal Upadhyaya, an RSS man and the general secretary of the BJS from its foundation in 1951 by Syama Mukherjee to 1967, when Upadhyaya became the party's president.[74] He was found dead under suspicious circumstances within a year. The organizational successor to the Hindu Mahasabha, the BJS was ideologically more closely affiliated with and indeed became the political wing of the supposedly nonpolitical RSS. In 1977, with the Emergency just lifted, the BJS merged into a cross-party opposition to Indira Gandhi's Congress that was called the Janata Party. When this dissolved in 1980, the Jana Sangh element regrouped as the Bharatiya Janata Party, or BJP. From Upadhyaya's first speech at the Jana Sangh's inauguration in Delhi in May 1952 onward, the party presented itself as a principled departure from the Congress status quo.[75]

Akhand Bharat was the Jana Sangh's foundational "first principle."[76] The undoing of Partition appealed in the refugee environment in Delhi in which the party was founded.[77] RSS members reputedly pray before a map of Akhand Bharat to this day, and "Akhand Bharat" is the closing line of the "Bharat Bhakti Stotra" that RSS members used to recite daily at the *shakha* even decades after Partition until the text was updated and tellingly rebranded "Ekatmata Stotra," "unity hymn."[78] Still, "Akhand Bharat" is hardly found in the indexes of monographs on either of the two Sanghs. Though the idea of Akhand Bharat is becoming more important every day, it remains understudied and its place in Hindu nationalist ideology poorly understood.[79] When the RSS launched its English weekly, the *Organiser,* with the express purpose of making their views on Partition widely available, the first issue, of July 3, 1947, carried an article by Mukherjee unambiguously titled "'Hindus Will Never Accept Partition.'"[80] It was reported that in Delhi in early 1948, the RSS held a rally attended by some fifty thousand people, in which their *saranghchalak,* Golwalkar, promised that the Sangh "will not rest until it has achieved *Akhand Hindustan* [. . .] and will finish any individual Government that stands in the way."[81] Mukherjee's inaugural speech as president of the Jana Sangh in 1951 called the creation of Pakistan "'a terrible blunder.'"[82] The following year, Upadhyaya accused those who viewed Partition as a real "obstacle" of a lack of "fervent devotion" to the mother country—a *bhakti* idiom.[83] In its election manifestos and its 1965 constitution, the Jana Sangh openly stated its objective to "end the separation of India and Pakistan and to bring the two together."[84] In 1964, along with the socialist Ram Manohar Lohia (1910–1967), Upadhyaya even advocated for an "Indo-Pak Confederation" as a first step toward Akhand Bharat.[85] For the party that issued Hindutva into the postindependence era, Pakistan was only an "artificial division."

In 1947, as Upadhyaya would declare some fifteen years later, only one part of the country had become free, while the other continued to be "enslaved"—by the Mughals, no less.[86] India's "political independence" would remain incomplete as long as the "remnant of slavery" endured with "the existence of Pakistan."[87] To "liberate" Pakistan in the same way as Hyderabad and Goa, and as the Jana Sangh advocated for Kashmir—namely by military action—was no act of aggression.[88] It was Bharat's "right."[89] "So far as India [wa]s concerned," wrote Upadhyaya in 1960 in the context of Nehru's visit to Pakistan, "the only question to be discussed with Pakistan inrespect [*sic*] of Kashmir" was when Pakistan would withdraw from "that part of Indian territory." Hari Singh, the Hindu maharaja of Jammu and Kashmir, had had the right to sign his princely state over to India; this decision must not be challenged. Upadhyaya was adamant: "If Pakistan wants to put the hands of [t]he clock back, let us go to June 3, 1947 and not to October 26, 1947." In other words, Mountbatten's plan for Partition, and not the accession of Muslim-majority Kashmir to Hindu-majority India, was up for revision.[90] 1947 was not the first time that Bharat had splintered into various "chunks," according to Upadhyaya. It had done so earlier under Muslim rule. But the ancestors had never accepted this division; they had kept on fighting.[91] Bharat had survived, crucially, because it was not a "polity" (*rajya, rashtra*) but an integral nationality.[92] This was a momentous turn away from the Hindu Crown of paramount emperors explored in the preceding chapter to an avowedly anti-statist form of sovereignty in keeping with RSS tradition. It was a turn from state to nation, from the territorial to the social.

The Jana Sangh proceeded to formalize its identity. Following months of intense internal discussion, at its annual plenary session in January 1965, the party adopted a draft of Upadhyaya's philosophy, titled "Principles and Policies," as its constitution.[93] The BJP inherited this constitution, and new party members are required to swear on it to this day. The text was standardized as a series of four speeches that Upadhyaya delivered in Bombay in April 1965 and titled *Integral Humanism* in English ("Ekatma Manavvad," also known as "Ekatmata Manavvad" or "Ekatma Manav Darshan" in Hindi) after its central concept. The average RSS *swayamsevak* may be shaky on some of the finer points of Upadhyaya's philosophy, according to the former BJP general secretary and high-ranking RSS functionary Ram Madhav (who wrote a book to remedy this).[94] But a copy of *Integral Humanism* can reportedly be found in every RSS household. Despite this, as well as frequent invocations of Upadhyaya and Integral Humanism under BJP-RSS prime minister Narendra Modi, there has been surprisingly little scholarly interest and no rigorous account of the foundational text of Hindu nationalism after *Essentials of Hindutva*.[95] This anonymity in, despite, and through ubiquity can be seen as the extraordinary achievement of a politician who preferred to operate in the shadows but made his vision the groundwork of a political movement.

Upadhyaya's four speeches in *Integral Humanism* build on each other. The first speech sets out the Indian problem: India (or "Bharat," as Upadhyaya called it, no longer Savarkar's "Hindusthan") had lost its "national identity" or "self" under colonialism and had been set adrift. Independence had won India freedom from the British but not recovered this self.[96] The second speech announces India's identity and charts its path: Bharat stood for the "integrated view point [*sic*]." The West propounded so-called universalisms, but its political ideals clashed and its philosophy compartmentalized man. Only Bharat revealed the human person, society, and life itself "as an integrated whole." The thrust was not against Europe and Eurocentrism, however, but aimed at Indian society.[97] The third and conceptually richest speech elaborates on the integral constitution of India's social fabric. Society was not artificially produced by social contract, as in the Western history of political thought. Rather, society was "self-born," given a mission and animated by a soul. It was called a nation. Society was king and sovereign. Society was sustained by *dharma,* or fundamental law. There was no inherent conflict between society and individuals (as in the liberal tradition), who, if discharging their duties properly, avoided conflict, clash, and strife.[98] The fourth speech turns to political economy, asking which economic system was best able to serve society and foster "the Integral Man." The essential element to note here is not the details of economic policy, of which Upadhyaya provided a rough sketch, but his fundamental rejection of both socialism and capitalism.[99]

Many things could be said about *Integral Humanism,* but at its core was the idea of "integrality" itself. The English word choice here is striking and crucial. In 1949, Sardar Patel had forced the secretive RSS out into the open by making it adopt a written constitution as a precondition to lift the ban imposed on it after Gandhi's murder. Upadhyaya was involved in the drafting of this constitution, whose preamble situated the RSS thus: "Whereas in the *disintegrated* conditions of the country it was necessary to have an Organisation."[100] Its stated objectives were unification and the integration (as erasure) of difference in Hindu society. Summing up the lesson of *Integral Humanism* at the end of his fourth speech some fifteen years after the constitution, Upadhyaya stated that India's diversity did not need to lead to "conflict" or endanger national unity along with democratic self-rule. That is, diversity was not a threat as long as India developed a backbone of steel around its unitary national soul (*chiti*).

Introduced by Upadhyaya into the glossary of contemporary Hindu nationalism, the concept of *chiti* is absent in Savarkar. It designates the nation's "inborn," imperishable, and, crucially, single "soul." It acts the part of "nature," out of which "national culture," or *sanskriti,* develops.[101] *Chiti* defines India's identity. A concept still waiting for the serious intellectual history it deserves, *chiti* asserts ownership and defines the content of India. It states that there is only one national culture in India, and this is Hindu—a core piece of RSS ideology. *Chiti* is undergirded by *dharma,* whose English translation as "religion" Upadhyaya rejected.[102] Religion was a narrow aspect of life, but *dharma* was "that which sustains" society and the world, making any transgression against the national ethos a crime against God-ordained nature itself. Upadhyaya gave *dharma* some local flavor as the particular set of laws needed to "sustain" a nation's *chiti*.[103] Still, the conviction held that India's particular in fact *was* the universal. Inward-looking and concerned with the remaking of Indian society though it is, where *chiti* is an adjunct of *dharma*, Hindu India may claim to have found the law that makes the world tick. Nineteenth-century Vedantins like Bankim took Hinduism not only for the universal religion but for a "*natural religion*," something like a natural law.[104] Postindependence Hindutva, however, is not about the discovery of Hindu *dharma* as "culture" but rather about the discovery of oneness itself.

"Integral" in the Hindi rendition of *Integral Humanism* is not rendered as *ekta*, "oneness" or "union," as one might expect, but as *ekatma* or *ekatmata*, literally translating as "one-soul" (*ek* plus *atma*) or "one-soulness," respectively. Crucially, and staggeringly, we have entered theological terrain: the matrix of Bharat's integrality is the unity of the *atman* and *brahman*. The soul (*atman*) is indivisible. It does not tolerate fragmentation. As Upadhyaya proceeded to explain in *Internal Humanism*, the Western viewpoint, as instanced by Hegel, Marx, and Darwin, had only developed up to "the principle of duality," *dvaita* in Hindi and in the Hindu theological sense.[105] Only Bharat recognized the internal "unity" behind the outward appearance of "diversity and plurality in life."[106] Bharat's "viewpoint" was *ekatmavadi*, the school of "monism"; the Western way was *dvaitavadi*, "dualism."[107] It could hardly get any clearer: Integral Humanism emulates the Vedanta.

"Integral" (understood as *ekatma*), then, is theologically grounded, but why pair it with "humanism"?[108] Upadhyaya was not alone in making a composite of either or both of these concepts. India's first vice-president, second president, and a professional Hindu philosopher in the Vedantic tradition, Sarvepalli Radhakrishnan (1888–1975), coined the self's fundamental experience of itself as an "integral experience" in 1923.[109] Sri Aurobindo pioneered "integral yoga" (*purna yoga*, or "complete yoga," in Hindi). "Integral Idealism" and "Critico-Integral Humanism" were in the offing by the 1950s.[110] The recovering socialist M. N. Roy actually used the term "Integral Humanism" in a first draft of his postwar turn away from Marxist class struggle later known as "Radical Humanism."[111] But spokespeople for the Sangh Parivar today cite Bipin Chandra Pal's (1858–1932) concept of *narayana*, or "universal humanity," as the forerunner of Integral Humanism, which Upadhyaya indeed referenced in the last paragraph of his fourth and final speech on the subject.[112] Pal was a Brahmo Samaji, who offered a monistic vision of the individual as organically integrated in society both at home and in the world as an alternative to capitalist civil society.[113] *Narayana,* according to him, was India's offering to the world of redemption and emancipation from the "law in the lower animal kingdom," which was the "anti-humanitarian" outgrowth of individualism and nationalism.[114]

Neo-Vedanta and humanism were proximate and mutually implicated in three overlapping ways. First, neo-Vedantins were able to reinterpret the realization of the deep union of the individual soul with the Absolute as the awakening of the latent divinity of man.[115] Second, "humanism" encapsulates India's ambition, reaffirmed in recent years, to be a *vishwaguru,* a teacher to all the world. Third, as Andrew Sartori put it, "India's awareness of the immanence of the divine spirit in all creation allowed it to pursue its national interest as a means toward realizing the universal rather than particularistically negating it."[116] This goes some way toward accounting for the afterlife of Hegelianism in Hindu nationalists like Upadhyaya and Dattopant Bapurao Thengadi (1920–2004), Upadhyaya's colleague and successor as the major exegete of Integral Humanism, and even Savarkar in his dubious "humanist" confessions.[117] Their philosophies assumed that nations contribute their individual "genius" to world history, that the most strident nationalism is conducted in the service of all of humanity, and that in India's case, there is no clash between nationalism and internationalism—or "humanity," as it was called.[118]

Upadhyaya's idea of integrality was already fully developed by the early 1950s, when he published an article on "Akhand Bharat: Goal and Means" in *Panchjanya,* the Hindi weekly magazine he had launched for the RSS in 1948. The article showcases how the concept of integrality was formulated out of the nonacceptance of Partition. It presents an object lesson on the many variations of the theme of "one," *ek,* in Hindi. There is *ekta,* "union" or "oneness," and *ekatmata,* as well as the slogan of Nehruvian India flagged prior, *anekta mein ekta,* "unity in diversity" (literally, "unity in disunity"). "Union" and "oneness" figure as philosophy, as something to be perceived with the visual senses and subject to cognitive realization, as well as capable of being grasped and experienced as a "feeling." But more than anything, the "feeling of unity" is rendered as "lack" or privation (*ekta ki anubhumi ke abhav*).[119]

This lack of feeling of oneness, and nothing else, had allowed the country to be partitioned in August 1947.[120] Strikingly and boldly, Upadhyaya's account leads away from the usual culprits of Partition: imperial machinations, Jinnah, Nehru, even Gandhi. In Upadhyaya's determination, the Congress approach to Hindu-Muslim "unity" (*ekya*) was artificial and had dead-ended in Partition:

one could not look to the path India's grand old party had charted over the last half century for solutions. Therefore, he continued, "If we want unity, then look at Indian nationality, which is Hindu nationality, and Indian culture, which is Hindu culture."[121] Bharat's "nature" (*prakriti*) and "culture" (*sanskriti*) were oneness personified; its motto was "Ekam sat viprah, bahudha vedanti" (Truth is One, though the Vedantins call it by different names).[122] I return to this point later. Bharat itself showed the way to "unite" (*ek karne*) what was divided, as the river streams that merged into the holy Ganges "became one" (*ekrup hona*).[123] As the "separatist" and "anti-national" (*arashtriya*) attitude of India's Muslims was the wedge that had split the feeling of unity, caused Partition, and at present still represented the "biggest obstacle in the path of a united India," as well as a great security threat, it was the Muslims that needed reforming. Short of expulsion, India's "six crore Muslims" would have to submit to being "assimilated" into "Indian life." Thus, what was "divided" (*khand*) would become "undivided" (*akhand*): geographically and geopolitically as regards Pakistan, for sure, but more than a revision of Partition was at stake here. Upadhyaya's thought illustrates how the creation of Pakistan gave Hindu nationalists license to impose their vision of national identity on India and demand complete self-erasure of Muslims in exchange for the right to remain. Pakistan proved that India was Hindu. In this sense, though never resigning itself to Partition as settled fact, postindependence Hindutva actually requires the (continued) existence of Pakistan as its prerequisite. The way to unification does not start with Pakistan; that is its final utopian aim. It starts with remaking Indian society.

Organicism was from the first ingrained in the RSS vision, as their stated aims were the unity and organization (*sangathan*) of Hindu society. As the RSS was always more religious than Savarkar's brand of Hindutva, monism could and indeed was made serviceable for their aims. For instance, the organization's founder, Keshav Hedgewar, used the term *ekatma* in the context of urging RSS volunteers, or *swayamsevaks*, to become one with the Sangh.[124] In 1938, his chosen successor, Golwalkar, who led the RSS for the duration of Upadhyaya's tenure with the BJS, urged volunteers to merge their individual identity with the nation, which, he averred, was not like death. Instead, "when you merge your personhood [*vyaktitva*] with the nation, you are no longer an individual but have become the nation." It was like merging with the "infinite" (*asim*)—a this-worldly reorientation of Vedantic eschatology.[125] In both examples, monistic merging figures as a demand put on the *svayamsevak*. It was only after 1947 that *ekatma* and *ekatmata* gained more prominence in Golwalkar's vocabulary and monism's orientation changed. This was when not only Partition but Indian independence itself forced a reckoning with RSS goals. Was the RSS to reorient itself or even disband now that independence was achieved? Golwalkar argued that it should not, for nothing had fundamentally changed. "Society" (*samaj*) had not changed. The negative unity brought about by the fight against a common enemy—the British—had proved ephemeral.[126] The fragmentation of society continued, and so did the need to have an organization fighting it.

In November 1948, in a press statement issued after his negotiations with the Indian government over lifting the RSS ban had broken down, Golwalkar laid out the raison d'être of the RSS. The "Motherland," he explained, had always been one, but its sheer scale had given rise to a diversity that over time had eroded the underlying unity. "Foreign invaders [coming to India] a thousand years ago"—unnamed but unmistakably Muslims—had consequently found Hindus a "disrupted people" easy to subjugate. A "thousand years' subjugation hastened the disintegrating process" to the point that all "memory of having been one people" was forgotten. The RSS, per Golwalkar, was set up to revive that memory of oneness and "build up an integrated, organized and disciplined corporate social life" when all around was disintegration.[127] Note that Golwalkar did not blame the Hindus' historical defeat on Muslims any more than Savarkar or indeed Hadgewar did. Rather, even the most rabid Muslim haters among Hindu nationalists tended to blame Hindu society itself for an inner weakness that had made Hindus easy prey for Muslims. Hindu society is always the first target of Hindu nationalism. The second stage is to remake Indian society in the image of Hindu society. Partition brought that opening.

Speaking in Pune in 1947 after Partition and independence, Golwalkar insisted that a nation contained only one "soul" *(atma)* but that Hindus had forgotten their soul (*atmavismriti*). Now more than ever, "unity" (*ekatma*) was needed.[128] Savarkar deserves the credit for naming Hindu identity, while Hedgewar set the parameters of the organization that would eventually succeed in organizing Hindu society. Golwalkar's achievement lies in making the RSS respectable again after the murder of Gandhi by one of its members. (To this end, he would even come to disown *We, or Our Nationhood Defined,* the book in which he applauded the Nazi approach to their Jewish minority that was published just before he became head of the RSS in 1940.)[129]

But Upadhyaya's legacy is as the theorist of the birth of independent India out of the spirit of the Hindu "one-soul."

Neo-Vedanta, which is associated with Rammohan Roy, Ramakrishna and Vivekananda, the Tagores, Gandhi, and Radhakrishnan, is convincingly identified with liberalism, universalism, tolerance, and humanism, and so it is with projects of domination and hegemony in Indian society.[130] Yet Upadhyaya's integral thinking was a departure from both the nineteenth-century pioneers and contemporaneous Hindu philosophy in several ways. Integral Humanism conceptually depended on the emergence of Indian and Pakistani statecraft and military capabilities. The ideology's monistic professions threatened violence and war to incorporate India's Muslims and Pakistan. Above all, the BJS philosopher utilized the tested means of organizing Hindu society into RSS cadres for an unprecedented drive for uniformity within Indian society. This welding of Indian society into one integrated unit, something that neither the Arya Samaj nor Savarkar nor the RSS pre-1947 had achieved even for Hindus, was, for Upadhyaya, the Akhand Bharat that the Jana Sangh took as its foundational principle.

Muslims and the Question of Hostility

India and Pakistan were again at war over Kashmir and the Rann of Kutch when the Jana Sangh adopted the "Principles and Policies" and Upadhyaya gave his famous four speeches. Upadhyaya had campaigned for war under the motto "'We must smash Rawalpindi's throne,'" meaning Pakistan's capital at the time and, for Upadhyaya, the new seat of Muslim power in the subcontinent after the fall of the Mughals at Delhi.[131] Against the backdrop of armed conflict in the spring of that year, Upadhyaya gave a speech elaborating on the "Muslim problem" that stood in the way of India's integrality. As noted, Upadhyaya developed Integral Humanism out of the monistic "feeling of oneness" or "integral feeling" (*ekatma ke bhav*) that pointed toward Akhand Bharat.[132] Nepal, Burma, and Sri Lanka were likewise part of Akhand Bharat, yet Upadhyaya had no issue with their separate political existence.[133] How was Pakistan different? The issue with Pakistan, as Upadhyaya here strikingly redefined it, was not that it was a separate state. Bharat's principle had never been "state" (*rajya*) and "citizenship" (*nagarikta*), he explained, but "nationality" (*rashtriyata*).[134] It had therefore never been necessary for those that shared "Bharatiya" nationality—Nepal, Burma, and Sri Lanka—to become one with the Indian state. Much like Savarkar, he argued that Nepal's independence had been a source of pride for Hindus under British rule and did not feel like a "partition" (*vibhajan*).[135]

The issue with Pakistan was that it had cut itself out of and acted as a continuous "refutation" of "Bharatiya" nationality.[136] Pakistan was not "a separate independent State," it was India's negation.[137] It represented "that attitude and tradition which wants to put an end to the national personality of India."[138] Bharat's "soul" and "essence" (*tattva*) was *ekatmata*, integrality or one-soulness itself; Pakistan's was "disintegration" (*vighatankari*) and "division" (*vibhed*). Pakistan was "poison" to and "deformation" of Bharat's "life."[139] That is why Bharat could not fully live as long as Pakistan endured. The antidote was "national assimilation" (*rashtriya atmasatikaran*). The existence of Pakistani statecraft meant that Savarkar's tested means of *shuddhi* and intermarriage could be dismissed as ineffective. They left residue difference, and besides—in a sharp turn against Savarkar—"who would marry their offspring?"[140] What was required for Bharat to regain its self-identity, according to Upadhyaya, was the total defeat of Pakistan and of Muslim "nationality" in India.[141]

However "muscular" the Hinduism of Vivekananda, this was something else. In its election manifestos of the 1950s and 1960s, the Jana Sangh coupled its vision of monistic unity in Akhand Bharat with sharp antagonism toward Pakistan, as long as it remained a "separate entity."[142] Integral Humanism was a militarized monism propped up by the "fundamental right" to bear arms, universal military training, and the nuclear bomb, an ethical contradiction that did not go unnoticed.[143] The calculus was that Pakistan's "worked-up hostility towards India" would somehow cease and Pakistanis return to the "*Bharatiya* nation," of which they were "basically" always a part.[144] Just how ramping up antagonism would give way to deep unity was not questioned. The RSS extolled harmony and Upadhyaya monism. How could they square this with their intense hostility toward Muslims? Hypocrisy is one answer, but a surface one. At a deeper level, the question is how Hindutva can desire to annex that which it hates. After all, it is not Pakistan that wants to reconquer India. Hindutva's attitude toward India's Muslims is characterized by a deep ambivalence between the desire to possess (love?) and hate that has psychoanalytical significance. The ambivalence is resolved by a desire for aggressive incorporation, a point on which Upadhyaya offered no more introspection than Savarkar. Instead, he bridged the gap between one-soulness and hostility by projection: it is the other that hates, negates, and partitions.

Gandhi had identified Allah with Ishwar (the Hindu personal God, as a manifestation of the Absolute) and was killed for it.[145] Yet surprisingly, Upadhyaya sided with him on the theological point. "We" Hindus, he opined, had always kept to the Vedic principle of "Truth is One, though the Vedantins call it by different names" (*Ekam sat vipra, bahudha vadanti*). From this viewpoint, the "veneration" (*puja*) of Mohammad was no different from the veneration of Ganesh as different "names" of the Absolute, Ishwar. Pointing out that Kabir and Nanak had extolled this truth before Gandhi, Upadhyaya relativized the Mahatma's contribution while fixing him in the Indic tradition of blurring the lines between Islam and Hinduism to which Upadhyaya remained deeply ambiguous even as he appropriated it.[146] In 1952, Upadhyaya had asked Muslims to model themselves after the Sufi poets Kabir, Jayasi, and Raskhan, if they wished to have a future in India.[147] Appropriating the devotionalism shared by Hindus and Muslims in the subcontinent for orthodox Vedanta and Upadhyaya's own Integral Humanism, in this sense, the conspicuously Hindu form of Hindutva that superseded Savarkar's after independence set itself up as the spiritual heir of the "grand soul" their ideology had murdered.[148] In this way paying a bizarre *Homage to the Mahatma*, Golwalkar spoke in 1969 of how Gandhi's *satyagraha* was rooted in Hinduism, whose ideal of "*ekam sadvipra bahudha vedanti*" "assumed flesh and blood in Gandhiji." "Sufism," Golwalkar added, "is taken to be nearest to Vedanta in philosophical outlook." But while Islam and communism promised "'one religion for all mankind,'" Hinduism alone united humanity by its "catholicity," its inbuilt pluralism built on the capacity to draw equivalences—"whether [of] Rama, Krishna, Allah or Christ."[149] Nevertheless, argued Upadhyaya, the Congress had woefully misunderstood the "Muslim problem" when it demanded Hindu-Muslim unity (*ekta*) on the basis of "'Ishwar, your name is Allah.'"[150]

The "Muslim problem," as Upadhyaya consequently framed it, was not "religious" (*dharmik*), it was "political."[151] In so arguing, *Integral Humanism*'s author reiterated a Hindu nationalist commonplace. Hindus stood for religious "tolerance."[152] However, "tolerance" is not the right word for what Upadhyaya meant, despite the incredibly successful recoinage of polytheism as tolerance in the nineteenth century.[153] "Tolerance" means an ethical commitment to respect and retain the other's difference. If Gandhi extolled the supreme "tolerance" of Hinduism, he fashioned out of this cliché a virtue of nonappropriation that he made the first principle of nonviolence.[154] By contrast, immense coercive power inhered in Upadhyaya's monistic assurance that "we are no one's enemy."[155] Upadhyaya's Hindutva conceived of Hinduism as a universal order of *dharma* in the signification of natural, "'Innate law.'"[156] Hinduism was more than *a* religion. It was *the* religion: a metareligion that subsumed all others as mere "sects" or "creeds" (*panth*). This ecumenism was about supremacy as well as sovereignty, especially recalling that the Mughals had pioneered ideas of universal sovereignty in India as being above religious divisions, which the British appropriated as religious noninterference.[157]

Hindus personified tolerance, but Muslims were "intolerant," Upadhyaya argued. They regarded non-Muslims as "kafir" and India as *darul harab*, "enemy land."[158] The problem with India's Muslims was therefore not their religious practice but that conversion had changed their "nature" (*prakriti*) and "nationality," turning them into "enem[ies]" of Bharat.[159] If this seems like acceptance of the two-nation theory, the bottom line was that religion could not serve as a basis for sovereign projects: Pakistan and Sikh separatism were wrong.[160] The existence of an antagonistic sovereign project necessitated a political fight, patterned on Shivaji, who had "smashed Delhi's throne."[161] For all of neo-Hindutva's monist confessions, this was pure Savarkar. And like Savarkar, Upadhyaya never forgave the Muslims for "their" history of conquest and "sovereignty" (*prabhuta*) in India. Muslim difference, he argued, was sustained by the "political aspiration" to establish "Political Supremacy" in India.[162] Upadhyaya wanted to extinguish in Muslims this spark of political domination of which Pakistan was only an "instrument" and a halfway house. There was no geopolitical solution for this. Though Upadhyaya wanted Pakistan's total defeat, the onus was really on India's Muslims, who, according to Hindu nationalists, propped up India's enemy, Pakistan, from within.[163] Akhand Bharat required a change in the consciousness of Indian Muslims. The existence of Pakistan gave Hindu nationalists license to make India Hindu.

The Jana Sangh was founded on the principle that Bharat contained only "one nationality" (*ekrashtravad*), no minorities, and that it had only "one culture" or "tradition" (*ek sanskriti*), which was indistinguishable from Hinduism.[164] Under Upadhyaya's aegis, Hindutva co-opted Indian statecraft to the extent that it could retire the word "Hindu." It was replaced with the figure of the "national" (*Bharatiya, rashtriya*), just as the Muslim was renamed the "unnational." Therefore, while it looks as though Hindutva finally admitted the two-nation theory, in reality this left only a purely negative, parasitic identity for India's Muslims, who represented negation and division. The Indian Muslim, post-Partition, is suspect, constantly asked to prove their loyalty to India.

But the litmus test of Indian nationality remains definitionally unpassable. The indeterminacy of the figure of the Indian Muslim, who is suspected of being a crypto-Pakistani, is one of the greatest sources of strength of Hindu nationalism today. Upadhyaya, for his part, gave a clear account of what is expected of India's Muslims after Pakistan: "national assimilation" (*rashtriya atmasatikaran*).[165] The assimilated Muslim would become completely "identical" (*ekrup hona*) with national society.[166] And here, finally, Upadhyaya revealed the incapacity of Hindu ecumenism to subsume and neutralize Muslim religious difference even in the distorted form of Muhammad veneration, which is not Islam: he let slip that assimilation entailed no longer feeling the need to go to mosque.[167] Total assimilation meant there would be no more Muslims. There would only be society.

Dharma Rajya and the Withering Away of the State

According to Upadhyaya, the society or collective was more than the sum of its parts (the individuals that constitute it), a claim he supported by the new psychology of "group mind."[168] Nevertheless, it was a quintessentially Indian view of society:

> In our view society is self-born. Like an individual, society comes into existence in an organic way. People do not produce society. It is not a sort of club, or some joint-stock company, or a registered cooperative of society. In reality, society is an entity with its own "SELF," its own life; it is a sovereign being like an individual; it is an organic entity.[169]

Bharat's ontological viewpoint was *ekatma*, revealing society as one integrated whole: one "body" consisting of a "nose," "eyes," and so on. Elsewhere, the imagery draws on kinship relations or the growth of a tree.[170] In a perfectly integrated society, there was perfect "harmony between the individual and the collectivity," which forestalled any clash of interests.[171] Social conflict results from a person's "inability to behave properly." It was a "perversion."[172] Upadhyaya related the example of a wife who, upon becoming a mother, cares more for her child than for her husband. Here, conflict arises from the woman "slipp[ing] in her duty" as a wife.[173] Further singled out in *Integral Humanism* as sources of conflict are, next to gender and just as tellingly, class and caste. However, when duties were integrated and equally discharged, there could be no clash of individual interests or class or caste conflict, as theorized in the West.[174]

In the West, explained Upadhyaya, society had come into existence as a "social contract," while the king claimed divine rights. The West had got it wrong. The true order of things was exactly reversed, as had been known in Bharat. In Bharat, the state was founded on contract as an instrument to serve society or "nation." But society or nation (synonyms in his usage) was not built on contract, it was "self-born."[175] Society was anterior to, and of a higher order than, the state. Likewise, Golwalkar explicitly relegated questions of the state and made the nation the central focus of *We*, the book in which he flirted with Nazi racial ideas.[176] Hitler himself viewed the state with contempt. Though he availed himself of all its brute force, he claimed that he did not like it. "The state," wrote Hitler in *Mein Kampf*, "is a means to an end." The state was a "container," whose "content" was race. A state could be considered good depending on how successfully it managed that content.[177] Golwalkar, in a speech of the early 1960s that showed the influence of Upadhyaya and is canonized in *Bunch of Thoughts*, revealed what society or nation was to him that the state could never be. It was not enough to approach God through definitions such as "*nirākār* (without form) or *nirguna* (without attributes)," he said. "We want a 'living' God."[178] That God was society. The concept of Hindu "nation" meant the realization of God in society.[179]

The state and nation were distinct, and of the two, it was not the state that was "supreme": "A watchman is not deemed greater than the treasure he is supposed to protect."[180] In fact, this relegation of the state, according to Upadhyaya, had allowed the nation to survive as the Indian state fell to foreign conquerors. But inattention to the state had become harmful. Ventriloquizing Ambedkar, Upadhyaya described how "our Gram Panchayats," the village self-governments through which society ruled itself, had become "so strong that we neglected the throne of Delhi." Finally, Ramdas, the architect of Shivaji's Hindu empire, recalled the important function that state power could serve for the nation. The state was a "limb" whose amputation may endanger the "body" as a whole, the nation.[181] Nevertheless, the state was still a compromise. The ideal and most ancient stage of history in Bharat was rule by *dharma*.

In the Kritiyuga, or Satyayuga ("age of truth"), described in the Mahabharata, the first, golden age where virtue ruled, there had been no need for either king or state; there was only society, wrote Upadhyaya.[182] Back then, *dharma* had been "sovereign."[183] Not state but *dharma* reigned "supreme," which sustained and protected the nation's soul, *chiti*. Destroy *dharma* and you destroy the nation's soul.[184] Thus, Upadhyaya reinstituted the sovereign rule of *dharma*, including but not restricted to the *virat purusha* representing the fourfold caste order. At the close of the golden age, *dharma* had declined, and "disorganisation" set in. Dismayed, the Rishis had sent for Brahma, who handed them "a treatise on 'Law and Functions of the State,' which he himself had written" (the Manusmriti), and appointed Manu as the first king. Countering the progression from the state of nature to civil society and the state in the European tradition, the Indian state emerged from the failure of human society. Initially, Manu had declined the kingship for fear of the sins he would accrue in this office. But then Brahma assured him that none of his actions as king would count as sin, as long as he enforced *dharma*.[185] In the West, wrote Upadhyaya, the king was sovereign. After the monarchy fell, it was the people. He stated, "Here, in our country neither the kings, nor the people, nor the parliament have had absolute sovereignty."[186] The Indian Constitution and the "majority" also did not rule.[187] *Dharma* alone was sovereign. The Indian "ideal of the state" was called "'Dharma Rajya.'"[188]

Dharma, more than anything, has the appearance of fixed law. Yet interestingly, Upadhyaya defined it as that which sustains integral harmony in society. Though he did not elaborate the consequences, this logically meant a reversal in the order of primacy. The discovery of integrality itself was a discovery in the order of a law of nature, like gravity.[189] But reworking Indian society on this basis was up to human management. Upadhyaya was clear: a return to the "golden age" was impossible. The Ganges "must inevitably flow onwards"; one could not "turn" "back" its waters.[190] The fundamentals of *dharma* were eternal, but the principles that derived from them needed to be "adapted to changing times and places." This ensured dynamism and scope for managerial decision-making, called "implementation."[191] The implementor was not actually the king. Instead, it was the *purohit*, the royal priest, classically put above the king, who ensured that the king remained true to *dharma* and punished him when he erred.[192] A Brahmin was needed to crown a Kshatriya king. For this reason, the Brahmin could strip away the sovereignty he bestowed. Savarkar's Hindutva weaponized the Kshatriya ideal, and Greater Indianists tracked kings. Now, under the RSS and BJS, came the time of the Brahmin.

The ideal of rule by *dharma* is core RSS ideology. But it was Upadhyaya who made this anti-political politics workable for a political party. Scholars have been appalled that a party in a democratic and republican system, the BJP, should be bound by oath to Integral Humanism and thus to a fundamentally undemocratic, metapolitical ethic that claims for itself the right to override the Indian Constitution and depose monarchs, as did the ancient Rishis.[193] Through its executors, the Rishis or *purohits* updated into RSS and BJS-BJP members, Upadhyaya envisioned *dharma* as bringing Indian society to heel. The role of the king was to ensure that *dharma* ruled society, and this made his role—the state's role—important.[194] Yet the ultimate aim was to disseminate *dharma* through society. This established sovereignty as immanent in society, corresponding to the RSS's specific, capillary mode of power that traditionally sidelines the state.[195] The *dharma*-state could find its people by making them. Dispersing itself as a Brahmin "monarch" in Shruti Kapila's sense, the state dissolved into society.[196]

Deliberately historicizing *Integral Humanism* after the fall of the fascist empires and disillusionment with Stalinist communism, Upadhyaya announced Bharat's monism to a world in crisis.[197] This in itself was nothing new. Indians had long advertised a native cure for Western ills like materialism and aggressive nationalism. The West, according to Upadhyaya, held clashing political ideals: nationalism, democracy, and socialism (which to him, as curiously to Bose, was another name for equality). Try to combine any two of them (like Hitler and Mussolini did in "nationalism-cum-socialism") and you will kick out the third (as they did to democracy).[198] Only Bharat's thought was able to harmonize all three. Marx is repeatedly mentioned in *Integral Humanism*—as a thinker of equality, as the author of a particularly seductive Ism in the jungle of Western "Isms" in which Indians were trapped, and as an archdualist thinker.[199] But if Upadhyaya had been less opposed to dialectics as a species of *dvaita*, Integral Humanism would perhaps have been the synthesis to Marx's antithesis of capitalist society.

Upadhyaya knew that according to Marxism-Leninism, the end stage, called communist society, would be achieved when, after an interlude of proletarian dictatorship, "the State will be replaced by a classless, stateless society."[200] Famously, the state would "wither away." Yet, as Upadhyaya remarked, the state in the communist regimes of his day showed no sign of withering away. Instead, it was becoming "more and more totalitarian."[201] Yet the ideal self-regulating society that would remain after the withering away of the state was much like the integrated society that Upadhyaya theorized. In fact, statelessness in the Kritiyuga looked a lot like anarchist communism.

Upadhyaya did not make the intellectual debt he owed explicit, but Golwalkar and Thengadi did.

In a speech in the Matunga locality of Bombay in February 1950, the RSS chief declared, "'Socialists and Communists talked of an ideal society and ideal human relations. But I am sure the objects of an ideal social order and the maximum of human happiness could be achieved through following the R.S.S. programme of nation-building.'"[202] Some fifteen years later, right around the time *Integral Humanism* was being etched out, Golwalkar explicitly dealt with the question of communism and the "withering away of the state."[203] Communism and capitalism, in his view, shared a basic conceptual flaw. Both viewed society and the individual as mutually opposed, held together only by contract: capitalism, defender of the rights of the individual, viewed society as the "enemy of the individual," and communism viewed the individual as the "enemy of society," which it, in turn, championed.[204] Communism aimed to satisfy basic needs and equalize society by force until there would be "no more room for mutual conflict, thus obviating the need for central authority." In theory, "the state withers away and a governmentless 'anarchic' society will come into being." But the communist state in Russia in its fifty years of existence had "not shown any signs of withering away but has grown all the more powerful." It could not bridge the gap from ubiquitous conflict to the "ideal state" of a stateless, self-governing society because its "theoretical base" was wrong.[205] The "highest aim of society" was not absolute "equality" but "harmony," Golwalkar averred. To illustrate what harmonized society would look like, he quoted the famous passage on *dharma rajya* from the Mahabharata: "*There existed no state, no king, no penalty and no criminal. All protected one another by virtue of dharma.*" *Dharma*, Golwalkar explained, "is the right code of conduct that awakens the Common Inner Bond, restrains selfishness, and keeps the people together in the harmonious state even without external authority."[206] The strangest of echoes of communism and anarchism as well as Gandhi, RSS-BJS theory offered its solution to the basic problem of how humans can live together peacefully: through societal self-rule.

A man of Upadhyaya's generation born just after the Russian Revolution, Dattopant Thengadi was a lifelong RSS *pracharak*, a politician, and the founder of one of India's biggest trade unions, the BMS, which is the labor organization of the RSS. Thengadi swore his union off revolution.[207] "Total revolution," he argued in essays and speeches that were collectively published in 1984, was invented by French and Russian revolutionaries for the specific requirements of France and Russia, where society needed "drastic alteration." But in India, no change beyond the superstructure was needed because Indian society was founded on *dharma*.[208] On this point, he drew up a confrontation between the Communist Party (CP) and what he curiously called the "Bharatiya Socio-Cultural Organisation," or BSCO for short: the CP "seeks to proletarianise all," while "BSCO seeks to acculturate all." The CP "believes that the State moulds the Society," while "BSCO believes that the Society moulds the State." The CP "stands for the totalitarian State," while BSCO "stands for the decentralisation of all authority." The CP viewed life as a conflict of interests, while BSCO viewed life as an "integrated" whole, where interests were harmonized and "mutually complementary."[209] As much as Muslims were their first hate, the RSS and Jana Sangh in independent India were animated by enmity toward the Indian Left, with whom they competed for India's soul.

In the 1970s, a book by the communist leader Bani Deshpande caused quite a stir in Communist Party of India circles. Published with a foreword by veteran party chairman Shripad Amrit Dange (who also happened to be Deshpande's father-in-law), *Universe of Vedanta* made Vedantists out of Marx and Engels and out of Shankara a dialectician.[210] Had he still lived, M. N. Roy would have surely suspected such "perverted" Hegelian dialectics of fascism. Deshpande's book was widely read and panned as reactionary, forcing the party to organize a conference to distance themselves from the author's views.[211] In the words of one contributor who pointed out the futility of turning to Shankara for a dualistic understanding of the universal *brahman*, "Bani Deshpande has been looking for tenets of dialectical materialism exactly where he should not."[212] But Thengadi appreciated Deshpande's book, in which he saw "Hindu genius" finally applying its synthesizing strength to the monumental synthesis of Marxism with Hindu Vedanta.[213] He wrote, "Stateless, self-governed society is the ideal of Bharatiya culture."[214] Thengadi, a man steeped in socialist, anarchist, and communist thought, also shows an alternative way of thinking through Integral Humanism's indebtedness to these traditions of thought.[215] In his view, the influence of communism and anarchism was triangulated by, and may have even come via, Islamist thought.

After World War II, Islam and communism were global faiths that Hinduism struggled to compete with. For instance, Aldred's *The Word* reported how the organizing secretary for the Ambala Hindu Mahasabha, Indra Sen, complained at a camp function of Savarkar supporters in 1950 that "while two of the world-wide ideologies—Communism and Islam—had states to give the fullest possible display to their merits, the third great ideology—Hinduism—which was Humanism par excellence, had not land where it could develop itself and flourish."[216] There was also a deeper conceptual connection, or competition, between Islam and communism. "According to Islam," wrote Thengadi, "sovereignty belongs to God only. No human being can claim that supreme position."[217] In this sense, Islam was "'totalitarian'" and "theocratic." But because Allah was sovereign and had made his divine law, the Shariat, binding upon society, rulers were not considered sovereigns but only "vice-regents" of God. Finally, because it was not individuals but the community of believers that had the right to govern as so many "Caliphs," though they may "concentrate their Caliphate in any one of them," Islam actually had a theory of "limited popular sovereignty": the Caliphate, which was a theory of "popular vice-regency." There was no room for true popular sovereignty, since God alone was sovereign, and even a "unanimous resolution of the National Parliament would be treated as null" if it contravened the Shariat.[218] But there was "no room" for communist dictatorship either, "since everyone is a Caliph."[219]

The Islam Thengadi described was not just any kind of Islam. It was the Islamism of Abul A'la Maududi (1903–1972), the founder of Pakistan's Jamat-e-Islami party, architect of the country's Islamization, and the archtheorist of the Islamic state. As historian Faisal Devji has demonstrated, the cornerstone of Maududi's Islamic political thought was that sovereignty rests in God alone, rather than in kings or majorities. The Caliphate the maulana envisioned with such lasting, global effect would do away with the state altogether, in a "bizarre" echo of Lenin's "'withering away' of the state."[220] Thengadi's conclusion on the politics of Islam was contained in the title of his essay: "Islam and Communism are Incompatible." This was true insofar as the Soviet Union sealed "the victory of communism over anarchism in Europe and America," as Devji writes.[221] But not so in South Asia, where colonial rule decapitated Hindu and Muslim kingship, driving South Asian thought away from "politics" and into areas beyond the reach of the state, toward the social and religious.[222] In South Asia, anarchism survived by drawing on religion. As Devji demonstrates, Maududi's rule by divine law in the Islamic state revived the essentially anarchist idea of "decentralized self-governance."[223] The same can be said of Upadhyaya's *dharma rajya,* coined at the same time as Maududi's Islamic state, after independence, in the early 1950s. The Jana Sangh was committed to *dharma rajya* from the moment of its foundation with its first election manifesto, drafted by Upadhyaya and adopted at the party's inaugural session on

October 21, 1951.[224] This was just after the Indian constitutional question had been settled, consigning India to a future without Hindu hegemony. Hindutva had failed to capture the Indian state (by which it had already faced persecution) and was hard-pressed to imagine new ways of establishing hegemony in society. The fruit of these labors was that society replaced the state.

The BJS's "Principles and Policies" assert unambiguously that "absolute sovereignty vests in *Dharma* alone" and further state,

> In the *Krita-yuga*, they say, all men were guided in their conduct towards one another by *Dharma*, so there was no State. That is our conception of the ideal state of society—stateless, and regulated entirely by *Dharma*. This is possible only when everyone becomes selfless and *Dharma-nishtha*. But ordinarily, the institution of State is necessary to maintain order and to assure to every individual all opportunity for following his *Dharma*. [. . .] *Dharma Rajya* does not recognise any individual or body as sovereign. Every individual is subject to certain obligations and regulations.[225]

The Jana Sangh's first election manifesto campaigned for "**Dharma Rajya—Not Theocracy but Rule of Law**." Though Hindu nationalists from the time of Savarkar to Upadhyaya to our own have decried Islam as theocratic and, indeed, made this a major point of contrast, there is no denying that *dharma rajya* looks a lot like the much-maligned Islamic "'Khilafat.'"[226] Upadhyaya addressed this similarity, declaring that "Dharma Rajya does not mean a theocratic state. Where a particular sect and its prophet or Guru, [*sic*] rule supreme, that is a theocratic state." Pakistan was a theocratic state, having adopted the title "Islamic Republic" under its 1956 constitution. In Pakistan, there was a "tie-up" between state and religion that relegated all non-Muslims as second-class citizens. By contrast, *dharma rajya* ensured religious freedom for all, but within the boundaries Upadhyaya defined by that old illustration of the harm principle in the liberal tradition: that the freedom to swing my fists ends when I hit someone else's nose.[227] This did not mean that *dharma rajya* indicated a "secular" state. A state could be no more "without dharma" (*nidharmi*) or "indifferent to dharma" (*dharmnirpeksh*) than fire could be without heat. If fire loses its heat, "it does not remain fire any longer." So would the state, whose purpose was to "maintain" *dharma*, cease to be a state if it neglected its purpose.[228]

According to Upadhyaya, "We have always vested sovereignty in Dharma."[229] The supremacy of divine law over constitution, parliament, and majority, though lambasted by Thengadi in the case of Islam, is the basic tenet to which BJP party members swear when they swear to Integral Humanism. *Dharma* encompasses all aspects of individual and social life. As much as a "withering away" of the state and a return of anarchism, *dharma rajya* marks the return of Law with a capital *L*. A similar route was taken by Maududi, for whom, Devji argues, the Shariat was meant to be in society, not in the state. No aspect of life was to remain outside it. God is an absent king, and it is his law that rules. Those learned in the law become his enforcers and vice-regents, whose task is to administer society in God's absence. In *dharma rajya*, a hyperreal idea of the Brahmin acts as society's keeper.

The Grassroots Transformation of Society

Maududi's Islamic Revolution aims to destroy the social order to rebuild it from scratch. The Islamic state would follow the Islamization of society. For Upadhyaya, in turn, the division that the Pakistani state represented would disappear once the work of integration in India was done and *dharma* ruled. If this was a revolution, its temporality was exceedingly slow. Golwalkar castigated the "short-cut mania" of his compatriots, who demanded, "'How long do you carry on like this? When will you be able to bring about the total transformation of society that you visualise?'"[230] Society's total transformation required slow and difficult work:

> The ultimate vision of our work, which has been the living inspiration for all our organisational efforts, is a perfectly organised state of our society wherein each individual has been moulded into a model of ideal Hindu manhood and made into a living limb of the corporate personality of society.
>
> Obviously, this is not a vision which can be realised within a few days or even a few years. It requires the untiring, silent endeavour of hundreds and thousands of dedicated missionaries.[231]

Such patient transformative work on society, rather than the quick fix of revolution, was "the technique that succeeds." Golwalkar explained how the idea of the vanguard ("a powerful group within society") had been explored in Russia,

Italy, Germany, and China. The military vanguard had also been experimented with (by Bose). But the Sangh had eschewed such "totalitarian" enterprises for India: "the Sangh has never entertained the idea of building an organization as a distinct and separate unit within society. Right from its inception the Sangh has clearly marked out as its goal the moulding of the whole of society, and not merely any one part of it, into an organised entity."[232] Savarkar's militant vanguardism had dead-ended. To bring about the total transformation of Indian society, the RSS had to *become* society, and Indian society had to become the RSS.

Upadhyaya showed the way to make the *dharma*-state immanent in a fictionalized biography of Shankara, the founder of the Advaita Vedanta tradition.[233] Published, significantly, in 1947, the book anticipated the interventions of *Integral Humanism* in several ways. The most important is through Upadhyaya's narration of Shankara's recognition that the appearance of "dissimilitude" (*bhed*) was "untruth" (*asatya*) and that truth was "non-distinction" (*abhed*).[234] Upon this realization, Upadhyaya's Shankara resolved to restore Vedic *dharma*. Yet Upadhyaya insisted that Shankara did not invent Advaita Vedanta but simply restored the forgotten essence of the Vedas by putting him into a direct guru-student transmission line leading all the way to the Vedic sage Maharishi Badarayana, the legendary author of the Brahma Sutra.[235]

The much-earlier context of Badarayana allowed Upadhyaya to target his intervention at Hindutva's long-standing enemy, Buddhism (and, though never designated as enemy in the same way, Jainism). From a "moral viewpoint," wrote Upadhyaya, the Buddha and Jainism's founder, Mahavira, were "very high" and unsurpassed, namely because of their uncompromising nonviolence. Yet both schools had neglected the force of tradition (*parampara*). As a result, they had broken with the one thing that united the countless schools of Hinduism: the Vedas. They had become *avaidik*.[236] The Buddha had formulated his *ahimsa* out of repulsion with Vedic society, whose loveless behavior he witnessed. But he was wrong to become repulsed by Vedic religion itself.[237] For Upadhyaya, echoing Savarkar's ambiguous praise, the Buddha was India's greatest sage for the depth of his concern for human welfare. His complete "boycott" of the Vedas, however, had given rise to "untruths" like "nihilism" (*shunyavad*).[238] Buddha regarded the world as suffering, so he showed the way out of the world, emphasizing relief from suffering and an ethic of quietude.[239] In this situation, wrote Upadhyaya, Badarayana had revived Advaita Vedanta. What Shankara did was revive the inner-worldly ideal of "service" (*karya*) for the nation, whose historical loss had made Vedic society uncaring.[240]

Thus, the challenge to the Brahmanic order that the Buddha represented vanished along with the situation that had called for it. What we call Hinduism today dates from this victory of Brahmanism over Buddhism.

Shankara's proper invention, as Upadhyaya saw it, was the *karm-sanyas,* or "work ascetic." This was a hybrid (or integrated) subject arising out of Shankara's own biographical conflict between his duty toward his mother—who wanted him to become a householder, marry, have children, and care for her—and his own wish to renounce the world.[241] In Upadhyaya's rendering, Shankara could eventually become a *sanyasi* because "society" (*samaj*) took over his filial duties toward his mother.[242] Already in the nineteenth century, the "bourgeois Vedantins," as Brian Hatcher has called them, confronted the problem of how to make Shankara's Vedanta this-worldly and fit for modernity and business.[243] Their answer was to upend Hinduism by canceling the ideal of the direct pursuit of liberation (*moksha*), making it reachable through work alone. Thus, they replaced the traditional ideal of the *sanyasi,* or renouncer, with the householder (*grihastha*) ideal.[244] Upadhyaya similarly centered the idea of work as the superior path to *moksha.*[245] His idea of work as service to society tapped into the well of *bhakti,* the path of devotion, which prefers a life of service to the divinity to the ultimate aim of release from rebirth and absorption into the Absolute. The *deshbhakt* (lit. "devotee of the country," "patriot") figured in Indian anticolonial nationalism and was associated with figures such as Ramakrishna and Aurobindo. More specifically, Upadhyaya's Shankara practically invented the *pracharak,* the RSS "full-timer," who dedicates his life, body, and reproductive future to his volunteer work.[246] Thus, Upadhyaya's vision retained much more of the ascetic than Hatcher's bourgeois Vedantins. After all, the RSS stays true to the *brahmacharya* ideal of celibacy and stepping out of family duties, whereas the bourgeois Vedantins became confirmed householders.

Upadhyaya concluded that Shankara, at some point in his life, must have pondered the question of Indian unity.[247] But the saint seemed to share Upadhyaya's own Partition context when he opined that "cultural unity" (*sanskritik ekta*) must precede "political unity" (*rajnitik ekta*).[248] The RSS showed the way to establish that unity through decades of patient work that elided the state before being able to capture it. Savarkar's theory of violence had proved inadequate to patch the split and defeat caused by Partition. What makes Upadhyaya the definitive architect of Hindutva post-Partition is his recalibration of Hindutva as oneness, which he aimed at the total remaking of

Indian society and the deferred aim of Akhand Bharat.[249] It was he who stood neo-Vedantic Hindutva on strong theoretical foundations.

Upadhyaya's Integral Humanism dispersed the immanent power of religion through society. It shared this quality with its namesake, Jacques Maritain's (1882–1973) *Humanisme Intégral* (1936), a connection made explicit by Upadhyaya's exegete Thengadi.[250] In his thought-provoking revision of the origin story of human rights, historian Samuel Moyn has credited the French Catholic thinker Maritain, above all others, with the tremendous "assertion of religious sovereignty over personal conscience," through which Catholic conservatism was able to reinvent itself as "humanism" in the postwar era.[251] Starting with Catholic discourses on the "dignity" of the human "person" in the 1930s, this postwar reinvention, Moyn argues, gave birth to the notion of "human rights" at the same time as it allowed Catholic conservatism to style itself as the only moral alternative to totalitarianism, disinheriting the secular inheritance of the "rights" of the French Revolution.[252] Though trivializing the connection between Upadhyaya and Maritain, Hindutva's Western scholar-convert Koenraad Elst nevertheless concludes that "Integral Humanism is most akin to the Christian-Democratic movement in Europe."[253] Of course, it is anything but that.

Maritain's humanism was "integral" in the sense that it was able to organically integrate and unify "numerous other truths."[254] This pluralization of "truth" is significant because it set off "Christian humanism" from the doctrine of salvation in competition against which it was formulated: "socialist humanism."[255] Unlike Marxism, which, according to Maritain, was "manichaean," "integral humanism [wa]s able to accept all, since it kn[ew] that *God has no opposite*."[256] In an English-language journal article of 1939, Maritain characterized dualism as one of the "worst vices of the modern world."[257] His major theological claim was that there was no opposition between the temporal and the sacred, "the impure" and "the pure."[258] This new offering of a monistic alternative in Christianity required Christians to launch themselves into temporal work, thereby helping the transcendent again take control of society, the economy, and politics, through which it was diffused. In some ways like Upadhyaya's "work ascetic," this reconfiguration of Christian ethics as immanent power was meant to put an end to Christian quietude and profoundly remake the world as well as Catholicism. Maritain, like Upadhyaya, asserted hegemony by simulating tolerance, as Catholicism realized its full potential by realizing the monistic unity in plurality. There were limits to pluralism, to be sure.[259] Not surprisingly, for Maritain, the "error" of exaggerating "*civil tolerance*" into "theological liberalism" and "*dogmatic tolerance,* which regards the liberty of error as in itself good," befell the "legislation of the Hindus."[260]

The introduction to Maritain's *Integral Humanism* admits humanism to be inseparable from the "pagans."[261] Through Ramanuja, the eleventh-century sage who inspired the *bhakti* tradition, Indian monism was ingrained into Maritain's vision of pagan humanism from the start. The book then proceeds to reclaim transcendence for Western humanism, which had become materialistic and irreligious (as in Comte's "kingdom of pure *humanity*"—a "secularisation of the Kingdom of God"), and reclaim humanism for Christianity.[262] This was framed as the restoration of humanism to its "first origins" in Christian spirituality.[263] After switching codes from the universality of the Christian God to the "universal religion," Maritain showed the way to achieving Catholic hegemony by making the Christian God immanent. In this light, the similarities between Maritain and Upadhyaya are an instance of discursive backflow as well as of linear "influence." Maritain fashioned the criticisms of the West that India had helped produce into the groundwork of his intervention, accounting for its soft and inaudible landing in Upadhyaya's ideology. Like the Catholic integralism of the late nineteenth and early twentieth centuries, the RSS-BJS subordinated the state to religion. Like Catholic integralism, they set out to capture society for their church. After a long history of indexing the antithesis of "the political" and sovereignty itself for modern Indian political thought—and especially for Hindutva's founder, Vinayak Savarkar—monism showed the way for Hindutva's massive assertion of this-worldly power and its violent deployment in India today.

EPILOGUE

One of the striking features of Indian political life in recent years is that saffron politicians have begun to publish books on ideology. In *Hindutva Paradigm* (2021), BJP politician Ram Madhav quotes the Mahabharata passage on the Kritiyuga, the Hindu golden age, that reads, "'There was no state; no king. There was none to be punished and none to punish. People have protected each other through the eternal principles of *Dharma*.'" He concludes, naming the tradition he expropriates, "Thus, aeons before Marx envisaged the 'withering away of the state,' the Indian nation had experienced such a state of statelessness. Yet, its national life had continued."[1] The Brahmin dissolves into society, but the king, state, or sovereign still has a role to play in the dark age in which we live. His role is to uphold *dharma* in society. Fascism is usually thought to be very much about the state. Yet Nazis, including Hitler, differentiated National Socialism from Italian Fascism by proclaiming their project to be about the nation (*Volk*), not the state, which was only a vessel for the *Volk*. In its professed attitude to the state, Nazism parallels post-Savarkar Hindutva, which, in keeping with RSS ideology but bizarrely for a political party, prioritizes society (*samaj*) over state power. But the BJP is no longer in opposition to the Indian state, as its forerunner was when Deendayal Upadhyaya formalized its ideology. Today, it owns the state and its institutions.[2] This past decade has witnessed the bending of the Indian state to its new purpose of enforcing Hindu *dharma* in Indian society, of bringing Indian society to heel.

Just before the COVID-19 pandemic ground the world to a halt in the spring of 2020, the book *The RSS: Roadmaps for the 21st Century* was published. Its title is its program. The fact that Mohan Bhagwat, the RSS *saranghchalak*, or chief leader, since 2009, launched the book at an event attended by other high-profile RSS and BJP figures counts as an official endorsement of the line taken by its author. In his introduction, the author, an RSS longtimer, reports what he finds to be the future vision of the RSS, which is worth quoting in full:

> After deliberating with RSS functionaries, the common answer I could gather was that India would continue to march on its mission as a Vishwa Guru, or World Teacher, to provide knowledge and direction to the world, while the Sangh would become indistinguishable from Indian society. The merger of the Sangh and Indian society would be as complete as the mixing of sugar in milk and just as the milk when stirred displays the characteristics of sugar, Indian society as a whole would start exhibiting the traits of the Sangh. So, the Sangh would become coterminous with all of Indian society and the need for it to exist as a distinct entity would be obviated.
>
> The Sangh does not want to be a separate power ruling over society [. . .]. To use a metaphor, just as the mighty rivers fall into oceans and have no separate existence, the Sangh's complete union with society is conceived as the ultimate goal. "*Sangh Samaj Banega*" [Sangh will become society] is a slogan, referring to the merging of Sangh with society, which is raised repeatedly in the RSS to reinforce this goal when Sangh and society become one.[3]

Likening the merger of Sangh and society to sugar mixing in milk is an old Golwalkar metaphor.[4] The RSS's aim, as unambiguously stated by Golwalkar and restated in the prior twenty-first-century roadmap, is to remake Indian society in its own image. Hindutva, we are further told, "is oneness."[5]

In 2016, the year celebrating the centennial of Upadhyaya's birth, under a BJP government, proposals were made for Race Course Road, where the Indian prime minister resides, to be renamed Ekatma Marg, after Upadhyaya's central concept, *ekatma manavvad,* or Integral Humanism. A compromise was reached, and it was renamed Lok Kalyan Marg, orienting India's leader to the "people's welfare" instead of to RSS-BJP ideology steeped in Hindu theology. Monism (Advaita Vedanta, the theory of divine oneness) also led the charge in earlier decades of Hindu nationalist ascendency. The 1980s, which opened with the emergence of the BJP from the Janata coalition, saw a new form of political pilgrimage called Ekatmata Yatra, invented and organized by one of the stalwarts of Hindutva today, the Vishva Hindu Parishad. Unity, or "one-soulness," was inscribed as its central idea and expressed in several ways: in the 1983 Yatra drawing pilgrims from Nepal, Bhutan, and Bangladesh, as well as India; in the pilgrimage route starting off the political map of India in Kathmandu and connecting the four corners of Hindu civilizational space (loosely, but larger than, India) to invariably culminate in Nagpur, the RSS headquarters in India's center; in the free mingling of pilgrims irrespective of caste; and in the mixing of holy water from the Ganges with river water found along the way.[6] The message: India was one, Hindus were one, and India was one with the Hindus.

What, then, of the other old dream of Hindutva after 1947, that of Akhand Bharat ("Undivided India")? Bhagwat made headlines in the winter of 2021 with statements not only committing the RSS to undoing Partition but intriguingly stating that "Akhand Bharat is possible not through force, but through Hinduism." An article in the RSS newspaper *Organiser* that discussed the RSS chief's statement reiterates the Rig Vedic verse that has become an RSS formula: "'*Ekam Sat Viprah Bahudha Vadanti*'" (Truth is one, though the Vedantins call it by different names).[7] The "creed" of Jews, Parsees, Christians, and even Muslims was only incidental to, and merged into, the metamatrix of the Hindu "one-truth." None could claim a separate status for themselves in view of this unipolar truth. Indeed, the author of the RSS twenty-first-century roadmap points to the Rig Vedic verse rendering "differences in the modes of worship" irrelevant as the "critical difference between the Sangh and The [*sic*] Hindu Mahasabha"—Savarkar's party. The latter, he argued, was partisan and sought representation on the basis of religion, while the former stood for nationalism "irrespective of religion." It was on this secular basis that the Sangh had opposed the Partition of the country "on religious lines."[8] "The Sangh," we are told, "never forgot the partition of the country and Guruji [Golwalkar] felt that unity and integrity of the country could not be fully secured unless Hindutva became the collective consciousness of our society—and this work is being done by the Sangh."[9]

Bhagwat has been incredibly prolific and public, especially of late and unperturbed by the pandemic. Among other things, he penned the foreword and gave publicity to a treatise on Akhand Bharat that credits Savarkar as *Veer Savarkar: The Man Who Could Have Prevented Partition*.[10] The book blames Partition on the Congress's "appeasement" of Muslims, and Savarkar emerges as the great seer who predicted this. Hence, Savarkar's tactics of threats and use of violence against Muslims to give up their political identity and beat them into submission are rehabilitated. Savarkar shows the way to undoing Partition and countering "divisive forces" in India today. According to Bhagwat, the authors show that Hindutva "isn't discriminatory by nature but inclusive"—again, that monism of steel that really is unlike Savarkar but instead typical of Upadhyaya and the RSS.[11] Sharing the stage with Indian defense minister Rajnath Singh at the book launch of *Veer Savarkar,* the RSS chief reiterated that Muslim separatism was an artificial division while Hindutva was about "unity" standing above religious division. Muslim "worship" (*puja*) may be different, he said; there were many religions in India, but in truth, they were "one" (*ek*). "Existence is one," he added in English. *That* was the meaning of Hindutva. No part of the essential oneness that is Bharat had a right to secession or special treatment ("appeasement") as a minority.[12]

The Citizenship Amendment Act (CAA), which was enacted in 2019 but came into force only in March 2024, demonstrates the contradictory nature of the dream of Akhand Bharat three generations on from Partition. The CAA opens a path to Indian citizenship for religious minorities from neighboring Pakistan, Afghanistan, and Bangladesh—provided they are non-Muslims. (Notable Muslim minorities in the region that also face religious persecution, such as the Ahmadiyya, Shias, and Myanmar's Rohingyas, are excluded.) Thus, for the first time, a religious stipulation was introduced into Indian citizenship law. As the forerunner of the BJP, the Jana Sangh's 1954 election manifesto already welcomed "any part of Pakistan" that was "disgusted" with its government and disenchanted with Partition "to establish relations with *Bharatwarsh,*" which covertly meant to return to it.[13] Given this history, the passage of the CAA is intelligible as a step toward Akhand Bharat and the undoing of Partition.

It is also intelligible as a step toward the fulfilment of Partition. Though never giving up on "Undivided India," the new Hindutva that took shape under Upadhyaya conceptually depended on Partition and the emergence of Pakistan. The ideological work that has gone into it, as well as the trauma of Partition, makes Pakistan more than just an instance of British "divide and rule," even and especially in the Hindu nationalist imagination. Even if patchily, the CAA would concentrate the non-Muslims of South Asia in India while, at the same time, preparations are underway to strip Muslim migrants from Bangladesh of Indian citizenship. So just as much as the erasure of Partition, the aim may be to complete the population transfer on religious lines that remained incomplete in 1947 and 1971, when Bangladesh emerged from Pakistan's eastern wing. There is a tension here that cannot be resolved.[14]

One of the intellectual motivations behind this book has been to understand Hindu nationalism in India today. Yet the more I felt that I understood Savarkar, the less I believed that all genealogical routes led to him. Savarkar would have laughed at the Ministry of Ayush (which covers the alternative medical systems of Ayurveda, yoga, naturopathy, Unani, Siddha, Sowa Rigpa, and homoeopathy) created by the Modi government in 2014. He would have heaped scorn on the government-funded SUTRA PIC (or Scientific Utilisation Through Research Augmentation-Prime Products from Indigenous Cows) program tasked with identifying the unique properties of the milk, urine, and dung of Desi cows and finding commercial application for them. He would have approved replacing mosques with temples, as was done at Ayodhya, but none ridiculed Hinduism or devout Hindus more than he. "Society" was not a mainstay of Savarkar's vocabulary, "culture" not half as important as it is today. What, then, is the relation between Savarkar and the Hindutva that has taken over India in our own time? To answer this question, this book turned to the thought of Upadhyaya, who built a political party from RSS ideology and wrote the decisive manifesto of Hindutva after Savarkar's *Essentials of Hindutva* (1923)—*Integral Humanism* (1965).

The conclusion is that twenty-first-century Hindutva is a potent blend of two distinct ideological threads of Hindutva. One is Savarkar's violence, and the other is the iron monism of the RSS. In either iteration, Hindutva is a claim to sovereignty, which is about disinheriting Muslim sovereignty. In centering its foremost ideologues, Vinayak Savarkar and Deendayal Upadhyaya, this book has tracked how Hindutva, which was initially ambiguous toward Hinduism, to say the least, came to endorse Hindu philosophy (Advaita Vedanta) and practice (*bhakti*) to the point that today, Hindutva and Hinduism are nearly indistinguishable. Savarkar's Hindutva was irreligious and irreverent of tradition. Its distinguishing feature was its fascination with violence. In this sense, the 2002 anti-Muslim pogrom in Gujarat proceeded distinctly along the lines of Savarkar. Savarkar brandished an ideology of antagonism (as an extreme case of what is traditionally dualism, or *dvaita*, in Hindu theology), and his tactic was escalation. The RSS and Upadhyaya played a longer game. They trusted in Hindu monism (*advaita*) and patience to bring about the transformation of Indian society. Savarkar remains potent, but the religious and conservative elements, as well as a good deal of grassroots work, were required to make

Hindutva hegemonic in Indian society. Prepared through decades of patient labor by the RSS and its political wing, the BJS and BJP, Hindutva today is poised to achieve, and perhaps has achieved, something that Savarkar never could: to make India Hindu.

Early in 2024, India's BJP prime minister, Narendra Modi, consecrated the Ram Mandir (temple) in Ayodhya in a controversial ceremony that sidelined not only religious authority but the idol itself, which had been worshipped there for seventy-five years, ever since its miraculous "appearance" inside the Babri Masjid (mosque) to reclaim Lord Rama's supposed birthplace. The destruction of the sixteenth-century mosque by a Hindu mob in 1992 first put Hindu nationalism on the map of scholars.[15] The culmination of a series of major retreats from the principle of Indian secularism, the consecration of the Ram temple has been interpreted as the final arrival of Hindu *rashtra*, the Hindu state.[16] It epitomizes the identification of Hindutva with the Hindu religion that became dominant after independence. Yet their merging was neither complete nor unopposed, as the temple reveals Hindutva's appropriation of Hinduism as an act of disinheritance.

Headlined by Modi, the consecration ceremony on January 22, 2024, was boycotted by the highest religious authorities in Hinduism: the four Shankaracharyas, the keepers of the Advaita Vedanta tradition of Shankara. Significantly, the four traditional protectors of *Sanatan dharma*, or the "eternal religion," objected to the consecration on the grounds that it broke religious law. The Hindu Shastras do not permit the consecration of a deity in a temple that is still under construction or the entering of the holiest of holies and the touching of the deity by a nonpriest—in this instance, Modi, who officiated in the *pran pratishtha* (religious consecration) ceremony. The Shankaracharyas further objected to the inauspicious date chosen for the consecration and to the sidelining of their religious authority (and that of others) throughout. In an interview, the Shankaracharya of Jyotish Peeth, Swami Avimukteshwaranand Saraswati, said, "The entire discussion around the temple is political, it has ceased to be religious. If it was about religion, we would have been consulted." The BJP and RSS, which forced the event, had "managed to divide the Hindus themselves" by "dividing the religious Hindus" from "the politicised Hindus."[17]

In addition, to forge a corridor through the ancient holy city of Varanasi (Kashi) linking the Vishwanath Temple to the bathing ghats, an expensive government project launched by Modi allegedly "broke important, ancient temples." The Shankaracharya reasoned, "We hate Aurangzeb because we were told he broke temples, then why will we forgive one of our own to do it?"[18] The amazing rendering of Modi as the new Aurangzeb that went viral in 2024 reveals Hindutva's potential to become the destroyer of Hinduism: it destroys temples, even as it hunts for temples underneath mosques. Though papered over by Upadhyaya, the gap that was once forged by Savarkar between the political subject he coined and the traditional religious subject incapable of incarnating "Hindutva" has reopened. Resistance to Hindutva now comes from some of Hinduism's traditional rulers ousted by an Indian state recalibrated, since 2014, to take on the stewardship of the Hindu religion in India. This is significant, as it suggests that Hindu *rashtra,* or the Hindu state that is the aim of Hindu nationalism, may not be the same as *Ram rajya,* the traditional ideal of Lord Rama's rule of righteousness. Ultimately, however, it remains unclear whether religious opposition has the will or power to break state-sanctioned Hindutva.

Certainly, *Fascism in India* holds lessons for contemporary India. The changing relationship between Hindutva and Hinduism is a case in point. "Love jihad" is the name we today give to what was in Savarkar's time the idée fixe of Muslims stealing Hindu women by *rakshasa* marriage. Caste continues to mark the frontier of the Hindu as a political subject, and Hindutva remains obsessed with Hindu sovereignty. More than eighty years ago, Benoy Sarkar and Subhas Bose questioned fascism's alterity not only from nationalism but from democracy. The same question persists today, not just in India but around the world, with the rise of ultra–right wing political movements by democratic means. However much it represses the voice of the opposition, Hindu nationalism today is exceedingly popular. Indeed, the nomenclature of "Hindu majoritarianism" we use to describe the change in Indian democracy points to the key problem of democratic theory: that the will of the majority may not be liberal or nice. And yet, as much as it speaks to the current moment, this book insists on the difference between the mid-twentieth century and our present. We know that we are dealing with thought that is different exactly because it surprises or disturbs us. It may bother us that Savarkar—who, depending on one's political inclination, stands for evil—was more radical in his thinking on intermarriage than is conceivable in India today. Or, to list another example, to crown the king of Nepal as emperor of an India divided into Hindu sovereign chunks seems ludicrous once the regime of territorial nation-states that arose from Partition was naturalized.

Readers may not be convinced that Hindu nationalism truly constitutes fascism. Such contention is only productive. Yet it was necessary to frame the thought described here as fascism in India. Europe's experiments with fascism demanded conceptual engagement in India, as they did globally in the twentieth century. Moreover, the book jettisons diffusionist models that view fascism as originating solely in Europe and inspiring only derivative forms elsewhere. This methodological move liberates Indian thought from the threshold set by the famous European cases, opening up the vista of what fascism might look like if charted from India. What comes into view, among others, is a philosophical tension between dualism and monism, a surprising articulation of miscegenous race, and an understanding of sovereignty that does not map onto the territory of the nation-state.

Though it did not give fascism its name, Nazi Germany has acted as an interlocutor for the Indian thought explored in this book. On race and sovereign territory, points of contrast outweigh points of contact with Nazi imaginaries of "blood and soil." Savarkar envisaged intermarriage and reproduction between Muslim women and Hindu men as a means to eradicate Muslims by absorption, in stark contrast to Nazi Germany, where, though racial theorizing did not assume Germans to be an unmixed race, the race that mattered—the Jews—was beyond the pale of miscegenation. As for soil, though there is overlap with the border-leveling expansionism of the Nazi ideology of *Lebensraum*, Hindu proponents of Greater India were concerned with unearthing a history of Hindu empire rather than with reconstituting it in the present; Savarkar identified Hindu sovereignty with spaces that were much smaller than Hindusthan; and Akhand Bharat was about making India Hindu as much as it was about reabsorbing Pakistan. But on the question of monism, there was surprising overlap, as Nazi thinkers fought German philosophy's deep attraction to Hindu thought, particularly Advaita Vedanta, which does not distinguish between self and other: distinctions that were fundamental for both Nazism's and Hindutva's enmities with Jews and Muslims. With caste, too, the Nazis domesticated an Indian problem. Nazi nationalism produced a vision of a casteless *Volk* that has a parallel in the integrated, "integral" society devised by the brand of Hindutva that gained prominence after Indian independence.

The question, then, is no longer whether Indian thought meets the standard set by someone else (producing a carbon copy of European fascism plus ethnic difference at best). It is what India can teach us about political thought in a global context defined by fascism. In other words, this book has aimed to push the boundaries of what was "thinkable" in the fascist age. Theorizing from India, the book has also explored India's capacity to universalize itself in several ways. The ideas of race it generated can broaden the recently and unhelpfully narrowed understanding of "race" that dominates global yet US-centric discourse. India's pattern of social exclusion, caste, has already proved its generalizability, namely by lending itself to analyses of rule and power in society, from Nazi Germany to the contemporary United States. Hindu nationalism, much like Nazism, showcases that the "people," or *demos,* of democracy is an abstraction only too often filled with *ethnos*—that is, ethnic or racial content. Deeply versed in the Western canon of political thought yet wholly original, Benoy Sarkar is the theorist who can help us think through the proximity of fascism and democracy today. With speculation over the rebirth of "fascism" in our own time abounding, he and Indian thinker-politicians Subhas Bose and M. N. Roy certainly felt that India had something new to say, and add, to that globalism of the middle decades of the twentieth century, fascism.

Hindutva was neither a copycat fascism in Savarkar's time nor today only an ethnic variant of the kind of populism or neofascism that appears to be stalking the globe. On the contrary, with its violent politics making international news, India today seems a trendsetter in a troubled age. Its identification of one community, group, or *ethnos*—the Hindus—with the nation is almost complete, while White supremacists are still struggling to achieve the same for their countries on both sides of the Atlantic. The liberal state that still prevents them from doing so in Euro-America is, in the Indian case, almost completely in the service of Hindu nationalism. And India's capacity for violence against its minorities is more formidable than even the border regimes of the United States and the European Union.

Is India's brand of violence also exportable or generalizable? Strikingly, Hindutva is characterized by its refusal to let go of the one it hates. Whether through genetic incorporation, religious subsumption, or the dream of undividing India, Hindutva has not made peace with its inability to neutralize Muslims by forcibly absorbing them. For Pakistan, Partition is the beginning of its sovereign existence as a nation, not the wound that will not heal. Likewise, on the part of India's Muslims, we see no comparable fixation with Hindus or a desire to appropriate them wholesale. Hindutva's desire for the one it hates is instructive and suggestive in an age of fractured discursive communities that nevertheless produce totalizing objectives. With Gandhi, friendship and the possibility of peace are built on relinquishing the desire to convert the other.

NOTES

All translations from German, Hindi, and French are my own.

Introduction

1. Shruti Kapila, *Violent Fraternity: Indian Political Thought in the Global Age* (Princeton, NJ: Princeton University Press, 2021), 229–71.
2. From the journalistic to the scholarly, see, for instance, Jason Stanley, "For Trump and Modi, Ethnic Purity Is the Purpose of Power," *The Guardian*, February 24, 2020, https://www.theguardian.com/commentisfree/2020/feb/24/trump-modi-citizenship-politics-fascism; Ajay Gudavarthy and Vijay Gudavarthy, "Populism, Fascism, Neoliberalism: Theorizing Contemporary India," in *Spectres of Fascism: Historical, Theoretical, and International Perspectives*, ed. Samir Gandesha (London: Pluto Press, 2020), 223–40; Jairus Banaji, ed., *Fascism: Essays on Europe and India* (New Delhi: Three Essays Collective, 2013); Sumit Sarkar, "The Fascism of the Sangh Parivar," *Economic and Political Weekly* 28, no. 5 (1993): 163–7; Christophe Jaffrelot, *The Hindu Nationalist Movement and Indian Politics, 1925 to the 1990s: Strategies of Identity-Building, Implantation and Mobilisation (With Special Reference to Central India)* (London: Hurst, 1996), 51–63; William Gould, *Hindu Nationalism and the Language of Politics in Late Colonial India* (Cambridge: Cambridge University Press, 2004), 153, 157–8, 178; Tobias Delfs, *Hindu-Nationalismus und europäischer Faschismus: Vergleich, Transfer- und Beziehungsgeschichte (Inklusive der ersten Auflage von M. S. Golwalkar's "We or Our Nationhood Defined" aus dem Jahre 1939 und mit einem Geleitwort von Hermann Kulke)* (Hamburg-Schenefeld, Germany: EB-Verlag, 2008); Chetan Bhatt, *Hindu Nationalism: Origins, Ideologies and Modern Myths* (Oxford: Berg, 2001).
3. François Furet and Ernst Nolte, *Fascism and Communism*, trans. Katherine Golsan (Lincoln: University of Nebraska Press, 2001), 35.
4. Ibid., 62.
5. Roger Griffin, "Decentering Comparative Fascist Studies," *Fascism* 4, no. 2 (2015): 108; Roger Griffin, *The Nature of Fascism* (London: The Printer Press, 1991).
6. See Christophe Jaffrelot, *Modi's India: Hindu Nationalism and the Rise of Ethnic Democracy* (Princeton: Princeton University Press, 2021).
7. Daniele Conversi, "Conceptualizing Nationalism: An Introduction to Walker Connor's Work," in *Ethnonationalism in the Contemporary World: Walker Connor and the Study of Nationalism*, ed. Daniele Conversi (London: Routledge, 2002), 2.
8. See Markus Daechsel, "Scientism and Its Discontents: The Indo-Muslim 'Fascism' of Inayatullah Khan Al-Mashriqi," *Modern Intellectual History* 3, no. 3 (2006): 443–72.

9. See Shruti Kapila, "Global Intellectual History and the Indian Political," in *Rethinking Modern European Intellectual History*, ed. Darrin M. McMahon and Samuel Moyn (Oxford: Oxford University Press, 2014), 253–74; Shruti Kapila and Faisal Devji, eds., *Political Thought in Action: The Bhagavad Gita and Modern India* (Cambridge: Cambridge University Press, 2013); Shruti Kapila, ed., *An Intellectual History for India* (Cambridge: Foundation Books, 2010); Samuel Moyn and Andrew Sartori, eds., *Global Intellectual History* (New York: Columbia University Press, 2013). A journal of *Gobal Intellectual History* has been running since 2016. On India, see, inter alia, Kapila, *Violent Fraternity*; Nazmul Sultan, *Waiting for the People: The Idea of Democracy in Indian Anticolonial Thought* (Cambridge, MA: Harvard University Press, 2024); Tejas Parasher, *Radical Democracy in Modern Indian Political Thought* (Cambridge: Cambridge University Press, 2023); Amar Sohal, The *Muslim Secular: Parity and the Politics of India's Partition* (Oxford: Oxford University Press, 2023); Prathama Banerjee, *Elementary Aspects of the Political: Histories from the Global South* (Durham, NC: Duke University Press, 2020); Faisal Devji, *The Impossible Indian: Gandhi and the Temptation of Violence* (Cambridge, MA: Harvard University Press, 2012); Faisal Devji, *Muslim Zion: Pakistan as a Political Idea* (Cambridge, MA: Harvard University Press, 2013); Ajay Skaria, *Unconditional Equality: Gandhi's Religion of Resistance* (Minneapolis: University of Minnesota Press, 2016).

10. Kapila, "Global Intellectual History," 261–2.

11. Vinayak Damodar Savarkar [A Maratha, pseud.], *Essentials of Hindutva* (Nagpur: V. V. Kelkar, 1923). Though Savarkar did not invent the word, he is rightly regarded as Hindutva's architect.

12. Sohal, *Muslim Secular*, 24.

13. See, for instance, Sheldon Pollock, "The Death of Sanskrit," *Comparative Studies in Society and History* 43, no. 2 (2001): 392–426.

14. Hannah Arendt, *On Violence* (New York: Houghton Mifflin Harcourt, 1970).

15. Devji, *Impossible Indian*.

16. Carl Schmitt, *Der Begriff des Politischen* (Munich: Duncker & Humblot, 1932); Kapila, *Violent Fraternity*, 1–13.

17. Kapila, *Violent Fraternity*, 4.

18. See Tanika Sarkar, "Semiotics of Terror: Muslim Children and Women in Hindu Rashtra," *Economic and Political Weekly* 37, no. 28 (2002): 2874–6.

19. Siobhán K. Fisher, "Occupation of the Womb: Forced Impregnation as Genocide," *Duke Law Journal* 46, no. 1 (1996): 91–133.

20. Dipesh Chakrabarty, *Provincializing Europe: Postcolonial Thought and Historical Difference* (Princeton, NJ: Princeton University Press, 2000).

21. Seminal contributions include Ernst Nolte, *Der Faschismus in seiner Epoche: Die Action francaise, der italienische Faschismus, der Nationalsozialismus* (Munich: R. Piper, 1963); Stanley G. Payne, *Fascism, Comparison and Definition* (Madison: University of Wisconsin Press, 1980); George L. Mosse, *The Crisis of German Ideology: Intellectual Origins of the Third Reich* (London: Weidenfeld and Nicolson, 1964); George L. Mosse, *The Fascist Revolution: Toward a General Theory of Fascism* (New York: H. Fertig, 1999); George L. Mosse, *International Fascism: New Thoughts and New Approaches* (London: Sage Publications, 1979); Griffin, *Nature of Fascism*; Zeev Sternhell, *Ni droite, ni gauche: L'idéologie fasciste en France* (Paris: Editions du Seuil, 1983); Zeev Sternhell, *The Birth of Fascist Ideology: From Cultural Rebellion to Political Revolution*, with Mario Sznajder and Maia Asheri, trans. David Maisel (Princeton, NJ: Princeton University Press, 1994); also, though later, Robert O. Paxton, *The Anatomy of Fascism* (New York: Knopf, 2004).

22. For totalitarianism's most famous theorist, Hannah Arendt, in *The Origins of Totalitarianism* (1951; repr., New York: Schocken Books, 2004), only Nazism and Stalinism qualify as properly "totalitarian." Italian Fascism, while authoritarian, falls short of meeting this standard.

23. Roger Griffin, "Palingenetischer Ultranationalismus: Die Geburtswehen einer neuen Faschismusdeutung," in *Der Faschismus in Europa: Wege der Forschung*, ed. Thomas Schlemmer

and Hans Woller (Berlin: De Gruyter, 2014), 28–9. For instance, one of the greatest historians of Italian Fascism, Emilio Gentile, distinguishes between "fascism" and National Socialism throughout: see, for example, Emilio Gentile, *The Origins of Fascist Ideology 1918–1925*, trans. Robert L. Miller (New York: Enigma Books, 2005), 360.

24. For the German *Historikerstreit* ("historians' dispute") of the 1980s over the place of the Holocaust in German history, see Rudolf Augstein, *Historikerstreit: Die Dokumentation der Kontroverse um die Einzigartigkeit der nationalsozialistischen Judenvernichtung* (Munich: Piper, 1987). For the 1975 Italian controversy over the historian Renzo de Felice's distinction between Italian Fascism as a movement, which was revolutionary, and as a regime once in power, see Michael A. Ledeen, "Renzo de Felice and the Controversy over Italian Fascism," *Journal of Contemporary History* 11, no. 4 (1976): 269–83.

25. On circulation, see, for instance, Arndt Bauerkämper and Grzegorz Rossolinski-Liebe, eds., *Fascism without Borders: Transnational Connections and Cooperation between Movements and Regimes in Europe from 1918 to 1945* (New York: Berghan Books, 2017); Sandrine Kott and Kiran Klaus Patel, eds., *Nazism across Borders: The Social Policies of the Third Reich and Their Global Appeal* (Oxford: Oxford University Press, 2018). On responses, see, for example, David Motadel, *Islam and Nazi Germany's War* (Cambridge, MA: Belknap Press of Harvard University Press, 2014); Francis R. Nicosia, *Nazi Germany and the Arab World* (New York: Cambridge University Press, 2015); Israel Gershoni, ed., *Arab Responses to Fascism and Nazism: Attraction and Repulsion* (Austin: University of Texas Press, 2014); Ulrike Freitag and Gershoni, eds., *Arab Encounters with Fascist Propaganda 1933–1945* (Göttingen, Germany: Vandenhoeck & Ruprecht, 2011); Jeffrey Herf, *Nazi Propaganda for the Arab World* (New Haven, CT: Yale University Press, 2007); Stefan Ihrig, *Atatürk in the Nazi Imagination* (Cambridge, MA: Belknap Press of Harvard University Press, 2014).

26. See, for instance, Eugene J. D'souza, "Nazi Propaganda in India," *Social Scientist* 28, no. 5/6 (2000): 77–90; Marzia Casolari, *In the Shade of the Swastika: The Ambiguous Relationship between Indian Nationalism and Nazi-Fascism* (Bologna, Italy: Il Libre de Emil, 2011); Maria Framke, *Delhi—Rom—Berlin: Die indische Wahrnehmung von Faschismus und Nationalsozialismus 1922–1939* (Darmstadt, Germany: WBG, 2012); Maria Framke, "Shopping Ideologies for Independent India? Taraknath Das's Engagement with Italian Fascism and German National Socialism," *Itinerario* 40, no. 1 (2016): 55–81; Maria Framke and Jana Tschurenev, "Umstrittene Geschichte: (Anti-)Faschismus und (Anti-)Kolonialismus in Indien," *Prokla* 158, no. 1 (2019): 67–83; Baijayanti Roy, "Hakenkreuz, Swastika and Crescent: The Religious Factor in Nazi Cultural Politics Regarding India," in *Religious Entanglements between Germans and Indians, 1800–1945*, ed. Isabella Schwaderer and Gerdien Jonker (Cham: Springer Nature, 2023), 253–82; Mario Prayer, "Italian Fascist Regime and Nationalist India, 1921–45," *International Studies* 28, no. 3 (1991): 249–71; Mario Prayer, "Creative India and the World: Bengali Internationalism and Italy in the Interwar Period," in *Cosmopolitan Thought Zones: South Asia and the Global Circulation of Ideas*, ed. Sugata Bose and Kris Manjapra (Basingstoke, UK: Palgrave Macmillan, 2010), 236–59. For older accounts, the literature is too numerous to cite. See, inter alia, Léon Poliakov, *The Aryan Myth*, trans. Edmund Howard (London: Chatto Heinemann for Sussex University Press, 1974); Dorothy M. Figueira, *The Exotic: A Decadent Quest* (Albany: State University of New York Press, 1994), 137–62; Dorothy M. Figueira, *Aryans, Jews, Brahmins: Theorizing Authority through Myths of Identity* (Albany: State University of New York Press, 2002); Nicholas Goodrick-Clarke, *The Occult Roots of Nazism: The Ariosophists of Austria and Germany 1890–1935* (Wellingborough, UK: Aquarian, 1985); Victor Trimondi and Victoria Trimondi, *Hitler, Buddha, Krishna: Eine unheilige Allianz vom Dritten Reich bis heute* (Vienna: Ueberreuter, 2002); Eric Kurlander, *Hitler's Monsters: A Supernatural History of the Third Reich* (New Haven, CT: Yale University Press, 2017); Eric Kurlander, "The Orientalist Roots of National Socialism? Nazism, Occultism, and South Asian Spirituality, 1919–1945," in *Transcultural Encounters*, ed. Joanne Miyang Cho, Kurlander, and Douglas T. McGetchin

(London: Routledge, 2014), 155–69; Sheldon Pollock, "Deep Orientalism? Notes on Sanskrit and Power beyond the Raj," in *Orientalism and the Postcolonial Predicament: Perspectives on South Asia*, ed. Carol A. Breckenridge and Peter van der Veer (Philadelphia: University of Pennsylvania Press, 1993), 96.

27. See Marzia Casolari, "Hindutva's Foreign Tie-Up in the 1930s: Archival Evidence," *Economic and Political Weekly* 35, no. 4 (2000): 218–28. Also see Walter Laqueur, *Fascism: Past, Present, Future* (New York: Oxford University Press, 1996), 173–5; Roger Griffin, "What Fascism Is Not and Is: Thoughts on the Re-inflation of a Concept," *Fascism* 2, no. 2 (2013): 260; Michael Mann, *Fascists* (Cambridge: Cambridge University Press, 2004), 372–4; Paxton, *Anatomy of Fascism*, 203–4; Stein Ugelvik Larsen, "Was There Fascism outside Europe? Diffusion from Europe and Domestic Impulses," in *Fascism outside Europe: The European Impulse against Domestic Conditions in the Diffusion of Global Fascism*, ed. Stein Ugelvik Larsen (Boulder, CO: Social Science Monographs, 2001), 749–53.

28. See Jan Kuhlmann, *Subhas Chandra Bose und die Indienpolitik der Achsenmächte* (Berlin: Schiler, 2003); Hans-Bernd Zöllner, *"Der Feind meines Feindes ist mein Freund": Subhas Chandra Bose und das zeitgenössische Deutschland unter dem Nationalsozialismus, 1933–1943* (Münster, Germany: Lit, 2000); Romain Hayes, *Subhas Chandra Bose in Nazi Germany: Politics, Intelligence and Propaganda 1941–43* (London: Hurst, 2011); Larsen, "Was There Fascism?," 753–8; Mann, *Fascists*, 373–2; Sugata Bose, *His Majesty's Opponent: Subhas Chandra Bose and India's Struggle against Empire* (Cambridge, MA: Harvard University Press, 2011), 98, 132.

29. I am grateful to Alison Bashford for suggesting the term "exposé." I am here thinking in particular of Benjamin Zachariah's works: "Global Fascisms and the *Volk*: The Framing of Narratives and the Crossing of Lines," *South Asia: Journal of South Asian Studies* 38, no. 4 (2015): 608–12; "A Voluntary Gleichschaltung? Perspectives from India towards a Non-Eurocentric Understanding of Fascism," *Transcultural Studies*, no. 2 (2014): 63–100; "At the Fuzzy Edges of Fascism: Framing the *Volk* in India," *South Asia: Journal of South Asian Studies* 38, no. 4 (2015): 639–55; "Rethinking (the Absence of) Fascism in India, c. 1922–1945," in *Cosmopolitan Thought Zones: South Asia and the Global Circulation of Ideas*, ed. Sugata Bose and Kris Manjapra (Basingstoke, UK: Palgrave Macmillan, 2010), 178–209. See also Satadru Sen, "Fascism without Fascists? A Comparative Look at Hindutva and Zionism," *South Asia: Journal of South Asian Studies* 38, no. 4 (2015): 690–711.

30. For a classic account, see Bauerkämper and Rossolinski-Liebe, eds., *Fascism without Borders*. For Indian case studies, see, for instance, Benjamin Zachariah, ed., "*Völkisch* and Fascist Movements in South Asia," special issue, *South Asia: Journal of South Asian Studies* 38, no. 4 (2015).

31. C. A. Bayly, *Recovering Liberties: Indian Thought in the Age of Liberalism and Empire* (Cambridge: Cambridge University Press, 2011), 3.

32. Vinayak Damodar Savarkar, *Mazzini charitra* (1907; repr., New Delhi: Prabhat Prakashan, 2009).

33. Ángel Alcalde, "The Transnational Consensus: Fascism and Nazism in Current Research," *Contemporary European History* 29, no. 2 (2020): 251.

34. Luna Sabastian, "Spaces on the Temporal Move: Weimar *Geopolitik* and the Vision of an Indian Science of the State, 1924–1945," *Global Intellectual History* 3, no. 2 (2018): 231–53.

35. For a discussion of its usefulness today, see Gilbert Allardyce, "What Fascism Is Not: Thoughts on the Deflation of a Concept," *American Historical Review* 84 (1979): 367–88; Mark Mazower, "Fascism and Democracy Today: What Use Is the Study of History in the Current Crisis?," *European Law Journal* 22, no. 3 (2016): 375–85; Griffin, "What Fascism Is Not and Is."

36. Allardyce, "What Fascism Is Not," 370; Mazower, "Fascism and Democracy," 376–8.

37. Friedrich Wilhelm Nietzsche, *Zur Genealogie der Moral: Eine Streitschrift* (Leipzig: C. G. Naumann, 1887), 71.

Chapter One: An Indian Theory of Fascism

1. See Leslie James, "Blood Brothers: Colonialism and Fascism as Relations in the Interwar Caribbean and West Africa," *American Historical Review* 127, no. 2 (2022): 634–63; Kasper Braskén, Nigel Copsey, and David Featherstone, eds., *Anti-Fascism in a Global Perspective: Transnational Networks, Exile Communities, and Radical Internationalism* (London: Routledge, 2021).

2. See Sugata Bose, *His Majesty's Opponent: Subhas Chandra Bose and India's Struggle against Empire* (Cambridge, MA: Harvard University Press, 2011), 2; Maria Framke, "Encounters with Fascism and National Socialism in Non-European Regions," *South Asia Chronicle* 2 (2012): 351; Faisal Devji, *The Impossible Indian: Gandhi and the Temptation of Violence* (Cambridge, MA: Harvard University Press, 2012), 119.

3. John Patrick Haithcox, "The Roy-Lenin Debate on Colonial Policy: A New Interpretation," *Journal of Asian Studies* 23, no. 1 (1963): 96–7.

4. François Furet, *The Passing of an Illusion: The Idea of Communism in the Twentieth Century*, trans. Deborah Furet (Chicago: University of Chicago Press, 1999), 219–22.

5. Vladimir Ilyich Lenin, *Imperialism: The Highest Stage of Capitalism: A Popular Outline*, rev. trans. (1917; repr., New York: International Publishers, 1935), 112.

6. Rajani Palme Dutt, *Fascism and Social Revolution* (London: Martin Lawrence, 1934); Rajani Palme Dutt, "The Question of Fascism and Capitalist Decay," *Communist International* 12, no. 14 (1935), Marxists Internet Archive, retrieved February 11, 2024, https://www.marxists.org/archive/dutt/articles/1935/question_of_fascism.htm.

7. Mark Mazower, "Fascism and Democracy Today: What Use Is the Study of History in the Current Crisis?," *European Law Journal* 22, no. 3 (2016): 376–8; Gilbert Allardyce, "What Fascism Is Not: Thoughts on the Deflation of a Concept," *American Historical Review* 84 (1979): 370.

8. John Patrick Haithcox, *Communism and Nationalism in India* (Princeton, NJ: Princeton University Press, 1971), 290.

9. For decolonization, see Vineeta Sinha, "Benoy Kumar Sarkar," in *Sociological Theory beyond the Canon*, by Syad Farid Alatas and Vineeta Sinha (London: Palgrave Macmillan, 2017), 303–35; Syad Farid Alatas, "The Role of Human Sciences in the Dialogue among Civilizations," in *East Meets West: Civilizational Encounters and the Spirit of Capitalism in East Asia*, ed. Kyong-Dong Kim and Hyun Chin Lim (Leiden, Netherlands: Brill, 2007), 113; see similarly, and earlier, Swapan Kumar Bhattacharyya, *Indian Sociology: The Role of Benoy Kumar Sarkar* (Burdwan, India: University of Burdwan, 1990), iii. For globalization, see Farah Godrej, *Cosmopolitan Political Thought: Method, Practice, Discipline* (Oxford: Oxford University Press, 2011); Martin J. Bayly, "Global Intellectual History in International Relations: Hierarchy, Empire, and the Case of Late Colonial Indian International Thought," *Review of International Studies* 49, no. 3 (2023): 442–5.

10. See, for example, Carolien Stolte, "Orienting India: Interwar Internationalism in an Asian Inflection, 1917–1937" (PhD diss., University of Leiden, 2013), 19, 78–92; Ali Raza, Franziska Roy, and Benjamin Zachariah, "Introduction: The Internationalism of the Moment—South Asia and the Contours of the Interwar World," in *The Internationalist Moment: South Asia, Worlds, and World Views, 1917–1939*, ed. Ali Raza, Franziska Roy, and Benjamin Zachariah (Los Angeles: Sage, 2015), xi–xii.

11. See Satadru Sen, *Benoy Kumar Sarkar: Restoring the Nation to the World* (New Delhi: Routledge, 2014); Manu Goswami, "Imaginary Futures and Colonial Internationalisms," *American Historical Review* 117, no. 5 (2012): 1461–8; Kris Manjapra, *Age of Entanglement: German and Indian Intellectuals across Empire* (Cambridge, MA: Harvard University Press, 2014), 210; Benjamin Zachariah, "Rethinking (the Absence of) Fascism in India, c. 1922–1945," in *Cosmopolitan Thought Zones: South Asia and the Global Circulation of Ideas*, ed. Sugata Bose and Kris Manjapra (Basingstoke, UK: Palgrave Macmillan, 2010), 185; Maria Framke, *Delhi—Rom—Berlin: Die indische Wahrnehmung von Faschismus und Nationalsozialismus 1922–1939* (Darmstadt, Germany:

Wissenschaftliche Buchgesellschaft, 2012); Mario Prayer, "Creative India and the World: Bengali Internationalism and Italy in the Interwar Period," in Bose and Manjapra, *Cosmopolitan Thought Zones*, 236–42; Bhattacharyya, *Indian Sociology*, ix–xi; Giuseppe Flora, *Benoy Kumar Sarkar and Italy* (New Delhi: Italian Embassy Cultural Centre, 1994), 93–7.

12. See Zachariah, "Rethinking (the Absence of) Fascism," 185; Bhattacharyya, *Indian Sociology*, ix–xi, quote at xi.

13. See Sen, *Benoy Kumar Sarkar*, 61, 185–6.

14. See Stephen Legg, "Interwar Spatial Chaos? Imperialism, Internationalism and the League of Nations," in *Spatiality, Sovereignty and Carl Schmitt: Geographies of the Nomos*, ed. Stephen Legg (London: Routledge, 2011), 114; Carlo Gallo, "Carl Schmitt and the Global Age," trans. Elizabath Fay, *Centennial Review* 10, no. 2 (2010): 3; John P. McCormick, *Carl Schmitt's Critique of Liberalism: Against Politics as Technology* (Cambridge: Cambridge University Press, 1997). Schmitt dismisses Versailles and Geneva internationalism, for example, in Carl Schmitt, *Der Begriff des Politischen* (Hamburg: Hanseatische Verlagsanstalt, 1933), 54, 111–15.

15. Bhattacharyya, *Indian Sociology*, 20–1.

16. Flora, *Benoy Kumar Sarkar*, 47.

17. Haridas Mukherjee, *Benoy Kumar Sarkar: A Study* (Calcutta: Das Gupta, 1953), 7.

18. Benoy Kumar Sarkar, *Social Insurance Legislation and Statistics: A Study in the Labour Economies and Business Organization of Neo-Capitalism* (Calcutta: Calcutta Publishers, 1936), ii, iv; Goswami, "Imaginary Futures," 1480; Flora, *Benoy Kumar Sarkar*, 66.

19. For Ida and Indira Sarkar, see Jessica Namakkal, "Decolonizing Marriage and the Family: The Lives and Letters of Ida, Benoy, and Indira Sarkar," *Journal of Women's History* 31, no. 2 (2019): 124–47.

20. For Sarkar's influence on Haushofer's Weimar *Geopolitik*, see Luna Sabastian, "Spaces on the Temporal Move: Weimar *Geopolitik* and the Vision of an Indian Science of the State, 1924–1945," *Global Intellectual History* 3, no. 2 (2018): 231–53.

21. Ibid., 236.

22. Benoy Kumar Sarkar, *The Political Philosophies since 1905: Their Origins and Tendencies: An Objective and Chronological Survey: Outline of a Course of Lectures Given at the Kashi Vidyapitha, Benares in October 1927* (Madras: B. G. Paul, 1928), x.

23. Ibid., 12.

24. B. D. Basu, foreword to Sarkar, *Political Philosophies since 1905*, xxiv.

25. Benoy Kumar Sarkar, "Democratic Ideals and Republican Institutions in India," *American Political Science Review* 12, no. 4 (1918): 581.

26. Benoy Kumar Sarkar, *The Futurism of Young Asia and Other Essays on the Relations between the East and the West* (Berlin: Julius Springer, 1922); Edward W. Said, *Orientalism* (New York: Pantheon Books, 1978). See Sinha, "Benoy Kumar Sarkar," 309; Sen, *Benoy Kumar Sarkar*, 13; Goswami, "Imaginary Futures," 1471.

27. First published as Benoy Kumar Sarkar, "The Futurism of Young Asia," *International Journal of Ethics* 28, no. 4 (1918): 521–41.

28. Dipesh Chakrabarty, *Provincializing Europe: Postcolonial Thought and Historical Difference* (Princeton, NJ: Princeton University Press, 2000), 8.

29. Sabastian, "Spaces on the Temporal Move"; Goswami, "Imaginary Futures."

30. Sarkar, *Futurism*, 31.

31. Ibid., 38, 67–8.

32. Sarkar's disbelief that the Great War sounded the death knell of colonialism was shared across the colonies, as timely revisions of historian Erez Manela's thesis of a postwar "Wilsonian moment" have shown. See Erez Manela, *The Wilsonian Moment: Self-Determination and the International Origins of Anticolonial Nationalism* (Oxford: Oxford University Press, 2007). For a critique, see Adom Getachew, *Worldmaking after Empire: The Rise and Fall of Self-Determination* (Princeton, NJ: Princeton University Press, 2019), 39–43; Hussein A. H. Omar, "The Arab

Spring of 1919," *London Review of Books* (blog), April 4, 2019, https://www.lrb.co.uk/blog/2019/april/the-arab-spring-of-1919.

33. Sarkar, *Futurism*, 31.

34. Ibid., 342.

35. Ibid., 341, 32.

36. Ibid., 32.

37. Schmitt, *Begriff des Politischen*, 37. I am grateful to Samuel Zeitlin for pointing me to this passage.

38. Benoy Kumar Sarkar, *The Political Philosophies since 1905*, vol. 2, *The Epoch of Neo-Democracy and Neo-Socialism (1924–1941)*, part 1 (Lahore, India: Motilal Banarsi Dass, 1941), 50–1.

39. One who successfully walks this tightrope is Kurt Weyland, who recently explained the "riptide of democratic breakdown" in Europe due to the attempt to avoid both communism and fascism, resulting in a littering of autocratic regimes across the continent: Kurt Weyland, *Assault on Democracy: Communism, Fascism, and Authoritarianism during the Interwar Years* (Cambridge: Cambridge University Press, 2021), 17–18, 25–6 on Nolte.

40. Benoy Kumar Sarkar, "Demo-Despotocracy and Freedom," *Calcutta Review* 70, no. 1 (1939): 91–2.

41. Benoy Kumar Sarkar, "Stalin as the Manager of Leninism No. II," *Calcutta Review* 68, no. 3 (1938): 305.

42. Ibid., 314–15.

43. Benoy Kumar Sarkar, "The Hitler-State: A Landmark in the Political, Economic and Social Remaking of the German People" (Calcutta: The Insurance and Finance Review, 1933), 4.

44. Sarkar, "Stalin as the Manager," 314, 317.

45. Ibid., 305–6. Sarkar dated the New Economic Policy to 1922, the year money was reintroduced.

46. Ibid., 305–6.

47. Furet, *Passing of an Illusion*, 131, 146, even speaks of "what we might term 'the second Bolshevism' of Stalin," "the Second Bolshevism—National Bolshevism, Stalinist Bolshevism, or whatever we decide to call it."

48. Benoy Kumar Sarkar, "Creative Disequilibrium and Freedom," *Calcutta Review* 74, no. 1 (1940), 27.

49. Sarkar, *Political Philosophies since 1905*, 329; Sarkar, *Political Philosophies since 1905*, 2:1:37–53.

50. Adolf Hitler, *Mein Kampf: Eine kritische Edition*, ed. Christian Hartmann, Thomas Vordermayer, Othmar Plöckinger, and Roman Töppel, 2 vols (1925–26; repr., Munich: Institut für Zeitgeschichte, 2016), 2:1001, see also 2:1000–1, 2:1001n23.

51. Benoy Kumar Sarkar, *Politics of Boundaries and Tendencies in International Relations* (Calcutta: N. M. Ray-Chowdhury, 1926).

52. I am much indebted to Dimitry Okropiridze, Katja Rakow, and Adrian Heinrich for our discussions on "utopia" and "heterotopia" at the University of Heidelberg many years ago.

53. Michael Bergunder, "'Östliche' Religionen und Gewalt," in *Religion, Politik und Gewalt: Kongressband des XII. Europäischen Kongresses für Theologie 18.–22. September 2005 in Berlin*, ed. Friedrich Schweitzer (Gütersloh, Germany: Gütersloher Verlagshaus, 2006), 144–5.

54. Alfred Rosenberg, *Der Mythus des 20. Jahrhunderts: Eine Wertung der seelisch-geistigen Gestaltenkämpfe unserer Zeit* (Munich: Hoheneichen, 1939), 147.

55. Richard Coudenhove-Kalergi, "Ein Appell an Europa," *Kölnische Zeitung*, December 19, 1927, BArch R 4902/812, Bundesarchiv, Berlin-Lichterfelde; Volker Zotz, "Zum Verhältnis von Buddhismus und Nationalsozialismus," *Zeitschrift für Religionswissenschaft* 25, no. 1 (2017): 9–10; Houston Stewart Chamberlain, *Arische Weltanschauung*, 3rd rev. and expanded ed. (1905; repr., Munich: F. Bruckmann, 1916), 42–6.

56. "Aufzeichung über die Unterredung zwischen dem Führer und dem indischen Nationalistenführer Bose in Berlin am 29. Mai 1942," in *Staatsmänner und Diplomaten bei Hitler:*

Vertrauliche Aufzeichnungen über Unterredungen mit Vertretern des Auslandes 1942–1944, ed. Andreas Hillgruber, 2 vols. (Frankfurt am Main: Bernard & Graefe Verlag für Wehrwesen, 1970), 2:86; Hitler, *Mein Kampf*, 2:1663–7.

57. Max Deeg, "Aryan National Religion(s) and the Criticism of Asceticism and Quietism in the Nineteenth and Twentieth Centuries," in *Asceticism and Its Critics: Historical Accounts and Comparative Perspectives*, ed. Oliver Freiberger (Oxford: Oxford University Press, 2006), 63–4.

58. Rolf-Peter Sieferle, "Indien und die Arier in der Rassentheorie," *Zeitschrift für Kulturaustausch* 37, no. 3 (1987): 458.

59. Rosenberg, *Mythus*, 267.

60. Sarkar, *Futurism*, 323, 340–2.

61. Schmitt, *Begriff des Politischen*.

62. Alfred Rosenberg, "Menschheitsdogmen: Auf gut Deutsch," December 3, 1920, in *Blut und Ehre: Ein Kampf für deutsche Wiedergeburt: Reden und Aufsätze von 1919–1933*, ed. Thilo von Trotha (Munich: Zentralverlag der NSDAP, F. Eher, 1939), 195.

63. Shruti Kapila, *Violent Fraternity: Indian Political Thought in the Global Age* (Princeton, NJ: Princeton University Press, 2021), building on Alain Badiou, *The Century*, trans. Alberto Toscano (Cambridge: Polity Press, 2007).

64. Sarkar, *Futurism*, 257, 267, 272; Benoy Kumar Sarkar, *Chinese Religion through Hindu Eyes: A Study in the Tendencies of Asiatic Mentality* (Shanghai: Commercial Press, 1916).

65. Sarkar, *Futurism*, 166 (italics and bold in the original).

66. See especially Jyotirmaya Sharma, *A Restatement of Religion: Swami Vivekananda and the Making of Hindu Nationalism* (New Haven, CT: Yale University Press, 2013).

67. Benoy Kumar Sarkar, *The Might of Man in the Social Philosophy of Ramakrishna and Vivekananda* (Madras: Sri Ramakrishna Math, 1945), 22; Benoy Kumar Sarkar, *The Aesthetics of Young India* (Calcutta: Kar, Majumder, 1922), quote at 10. For non-Vedantic and tantric aspects of Ramakrishna and Vivekananda, see Ruth Harris, *Guru to the World: The Life and Legacy of Vivekananda* (Cambridge, MA: Belknap Press of Harvard University Press, 2022).

68. Ruth Harris, "Vivekananda: Indian Swami and Global Guru," *Religions* 14, no. 8 (2023): 1041; Ruth Harris, "Broken Friendship and the History of South Asian Religious Modernisms: The Case of Swami Vivekananda and Anagarika Dharmapala," *International Journal of Hindu Studies* 29 no. 1 (2025): 64.

69. See Pradip Kumar Datta, "Rabindranath Tagore's Theology of Work," *Economic and Political Weekly* 52, no. 19 (2017): 40–5.

70. See Vishwanath Prasad Varma, *Modern Indian Political Thought* (Agra, India: Lakshmi Narain Agarwal, 1961), 105–7; for Tagore on harmony, see Pradip Kumar Datta, "Tagore and the Theology of the Global," June 16, 2016, Asian Studies Centre, University of Oxford, podcast, http://podcasts.ox.ac.uk/tagore-and-theology-global.

71. For conceptions of the oneness of the *brahman* in nineteenth-century Bengal, see Brian A. Hatcher, *Bourgeois Hinduism, or The Faith of the Modern Vedantists: Rare Discourses from Early Colonial Bengal* (Oxford: Oxford University Press, 2008), 92–7.

72. Sarkar, *Chinese Religion*, 303, 279.

73. Benoy Kumar Sarkar, "Creative Disequilibrium and Freedom," *Calcutta Review* 74, no. 1 (1940): 29–30.

74. Benoy Kumar Sarkar, *Villages and Towns as Social Patterns* (Calcutta: Chuckervertty, Chatterjee, 1941), vii.

75. Subhas Chandra Bose, *An Indian Pilgrim*, in Subhas Chandra Bose, *Netaji: Collected Works*, ed. Sisir Kumar Bose and Sugata Bose, 12 vols. (Calcutta: Netaji Research Bureau, 1980–2007), 1:122.

76. Ibid., 1:70, 63.

77. Ibid., 1:78.

78. Vinayak Damodar Savarkar, *My Transportation for Life* (1927; repr., Bombay: Veer Savarkar Prakashan, 1984), 273, quoted in Tobias Delfs, *Hindu-Nationalismus und europäischer Faschismus:*

Vergleich, Transfer- und Beziehungsgeschichte (Inklusive der Ersten Auflage von M. S. Golwalkar's "We or Our Nationhood defined" aus dem Jahre 1939 und mit einem Geleitwort von Hermann Kulke (Hamburg-Schenefeld, Germany: EB-Verlag, 2008), 58n14.

79. Bose to Dilip Kumar Roy, October 9, 1925, in Bose, *Netaji*, 2:132.

80. Bose, *Indian Pilgrim*, 121, 123–4; Subhas Chandra Bose, "My Personal Testament," November 29, 1940, in Bose, *Netaji*, 10:141–2.

81. Sarkar, "Creative Disequilibrium and Freedom," 29.

82. Sarkar, *Villages and Towns*, 525.

83. Ibid., 246, 127.

84. Sarkar, "Hitler-State," 1–2, quotes at 5 and 6.

85. Furet, *Passing of an Illusion*, 22.

86. See Reinhart Koselleck, "Die Verzeitlichung der Utopie," in *Utopieforschung: Interdisziplinäre Studien zur neuzeitlichen Utopie*, ed. Wilhelm Vosskamp (Stuttgart: Metzler, 1982), 3:1–14; Goswami, "Imaginary Futures," 1462–3.

87. Kris Manjapra, *M. N. Roy: Marxism and Colonial Cosmopolitanism* (Delhi: Routledge, 2010), 20.

88. M. N. Roy, *M. N. Roy's Memoirs* (Bombay: Allied Publishers, 1960), 503.

89. Haithcox, *Communism and Nationalism*, 288, 290.

90. Manjapra, *M. N. Roy*, 128–34.

91. M. N. Roy, *Fascism: Its Philosophy, Professions and Practice* (Calcutta: D. M. Library, 1938).

92. Ibid., 3–4.

93. Ibid., 7.

94. Ibid., 42.

95. Ibid., 44.

96. Hatcher, *Bourgeois Hinduism*.

97. Roy, *Fascism*, 44–45.

98. Ibid., 55. The reference is to Hitler's speech at a rally in Erfurt on June 18, 1933, which was reported in the Anglophone press in identical wording: Sidney B. Fay, "The Nazi 'Totalitarian' State," *Current History (1916–1940)* 38, no. 5 (1933): 615. The original German text read: "[Wir] verdienen, dass man uns einst auf die Grabsteine schreibt: Sie sind oft rauh gewesen, sie sind hart gewesen, sie waren rücksichtslos, aber sie sind gewesen: Gute Deutsche," cited in "Das neue Erfurter Programm: Der Führer bei der Gautagung der N.S.D.A.P.-Thüringen: Aufmarsch von 60,000 S.A.- und S.S.-Männern und der Hitler-Jugend in Erfurt," *Völkischer Beobachter* (North German edition) 46, no. 171 (1933): 1.

99. Roy, *Fascism*, 55.

100. Ibid., 48–50.

101. Shruti Kapila, "Ambedkar's Agonism: Sovereign Violence and Pakistan as Peace," *Comparative Studies of South Asia, Africa and the Middle East* 39, no. 1 (2019): 188.

102. Roy, *Fascism*, 47.

103. For Tilak's Gita, see Shruti Kapila, "A History of Violence," *Modern Intellectual History* 7, no. 2 (2010): 437–57.

104. Roy, *Fascism*, 64.

105. Ibid., 14.

106. Ibid., 19.

107. Ibid., 17.

108. Ibid., 18.

109. Ibid., 17.

110. Ibid., 18.

111. Henri Bergson, *Creative Evolution*, trans. Arthur Mitchell (1907; repr., New York: Henry Holt, 1911), 272–98.

112. Ibid., 276.

113. Ibid., 286–7.

114. Ibid., 290.
115. Gilles Deleuze, *Bergsonism*, trans. Hugh Tomlinson and Barbara Habberjam (New York: Zone Books, 1991), 103.
116. Roy, *Fascism*, 20–1.
117. Subhas Chandra Bose, "The Need for Transformation in Freedom's Cause," December 1, 1929, in Bose, *Netaji*, 6:83; Sarkar, *Might of Man*, 33.
118. Christopher Balcom, "From Communist Internationalism to a 'New Humanism': On M. N. Roy's Confrontation with Fascism," *South Asia: Journal of South Asian Studies* 46, no. 2 (2023): 353–69.
119. Haithcox, *Communism and Nationalism*, 298; Balcom, "From Communist Internationalism"; Disha Karnad Jani, "The Concept of Fascism in Colonial India: M. N. Roy and The Problem of Freedom," *Global Histories* 3, no. 2 (2017): 128–35.
120. Ernst Nolte, *Der europäische Bürgerkrieg 1917–1945: Nationalsozialismus und Bolschewismus* (Berlin: Propyläen Verlag, 1987).
121. Often overlooked is the competition of Leftist causes, as fighting fascism in Europe sapped European Leftist support for fighting colonialism out in the world: see Tom Buchanan, "'The Dark Millions in the Colonies Are Unavenged': Anti-Fascism and Anti-Imperialism in the 1930s," *Contemporary European History* 25, no. 4 (2016): 645–65.
122. Of course, this was a question already asked by contemporaries: Hira Lal Seth, *Personality and Political Ideals of Subhas Chandra Bose: Is He Fascist?* (Lahore, India: Hero Publications, 1944).
123. For Bose's biography, see Bose, *His Majesty's Opponent*; Bose, *Indian Pilgrim*.
124. Whether Bose and Schenkl underwent a legal marriage ceremony is disputed but beside the point. He acknowledged her and their child: see Leonard A. Gordon, *Brothers against the Raj: A Biography of Indian Nationalists Sarat and Subhas Chandra Bose* (New York: Columbia University Press, 1990), 344–45, 447.
125. Bose to Amrita Bazar Patrika, March 9, 1935, in Bose, *Netaji*, 8:290.
126. Bose to Franz Thierfelder, March 25, 1935, in Bose, *Netaji*, 8:165.
127. Bose to Thierfelder, November 7, 1935, in Bose, *Netaji*, 8:113; see also Subhas Chandra Bose, "Germany and India," to C. R. Prufer, April 5, 1934, in Bose, *Netaji*, 8:62–4.
128. Subhas Chandra Bose, "Statement," *Āzād Hind*, no. 3/4 (1942): 15; Subhas Chandra Bose, "Bose's Statement (over Berlin Short-Wave Station)," *Āzād Hind*, no. 5/6 (1942): 7.
129. Subhas Chandra Bose, "The Tripuri Address," March 1939, in Bose, *Netaji*, 9:92–3.
130. Gandhi to Bose, April 2, 1939, in Bose, *Netaji*, 9:145.
131. Bose to Gandhi, March 25, 1939, in Bose, *Netaji*, 9:128.
132. Gandhi to Bose, April 2, 1939, in Bose, *Netaji*, 9:144.
133. Bose to Gandhi, April 13, 1939, in Bose, *Netaji*, 9:171–2.
134. Gandhi to Bose, April 17, 1939, in Bose, *Netaji*, 9:176.
135. Subhas Chandra Bose, "Forward Bloc: Its Justification," March 22, 1941, in Bose, *Netaji*, 11:19; Subhas Chandra Bose, "A Reminder," in Bose, *Netaji*, 10:50.
136. Subhas Chandra Bose, *The Indian Struggle, 1920–1942*, in Bose, *Netaji*, 2:30.
137. Ibid., 77.
138. Ibid., 252.
139. Ibid., 327.
140. Ibid., 328.
141. Bose, "Forward Bloc," 13.
142. Jawaharlal Nehru to Bose, February 4, 1939, in Bose, *Netaji*, 9:185.
143. Nehru to Bose, April 3, 1939, in Bose, *Netaji*, 9:225.
144. Subhas Chandra Bose, "Whom They Fight?," November 25, 1939, in Bose, *Netaji*, 10:40; see also Subhas Chandra Bose, "Forward Bloc in Perspective," in July to December 1940, in Bose, *Netaji*, 10:136–7.
145. Bose, *Indian Struggle*, 342.

146. Subhas Chandra Bose, "Full Support to Gandhi," August 1942, in Bose, *Netaji*, 11:123.
147. Bose, "Forward Bloc," 19.
148. Subhas Chandra Bose, "The Ramgarh Address," March 19, 1940, in Bose, *Netaji*, 10:87.
149. Bose, "Forward Bloc," 27.
150. Ibid., 18, 27.
151. Bose, *His Majesty's Opponent*, 234; Bose, *Indian Struggle*, 377.
152. "Aufzeichnung über die Unterredung," 81.
153. Subhas Chandra Bose, "An Address to Students of India," January 1940, in Bose, *Netaji*, 10:58–9.
154. See, for example, Hans-Bernd Zöllner, *"Der Feind meines Feindes ist mein Freund": Subhas Chandra Bose und das zeitgenössische Deutschland unter dem Nationalsozialismus, 1933–1943* (Münster, Germany: Lit, 2000); Jan Kuhlmann, *Subhas Chandra Bose und die Indienpolitik der Achsenmächte* (Berlin: Schiler, 2003); Romain Hayes, *Subhas Chandra Bose in Nazi Germany: Politics, Intelligence and Propaganda 1941–43* (London: Hurst, 2011); Milan Hauner, *India in Axis Strategy: Germany, Japan and Indian Nationalists in the Second World War* (Stuttgart: Klett-Cotta, 1981).
155. On the "event," see Kapila, *Violent Fraternity*, 40–2.
156. Subhas Chandra Bose, "Europe—Today and Tomorrow," September 1937, in Bose, *Netaji*, 8:398.
157. Subhas Chandra Bose, "The Nagpur Address," June 18, 1940, in Bose, *Netaji*, 10:121; Bose, *Indian Pilgrim*, 91–2.
158. For Shedai and the Battaliogne Azad Hindoustan (Free India Battalion) in Italy, see Kuhlmann, *Subhas Chandra Bose*, 111–15, 182–6, 241–3, 276–92.
159. Vinayak Damodar Savarkar [An Indian Nationalist, pseud.], *The Indian War of Independence of 1857* (S.l.: s.n., 1909); Subhas Chandra Bose, "Subhas Chandra Bose's Speech on the Occasion of the Independence Day on January 26, 1943 in Berlin, 'Haus der Flieger,'" *Āzād Hind*, no. 1/2 (1943): 17. On the Ghadr, see Kapila, *Violent Fraternity*, 53–88.
160. Bose, "Subhas Chandra Bose's Speech on the Occasion of the Independence Day."
161. Mukund R. Vyas, *Passage through a Turbulent Era: Historical Reminiscences of the Fateful Years 1937–47* (Bombay: Indo-Foreign Publications & Publicity, 1982), 269–71.
162. Bose, "Ramgarh Address," 85.
163. Ibid., 86.
164. Ibid., 87.
165. See Kapila, *Violent Fraternity*.
166. Subhas Chandra Bose, "Subhas Chandra Bose's Speech on the Occasion of the Foundation of the Indo-German Society in Hamburg," *Azad Hind*, no. 7/8 (1942): 8.
167. Bose, "Address to Students," 63.
168. Bose, *His Majesty's Opponent*, 188.
169. Vyas, *Passage*, 276; Bhagat Ram Talwar, "The Great Escape: My Fifty-Five Days with Netaji Subhas Chandra Bose," in *Netaji and India's Freedom: Proceedings of the International Netaji Seminar, 1973*, ed. Sisir Kumar Bose (Calcutta: Netaji Research Bureau, 1975), 156. For Germany as the destination, see Bose, *His Majesty's Opponent*, 195. This interpretation is borne out by another companion of the Kabul period: "Report of Mr. Santimoy Ganguli," in appendix 2 of Vyas, *Passage*, 248.
170. Alexander Werth, "An Assessment of Netaji's Policy of Cooperation with the Axis Powers during World War II," in Bose, *Netaji and India's Freedom*, 255–6.
171. Bose, *His Majesty's Opponent*, 205.
172. Joseph Goebbels, April 5, 1942, in *Die Tagebücher von Joseph Goebbels*, ed. Elke Fröhlich for the Institute of Zeitgeschichte, 31 vol. (Munich: K. G. Saur, 1993–2008), part 2, 4:51.
173. Hauner, *India in Axis Strategy*, 29–31, 365, 434–6.
174. Vyas, *Passage*, 326; Gordon, *Brothers against the Raj*, 468, 470.

175. Subhas Chandra Bose, "Presidential Address at the Maharashtra Provincial Conference, Poona," May 3, 1928, in Bose, *Netaji,* 5:250.
176. Bose, *His Majesty's Opponent,* 78.
177. Subhas Chandra Bose, "My Death Is Perhaps an Instance of Wishful Thinking," March 25, 1942, in Bose, *Netaji,* 11:77.
178. Mohandas Karamchand Gandhi, *Hind Swaraj, or: Indian Home Rule* (1909; repr., Madras: G.A. Natesan, 1921), 26.
179. Subhas Chandra Bose, "Speech from Tokyo," 1943, https://archive.org/details/HindSwaraj-Speech-02-8.
180. Archibald Wavell to Frederick Pethik-Laurence, October 22, 1945, "Private and Secret Weekly Letters between the Secretary of State for India and the Viceroy (Printed)," January–December 1945, vol. 2, p. 286, IOR/L/PO/10/22, India Office Records and Private Papers, British Library.
181. Hayes, *Subhas Chandra Bose,* 121; Gordon, *Brothers Against the Raj,* 459–60; Rudolf Hartog, *Im Zeichen des Tigers: Die Indische Legion auf deutscher Seite, 1941–1945* (Herford, Germany: Busse Seewald, 1991), 71–4.
182. Devji, *Impossible Indian,* 29.
183. Subhas Chandra Bose, "Towards Communal Unity," February 24, 1940, in Bose, *Netaji,* 10:8–1.
184. Nehru, April 12, 1942, cited in Hayes, *Subhas Chandra Bose,* 102.
185. Subhas Chandra Bose, "The Quit India Movement," August 17, 1942, in Bose, *Netaji,* 11:128.
186. Ibid., 130.
187. Subhas Chandra Bose, "The Pledge of the INA," June 1942, in Bose, *Netaji,* 11:107.
188. Subhas Chandra Bose, "The Bluff and Bluster Corporation of British Imperialists," March 1, 1943, in Bose, *Netaji,* 11:188.
189. Sri Aurobindo, *The Complete Works of Sri Aurobindo,* vol. 35, *Letters on Himself and the Ashram* (Pondicherry: Sri Aurobindo Ashram Press, 2011), 195.
190. Bose, *His Majesty's Opponent,* 251.
191. Jawaharlal Nehru, foreword to *My Memories of I.N.A. & Its Netaji,* by Shah Nawaz Khan (Delhi: Rajkamal Publications, 1946).
192. Netaji Papers, National Archives of India. Accessible online at https://nationalarchives.nic.in/online-records-national-archives-india/netaji-papers.
193. Bose, *Indian Struggle,* 351–2.
194. Ibid., 398–9.
195. For sympathetic scholars, see, for example, Kuhlmann, *Subhas Chandra Bose,* 22–3. For his retraction, see Maria Tumiotto, "Strategy or Fascination? Subhas Chandra Bose's Relations with Fascist Italy and Nazi Germany, and the Making of *Sāmyavāda* (1930s–1940s)," *Global Intellectual History* (2023): 10.
196. Subhas Chandra Bose, "The Mayoral Address," September 27, 1930, in Bose, *Netaji,* 6:128.
197. Subhas Chandra Bose, "The Fundamental Problems of India," November 1944, in Bose, *Netaji,* 12:298–9.
198. Bose, *Indian Struggle,* 351.
199. Tumiotto, "Strategy or Fascination?," 3; Bose, *His Majesty's Opponent,* 98.
200. Subhas Chandra Bose, "India Freed Means Humanity Saved," May 26, 1931, in Bose, *Netaji,* 6:181–5, quote at 185.
201. Subhas Chandra Bose, "The Anti-Imperialist Struggle and Samyavada," June 10, 1933, in Bose, *Netaji,* 8:256.
202. Subhas Chandra Bose, "India's History Mission," April 5, 1931, in Bose, *Netaji,* 6:152; Bose, "India Freed," 181.
203. Bose, *Indian Struggle,* 352.
204. Bose, "Fundamental Problems," 299.

205. Bose, "My Personal Testament," 140.
206. Ibid., 142.
207. Bose, "Subhas Chandra Bose's Speech on the Occasion of the Independence Day," 15.
208. M. R. Vyas, "The Future of Communism in India," *Āzād Hind*, no. 2 (1942): 28.
209. Gautam Chattopadhyay, *Subhas Chandra Bose and Indian Communist Movement: Study of Cooperation and Conflict* (New Delhi: People's Publishing House, 1973), 8.
210. Bose, "Fundamental Problems," 295.
211. Bose, "Anti-Imperialist Struggle," 256.
212. Subhas Chandra Bose, "What Romain Rolland Thinks," July 2, 1935, in Bose, *Netaji*, 8:305.
213. Bose, "Anti-Imperialist Struggle," 255; Bose, "Fundamental Problems," 295.
214. Bose, "What Romain Rolland," 305.
215. Bose, "Anti-Imperialist Struggle," 262–3.
216. Bose, *Indian Struggle*, 352; Bose to Kitty Kurti, February 23, 1934, in Bose, *Netaji*, 8:56. For Kurti and Bose's association, see Kitty Kurti, *Subhas Chandra Bose as I Knew Him* (Calcutta: Firma K. L. Mukhopadhyay, 1966).
217. Bose, "Anti-Imperialist Struggle," 263.
218. Bose to Kurti, 8:56.
219. Bose, "Anti-Imperialist Struggle," 261–2; also Bose, *Indian Struggle*, 329.
220. Subhas Chandra Bose, "The Role of the Young in Our National Life," November 29, 1929, in Bose, *Netaji*, 6:64–6, quote at 66.
221. Bose, "Fundamental Problems," 295.
222. Bose, *Indian Struggle*, 350; Bose, "Fundamental Problems," 295.
223. Bose, "Fundamental Problems," 298; Bose, *Indian Struggle*, 352; contrast my reading with Tumiotto, "Strategy or Fascination."
224. Bose, "Fundamental Problems," 289–9.
225. Bose, "India Freed," 182.
226. Bose, "Fundamental Problems," 299.
227. Ibid.
228. Subhas Chandra Bose, "Heart Searching," October 28, 1938, in Bose, *Netaji*, 10:18–20.
229. Bose, *Indian Pilgrim*, 4–6.
230. Bose to Anil Chandra Ganguli, August 8, 1937, in Bose, *Netaji*, 8:216.
231. On *vishwashakti*, see also Sen, *Benoy Kumar Sarkar*, 9; Giuseppe Flora, *The Evolution of Positivism in Bengal: Jogendra Chandra Ghosh, Bakimchandra Chattopadhyay, Benoy Kumar Sarkar* (Naples, Italy: Istituto Universitario Orientale, 1993).
232. Gordon, *Brothers against the Raj*, 614.
233. Sarkar, "Stalin as the Manager," 314–15.
234. Benoy Kumar Sarkar, "The People and the State in Neo-Democracy," *Calcutta Review* 60, no. 1 (1936): 64.
235. Otto Koellreutter, *Grundriß der allgemeinen Staatslehre* (Tübingen, Germany: J. C. B. Mohr [Paul Siebeck], 1933), 41; Sarkar, "People and the State," 64.
236. Sarkar, "People and the State," 65.
237. Koellreutter, *Grundriß der allgemeinen Staatslehre*, 185.
238. Furet, *Passing of an Illusion*, 206.
239. See Herlinde Pauer-Studer, introduction to *Rechtfertigungen des Unrechts: Das Rechtsdenken im Nationalsozialismus in Originaltexten*, ed. Pauer-Studer and Julian Fink (Berlin: Suhrkamp, 2014), 42–50, esp. 43.
240. Sarkar, "People and the State," 65–6.
241. Koellreutter, *Grundriß der allgemeinen Staatslehre*, 15.
242. Sarkar, "Hitler-State," 3–4.
243. "Index to Proscribed Literature for the Years 1946–52," in "Publication of—and up to Date List of Prescribed Literature," 1934, serial no. 232, file no. 1654/34, p. 27, Intelligence Branch Files, State Archives of West Bengal, Kolkata.

244. Sarkar, "Demo-Despotocracy and Freedom," 93.
245. Sarkar, *Villages and Towns,* 97; Geoffrey T. Garratt, *Europe's Dance of Death* (London: Gallen & Unwin, 1940), 133.
246. See S. E. Finer, "Pareto and Pluto-Democracy: The Retreat to Galapagos," *American Political Science Review* 62, no. 2 (1968): 440–50.
247. Garratt, *Europe's Dance of Death,* 105, 141.
248. Edmund Fawcett, *Liberalism: The Life of an Idea* (Princeton, NJ: Princeton University Press, 2015), 21; Carl Schmitt, *Die geistesgeschichtliche Lage des heutigen Parlamentarismus,* 2nd ed. (Munich: Duncker & Humblot, 1926), 5–23.
249. Sarkar, *Villages and Towns,* 92.
250. Sarkar, "Demo-Despotocracy and Freedom," 91–2.
251. See Sen, *Benoy Kumar Sarkar,* 152, 2.
252. Emma Hunter, "Languages of Freedom in Decolonising Africa," *Transactions of the Royal Historical Society* 27 (2017): 268.
253. Geoffrey T. Garratt, *Mussolini's Roman Empire* (Harmondsworth, UK: Penguin, 1938), 22–3; Richard J. Overy, *The Morbid Age: Britain and the Crisis of Civilisation* (London: Penguin, 2010), 356.
254. Sarkar, *Political Philosophies since 1905,* 125, 127. He discusses Hugo Krabbe, *Die Lehre der Rechtssouveränität: Beitrag zur Staatslehre* (Groningen, Netherlands: W. B. Wolters, 1906), and Hugo Krabbe, *Die moderne Staatsidee* (Leiden, Netherlands: Nijhoff, 1915).
255. Sarkar, *Political Philosophies since 1905,* 127–8.
256. Schmitt, *Politische Theologie: Vier Kapitel zur Lehre von der Souveränität,* 8th ed. (1922; repr., Berlin: Duncker & Humblot, 2004), 14–29.
257. Sarkar, *Political Philosophies since 1905,* 128.
258. Cf. Sen, *Benoy Kumar Sarkar,* 24.
259. Sarkar, *Political Philosophies since 1905,* vol. 2, three parts.
260. Benito Mussolini, *The Doctrine of Fascism,* trans. E. Cope, 3rd ed. (Florence, Italy: Vallecchi, 1938).
261. Benoy Kumar Sarkar, "Miscellany: The Corporative State as an Expression of Fascist Totalitarianism," *Calcutta Review* 68, no. 2 (1938): 233; Mussolini, *Doctrine of Fascism,* 38.
262. Sarkar, "Corporative State," 233–4.
263. Mussolini, *Doctrine of Fascism,* 33–4.
264. Ibid., 40.
265. Ibid., 14.
266. Sarkar, "Stalin as the Manager," 317.
267. Sarkar, *Political Philosophies since 1905,* 2:1:53.
268. Sarkar, "People and the State," 64.
269. Hannah Arendt, *The Origins of Totalitarianism* (1951; repr., New York: Schocken Books, 2004), 415; Jacob L. Talmon, *The Origins of Totalitarian Democracy* (London: Secker & Warburg, 1952), 6. However, Talmon reserved the phrase "democratic totalitarianism" for totalitarianism on the Left.
270. Sarkar, "Demo-Despotocracy and Freedom," 94, 96.
271. Ibid., 88.
272. Ibid., 93.
273. Ibid., 88.
274. Ibid., 77; Benoy Kumar Sarkar, "Hindu Theory of International Relations," *American Political Science Review* 13, no. 3 (1919): 408, Sen, *Benoy Kumar Sarkar,* 106, 112, 154.
275. See Kinch Hoekstra, "The *De Facto* Turn in Hobbes's Political Philosophy," in *Leviathan after 350 Years,* ed. Tom Sorell and Luc Foisneau (Oxford: Clarendon, 2004), 51–4, 57.
276. Benoy Kumar Sarkar, "Hindu Political Philosophy," *Political Science Quarterly* 33, no. 4 (1918): 498.

277. Benoy Kumar Sarkar, "Democratic Ideals and Republican Institutions in India," *American Political Science Review* 12, no. 4 (1918): 584; see also Benoy Kumar Sarkar, review of *Indian Constitutional Reform,* by Vicent A. Smith; *The Government of India,* by J. Ramsay MacDonald; and *The Political Future of India,* by Lala Lajpat Rai, all in *Political Science Quarterly* 35, no. 2 (1920): 298–9.
278. Benoy Kumar Sarkar, review of *A History of the Indian Nationalist Movement,* by Verney Lovett, *Political Science Quarterly* 36, no. 1 (1921): 137.
279. See Richard Tuck, *The Sleeping Sovereign: The Invention of Modern Democracy* (Cambridge: Cambridge University Press, 2016), 104–6, 126–41.
280. Benoy Kumar Sarkar, *The Political Institutions and Theories of the Hindus: A Study in Comparative Politics* (Leipzig: Markert & Petters, 1922), 1.
281. Sarkar, "Demo-Despotocracy and Freedom," 89.
282. Quentin Skinner, "Thomas Hobbes's Antiliberal Theory of Liberty," in *Liberalism without Illusions: Essays on Liberal Theory and the Political Vision of Judith N. Shklar,* ed. Bernard Yack (Chicago: University of Chicago Press, 1996), 161–4; see also Hoekstra, "*De Facto* Turn," 56–7. For Sarkar's view, see Sarkar, "Demo-Despotocracy and Freedom," 89.
283. Sarkar, "Demo-Despotocracy and Freedom," 87, 89.
284. Ibid., 92, 104.
285. Sarkar, *Social Insurance Legislation,* i.
286. Sarkar, *Villages and Towns,* 481, quote at 487.
287. Sarkar, *Political Philosophies since 1905,* 2:1:185.
288. Sarkar, *Social Insurance Legislation,* i.

Chapter Two: Savarkar's Miscegenous Race

1. Prem Datta Sharma to Vinayak Damodar Savarkar, July 26, 1940, reel no. 6, file no. c-7-38, p. 317, Veer Savarkar Papers, Nehru Memorial Museum and Library, New Delhi.

A note on the Veer Savarkar Papers is in order. First, microfilm reels one to five are damaged and no longer accessible to researchers, at least not to me. Second, the catalogue does not reflect the actual state of disarray of files contained on each microfilm reel. For citing a particular item, the library staff recommend a system of *approx karna* ("to approximate"). A system in this spirit but offering maximum guidance to future researchers was followed here. My system notes the reel number, page number, and date, as well as the file number that would be expected from the catalogue, except in cases where a particular folio could be unambiguously identified to belong to a different file, where a file number is given instead.
2. By order of the President Savarkar to Sharma, August 5, 1940, reel no. 6, file no. 3-c-15-46, p. 136, Veer Savarkar Papers.
3. Vinayak Damodar Savarkar [A Maratha, pseud.], *Essentials of Hindutva* (Nagpur, India: V. V. Kelkar, 1923).
4. For Savarkar's biography, see Dhananjay Keer, *Savarkar and His Times* (Bombay: A. V. Keer, 1950); Vikram Sampath, *Savarkar: Echoes from a Forgotten Past 1883–1924* (Gurgaon, India: Penguin Viking, 2019); Vikram Sampath, *Savarkar: A Contested Legacy, 1924–1966* (New Delhi: Penguin, 2021). For the early, revolutionary years, see Harindra Srivastava, *Five Stormy Years: Savarkar in London (June 1906—June 1911): A Centenary Salute to Swatantrayaveer Vinayak Damodar Savarkar* (New Delhi: Allied, 1983); Vinayak Chaturvedi, "A Revolutionary's Biography: The Case of V D Savarkar," *Postcolonial Studies* 16, no. 2 (2013): 124–39; John Pincince, "On the Verge of *Hindutva*: V. D. Savarkar, Revolutionary, Convict, Ideologue, c. 1905–1924" (PhD diss., University of Hawai'i at Mānoa, 2007); see also Vinayak Damodar Savarkar [Chitragupta, pseud.], *The Life of Barrister Savarkar* (Madras: B. G. Paul, 1926).
5. For Tilak's political thought, see Shruti Kapila, "A History of Violence," *Modern Intellectual History* 7, no. 2 (2010): 437–57.
6. Luna Sabastian, "History, International Radicalism and the Revolutionary in the Political Thought of Vinayak Damodar Savarkar, ca. 1906–1923" (MPhil diss., University of Cambridge,

2015), 22–42; Gita Srivastava, *Mazzini and His Impact on the Indian National Movement* (Allahabad, India: Chugh Publications, 1982), 238–43; Enrico Fasana, "Deshbhakta: The Leaders of the Italian Independence Movement in the Eyes of Marathi Nationalists," in *Writers, Editors and Reformers: Social and Political Transformations of Maharashtra, 1830–1930*, ed. N. K. Wagle (New Delhi: Manohar, 1999), 45–9; Chaturvedi, "A Revolutionary's Biography," 132–3.

7. For Krishnavarma's India House, see Harald Fischer-Tiné, *Sanskrit, Sociology and Anti-Imperial Struggle: The Life of Shyamji Krishnavarma (1857–1930)* (Delhi: Routledge India, 2014); Alex Tickell, *Terrorism, Insurgency and Indian-English Literature, 1830–1947* (New York: Routledge, 2012).

8. Guy Aldred, "'Hindu' Defined," *The Word* 8, no. 10 (1947): 118.

9. V. Krishnaswamy Iyer, in *Essentials of Hinduism* (Madras: G. A. Natesan, [1912]), 39–40.

10. Thomas Blom Hansen, *The Saffron Wave: Democracy and Nationalism in Modern India* (Princeton, NJ: Princeton University Press, 1999), 60–5, 77–80; Shruti Kapila, *Violent Fraternity: Indian Political Thought in the Global Age* (Princeton, NJ: Princeton University Press, 2021), 96–104.

11. Though the term "Hindutva" circulated in Bengal even prior to Chandranath Basu penning a work of that name in 1892 (on this, see Amiya P. Sen, ed., *Hindutva before Hindutva: Writings and Discourses of Chandranath Basu* [Abingdon, UK: Routledge, 2025]), Savarkar coined the current meaning of the term. He, not Basu, is the "father" of Hindutva. "Hindutva" is traditionally regarded as a compound of "Hindu" and *tva*, or "-ness." A different etymology has been proposed by Vinayak Chaturvedi, *Hindutva and Violence: V. D. Savarkar and the Politics of History* (Albany: State University of New York Press, 2022), 141, that combines "Hindu" with *tattva*, or "essence," to form "the Hindu's essence."

12. Blom Hansen, *Saffron Wave*, 60–5, 77–80.

13. Savarkar, *Essentials of Hindutva*, 95, 92.

14. See, for example, Janaki Bakhle, "Country First? Vinayak Damodar Savarkar (1883–1966) and the Writing of *Essentials of Hindutva*," *Public Culture* 22, no. 1 (2010): 177, 179–80; Chetan Bhatt, *Hindu Nationalism: Origins, Ideologies and Modern Myths* (Oxford: Berg, 2001), 98–9; Siegfried Wolf, "Die Konstruktion einer kollektiven Identität: Vinayak Damodar Savarkar und sein Hindutva-Konzept" (PhD diss., Ruprecht-Karls Universität Heidelberg, 2009), 133, 345.

15. Savarkar, *Essentials of Hindutva*, 99–100.

16. For a scholarly example, see Bakhle, "Country First?," 169–71, 177. For a contemporary example, see Ayaz S. Peerbhoy to Guy Aldred, December 4, 1948, in "Savarkar: Past and Present: A Socialist Estimate," *The Word* 10, no. 5 (1949): 61. Vinayak Damodar Savarkar [An Indian Nationalist, pseud.], *The Indian War of Independence of 1857* (S.l.: s.n., 1909).

17. Savarkar, *Indian War of Independence*, 233–4; Vinayak Damodar Savarkar, "The Following Statement Is Issued by Br. Savarkar, the President of the Hindu Mahasabha in Reply to the Article Published by the Maha Raja Sir Kishan Prasad of Hyderabad Regarding the Nizam Civil Resistance Movement," May 4, 1939, reel no. 23, serial no. 2, p. 549, Veer Savarkar Papers; Vinayak Damodar Savarkar, *Hindu Rashtra Darshan: Collection of the Presidential Speeches Delivered from the Hindu Mahasabha Platform* ([Bombay: L. G. Khare], 1949), 40–1; Vikram Visana, "Savarkar before Hindutva: Sovereignty, Republicanism, and Populism in India, c. 1900–1920," *Modern Intellectual History* 18, no. 4 (2021): 1126.

18. Vinayak Damodar Savarkar, *Hindu-Pad-Padashahi, or: A Review of the Hindu Empire of Maharashtra* (Madras: B. G. Paul, 1925).

19. Chaturvedi, Hindutva and Violence, 389.

20. Kapila, *Violent Fraternity*, 98–108.

21. I follow Savarkar's convention of spelling "Hindustan" with an *h*, assuming the Sanskrit suffix *-sthana* rather than the Persian *-stan*: see Manan Ahmed Asif, *The Loss of Hindustan: The Invention of India* (Cambridge, MA: Harvard University Press, 2020), 10.

22. Janaki Bakhle, *Savarkar and the Making of Hindutva* (Princeton, NJ: Princeton University Press, 2024), 109.

23. Savarkar, *Indian War of Independence*, 62–3.

24. Arjun Appadurai, "Number in the Colonial Imagination," in *Orientalism and the Postcolonial Predicament,* ed. Carol Breckenridge and Peter van der Veer (Philadelphia: University of Pennsylvania Press, 1993), 314–39; Bernard Cohn, "The Census, Social Structure and Objectification in South Asia," in *An Anthropologist among the Historians and Other Essays* (Oxford: Oxford University Press, 1990), 224–54.
25. Chris J. Fuller, "Colonial Anthropology and the Decline of the Raj: Caste, Religion and Political Change in India in the Early Twentieth Century," *Journal of the Royal Asiatic Society* 26, no. 3 (2016): 466–7.
26. Faisal Devji, *Muslim Zion: Pakistan as a Political Idea* (Cambridge, MA: Harvard University Press, 2013), 49–51, 83–7.
27. Pradip Kumar Datta, "'Dying Hindus': Production of Hindu Communal Common Sense in Early 20th Century Bengal," *Economic and Political Weekly* 28, no. 25 (1993): 1303–19.
28. Jyotirmaya Sharma, "Digesting the 'Other': Hindu Nationalism and the Muslims in India," in *Political Hinduism,* ed. Vinay Lal (Oxford: Oxford University Press, 2009), 150–72, explores another aspect of Hindutva in relation to imbibition: the fantasy of tearing apart and eating up the Muslim.
29. Chaturvedi, *Hindutva and Violence,* 186–96; Luna Sabastian, "Indian Political Thought and Germany's Fascism" (PhD diss., University of Cambridge, 2020), 86–139.
30. Cf. Marzia Casolari, "Hindutva's Foreign Tie-Up in the 1930s: Archival Evidence," *Economic and Political Weekly* 35, no. 4 (2000): 218–28; Bhatt, *Hindu Nationalism,* 105–8. "Race" was neither monolithic nor self-evident in Nazi Germany either: see Devan O. Pendas, Mark Roseman, and Richard F. Wetzell, eds., *Beyond the Racial State: Rethinking Nazi Germany* (Cambridge: Cambridge University Press, 2017).
31. Mohandas Karamchand Gandhi, "A Shame" [from Gujarati], *Navajivan,* February 1, 1925, in *The Collected Works of Mahatma Gandhi,* 6th ed. (1960–1994; repr., New Delhi: Publications Division, Ministry of Information and Broadcasting, Government of India, 2000), 30:165–7. I am grateful to Chris Wilson for pointing me to this source.
32. Gandhi, quoted in Pradip Kumar Datta, *Carving Blocs: Communal Ideology in Early Twentieth-Century Bengal* (Oxford: Oxford University Press, 1999), 196n159.
33. See Gyanendra Pandey, *A History of Prejudice: Race, Caste, and Difference in India and the United States* (Cambridge: Cambridge University Press, 2013); Nico Slate, *Colored Cosmopolitanism: The Shared Struggle for Freedom in the United States and India* (Cambridge, MA: Harvard University Press, 2017); Shefali Chandra, "Whiteness on the Margins of Native Patriarchy: Race, Caste, Sexuality, and the Agenda of Transnational Studies," *Feminist Studies* 37, no. 1 (2011): 127–53; and the bestselling Isabel Wilkerson, *Caste: The Origins of Our Discontents* (New York: Random House, 2020), recommended by Oprah, no less.
34. Vinayak Damodar Savarkar, *Six Glorious Epochs of Indian History,* trans. S. T. Godbole (1963; repr., Bombay: Bal Savarkar, 1971), 180–1. Cf. Tanika Sarkar, "Semiotics of Terror: Muslim Children and Women in Hindu Rashtra," *Economic and Political Weekly* 37, no. 28 (2002): 2874–6; Megha Kumar, *Communalism and Sexual Violence in India: The Politics of Gender, Ethnicity and Conflict* (London: I. B. Tauris, 2016), 13; Sudhir Kakar, *Intimate Relations: Exploring Indian Sexuality* (New Delhi: Penguin, 1990), 13.
35. Savarkar, *Essentials of Hindutva,* 73–4; Chaturvedi, *Hindutva and Violence,* 186–96.
36. Tobias Delfs, *Hindu-Nationalismus und europäischer Faschismus: Vergleich, Transfer- und Beziehungsgeschichte (Inklusive der ersten Auflage von M. S. Golwalkar's "We or Our Nationhood Defined" aus dem Jahre 1939 und mit einem Geleitwort von Hermann Kulke)* (Hamburg-Schenefeld, Germany: EB-Verlag, 2008), 105.
37. Christophe Jaffrelot, "The Idea of the Hindu Race in the Writings of Hindu Nationalist Ideologues in the 1920s and 1930s: A Concept between Two Cultures," in *The Concept of Race in South Asia,* ed. Peter Robb (Delhi: Oxford University Press, 1995), 335n32.
38. Vinayak Damodar Savarkar, *The Story of My Transportation for Life: A Biography of Black Days of Andamans,* trans. V. N. Naik (1927 in Marathi; trans. Bombay: Sadbhakti Publications, 1950), 461.

39. East India (Jails Committee), *Report of the Indian Jails Committee, 1919–20* (London: His Majesty's Stationary Office, 1921), 276; Savarkar, *Story of My Transportation,* 459.

40. Savarkar, *Six Glorious Epochs,* 175–6. For women as biocapital in anthropology, see Sarah Franklin and Helena Ragoné, introduction to *Reproducing Reproduction: Kinship, Power, and Technological Innovation,* ed. Sarah Franklin and Helena Ragoné (Philadelphia: University of Pennsylvania Press, 1998), 1–2.

41. "Annual Report of the Hindu Mahasabha [for 1939]," reel no. 7, serial no. D-22-22, p. 10, Veer Savarkar Papers.

42. For the latter, see Rolf-Peter Sieferle, "Indien und die Arier in der Rassentheorie," *Zeitschrift für Kulturaustausch* 37, no. 3 (1987): 448, 452, 460.

43. M. S. Golwalkar, *We, or: Our Nationhood Defined* (Nagpur, India: Bharat Publications, 1939), repr. in Shamsul Islam, *Golwalkar's We or Our Nationhood Defined: A Critique* (New Delhi: Pharos, 2006), 6, 8. For other Aryan repatriations, see Madhav M. Deshpande, "Aryan Origins: Arguments from the Nineteenth-Century Maharashtra," in *The Indo-Aryan Controversy: Evidence and Inference in Indian History,* ed. Edwin F. Bryant and Laurie L. Patton (London: Routledge, 2005), 429–30; Narayan Bhavanrao Pavgee, *Vedic Fathers of Geology* (Pune, India: Arya-Bhushan Press, 1912).

44. For racial Aryanism in India, see Romila Thapar, "The Theory of Aryan Race and India: History and Politics," *Social Scientist* 24, no. 1/3 (1996): 7–8; see also Romila Thapar, "Durkheim and Weber on Theories of Society and Race Relating to Pre-Colonial India," in *Sociological Theories: Race and Colonialism* (Paris: UNESCO, 1980), 96–7.

45. Rosalind O'Hanlon, "Caste and Its Histories in Colonial India: A Reappraisal," in "New Directions in Social and Economic History: Essays in Honour of David Washbrook," special issue, *Modern Asian Studies* 51, no. 2 (2017): 455. For Jotirao Phule's influential anti-Brahmin reinterpretation of the Aryan conquest in nineteenth-century Maharashtra, see Rosalind O'Hanlon, *Caste, Conflict and Ideology: Mahatma Jotirao Phule and Low Caste Protest in Nineteenth-Century Western India* (Cambridge: Cambridge University Press, 1985), 141–51; see also Anupama Rao, *The Caste Question: Dalits and the Politics of Modern India* (Berkeley: University of California Press, 2009), 12–13, 40–9.

46. Savarkar, *Essentials of Hindutva,* 5–6.

47. Ibid., 9.

48. Thapar, "Theory of Aryan Race," 5; Crispin Bates, "Race, Caste and Tribe in Central India: The Early Origins of Indian Anthropometry," in Robb, *Concept of Race in South Asia,* 165–218, 241; Susan Bayly, "Caste and 'Race' in Colonial Ethnography," in Robb, *Concept of Race in South Asia,* 165–218.

49. Savarkar, *Essentials of Hindutva,* 74.

50. Ibid., 75.

51. Ibid., 78.

52. Ibid., 63–4.

53. Ibid., 79. The identification of Hindus (rather than Muslims) with Jews may be surprising to some readers but was taken for granted by Savarkar and many of his ilk, and it still is today. I expect the perceived affinity is in their religions based on descent rather than conversion, civilizational longevity, and national survival amid and despite persecution and the loss of political power.

54. Oliver C. Cox, "Race and Caste: A Distinction," *American Journal of Sociology* 50, no. 5 (1945): 368. For the history of African American and Indian comparisons of race and caste since the nineteenth century, see Nico Slate, "Translating Race and Caste," *Journal of Historical Sociology* 24, no. 1 (2011): 62–79.

55. Cox, "Race and Caste," 366.

56. Radhakamal Mukerjee, *Regional Sociology* (New York: Century, 1926), 240–2, 248–9; Robert V. Russell, *The Tribes and Castes of the Central Provinces of India,* 4 vols. (London: Macmillan,

1916), 2:263–4; Govind Sadashiv Ghurye, *Caste and Race in India* (London: Kegan Paul, Trench, Trubner, 1932), 76–80, 96–7. For a discussion, see Barbara Celarent, "Caste and Race in India by G. S. Ghurye," *American Journal of Sociology* 116, no. 5 (2011): 1716–7. See also Morton Klass, *Caste: The Emergence of the South Asian Social System* (Philadelphia: Institute for the Study of Human Issues, 1980), 37–39.

57. Shridhar Venkatesh Ketkar, *History of Caste in India* (1909; repr., Jaipur, India: Rawat Publications, 1979), 15–17.

58. Deshpande, "Aryan Origins," 456.

59. See Bates, "Race, Caste and Tribe in Central India," 241; Herbert Hope Risley, *The Tribes and Castes of Bengal: Anthropometric Data,* 2 vols. (Calcutta: Bengal Secretariat Press, 1891).

60. Herbert Risley, *The People of India,* 2nd ed. (Calcutta: Thacker, Spink, 1908; repr., London: W. Thacker, 1915), 55.

61. See Jayanta Ghosh, Pulahesh Maiti, and Anil K. Bera, "Indian Statistical Institute: Numbers and Beyond, 1931–47," in *Science and Modern India: An Institutional History, c. 1784–1947,* ed. Uma Das Gupta (Delhi: Pearson Longman, 2011), 1025, 1055.

62. For the "Modern Synthesis," see Sahotra Sarkar, "Evolutionary Theory in the 1920s: The Nature of the 'Synthesis,'" *Philosophy of Science* 71, no. 5 (2004): 1215–26.

63. For instance: S. N. Roy, "How to Make a Child Beautiful," *Man in India* 7, no. 2 and 3 (1927): 196–9; S. S. Mehta, "Laws of Eugenics and the Institution of Marriage amongst the Hindus," *Man in India* 8, no. 2 and 3 (1928): 168–77.

64. Projit Bihari Mukharji, *Brown Skins, White Coats: Race Science in India, 1920–66* (Chicago: University of Chicago Press, 2022), 61–2.

65. Benoy Kumar Sarkar, "The Sociology of the Poor and the Pariah," *Man in India* 20, no. 3 (1940): 165–6. For Sarkar's view of ubiquitous miscegenation, see also Satadru Sen, *Benoy Kumar Sarkar: Restoring the Nation to the World* (New Delhi: Routledge, 2014), 50–5, 86, who, however—in my opinion—incorrectly assumes that Sarkar linked miscegenation to deracination.

66. Savarkar, *Essentials of Hindutva,* 63–4.

67. Sampath, *Savarkar,* 41–68. This point had already been made seventy years earlier by Keer, *Savarkar and His Times,* 132, 156–8, 160–72. Until recently, scholars have nevertheless tended to overestimate Brahmin supremacism (as a perpetuation of Aryanism) within Hindu nationalist ideas of the Hindu "race": see, for example, Bhatt, *Hindu Nationalism,* 88, 94–5; Prabhu Bapu, *Hindu Mahasabha in Colonial North India, 1915–1930: Constructing Nation and History* (London: Routledge, 2013), 68–9.

68. "Session of All India Hindu Mahasabha" [translated from the Arabic], *Oudh Akhbar* (Lucknow), January 6, 1923, in "Newspaper Extracts Relating to the Hindu Mahasabha," 1924, file no. 198, p. 9, Home (Political), National Archives of India, New Delhi.

69. Savarkar to Raja Ram Sabir, January 21, 1943, reel no. 11, serial no. 15, p. 208, Veer Savarkar Papers.

70. Raja Ram Sabir to Savarkar, January 15, 1943, reel no. 26, serial no. 14, p. 271–2, Veer Savarkar Papers.

71. Savarkar to Raja Ram Sabir, 208.

72. [Savarkar's] Presidential Office, Hindu Mahasabha, press note, April 15, 1942, reel no. 6, file no. c-55-86, p. 48, Veer Savarkar Papers.

73. Cf. Bakhle, *Savarkar and the Making of Hindutva,* 204, 205.

74. Vikram Visana, "Glory and Humiliation in the Making of V. D. Savarkar's Hindu Nationalism," *Historical Journal* 66, no. 1 (2023): 165–85.

75. A. B. Mahajan to Savarkar, December 25, 1940, reel no. 14, serial no. 10, p. 316, Veer Savarkar Papers.

76. S. M. Pavande to R. M. Deshmukh, [October 1940], copy, reel no. 7, file no. c-10-41, p. 160, Veer Savarkar Papers.

77. Fergus D'Arcy, "The Malthusian League and the Resistance to Birth Control Propaganda in Late Victorian Britain," *Population Studies* 31, no. 3 (1977): 429.
78. Savarkar, *Essentials of Hindutva*, 117–18.
79. Ibid., 116.
80. Savarkar to Savitri Devi, June 3, 1941, reel no. 10, file no. c-38-69, p. 5, Veer Savarkar Papers.
81. Savitri Devi to Savarkar, December 1, 1944, reel no. 31, file no. B 16/143, p. 34, Veer Savarkar Papers.
82. Nicholas Goodrick-Clarke, *Hitler's Priestess: Savitri Devi, the Hindu-Aryan Myth, and Neo-Nazism* (New York: New York University Press, 1998), 27, 120.
83. Ibid., 69–71.
84. Savitri Devi to Savarkar, 33.
85. John Dawson Mayne, *A Treatise on Hindu Law and Usage* (Madras: Stevens and Haynes, 1878), 396; Krishna Kamal Bhattacharyya, *The Law Relating to the Joint Hindu Family*, Tagore Law Lectures 1884–85 (Calcutta: Thacker, Spink, 1885), 125–6, 140; Thenkari Pichu Iyer Gopalakrishnan, *Hindu Marriage Law: Containing Exhaustive Commentaries on the Hindu Marriage Act, 25 of 1955, and a Detailed Exposition of Hindu Marriage Law from Earliest Times to Date: With Useful Appendices* (Allahabad, India: Law Book, 1957), 35.
86. Indrani Chatterjee, *Gender, Slavery and Law in Colonial India* (New Delhi: Oxford University Press, 1999), 12.
87. Savarkar, *Indian War of Independence*, 17–21, 27.
88. Savarkar, *Essentials of Hindutva*, 75.
89. Savarkar, *Six Glorious Epochs*, 37.
90. Ibid., 38.
91. Ibid., 39.
92. Savarkar, *An Echo from Andamans: Letters Written by Veer Savarkar during His Captivity to His Brother Dr. Savarkar* (Pune, India: Venus Book Stall, 1947),13.
93. Ronald Inden, *Imagining India* (Cambridge, MA: Blackwell, 1990), 88.
94. Savarkar, "Message," August 26, [193]9, reel no. 12, serial no. 4, p. 38, Veer Savarkar Papers; Savarkar, *Essentials of Hindutva*, 31n.
95. Savarkar to P. R. Gopalkrishna Rao, July 5, 1941, reel no. 10, file no. c-38-69, p. 15, Veer Savarkar Papers.
96. Swami Shraddhanand, *Hindu Sangathan: Saviour of the Dying Race* (Delhi: Shraddhananda Sanyasi, 1926), 1.
97. See Chaturvedi, *Hindutva and Violence*, 11, 22–3.
98. Savarkar, "Message."
99. Savarkar, *Essentials of Hindutva*, 117.
100. Mukund Wamanrao Burway, *Shri Ramagita* (Indore: M. W. Burway, 1928), 135–43.
101. Indra Prakash, *A Review of The History and Works of the Hindu Mahasabha and the Hindu Sanghatan Movement* (New Delhi: Akhil Bharatiya Hindu Mahasabha, 1938), 344–7; "Final Rights Make Miss Miller Hindu," *New York Times*, March 14, 1928, 3, ProQuest. Rudolf Otto sought a unifying principle behind all religious experience, which he called "the numinous" (*das Numinose*): Rudolf Otto, *Das Heilige: Über das Irrationale in der Idee des Göttlichen und sein Verhältnis zum Rationalen* (Wrocław, Poland: Trewendt & Granier, 1917), published in English as *The Idea of the Holy: An Inquiry into the Non-Rational Factor in the Idea of the Divine and Its Relation to the Rational*, trans. John Wilfred Harvey (London: Humphrey Milford, Oxford University Press, 1923).
102. Burway, *Shri Ramagita*, 136.
103. Ibid.
104. "Final Rights."
105. Burway, *Shri Ramagita*, 136.

106. "Final Rights."
107. "Miss Miller to Embrace Hinduism Tomorrow; Will Be Married to Ex-Maharajah Saturday," *New York Times,* March 12, 1928, 1, ProQuest.
108. Christophe Jaffrelot, *The Hindu Nationalist Movement and Indian Politics, 1925 to the 1990s: Strategies of Identity-Building, Implantation and Mobilisation (With Special Reference to Central India)* (London: Hurst, 1996), 23.
109. See Kenneth Jones, *Arya Dharm: Hindu Consciousness in 19th-Century Punjab* (Berkeley: University of California Press, 1976), 129–30; Charu Gupta, "Anxious Hindu Masculinities in Colonial North India: 'Shuddhi' and 'Sangathan' Movements," *CrossCurrents* 61, no. 4 (2001): 441–56.
110. Vinayak Damodar Savarkar, "The 'Suffering' Muslims of Kohat," *Mahratta,* March 1, 1925, 110.
111. Savarkar to Gopalkrishna Rao.
112. Gupta, "Anxious Hindu Masculinities," 446–7; Walter Andersen, "The Rashtriya Swayamsevak Sangh: II: Who Represents the Hindus?," *Economic and Political Weekly* 7, no. 12 (1972): 635.
113. Muhammad Ali Jinnah, "Qu'id-e-Azam Explains Political Situation," *The Dawn* 2, no. 1 (1942): 1–2, 8, 10–11.
114. By order of the President [Savarkar] to Vishwanathji Agrawal, August 10, 1944, reel no. 29, p. 16, Veer Savarkar Papers.
115. Sister Nivedita, "The Present Condition of Woman," in *Papers on Inter-Racial Problems: Communicated to the First Universal Races Congress, Held at the University of London, July 26–29, 1911,* ed. Gustav Spiller (London: P. S. King & Son and The World's Peace Foundation, 1911), 90–3.
116. Sister Nivedita, "Hinduism and Organisation," in *The Complete Works of Sister Nivedita: Birth Centenary Publication,* 5 vols. (Calcutta: Sister Nivedita's Girls School, 1955), 3:400.
117. Sister Nivedita, "Islam in India," in *Complete Works,* 2:207–8.
118. Sister Nivedita, "Islam in Asia," in *Complete Works,* 2:479–80.
119. Savarkar, *Six Glorious Epochs,* 154–5, 178–9. For the enmity of intimacy, see Kapila, *Violent Fraternity,* 89–129.
120. Savarkar, *Essentials of Hindutva,* 37–8.
121. Savarkar, *Six Glorious Epochs,* 155–6.
122. Savarkar, *Hindu Rashtra Darshan,* 54.
123. "Being Interviewed in Connection with the Controversy of 'TWO NATION THEORY Regarding Moslems' Dr. B. S. Moonje Has Issued the Following Press Interview," August 28, 1943, reel no. 28, p. 123, Veer Savarkar Papers.
124. Savarkar, *Hindu Rashtra Darshan,* 58–61.
125. Ibid., 50–1.
126. "Being Interviewed in Connection," 123.
127. Savitri Devi, *The Non-Hindu Indians and Indian Unity* (Calcutta: Hindu Mission, 1940), 6 (italics in the original).
128. Savarkar, *Hindu Rashtra Darshan,* 64–5, 69–70.
129. Golwalkar, *We,* 35, 47–8.
130. For the gendering, even queering, of sovereignty, see Teemu Ruskola, "Raping Like a State," *UCLA Law Review* 57, no. 5 (2010): 1479, 1481–2; Ashis Nandy, *The Intimate Enemy: Loss and Recovery of Self under Colonialism* (1983; repr., New Delhi: Oxford University Press, 1988), 4.
131. Muhammad Qasim Zaman, *The Ulama in Contemporary Islam: Custodians of Change* (Princeton, NJ: Princeton University Press, 2002), 28–9; Muhammad Khalid Masud, "Apostacy and Judicial Separation in British India," in *Islamic Legal Interpretation: Muftis and Their Fatwas,* ed. Muhammad Khalid Masud, Brinkley Messick, and David Powers (Cambridge, MA: Harvard University Press, 1996), 193–203.
132. Vinayak Damodar Savarkar, "Draft: Barrister Savarkar President of the All India Hindu Mahasabha Has Released the Following Statement to the Press on the Muslim Dissolution of Marriage Bill," reel no. 23, serial no. 1, p. 75–7, Veer Savarkar Papers.

133. Charu Gupta, *Sexuality, Obscenity, Community: Women, Muslims and the Hindu Public in Colonial India* (Delhi: Permanent Black, 2001), 241; Pradip Kumar Datta, *Heterogeneities: Identity Formations in Modern India* (New Delhi: Tulika Books, 2010), 164. I am grateful to Datta for supplying me with a digital copy of his book.

134. Datta, *Heterogeneities,* 155–213; also Datta, *Carving Blocs,* 148–237.

135. A. Montgomery to H. Tonkinson, May 6, 1925, file no. 91/I, 1925, p. 6, Home (Political), National Archives of India.

136. Savarkar, "'Suffering' Muslims of Kohat"; see also Luna Sabastian, "Women, Violence, Sovereignty: 'Rakshasa' Marriage by Capture in Modern Indian Political Thought," *Modern Intellectual History* 19, no. 3 (2022): 777. For a discussion of the significance of the Kohat riots, see Neeti Nair, *Changing Homelands: Hindu Politics and the Partition of India* (Cambridge, MA: Harvard University Press, 2011), 51–70.

137. Savarkar, "'Suffering' Muslims of Kohat," 110.

138. Savarkar to J. A. Shillidy, April 6, 1925, file no. 91/I, 1925, p. 8, Home (Political), National Archives of India.

139. D. O'Flynn to Savarkar, May 6, 1925, file no. 91/I, 1925, p. 10, Home (Political), National Archives of India.

140. "Allegation of Conversion of Starving Hindu [*sic*] in Bengal to Muslim Faith Made by Mr. V. D. Savarkar of the Hindu Mahasabha, Regarding Bengal Famine and Contradiction of the Allegations and Question of Prosecuting Mr. Savarkar for the Statement," 1943, file no. 87/43-Poll (I), Home (Political), National Archives of India.

141. Gupta, *Sexuality, Obscenity, Community,* 246–8; Pradip Kumar Datta, "'Abductions' and the Constellation of a Hindu Communal Bloc in Bengal of the 1920s," *Studies in History* 14, no. 1 (1998): 37–88; Shashi Joshi and Bhagwan Josh, *Struggle for Hegemony in India 1920–47,* vol. 3, *Culture, Community, and Power, 1941–47* (New Delhi: Sage Publications, 1992), 206–14.

142. Ishita Pande, "Loving Like a Man: The Colourful Prophet, Conjugal Masculinity and the Politics of Hindu Sexology in Late Colonial India," *Gender & History* 29 (2017): 675–92.

143. Maria Framke, "The Politics of Gender and Community: Non-Governmental Relief in Late Colonial and Early Postcolonial India," in *Gendering Global Humanitarianism in the Twentieth Century: Practice, Politics and the Power of Representation,* ed. Esther Möller, Johannes Paulmann, and Katharina Stornig (Basingstoke, UK: Palgrave Macmillan, 2020), 143–59.

144. "Annual Report of the Hindu Mahasabha [for 1939]," reel no. 7, serial no. D-22-22, p. 12–13, Veer Savarkar Papers; "The Following Statement, Regarding the Recent Hindu-Muslim Riots in Behar [*sic*], Has Been Issued by Barrister Savarkar, the President of the Hindu Maha Sabha, to Be Released to the Press, Dadar, Bombay," May 10, 1941, reel no. 10, serial no. c-37–68, quote at p. 180, Veer Savarkar Papers.

145. Savarkar, *Six Glorious Epochs,* 152 and elsewhere. See "Report from Bombay: Extract from the Fortnightly Report from Bombay for the Second Half of May 1947, 3 June 1947: Home Pol (I), File No. 18/5/47, NAI," in *1947,* ed. Sucheta Mahajan, vol. 10, part 2 of *Towards Freedom: Documents on the Movement for Independence in India,* ed. Sabyasachi Bhattacharya (New Delhi: Oxford University Press, 2015), 2093.

146. Savarkar, *Six Glorious Epochs,* 255.

147. Visana, "Glory and Humiliation"; Sharma, "Digesting the 'Other.'"

148. Savarkar, *Six Glorious Epochs,* 178–9.

149. Har Bilas Sarda, *Hindu Superiority: An Attempt to Determine the Position of the Hindu Race in the Scale of Nations* (Ajmer, India: Rajputana Printing Works, 1906), 61–3. The book is cited in Savarkar, *Six Glorious Epochs,* 4n6, and Savarkar to Gauri Shankar Prasad, May 3, 1945, reel no. 32, file no. B 13/140, p. 128, Veer Savarkar Papers. For Sarda, see Christophe Jaffrelot, ed., *Hindu Nationalism: A Reader* (Princeton, NJ: Princeton University Press, 2007), 50–1.

150. Sarda, *Hindu Superiority,* 54, 62.

151. Sabastian, "Women, Violence, Sovereignty."

152. Mayne, *A Treatise on Hindu Law and Usage*, 69, 66, quoted in Sabastian, "Women, Violence, Sovereignty," 757.
153. See Thomas R. Trautmann, *Lewis Henry Morgan and the Invention of Kinship* (Berkeley: University of California Press, 1987), 179–204. For a good general overview of Victorian anthropology that puts primitive polygamy and matriarchy theories into the context of Victorian attitudes to sex and gender, see George W. Stocking Jr., *Victorian Anthropology* (New York: Free Press, 1991), 197–208.
154. John Ferguson McLennan, *Primitive Marriage: An Inquiry into the Origin of the Form of Capture in Marriage Ceremonies* (Edinburgh: Adam and Charles Black, 1865).
155. See Kapila, "Self, Spencer and Swaraj: Nationalist Thought and Critiques of Liberalism, 1890–1920," *Modern Intellectual History* 4, no. 1 (2007): 115; Chaturvedi, *Hindutva and Violence*, 127–8.
156. Herbert Spencer, *The Principles of Sociology*, 2nd ed., 3 vols. (1874; repr., London: Williams and Norgate, 1877), 1:640–59.
157. McLennan, *Primitive Marriage*, 138–9.
158. Spencer, *Principles of Sociology*, 1:651, 1:657, 1:659.
159. Ritu Menon and Kamla Bhasin, *Borders and Boundaries: Women in India's Partition* (New Brunswick, NJ: Rutgers University Press, 1998); Urvashi Butalia, *The Other Side of Silence: Voices from the Partition of India* (New Delhi, London: Penguin, 1998); Veena Das, *Life and Words: Violence and the Descent into the Ordinary* (Berkeley: University of California Press, 2007), 19–37.
160. Bhimrao Ramji Ambedkar, *Riddles in Hinduism: An Exposition to Enlighten the Masses*, in *Dr. Babasaheb Ambedkar: Writings and Speeches*, ed. Vasant Moon, 17 vols. (Bombay: Education Department, Government of Maharashtra, 1979–2003), 4:227–8.
161. See Jesús Francisco Cháirez-Garza, "B. R. Ambedkar, Franz Boas and the Rejection of Racial Theories of Untouchability," *South Asia: Journal of South Asian Studies* 41, no. 2 (2018): 288; Christophe Jaffrelot, *Dr Ambedkar and Untouchability: Analysing and Fighting Caste*, rev. ed. (2000; repr., London: Hurst, 2005), 32.
162. B. R. Ambedkar, "Castes in India: Their Mechanism, Genesis, and Development," in Moon, *Dr. Babasaheb Ambedkar*, 1:20 (italics in the original); see also Jaffrelot, *Dr Amebedkar and Untouchability*, 38.
163. Ambedkar, "Castes in India," 9.
164. Ambedkar, *Riddles in Hinduism*, 4:229–30.
165. Ibid., 4:229–30.
166. Ibid., 4:232. Ambedkar (or his editors) misspell this as "Patna Potestas."
167. McLennan, *Primitive Marriage*, 48, 48n; see also Sabastian, "Women, Violence, Sovereignty," 766.
168. McLennan, *Primitive Marriage*, 146.
169. See Sabastian, "Women, Violence, Sovereignty."
170. Vinayak Damodar Savarkar, "Statement Issued Regarding the Burmese Muslim Riots in Rangoon," September 11, 1938, reel no 23, serial no. 1, p. 226, Veer Savarkar Papers.
171. Savarkar, *Story of My Transportation*, 235–6.
172. Savarkar, *Six Glorious Epochs*, 176–7.
173. Ibid., 176.
174. McLennan, appendix to *Primitive Marriage*, 310.
175. For Rama's medieval rise to his present status as ideal king-god, see Sheldon Pollock's classic statement "Rāmāyaṇa and Political Imagination in India," *Journal of Asian Studies* 52, no. 2 (1993): 261–97.
176. Savarkar, *Six Glorious Epochs*, 175–6.
177. Ibid., 245.
178. Savarkar to Lala Ganpat Rai, March 16, 1945, reel no. 32, file no. B 13/140, p. 142, Veer Savarkar Papers.

179. See Roger Jeffery and Patricia Jeffery, "Saffron Demography, Common Wisdom, Aspirations and Uneven Governmentalities," *Economic and Political Weekly* 40, no. 5 (2005): 449; Pande, "Loving Like a Man," 683–4.
180. B. S. Moonje, "Baroda Hindu Sabha Conference, Presidential Address," in *The Making of India and Pakistan: Select Documents*, ed. S. R. Bakshi, vol. 3, *Ideology of Hindu Mahasabha and Other Political Parties* (New Delhi: Deep & Deep, 1997), 564.
181. All-India Hindu Mahasabha, Madras Branch, in *Written Statement Submitted to the Hindu Law Committee 1945*, 2 vols. (Madras: Superintendent Government Press, 1947), 2:347 (italics in the original).
182. Ibid., 2:347.
183. Savarkar to Ganpat Rai, 142.
184. Savarkar, *Six Glorious Epochs*, 189–91, 175.
185. Ibid., 191.
186. Ibid., 119.
187. Ibid., 156.
188. Ibid., 159, 157.
189. Ibid., 193.
190. Ibid., 162.
191. Ibid., 160–1.
192. Ibid., 190.
193. Lala Lajpat Rai, "Women's Problems," *Stri Dharma: Official Organ of the Women's Indian Association* 11, no. 4 (1928): 51.
194. Swami Shraddhanand, "Extracts from Hindu Sangathan: Saviour of the Dying Race," in Jaffrelot, *Hindu Nationalism*, 49–50.
195. See Priyanath Sen, *The General Principles of Hindu Jurisprudence*, Tagore Law Lectures 1909 ([Calcutta]: University of Calcutta, 1918), 270; Pandurang Vaman Kane, *History of Dharmasastra (Ancient and Mediaeval, Religious and Civil Law)*, 8 vols. (Pune, India: Bhandarkar Oriental Research Institute, 1941), 2:1:520.
196. Savarkar, *Six Glorious Epochs*, 190, 192.
197. See Veena Das, *Critical Events: An Anthropological Perspective on Contemporary India* (Delhi: Oxford University Press, 1995), 66, 68.
198. Ibid., 70, 80.
199. Ibid., 81.
200. Sabastian, "Women, Violence, Sovereignty," 777, 781; Savarkar, "'Suffering' Muslims of Kohat," 110.
201. Suzanne Miers and Igor Kopytoff, "Introduction: African 'Slavery' as an Institution of Marginality," in *Slavery in Africa: Historical and Anthropological Perspectives*, ed. Suzanne Miers and Igor Koptyoff (Madison: University of Wisconsin Press, 1977), 11; Chatterjee, *Gender, Slavery, and Law*, 26.
202. Chatterjee, *Gender, Slavery, and Law*, 18–19.
203. Savarkar, *Six Glorious Epochs*, 183.
204. Vinayak Damodar Savarkar, "Hearty Congratulations to Pandit Anand Priya for Converting Muslims to Hinduism," May 25, 1947, in Vinayak Damodar Savarkar, *Historic Statements*, ed. S. S. Savarkar and G. M. Joshi (Bombay: Popular Prakashan, 1967), 196–7.
205. Vinayak Damodar Savarkar, *Savarkar Samagra*, 10 vols. (Delhi: Prabhat Prakashan, 2000–3), 2:646.
206. Gary Gerstle, *American Crucible: Race and Nation in the Twentieth Century* (Princeton, NJ: Princeton University Press, 2017), 20–4, 42–3.
207. Marilyn Strathern, *Reproducing the Future: Essays on Anthropology, Kinship and the New Reproductive Technologies* (Manchester, UK: Manchester University Press, 1992), 55.
208. Benoy Kumar Sarkar, *Villages and Towns as Social Patterns* (Calcutta: Chuckervertty, Chatterjee: 1941), 452, 442; Houston Stewart Chamberlain, *Die Grundlagen des neunzehnten*

Jahrhunderts, 2 vols (Munich: F. Bruckmann, 1899) 1:281, 1:291. For Cedric Dover, see Nico Slate, *The Prism of Race: W. E. B. du Bois, Langston Hughes, Paul Robeson, and the Coloured World of Cedric Dover* (Basingstoke, UK: Palgrave Macmillan, 2014), 15, 17; Nico Slate, "A Colored Cosmopolitanism: Cedric Dover's Reading of the Afro-Asian World," in *Cosmopolitan Thought Zones: South Asia and the Global Circulation of Ideas,* ed. Sugata Bose and Kris Manjapra (Basingstoke, UK: Palgrave Macmillan, 2010), 213–35.

209. Oswald de Andrade, "Cannibalist Manifesto," 1928, trans. Leslie Bary, *Latin American Literary Review* 19, no. 38 (1991): 38–47; José Vasconcelos, "The Cosmic Race," in *Modern Art in Africa, Asia and Latin America: An Introduction to Global Modernisms,* ed. Elaine O'Brien, Everlyn Nicodemus, Melissa Chiu, Benjamin Genocchio, Mary K. Coffey, and Roberto Tejada (1925; repr., Chichester, UK: Wiley-Blackwell, 2013), 402–12.

210. Cedric Dover, *Half-Caste* (London: M. Secker & Warburg, 1937), 269–71.

211. See Damon Ieremia Salesa, *Racial Crossings: Race, Intermarriage, and the Victorian British Empire* (Oxford: Oxford University Press, 2011); Thomas E. Skidmore, *Black into White: Race and Nationality in Brazilian Thought* (Oxford: Oxford University Press, 1974).

212. See, for instance, Daniela Moraes Traldi, "Christian Political Hypermasculinity: Brazilian Fascism in the 1930s," *Gender & History* 36, no. 2 (2024), 580–601; Aristotle Kallis, "Envisioning the New Man in 1930s Brazil," in *The "New Man" in Radical Right Ideology and Practice, 1919–45,* ed. Jorge Dagnino, Matthew Feldman, and Paul Stocker (London: Bloomsbury, 2018), 169–92.

213. See Kathryn Burns, "Gender and the Politics of Mestizaje: The Convent of Santa Clara in Cuzco, Peru," *Hispanic American Historical Review* 78, no. 1 (1998): 13–15.

214. I am grateful to Nick Stargardt for pointing this parallel out to me.

215. Heinrich Himmler, "Rede vor Gauleitern und anderen Parteifunktionären am 29.2 [*sic*].1940," in Heinrich Himmler, *Heinrich Himmler: Geheimreden, 1933 bis 1945, und andere Ansprachen,* ed. Bradley F. Smith and Agnes F. Peterson (Frankfurt am Main: Propyläen Verlag, 1974), 124.

216. Kapila, *Violent Fraternity,* 129; see also Joseph Alter, "Celibacy, Sexuality, and the Transformation of Gender into Nationalism in North India," *Journal of Asian Studies* 53, no. 1 (1994): 45–66; Joseph Alter, "Somatic Nationalism: Indian Wrestling and Militant Hinduism," *Modern Asian Studies* 28, no. 3 (1994): 557–88.

217. Tanika Sarkar and Urvashi Butalia, eds., *Women and the Hindu Right: A Collection of Essays* (New Delhi, India: Kali for Women, 1995). For the reproduction of RSS volunteers, see also Shubh Mathur, *The Everyday Life of Hindu Nationalism: An Ethnographic Account* (New Delhi: Three Essays Collective, 2008), 96.

218. See Dan Stone, "Race Science, Race Mysticism, and the Racial State," in Pendas, Roseman, and Wetzell, *Beyond the Racial State,* 178–9.

219. Cecil Roth, "The Nazi Delusion: Aryan versus Semitic," *Aryan Path* 5, no. 10 (1934): 614.

220. María Elena Martínez, *Genealogical Fictions: Limpieza de Sangre, Religion, and Gender in Colonial Mexico* (Stanford, CA: Stanford University Press, 2008), 27–8; Andrew C. Hess, "The Moriscos: An Ottoman Fifth Column in Sixteenth-Century Spain," *American Historical Review* 74, no. 1 (1968): 3–4. For evidence of New Christians defending their Jewish religious and cultural practices in the private sphere, see José Pedro Paiva, "The New Christian Divide in the Portuguese-Speaking World (Sixteenth to Eighteenth Centuries)," in *Racism and Ethnic Relations in the Portuguese-Speaking World,* ed. Francisco Bethencourt and Adrian J. Pearce (Oxford: Oxford University Press, 2012), 274–5.

221. Martínez, *Genealogical Fictions,* 9–11; Verena Stolcke, "Invaded Women: Sex, Race and Class in the Formation of Colonial Society," *European Journal of Development Research* 6, no. 2 (1994): 10–16; Dirk Rupnow, "Racializing Historiography: Anti-Jewish Scholarship in the Third Reich," in Pendas, Roseman, and Wetzell, *Beyond the Racial State,* 295.

Chapter Three: The Nazi *Volk* against *Kaste*

1. See, for example, Frank Bajohr and Michael Wildt, eds., *Volksgemeinschaft: Neue Forschungen zur Gesellschaft des Nationalsozialismus* (Frankfurt am Main: Fischer, 2009); David Welch,

"Nazi Propaganda and the *Volksgemeinschaft*: Constructing a People's Community," *Journal of Contemporary History* 39, no. 2 (2004): 213–38.

2. Marilyn Lake and Henry Reynolds, *Drawing the Global Colour Line: White Men's Countries and the International Challenge of Racial Equality* (Cambridge: Cambridge University Press, 2008), 66.

3. Carl Schmitt, *Die geistesgeschichtliche Lage des heutigen Parlamentarismus*, 2nd ed. (Munich: Duncker and Humblot, 1926), 13–14.

4. See Isabel Wilkerson, *Caste: The Origins of Our Discontents* (New York: Random House, 2020); Gyanendra Pandey, *A History of Prejudice: Race, Caste, and Difference in India and the United States* (Cambridge: Cambridge University Press, 2013); Nico Slate, *Colored Cosmopolitanism: The Shared Struggle for Freedom in the United States and India* (Cambridge, MA: Harvard University Press, 2017); Shefali Chandra, "Whiteness on the Margins of Native Patriarchy: Race, Caste, Sexuality, and the Agenda of Transnational Studies," *Feminist Studies* 37, no. 1 (2011): 127–53.

5. Slate, *Colored Cosmopolitanism*, 7, 11–20; Nico Slate, "Translating Race and Caste," *Journal of Historical Sociology* 24, no. 1 (2011): 62–79; Ania Loomba, "Racism in India," in *The Routledge Companion to the Philosophy of Race*, ed. Linda Martín Alcoff, Luvell Anderson, and Paul C. Taylor (New York: Routledge, 2018), 186–7, 194.

6. John Stuart Mill, *On Liberty* (1859; repr., Cambridge: Cambridge University Press, 2011), 8.

7. The historiography on the colonial "construction" of caste is immense. After Ronald Inden's overstatement of the constructivist case in *Imagining India* (Cambridge, MA: Blackwell, 1990), a seminal, nuanced articulation is Nicholas B. Dirks, *Castes of Mind: Colonialism and the Making of Modern India* (Princeton, NJ: Princeton University Press, 2001).

8. Ursula Sharma, *Caste* (Buckingham, UK: Open University Press, 1999), 5–30. For the American South, see Chris Fuller, "Caste, Race, and Hierarchy in the American South," *Journal of the Royal Anthropological Institute* 17, no. 3 (2011): 605–6, 612–13; Loomba, "Racism in India," 186.

9. Fuller, "Caste, Race," 617–19.

10. Moiz Tundawala and Salmoli Choudhuri, "Ambedkar's Liberty Concept in Comparative Constitutional Thought," in *The Indian Yearbook of Comparative Law 2016*, ed. Mahendra Pal Singh (Oxford: Oxford University Press, 2016), 72–3.

11. Wilkerson, *Caste*. For the motion picture, see *Origin*, directed by Ava DuVernay (2023).

12. See Arjun Appadurai, "Comparing Race to Caste Is an Interesting Idea, but There Are Crucial Differences between Both," *The Wire*, September 12, 2020.

13. For the racial connotation of "caste," see Fuller, "Caste, Race," 614.

14. See Maja Suderland, *Inside Concentration Camps: Social Life at the Extremes*, trans. Jessica Spengler (Cambridge: Polity Press, 2013), 91–2; Wilkerson, *Caste*, 78–88.

15. First noted by Josef Ackermann, *Heinrich Himmler als Ideologe* (Göttingen, Germany: Musterschmidt, 1970), 36; see also Peter Padfield, *Himmler: A Biography* (London: Macmillan, 1990), 90, 364, 402; Eckart Conze, "Adel unter dem Totenkopf: Die Idee eines Neuadels in den Gesellschaftsvorstellungen der SS," in *Adel und Moderne: Deutschland im europäischen Vergleich im 19. und 20. Jahrhundert*, ed. Eckart Conze and Monika Wienfort (Cologne: Böhlau, 2004), 165–6.

16. See, inter alia, Dorothy M. Figueira, *The Exotic: A Decadent Quest* (Albany: State University of New York, 1994), 154–6; Eric Kurlander, *Hitler's Monsters: A Supernatural History of the Third Reich* (New Haven, CT: Yale University Press, 2017), 22, 187; Michael Mann, *Fascists* (Cambridge: Cambridge University Press, 2004), 372. For Manu and Nazi eugenics, see Sheldon Pollock, "Deep Orientalism? Notes on Sanskrit and Power beyond the Raj," in *Orientalism and the Postcolonial Predicament: Perspectives on South Asia*, ed. Carl A. Breckenridge and Peter van der Veer (Philadelphia: University of Pennsylvania Press, 1993), 111; see also Lucia Staiano-Daniels, "The Melancholy of the Thinking Racist: India and the Ambiguities of Race in the Work of Hans F. K. Günther," in *Transcultural Encounters between Germany and India: Kindred Spirits in the Nineteenth and Twentieth Centuries*, ed. Joanne Miyang Cho, Eric Kurlander, and Douglas T. McGetchin (London: Routledge, 2014), 175–6. For a classic view of Nietzsche's Manu as a

precursor to Nazi eugenics, see Peter Emil Becker, *Wege ins Dritte Reich,* 2 vols. (Stuttgart: Georg Thieme, 1988–1990), 2:37–8.

17. Wilfried Daim, *Der Mann, der Hitler die Ideen gab: Von den religiösen Verirrungen eines Sektierers zum Rassenwahn des Diktators* (Munich: Isar, 1958). For Daim and his works, see Peter Diem, *Wilfried Daim: Querdenker zwischen Rot und Schwarz* (Vienna: Edition Steinbauer, 2011).

18. Wilfried Daim, *Die kastenlose Gesellschaft* (Munich: Manz, 1960).

19. Ibid., 302.

20. Ibid., 376.

21. Ibid.

22. See, paradigmatically, Michael Burleigh and Wolfgang Wippermann, *The Racial State: Germany 1933–1945* (Cambridge: Cambridge University Press, 1991). For critiques, see Devin O. Pendas, Mark Roseman, and Richard F. Wetzell, eds., *Beyond the Racial State: Rethinking Nazi Germany* (Cambridge: Cambridge University Press, 2017); Mark Mazower, *Hitler's Empire: Nazi Rule in Occupied Europe* (London: Allen Lane, 2008).

23. Peter Fritzsche, "Die Idee des Volkes und der Aufstieg der Nazis," in *Attraktion der NS-Bewegung,* ed. Gudrun Brockhaus (Essen, Germany: Klartext, 2014), 162. For consent to Nazi rule, see, inter alia, Thomas Kühne, *Belonging and Genocide: Hitler's Community, 1918–1945* (New Haven, CT: Yale University Press, 2010); Robert Gellately, *Backing Hitler: Consent and Coercion in Nazi Germany* (Oxford: Oxford University Press, 2001); Peter Fritzsche, *Germans into Nazis* (Cambridge, MA: Harvard University Press, 1999); Gudrun Brockhaus, ed., *Attraktion der NS-Bewegung* (Essen, Germany: Klartext, 2014); Götz Aly, *Hitlers Volksstaat: Raub, Rassenkrieg und nationaler Sozialismus* (Frankfurt am Main: S. Fischer, 2005); Ian Kershaw, *The "Hitler Myth": Image and Reality in the Third Reich* (Oxford: Oxford University Pres, 1987); Daniel Jonah Goldhagen, *Hitler's Willing Executioners* (London: Little, Brown, 1996).

24. Cf. Kris Manjapra, *Age of Entanglement: German and Indian Intellectuals across Empire* (Cambridge, MA: Harvard University Press, 2014), esp. 79; also Andrew Sartori, "Beyond Culture-Contact and Colonial Discourse: 'Germanism' in Colonial Bengal," in *An Intellectual History for India,* ed. Shruti Kapila (Cambridge: Cambridge University Press, 2010), 66–4.

25. The literature here is immense. See, for example, Pollock, "Deep Orientalism?" and the subsequent "Indologiestreit" between Vishwa Adluri and Reinhold Grünendahl: Karla Poewe and Irving Hexham, "Surprising Aryan Mediations between German Indology and Nazism: Research and the Adluri/Grünendahl Debate," *International Journal of Hindu Studies* 19, no. 3 (2015): 263–300; Figueira, *Exotic,* 137–62; Dorothy M. Figueira, *Aryans, Jews, Brahmins: Theorizing Authority through Myths of Identity* (Albany: State University of New York Press, 2002); Nicholas Goodrick-Clarke, *The Occult Roots of Nazism: The Ariosophists of Austria and Germany 1890–1935* (Wellingborough, UK: Aquarian, 1985); Victor Trimondi and Victoria Trimondi, *Hitler, Buddha, Krishna: Eine unheilige Allianz vom Dritten Reich bis heute* (Vienna: Ueberreuter, 2002); Eric Kurlander, *Hitler's Monsters*; Eric Kurlander, "The Orientalist Roots of National Socialism? Nazism, Occultism, and South Asian Spirituality, 1919–1945," in Cho, Kurlander, and McGetchin, *Transcultural Encounters,* 155–69; Karla O. Poewe, *New Religions and the Nazis* (New York: Routledge, 2006). See also the classic polemic: Amaury de Riencourt, *The Soul of India* (London: Jonathan Cape, 1960), 258–81.

26. For this, see Léon Poliakov, *The Aryan Myth,* trans. Edmund Howard (London: Chatto Heinemann for Sussex University Press, 1974); George Mosse, *The Crisis of German Ideology: Intellectual Origins of the Third Reich* (1964; repr., New York, 1966), 89–90; Jürgen Lütt, "Indische Wurzeln des Nationalsozialismus?," *Zeitschrift für Kulturaustausch* 37, no. 3 (1987): 469–79. Good general accounts of Aryanism and German orientalism are Stefan Arvidsson, *Aryan Idols: Indo-European Mythology as Ideology and Science,* trans. Sonia Wichmann (Chicago: University of Chicago Press, 2006); Suzanne Marchand, *German Orientalism in the Age of Empire: Religion, Race, and Scholarship* (Cambridge: Cambridge University Press, 2009).

27. Dayananda Sarasvati, *An English Translation of the Satyarth Prakash, Literally: Exposé of Right Sense (of Vedic Religion) of Maharshi Swami Dayanand Saraswati, "The Luther of India"; Being a Guide to Vedic Hermeneutics,* trans. Durga Prasad (1875; repr., Lahore, India: Virganand Press,

1908), 135. For Dayananda on caste, see J. Barton Scott, *Spiritual Despots: Modern Hinduism and the Genealogies of Self-Rule* (Chicago: University of Chicago Press, 2016), 171–2; see also Christophe Jaffrelot, "Hindu Nationalism: Strategic Syncretism in Ideology Building," *Economic and Political Weekly* 28, no. 12/13 (1993): 518.

28. Shruti Kapila, "Ambedkar's Agonism, Sovereign Violence and Pakistan as Peace," *Comparative Studies of South Asia, Africa and the Middle East* 39, no. 1 (2019): 184–95.

29. Ibid., 190–1.

30. See ibid., 193.

31. See Morton Klass, *Caste: The Emergence of the South Asian Social System* (Philadelphia: Institute for the Study of Human Issues, 1980), 26; Sanjay Subrahmanyam, *The Political Economy of Commerce: Southern India 1500–1650* (Cambridge: Cambridge University Press, 1990), 327–9.

32. See María Elena Martínez's masterful account: *Genealogical Fictions: Limpieza de Sangre, Religion, and Gender in Colonial Mexico* (Stanford, CA: Stanford University Press, 2008); see also Kathryn Burns, "Unfixing Race," in *Rereading the Black Legend: The Discourses of Religious and Racial Difference in the Renaissance Empires,* ed. Margaret R. Greer, Walter D. Mignolo, and Maureen Quilligan (Chicago: University of Chicago Press, 2000), 188–202.

33. See Gita Dharampal-Frick, *Indien im Spiegel deutscher Quellen der frühen Neuzeit (1500–1750): Studien zu einer interkulturellen Konstellation* (Tübingen, Germany: Max Niemayer, 1994), 176; Ronald Inden, *Imagining India* (Cambridge, MA: Blackwell, 1990), 53.

34. Dharampal-Frick, *Indien im Spiegel,* 184.

35. Werner Conze, "Adel, Aristokratie," in *Geschichtliche Grundbegriffe: Historisches Lexikon zur politisch-sozialen Sprache in Deutschland,* ed. Otto Brunner, Werner Conze, and Reinhart Koselleck (Stuttgart: Ernst Klett, 1972), 1:30n133. First noted by Albert Gombert, "Weitere Belege zu farbigen Worten," *Zeitschrift für deutsche Wortforschung* 7, no. 2 (1905): 148–9; see also Dharampal-Frick, *Indien im Spiegel,* 184n32.

36. Blake Smith, "Myths of Stasis: South Asia, Global Commerce and Economic Orientalism in Late Eighteenth-Century France" (PhD diss., Northwestern University and L'École des Hautes Études en Sciences Sociales, 2017), 148–87. I thank the author for sharing a manuscript of the relevant fourth chapter with me, titled "South Asia in the French Revolution." All references follow the pagination of the chapter manuscript, which differs from the prior page range.

37. Cf. Ibid., 16.

38. See Conze, "Adel, Aristokratie," 1:30n133; Dharampal-Frick, *Indien im Spiegel,* 184n32; Gombert, "Weitere Belege," 149; Christoph Martin Wieland, *Der goldne Spiegel oder die Könige von Scheschian: Eine wahre Geschichte; Aus dem Scheschianischen übersetzt* (Leipzig: Weidmann, Reich 1772). Citations refer to the second, revised edition: Christoph Martin Wieland, *Der goldene Spiegel: Zweyter Theil,* vol. 7 of *C. M. Wielands sämmtliche Werke* (1794; repr., Leipzig: Georg Joachim Göschen, 1795), 278–80. For the politics of Wieland's *Golden Mirror,* see Herman Meyer, "Christoph Martin Wieland: 'Der Goldene Spiegel' und 'Die Geschichte des weisen Danischmend,'" in *Christoph Martin Wieland,* ed. Hans Jörg Schelle (Darmstadt, Germany: Wissenschaftliche Buchgesellschaft, 1981), 131.

39. Wieland, *Goldene Spiegel,* 278–80.

40. For Wieland's attitude toward the French Revolution, see Gonthier-Louis Fink, "Wieland und die Französische Revolution," in Schelle, *Christoph Martin Wieland,* 407–43, esp. 412–13, 422–3; see also Martin Holtermann, *Der deutsche Aristophanes: Die Rezeption eines politischen Dichters im 19. Jahrhundert* (Göttingen, Germany: Vandenhoeck & Ruprecht, 2004), 80–2.

41. Hugo Wehrle and Anton Schlessing, *Schlessing-Wehrle deutscher Wortschatz: Ein Hilfs- und Nachschlagebuch sinnverwandter Wörter und Ausdrücke der deutschen Sprache; Mit einem ausführlichen Wort- und Sachverzeichnis,* 6th ed. (Stuttgart: E. Klett, 1927), 103, 223; Friedrich Kluge, *Etymologisches Wörterbuch der deutschen Sprache,* 11th ed., ed. Alfred Götze (Berlin: De Gruyter, 1934), 289.

42. Alfred Götze, *Trübners deutsches Wörterbuch: Im Auftrag der Arbeitsgemeinschaft für deutsche Wortforschung herausgegeben von Alfred Götze,* 4 vols. (Berlin: De Gruyter, 1943), 4:104; Gombert, "Weitere Belege," 148–9.

43. Horst Grünert, *Sprache und Politik: Untersuchungen zum Sprachgebrauch der "Paulskirche"* (Berlin: De Gruyter, 1974), 241, 224.

44. Ibid., 261.

45. See Poliakov, *Aryan Myth,* 189–214; Thomas Trautmann, *Aryans and British India* (Berkeley: University of California Press, 1997), 38–9, 172–6, 194–7; Rolf-Peter Sieferle, "Indien und die Arier in der Rassentheorie," *Zeitschrift für Kulturaustausch* 37, no. 3 (1987): 453; Romila Thapar, "The Theory of Aryan Race and India: History and Politics," *Social Scientist* 24, no. 1/3 (1996): 3–29; Romila Thapar, "Durkheim and Weber on Theories of Society and Race Relating to Pre-Colonial India," in *Sociological Theories: Race and Colonialism* (Paris: UNESCO, 1980), 96–8; Becker, *Wege ins Dritte Reich,* 2:519. For Indian spins on Aryan theorizing, see Joan Leopold, "The Aryan Theory of Race," *Indian Economic and Social History Review* 7, no. 2 (1970): 271–97.

46. Theodor Matthias, *Das neue deutsche Wörterbuch: Unter besonderer Berücksichtigung der Rechtschreibung sowie der Herkunft, Bedeutung und Fügung der Wörter, auch der Lehn- und Fremdwörter,* ed. Joseph Lammerz and Karl Quenzel (Leipzig: Hesse & Becker, 1930), 179.

47. *Meyers Handlexikon,* 7th, completely rev. ed. (Leipzig: Bibliographisches Institut, 1920), 376.

48. See Thapar, "Durkheim and Weber," 98–9; Inden, *Imagining India,* 72; Karuna Mantena, *Alibis of Empire: Henry Maine and the Ends of Liberal Imperialism* (Princeton, NJ: Princeton University Press, 2010), esp. 160–1, 121.

49. Francis Fukuyama, *The Origins of Political Order: From Prehuman Times to the French Revolution* (London: Profile Books, 2012), 175.

50. *Meyers Konversations-Lexikon,* 4th ed., 19 vols. (1840–55; repr., Leipzig: Verlag des Bibliographischen Instituts, 1888), 9:596; see similarly Joseph von Held, *Staat und Gesellschaft vom Standpunkte der Geschichte der Menschheit und des Staats: Mit besonderer Rücksicht auf die politisch-socialen Fragen unserer Zeit,* vol. 1, *Grundanschauungen über Staat und Gesellschaft* (Leipzig: F. A. Brockhaus, 1861), 114–5.

51. Christian Lassen, *Indische Alterthumskunde,* 2nd, corrected and much enlarged ed., 4 vols. (1847; repr., Leipzig: L. A. Kitter, 1867), 1:942–3.

52. Albert Reibmayr, *Inzucht und Vermischung beim Menschen* (Leipzig: Franz Deuticke, 1897), 35–6.

53. See, paradigmatically, Louis Dumont, *Homo Hierarchicus: The Caste System and Its Implications,* complete rev. English ed. (1966; repr., Chicago: University of Chicago Press, 1980); Michael Moffat, *An Untouchable Community in South India: Structure and Consensus* (Princeton, NJ: Princeton University Press, 1979), 303. For a critique, see Dipankar Gupta, "Caste and Politics: Identity over System," *Annual Review of Anthropology* 34, no. 1 (2005): 410–13.

54. India's ethnographic record has provided ample refutation of the equation of caste with (a single) hierarchy: see, notably, Dipankar Gupta, *Interrogating Caste: Understanding Hierarchy and Difference in Indian Society* (New Delhi: Penguin Books, 2000); see also M. N. Srinivas's influential concept of a "dominant caste" at the village level, first presented in "The Dominant Caste in Rampura," *American Anthropologist* 61, no. 1 (1959): 1–16; see also Gloria Goodwin Raheja, "Centrality, Mutuality and Hierarchy: Shifting Aspects of Inter-Caste Relationships in North India," *Contributions to Indian Sociology* 23, no. 1 (1989): 79–101.

55. Friedrich Wilhelm Nietzsche, *Jenseits von Gut und Böse,* Division 6, vol. 2 of *Nietzsche Werke: Kritische Gesamtausgabe,* ed. Giorgio Colli and Mazzino Montinari (1886; repr., Berlin: De Gruyter, 1968), 215–16; Friedrich Wilhelm Nietzsche, *Zur Genealogie der Moral,* Division 6, vol. 2 of *Nietzsche Werke* (1887; repr., Berlin: De Gruyter, 1968), 277.

56. Michel Foucault, *"Society Must De Defended": Lectures at the Collège de France, 1975–6,* ed. Mauro Bertani and Alessandro Fontana, trans. David Macey (1992; repr., New York, 2003), 115–40, esp. 123–6; Poliakov, *Aryan Myth,* 17–18, 45–8. See also Ann Laura Stoler, *Race and*

the Education of Desire: Foucault's History of Sexuality and the Colonial Order of Things (Durham, NC: Duke University Press, 1995), 55–94, who recovered Foucault's lectures on race for an Anglophone audience.

57. Foucault, *"Society Must Be Defended,"* 26, quote at 79.

58. Ibid., 90–93, 79.

59. For a critique, see Vanita Seth, "The Origins of Racism: A Critique of the History of Ideas," *History and Theory* 59, no. 3 (2020): 363.

60. Foucault, *"Society Must Be Defended,"* 211, 217–18.

61. Contrast with Smith, "Myths of Stasis," 14–16.

62. Emmanuel Joseph Sieyès, *Qu'est-ce que le Tiers-État?*, 3rd ed. (1789; repr., S.l.: s.n., 1789), 12n1.

63. Ibid., 16–17.

64. On "class-racism," see Étienne Balibar, "Class-Racism," trans. Chris Turner, in *Race, Nation, Class: Ambiguous Identities*, by Étienne Balibar and Immanuel Maurice Wallerstein (London: Verso, 1991), 207–8.

65. Poliakov, *Aryan Myth*, 37–53; Foucault, *"Society Must Be Defended,"* 26, 126–7, 134, quote at 79. For the two "races" in France, see Jacques Martin Barzun, *The French Race: Theories of Its Origins and Their Social and Political Implications Prior to the Revolution* (New York: Columbia University Press, 1932), 135, 140–6.

66. Arthur de Gobineau, *Essai sur l'inégalité des races humaines*, 2 vols. (Paris: Didot Frères, 1853), 2:17; see Edward J. Young, *Gobineau und der Rassismus: Eine Kritik der anthropologischen Geschichtstheorie* (Meisenheim am Glan, Germany: Anton Hain, 1968), 127; Michael D. Biddiss, *Father of Racist Ideology: The Social and Political Thought of Count Gobineau* (New York: Weybright & Talley, 1970), 164–5.

67. Hannah Arendt, *The Origins of Totalitarianism*, 2nd, enlarged ed. (1951; repr., London: George Allen & Unwin, 1958), 171–2, quoted in Biddiss, *Father of Racist Ideology*, 105.

68. Hildegard Châtellier, "Wagnerismus in der Kaiserzeit," in *Handbuch zur "Völkischen Bewegung" 1871–1918*, ed. Uwe Puschner, Walter Schmitz, and Justus H. Ulbricht (Munich: De Gruyter Saur, 1996), 589–91, 599; Uwe Puschner, *Die völkische Bewegung im wilhelminischen Kaiserreich: Sprache—Rasse—Religion* (Darmstadt, Germany: WBG, 2001), 16, 71, 78–82; also see Becker, *Wege ins Dritte Reich*, 2:30–8, 59–60; Young, *Gobineau und der Rassismus*, 32–8, 59–61; Biddiss, *Father of Racist Ideology*.

69. Houston Stewart Chamberlain, *Die Grundlagen des neunzehnten Jahrhunderts*, 2 vols. (Munich: F. Bruckmann, 1899).

70. In keeping with German convention, Chamberlain uses the terms "English" and "England" throughout, the connotation being "British" and "Britain." I cleave to Chamberlain's usage. See Houston Stewart Chamberlain, "England," in *Kriegsaufsätze*, 11th ed. (1914; repr., Munich: F. Bruckmann, 1915), 44–67.

71. For a historical refutation, which argues that early modern celebrations of "England's mongrel nationhood" indigenized the Norman conquest, see Colin Kidd, *British Identities before Nationalism: Ethnicity and Nationhood in the Atlantic World, 1600–1800* (Cambridge: Cambridge University Press, 1999), 76–8, 287–91; see also Poliakov, *Aryan Myth*, 37–53, esp. 52.

72. Chamberlain, "England," 48.

73. Ibid., 47.

74. Ibid., 48.

75. See Poliakov, *Aryan Myth*, 38; Chamberlain, "England," 49, 48.

76. Chamberlain, "England," 48.

77. See Châtellier, "Wagnerismus in der Kaiserzeit," 602–3; Becker, *Wege ins Dritte Reich*, 2:180–1, 2:11–60. For Chamberlain's views on Gobineau, see also Geoffrey G. Field, *Evangelist of Race: The Germanic Vision of Houston Stewart Chamberlain* (New York: Columbia University Press, 1981), 178, 234–5, 340–1.

78. Hildegard Châtellier, "Rasse und Religion bei Houston Stewart Chamberlain," in *Völkische Religion und Krisen der Moderne: Entwürfe "arteigener" Glaubenssysteme seit der Jahrhundertwende,* ed. Stefanie von Schnurbein and Justus H. Ulbricht (Würzburg, Germany: Königshausen & Neumann, 2001), 189–90; Chamberlain, *Grundlagen des neunzehnten Jahrhunderts,* 1:374.

79. The foundational text was Johann Plenge, *1789 und 1914: Die symbolischen Jahre in der Geschichte des politischen Geistes* (Berlin: J. Springer, 1916). For a discussion, see Klaus von See, *Freiheit und Gemeinschaft: Völkisch-nationales Denken in Deutschland zwischen Französischer Revolution und Erstem Weltkrieg* (Heidelberg, Germany: Winter, 2001); Jeffrey Verhey, *The Spirit of 1914: Militarism, Myth, and Mobilization in Germany* (Cambridge: Cambridge University Press, 2000); Wolfgang J. Mommsen, *Der autoritäre Nationalstaat: Verfassung, Gesellschaft und Kultur des deutschen Kaiserreiches* (Frankfurt am Main: Fischer Taschenbuch, 1990), 407–21; Hans Ulrich Wehler, *Deutsche Gesellschaftsgeschichte,* vol. 4, *Vom Beginn des Ersten Weltkriegs bis zur Gründung der beiden deutschen Staaten 1914–1949* (Munich: C. H. Beck, 1987), 16–21.

80. Chamberlain, "England," 44.

81. Ibid., 45–6. Cf. Field, *Evangelist of Race,* 223.

82. Chamberlain, "England," 46.

83. Contrast with Field, *Evangelist of Race,* 378–89. For German Jews during World War I, see Patrick Dassen, "The German Nation as a Secular Religion in the First World War? About the Problem of Unity in Modern German History," in *Political Religion beyond Totalitarianism: The Sacralization of Politics in the Age of Democracy,* ed. Joost Augusteijn, Dassen, and Maartje Janse (Basingstoke, UK: Palgrave Macmillan, 2013), 177; Michael Wildt, *Volksgemeinschaft als Selbstermächtigung: Gewalt gegen Juden in der deutschen Provinz 1919 bis 1939* (Hamburg: Hamburger Edition, 2007), 32.

84. Chamberlain, "England," *North American Review* 202, no. 716 (1915): 35–52. Subsequent references are still to the German version of Chamberlain's "England."

85. John McF. Howie, Alfred B. Cruikshank, and H. Michaelyan, "Mr. Chamberlain's 'England,'" *North American Review* 202, no. 717 (1915): 296; Chamberlain, "England," 53.

86. Chamberlain, "Deutsche Freiheit," in *Kriegsaufsätze,* 17.

87. Karuna Mantena, "The Crisis of Liberal Imperialism," in *Victorian Visions of Global Order: Empire and International Relations in Nineteenth-Century Political Thought,* ed. Duncan Bell (Cambridge: University of Cambridge, 2007), 126.

88. Henry Sumner Maine, "The Effect of Observation of India on European Thought," in *Village-Communities in the East and West, the Rede Lecture of 1875* (London: John Murray, 1876), 233, quoted in Mantena, "Crisis of Liberal Imperialism," 114.

89. See Kapila, "Ambedkar's Agonism," 187.

90. For Mahraun, see Clifton Greer Ganyard, *Artur Mahraun and the Young German Order: An Alternative to National Socialism in Weimar Political Culture* (Lewiston, NY: Edwin Mellen Press, 2008).

91. Artur Mahraun, *Das Jungdeutsche Manifest: Volk gegen Kaste und Geld; Sicherung des Friedens durch Neubau der Staaten* (Berlin: Jungdeutscher Verlag, 1927), 30.

92. See Verhey, *Spirit of 1914,* 213; Michael Wildt, "'Volksgemeinschaft': Eine Antwort auf Ian Kershaw," *Zeithistorische Forschungen/ Studies in Contemporary History* 8 (2011): 104.

93. Erich Everth, *Das innere Deutschland nach dem Kriege* (Jena, Germany: Eugen Diedrichs, 1916), 153.

94. Carl Schmitt, *Der Begriff des Politischen* (Hamburg: Hanseatische Verlagsanstalt, 1933); Everth, *Innere Deutschland,* 45–6.

95. Everth, *Innere Deutschland,* 45–6.

96. See Verhey, *Spirit of 1914,* 216–18, 223–27; Dassen, "German Nation," 163, 180–1; Bajohr and Wildt, introduction to *Volksgemeinschaft,* 13; Alexander Meschnig, "Die Sendung der Nation: Vom Grabenkrieg zur NS-Bewegung," in Brockhaus, *Attraktion der NS-Bewegung,* 33–40; Wildt, *Volksgemeinschaft als Selbstermächtigung,* 26–30.

97. For Jung, see Roshan Magub, *Edgar Julius Jung: Right-Wing Enemy of the Nazis: A Political Biography* (Rochester, NY: Camden House, 2017).
98. Edgar Julius Jung, "Deutschland und die Konservative Revolution," in *Deutsche über Deutschland: Die Stimme des unbekannten Politikers; Mit zusammenfassendem Nachwort; Deutschland und die Konservative Revolution* (Munich: Albert Langen/Georg Müller, 1932), 381.
99. Ibid.
100. See Bernhard Jenschke, *Zur Kritik der konservativ-revolutionären Ideologie in der Weimarer Republik: Weltanschauung und Politik bei Edgar Julius Jung* (Munich: C. H. Beck, 1971), 129–36; Sebastian Maass, *Die andere deutsche Revolution: Edgar Julius Jung und die metaphysischen Grundlagen der konservativen Revolution* (Kiel, Germany: Regin-Verlag, 2009), 96–98. For "Conservative Revolutionaries" on hierarchy and aristocracy, see Kurt Sontheimer, *Antidemokratisches Denken in der Weimarer Republik: Die politischen Ideen des deutschen Nationalismus zwischen 1918 und 1933* (Munich: Nymphenburger Verlagshandlung, 1962), 173, 180, 253–60; Klemens von Klemperer, *Germany's New Conservatism: Its History and Dilemma in the Twentieth Century* (Princeton, NJ: Princeton University Press, 1957), 120–4.
101. Edgar Julius Jung, *Die Herrschaft der Minderwertigen: Ihr Zerfall und ihre Ablösung durch ein neues Reich*, 3rd ed. (1927; repr., Berlin: Verlag Deutsche Rundschau, 1930), 262.
102. Ibid., 171.
103. Klemperer, *Germany's New Conservatism*, 212.
104. Quentin Skinner, "Meaning and Understanding in the History of Ideas," *History and Theory* 8, no. 1 (1969): 3–53; Quentin Skinner, "Some Problems in the Analysis of Political Thought and Action," *Political Theory* 2, no. 3 (1974): 277–303.
105. *Triumpf des Willens*, directed by Leni Riefenstahl (1935).
106. See Michael Wildt, "Die Ungleichheit des Volkes: 'Volksgemeinschaft' in der politischen Kommunikation der Weimarer Republik," in Bajohr and Wildt, *Volksgemeinschaft*, 36.
107. Reinhart Koselleck, "Volk, Nation, Nationalismus, Masse: XIII. Lexikalischer Rückblick," in Brunner, Conze, and Koselleck, *Geschichtliche Grundbegriffe*, 7:390. For the political semantics of "nation," "Volk," and "race," see also Peter Walkenhorst, *Nation, Volk, Rasse: Radikaler Nationalismus im deutschen Kaiserreich 1890–1914* (Göttingen, Germany: Vandenhoeck & Ruprecht, 2007), 80–165; Reinhart Koselleck, "Volk, Nation, Nationalismus, Masse," in Brunner, Conze, and Koselleck, *Geschichtliche Grundbegriffe*, 7:149.
108. Adolf Hitler, *Sämtliche Aufzeichnungen 1905–1924*, ed. Eberhard Jäckel and Axel Kuhn (Stuttgart: Deutsche Verlagsanstalt, 1980); Adolf Hitler, *Hitler: Reden, Schriften, Anordnungen: Februar 1925 bis Januar 1933*, ed. Institut für Zeitgeschichte, Clemens Vollnhans, Bärbel Dusik, Konstantin Goschler, Christian Hartmann, Klaus A. Lankheit, Lother Gruchman et al., 7 vols. (Munich: K. G. Saur, 1992–2003).
109. *Kampfzeit* appears in the title of a collection of Hitler speeches: Adolf Hitler, *Adolf Hitler in Franken: Reden aus der Kampfzeit* (n.p.: 1939).
110. Max Domarus and Adolf Hitler, *Hitler: Reden und Proklamationen 1932–1945: Kommentiert von einem deutschen Zeitgenossen*, 4 vols. (Leonberg, Germany: Pamminger & Partner, 1973), 1:349.
111. Hitler, "10. September 1930: 'Aufruf an das deutsche Volk: Was haben die alten Parteien versprochen, was haben sie gehalten?:' Artikel," in Institut für Zeitgeschichte and Hartmann, *Hitler*, 3:3:405.
112. Götze, *Trübners deutsches Wörterbuch*, 4:104. The pioneering dictionary writers of the nineteenth century, the Brothers Grimm, ignored the term's political function: *Deutsches Wörterbuch von Jacob Grimm und Wilhelm Grimm*, ed. Dr. Rudolf Hildebrand, vol. 5, *K* (Leipzig: Hirzel, 1873; repr., Munich: Deutscher Taschenbuch Verlag, 1984), 270.
113. Hitler, "10. September 1930," 405.
114. Hitler, "27. Februar 1925: 'Deutschlands Zukunft und unsere Bewegung'; Rede auf NSDAP-Versammlung in München," in Institut für Zeitgeschichte and Vollnhans, *Hitler*, 1:17.

115. Hitler, "Rede auf einer NSDAP Versammlung," January 3, 1923, in Hitler, *Sämtliche Aufzeichnungen,* 778.
116. Hitler, "3. März 1928: 'Tageskampf oder Schicksalskampf;' Rede auf NSDAP-Versammlung in Karlsruhe," in Institut für Zeitgeschichte and Dusik, *Hitler,* 2:2:738 (italics in original).
117. Cornelia Schmitz-Berning, *Vokabular des Nationalsozialismus* (Berlin: De Gruyter, 1998), 422; Rudolf Jung, *Der nationale Sozialismus: Seine Grundlagen, sein Werdegang und seine Ziele,* 3rd ed. (1919; repr., Munich: Deutscher Volksverlag Dr. E. Boepple, 1922).
118. Jung, *Der nationale Sozialismus,* 107.
119. Hitler, "13. November 1930: Rede auf NSDStB-Versammlung in Erlangen," in Institut für Zeitgeschichte and Goschler, *Hitler,* 4:1:99–100.
120. Hitler, "Die 'Hetzer' der Wahrheit," in *Adolf Hitlers Reden,* ed. Ernst Boepple (Munich: Deutscher Volksverlag Dr. E. Boepple, 1925), 23 (italics mine); slight variation in Hitler, *Sämtliche Aufzeichnungen,* 621, which adds, after "natives," "The same happened in Egypt and also in Rome."
121. Adolf Hitler, January 12–13, 1942, in Heinrich Heim and Adolf Hitler, *Monologe im Führerhauptquartier 1941–1944,* ed. Werner Jochmann (Hamburg: Knaus, 1980), 196.
122. *Adolf Hitler spricht: Ein Lexikon des Nationalsozialismus* (Leipzig: R. Kittler, 1934), 16.
123. Hitler, "'Hetzer' der Wahrheit," 23.
124. Hitler, "7. September 1932: 'Die politische Lage'; Rede auf NSDAP-Versammlung in Munich," in Institut für Zeitgeschichte and Lankheit, *Hitler,* 5:1:344.
125. Hitler, "27. Februar 1925," 1:18–20, quote at 18.
126. Hitler, "Parteipolitik und Judenfrage: Stichworte zu einer Rede," December 8, 1920, in Hitler, *Sämtliche Aufzeichnungen,* 275 (underlined in original).
127. Jacob Friedrich Fries, *Ueber die Gefährdung des Wohlstandes und Charakters der Deutschen durch die Juden* (Heidelberg: Mohr & Winter, 1816), 16, 18.
128. On the Jewish "enemy," see Jeffrey Herf, *The Jewish Enemy: Nazi Propaganda during World War II and the Holocaust* (Cambridge, MA: Harvard University Press, 2006).
129. For the events of the Nazi "seizure of power," see Richard J. Evans, *The Coming of the Third Reich* (London: Allen Lane, 2003), 247–308.
130. See Bernd A. Rusinek, "Die *Nationalsozialistischen Monatshefte* und *Volkstum und Heimat,*" in *Le milieu intellectuel conservateur en Allemagne: Sa presse et ses réseaux, 1890–1960 / Das konservative Intellektuellen-Milieu in Deutschland: Seine Presse und Seine Netzwerke, 1890–1960,* ed. Michel Grunewald and Use Puschner (Bern, Switzerland: Peter Lang, 2003), 575–616, quote at 577.
131. Alfred Rosenberg, "Der Konflikt zwischen Kaste und Volk," *Nationalsozialistische Monatshefte* 3, no. 31 (1932): 432–35.
132. See Dorothee Schlütter, *Vom Kampfblatt zur Staatspropaganda: Die auswärtige Pressearbeit der NSDAP dokumentiert am Beispiel der NS-Wochenzeitschrift* Westküsten-Beobachter *aus Chile* (Göttingen, Germany: Vandenhoeck & Ruprecht, 2016), 144.
133. Rosenberg, "Konflikt zwischen Kaste," 434–5.
134. Hitler, "7. September 1932," 343–4.
135. See Evans, *Coming of the Third Reich,* 38–9.
136. Alfred Rosenberg, *Der Mythus des 20. Jahrhunderts: Eine Wertung der seelisch-geistigen Gestaltenkämpfe unserer Zeit* (Munich: Hoheneichen, 1939 [1930]), 457.
137. For the Nazi "revolution," see Chris Clark, *Time and Power: Visions of History in German Politics, from the Thirty Years' War to the Third Reich* (Princeton, NJ: Princeton University Press, 2019), 171–210.
138. Hitler, "8. Oktober 1925: 'Heute, da jeder Lump und Franzose in Deutschland reden darf, ist ein Redeverbot eine Ehre'; Rede auf NSDAP-Versammlung in Wismar," in Institut für Zeitgeschichte and Vollnhans, *Hitler,* 1:171.

139. Hitler, "6. Oktober 1925: 'Rede auf NSDAP-Versammlung in Plauen,'" in Institut für Zeitgeschichte and Vollnhans, *Hitler,* 1:170.

140. See also Klaus von See, *Deutsche Germanen-Ideologie vom Humanismus bis zur Gegenwart* (Frankfurt am Main: Athenräum, 1970), 70–2; Uriel Tal, *Religion, Politics and Ideology in the Third Reich* (London: Routledge, 2004), 2–4; Timothy Stanton, "Popular Sovereignty in an Age of Mass Democracy," in *Popular Sovereignty in Historical Perspective,* ed. Richard Bourke and Quentin Skinner (Cambridge: Cambridge University Press, 2016), 320–58.

141. "Sendemanuscripte: 'The Social Policy of New Germany,'" February 3, 1941, BArch R 901/48007, p. 132, Bundesarchiv, Berlin-Lichterfelde. Cf. my discussion with Jan Kuhlmann, *Subhas Chandra Bose und die Indienpolitik der Achsenmächte* (Berlin: Schiler, 2003), 76.

142. Hitler, "7. September 1932," 343.

143. Ibid.

144. Benito Mussolini, "Trenchocracy," in *Fascism,* ed. Roger Griffin (Oxford: Oxford University Press, 1995), 28; see Roger Griffin, *The Nature of Fascism* (1991; repr., London: Routledge, 1993), 66, 92–3.

145. Stefan Breuer, *Ordnungen der Ungleichheit: Die deutsche Rechte im Widerstreit ihrer Ideen 1871–1945* (Darmstadt, Germany: Wissenschaftliche Buchgesellschaft, 2001).

146. See, paradigmatically, Conze, "Adel unter dem Totenkopf," 166; Alexandra Gerstner, *Neuer Adel: Aristokratische Elitekonzeptionen zwischen Jahrhundertwende und Nationalsozialismus* (Darmstadt, Germany: Wissenschaftliche Buchgesellschaft, 2008), esp., 331–9; Stephan Malinowski, *Vom König zum Führer: Sozialer Niedergang und politische Radikalisierung im deutschen Adel zwischen Kaiserreich und NS-Staat* (Berlin: Akademie Verlag, 2003).

147. See Charles de Miramon, "Noble Dogs, Noble Blood: The Invention of the Concept of Race in the Late Middle Ages," in *The Origins of Racism in the West,* ed. Miriam Eliav-Feldon, Benjamin H. Isaac, and Joseph Ziegler (Cambridge: Cambridge University Press, 2009), 200–14. For a critique of tracing "race" and racism to premodern European origins, thus eliding the histories of colonialism, plantation slavery, and biological racism, see Seth, "Origins of Racism," 359–63, 366–7.

148. Guillaume Aubert, "'The Blood of France': Race and Purity of Blood in the French Atlantic World," *William and Mary Quarterly* 61, no. 3 (2004): 449; Wolfgang Mager, "Von der Noblesse zur Notabilité: Die Konstituierung der französischen Notabeln im Ancien Régime und die Krise der Absoluten Monarchie," *Geschichte und Gesellschaft: Sonderheft* 13 (1990): 272.

149. See Breuer, *Ordnungen der Ungleichheit,* 71–2.

150. Karl August Graf von Drechsel, *Über Entwürfe zur Reorganisation des deutschen Adels im 19. Jahrhundert* (Ingolstadt, Germany: Ganghofer, 1912),108–111, quoted in Malinowski, *Vom König zum Führer,* 300.

151. Sister Nivedita, "Noblesse Oblige: A Study of Indian Caste," in *The Complete Works of Sister Nivedita: Birth Centenary Publication,* 5 vols. (Calcutta: Sister Nivedita's Girls School, 1955), 2:120.

152. Ibid., 105.

153. Ibid., 121.

154. Ibid., 118.

155. Rainer Zitelmann, *Hitler: Selbstverständnis eines Revolutionärs* (Hamburg: Berg, 1987), 92–115; Hitler, "Die Proklamation des Führers," in *Reden des Führers am Parteitag der Arbeit 1937* (Munich: Zentralverlag der NSDAP, Franz Eher, 1938), 16.

156. For this trope, see Ian Wood, *The Modern Origins of the Early Middle Ages* (Oxford: Oxford University Press, 2013), 16–17, 174–5.

157. Richard Walther Darré, *Neuadel aus Blut und Boden* (Munich: J. F. Lehmann, 1930), 10–11. For Darré and Nazi breeding fantasies, see Becker, *Wege ins Dritte Reich,* esp. 1:268–271; Peter Weingart, Jürgen Kroll, and Kurt Bayertz, *Rasse, Blut und Gene: Geschichte der Eugenik in Deutschland* (Frankfurt am Main: Suhrkamp, 1992), esp. 34, 139–42, 454–5.

158. Darré, *Neuadel aus Blut,* 15.

159. Joseph von Held, *Staat und Gesellschaft,* vol. 2, *Volk und Regierung mit besonderer Rücksicht auf die Entwicklung der Gesellschaft und des Staats in Deutschland* (Leipzig: Brockhaus, 1863), 438–42.

160. See Conze, "Adel, Aristokratie," 1.

161. Friedrich Hertz, *Rasse und Kultur: Eine kritische Untersuchung der Rassentheorien,* 2nd, reworked and enlarged ed. of *Moderne Rassentheorien* (1904; repr., Leipzig: Alfred Kröner, 1915), 29.

162. For Darré's influence by Günther, see Horst Gies, *Richard Walther Darré: Der "Reichsbauernführer", die nationalsozialistische "Blut und Boden"-Ideologie und Hitlers Machteroberung* (Vienna: Böhlau, 2019), 74–88; Hans-Jürgen Lutzhöft, *Der nordische Gedanke in Deutschland 1920 bis 1940* (Stuttgart: Klett, 1971), 52–4.

163. Hans F. K. Günther, *Adel und Rasse* (Munich: J. F. Lehmann, 1927), 27–39, quote at 39.

164. Staiano-Daniels, "Melancholy of the Thinking," 176, 178.

165. Günther, *Adel und Rasse,* 104, 39.

166. Darré, *Neuadel aus Blut,* 153–4.

167. Ibid., 153.

168. Herbert Meyer, *Rasse und Recht bei den Germanen und Indogermanen* (Weimar, Germany: Hermann Böhlaus, 1937), 5; Günther, *Führeradel durch Sippenpflege* (Munich: J. F. Lehmann, 1936). For Meyer as a "Germanist" jurist, see Hans-Jürgen Becker, "Neuheidentum und Rechtsgeschichte," in *Die deutsche Rechtsgeschichte in der NS-Zeit: Ihre Vorgeschichte und ihre Nachwirkungen,* ed. Joachim Rückert and Dietmar Willoweit (Tübingen, Germany: J. C. B. Mohr, 1995), 19.

169. Günther, quoted in Meyer, *Rasse und Recht,* 65. The quotation is very likely drawn from Günther, *Rasse und Adel,* 17.

170. Meyer, *Rasse und Recht,* 68.

171. Ibid., 5.

172. For the Nazi rejection of ideas of a "German race," see Richard Wetzell, "Eugenics, Racial Science, and Nazi Biopolitics: Was There a Genesis of the 'Final Solution' from the Spirit of Science?," in Pendas, Roseman, and Wetzell, *Beyond the Racial State,* 154–8.

173. Rosenberg, *Mythus,* 576–7.

174. Contrast this with the prevalent scholarly view that Nietzsche wished to breed four castes, or "races," first discussed by Annemarie Etter, "Nietzsche und das Gesetzbuch des Manu," *Nietzsche-Studien* 16, no. 1 (1987): 341; see also Roger Berkowitz, "Friedrich Nietzsche, the Code of Manu, and the Art of Legislation Symposium: Nietzsche and Legal Theory (Part II)," *Cardozo Law Review* 24, no. 3 (2003–2002): 1139–40; Koenraad Elst, "Manu as a Weapon against Egalitarianism: Nietzsche and Hindu Political Philosophy," in *Nietzsche, Power and Politics, Rethinking Nietzsche's Legacy for Political Thought,* ed. Herman Siemens and Vasti Roodt (Berlin: De Gruyter, 2009), 557; Thomas Paul Bonfiglio, "Toward a Genealogy of Aryan Morality: Nietzsche and Jacolliot," *New Nietzsche Studies* 6, no. 3/4, and 7, no. 1/2 (2005–2006): 173–4; Dorthy M. Figueira, "Aryan Aristocrats and Übermenschen: Nietzsche's Reading of the *Laws of Manu,*" *Comparatist* 23 (1999): 10. For the contrasting view that Nietzsche ultimately rejected both Manu and caste breeding, see Gerd Schank, *"Rasse" und "Züchtung" bei Nietzsche* (Berlin: De Gruyter, 2011), 62–5; also Thomas H. Brobjer, "The Absence of Political Ideals in Nietzsche's Writings: The Case of the Laws of Manu and the Associated Caste-Society," *Nietzsche-Studien* 27, no. 1 (1998): 304, 313; Thomas H. Brobjer, "Nietzsche and the Laws of Manu," in *Eastern Influences on Western Philosophy: A Reader,* ed. Alexander Lyon Macfie (Edinburgh: Edinburgh University Press, 2003), 261, 271.

175. For Härtle's "popular handbook": Max Whyte, "The Uses and Abuses of Nietzsche in the Third Reich: Alfred Baeumler's 'Heroic Realism,'" *Journal of Contemporary History* 43, no. 2 (2008): 187.

176. Georg Brandes, "Aristokratischer Radikalismus: Eine Abhandlung über Nietzsche. In: *Deutsche Rundschau.* Berlin, Bd. 16, Nr. 7, April 1890, S. 52–89," in *Rezensionen und Reaktionen zu Nietzsches Werken: 1872–1889,* ed. Hauke Reich (Berlin: De Gruyter, 2013), 927.
177. Heinrich Härtle, *Nietzsche und der Nationalsozialismus* (1937; repr., Munich: Zentralverlag der NSDAP, 1942), 141.
178. Alfred Rosenberg, *Das Verbrechen der Freimaurerei: Juden, Jesuitismus, deutsches Christentum* (Munich: Hoheneichen, 1921), 22–3; identically, see Alfred Rosenberg, "Menschheitsdogmen: Auf gut Deutsch," December 3, 1920, in *Blut und Ehre: Ein Kampf für deutsche Wiedergeburt: Reden und Aufsätze von 1919–1933,* ed. Thilo von Trotha (Munich: Zentralverlag der NSDAP, Franz Eher, 1939), 195–6; similarly, see Rosenberg, *Mythus,* 28–31.
179. Rosenberg, *Verbrechen,* 22–3, 169.
180. Ibid., 22.
181. Ibid., 22–3; Rosenberg, *Mythus,* 28–32, quote at 31.
182. See Staiano-Daniels, "Melancholy of the Thinking," 176.
183. Günther, *Die nordische Rasse bei den Indogermanen Asiens* (Munich: Lehmann, 1934), 34–6, quotes at 36.
184. Fuller, "Caste, Race," 606.
185. Indrani Chatterjee, *Gender, Slavery and Law in Colonial India* (New Delhi: Oxford University Press, 1999), 6.
186. Rupa Viswanath, *The Pariah Problem: Caste, Religion, and the Social in Modern India* (New York: Columbia University Press, 2014), 3–1, 23–4, 241–2.
187. Roy, *Fascism,* 48–51.
188. Whyte, "Uses and Abuses," 174, 187.
189. Härtle, *Nietzsche und der Nationalsozialismus,* 156.
190. Ibid., 158.
191. Ibid., 30–1, 158.
192. Ibid., 27, 30–1.
193. For the French revolutionary notion of "the people," see Bryan Garsten, "From Popular Sovereignty to Civil Society in Post-Revolutionary France," in Bourke and Skinner, *Popular Sovereignty,* 236–69.
194. See Whyte, "Uses and Abuses," 173, 180.
195. Friedrich Wilhelm Nietzsche, *Der Wille zur Macht: Versuch einer Umwertung aller Werte,* ed. Alfred Baeumler (Leipzig: Alfred Kröner Verlag, 1930), 134.
196. Ibid., 637.
197. Friedrich Wilhelm Nietzsche, *Die Unschuld des Werdens: Der Nachlass,* ed. Alfred Baeumler, 2 vols. (Leipzig: Alfred Kröner, 1931), 2:252.
198. Ibid., 2:433.
199. Härtle, *Nietzsche und der Nationalsozialismus,* 68.
200. Ibid., 74.
201. Ibid., 73, 68.
202. Ibid., 86.
203. Ibid., 76.
204. Lutzhöft, *Nordische Gedanke in Deutschland,* 137, 146, 152.
205. Härtle, *Nietzsche und der Nationalsozialismus,* 74.
206. See Lutzhöft, *Nordische Gedanke in Deutschland,* 138.
207. Günther, *Nordische Rasse,* 26.
208. See Rosalind O'Hanlon, *Caste, Conflict and Ideology: Mahatma Jotirao Phule and Low Caste Protest in Nineteenth-Century Western India* (Cambridge: Cambridge University Press, 1985), 141–51; Anupama Rao, *The Caste Question: Dalits and the Politics of Modern India* (Berkeley: University of California Press, 2009), 12–13, 40–9. For anti-Brahmanic reinterpretations of the Aryan conquest in the Tamil-speaking South, see Michael Bergunder, "Umkämpfte Vergangenheit: Anti-brahmanische und Hindu-nationalistische Rekonstruktion der

frühen indischen Religionsgeschichte," in *"Arier" und "Draviden": Konstruktion der Vergangenheit als Grundlage für Selbst- und Fremdwahrnehmungen Südasiens,* ed. Michael Bergunder and Rahul Peter Das (Halle, Germany: Verlag der Frankeschen Stiftungen zu Halle, 2002), 143–9.

209. Here, I especially draw on medievalist Klaus von See's works: *Barbar, Germane, Arier: Die Suche nach der Identität der Deutschen* (Heidelberg: C. Winter, 1994); *Freiheit und Gemeinschaft; Deutsche Germanen-Ideologie*; see also Gerhard Dilcher, *Die Germanisten und die historische Rechtsschule: Bürgerliche Wissenschaft zwischen Romantik, Realismus und Rationalisierung* (Frankfurt am Main: Vittorio Klostermann, 2017), 152–3; Dietmar Willoweit, "Freiheit in der Volksgemeinde: Geschichtliche Aspekte des Freiheitsbegriffs in der deutschen rechtshistorischen und historischen Forschung des 19. und 20. Jahrhunderts," in Rückert and Willoweit, *Deutsche Rechtsgeschichte,* 303–4, 306, 310–19.

210. T. L. Vaswani, *Ecstasy and Experiences: A Mystical Journey,* trans. Aruna Jethwani (New Delhi: Sterling Paperbacks, 2011), 71.

211. T. L. Vaswani, *Die Gestalter der Zukunft und das arische Ideal* (Stuttgart: W. Kohlhammer, 1926), 176.

212. Rosenberg, *Mythus.*

213. Karl Haushofer, "Das Indien von heute," *Süddeutsche Monatshefte* 24, no. 2 (1926): 123.

214. He is mentioned in passing in Max Deeg, "Aryan National Religion(s) and the Criticism of Asceticism and Quietism in the Nineteenth and Twentieth Centuries," in *Asceticism and Its Critics: Historical Accounts and Comparative Perspectives,* ed. Oliver Freiberger (Oxford: Oxford University Press, 2006), 67; Poewe and Hexham, "Surprising Aryan Mediations," 288.

215. Günther, *Adel und Rasse,* 9.

216. Ibid., 17, quote at 20.

217. Ibid., 20–2.

218. Alfred Baeumler, *Nietzsche: Der Philosoph und Politiker* (Leipzig: Phillip Reclam, 1931), 91.

219. Härtle, *Nietzsche und der Nationalsozialismus,* 156.

220. Ibid., 158; see also Lutzhöft, *Nordische Gedanke in Deutschland,* 141.

221. Härtle, *Nietzsche und der Nationalsozialismus,* 125.

222. Ibid., 129.

223. For Nazi ideas of Europe, see Mazower, *Hitler's Empire*; Paolo Giaccaria and Claudio Minca, eds, *Hitler's Geographies: The Spatialities of the Third Reich* (Chicago: Chicago University Press, 2016); Johannes Dafinger and Dieter Pohl, eds., *A New Nationalist Europe under Hitler: Concepts of Europe and Transnational Networks in the National Socialist Sphere of Influence, 1933–1945* (New York: Routledge, 2019); Walter Lipgens, ed., *Documents on the History of European Integration,* vol. 1, *Continental Plans for European Union 1939–1945 (Including 250 Documents in Their Original Language on 6 Microfiches)* (Berlin: De Gruyter, 1985).

224. The term *Bauer* ("peasant") had no pejorative meaning. For Darré, it implied descent from a long line of farmers and possession of a hereditary farmstead: see Gustavo Corni and Horst Gies, *"Blut und Boden": Rassenideologie und Agrarpolitik im Staat Hitlers* (Idstein, Germany: Schulz-Kirchner, 1994), 36.

225. See Gies, *Richard Walter Darré,* 408–10, 416–18, revising his earlier position in Corni and Gies, *"Blut und Boden,"* 22–3, 34–6.

226. See Gies, *Richard Walter Darré,* 297–303; cf. Peter Longerich, *Heinrich Himmler,* trans. Jeremy Noakes and Lesley Sharpe (Oxford: Oxford University Press, 2012), 415–16, 435.

227. Longerich, *Heinrich Himmler,* 415, 435; Corni and Gies, *"Blut und Boden,"* 23–4.

228. Longerich, *Heinrich Himmler,* 415–23, 434–6, 441, quote at 415; see also Michael Wildt, "Himmlers Terminkalender aus dem Jahr 1937," *Vierteljahreshefte für Zeitgeschichte* 52, no. 4 (2004): 673; Georg Lilienthal, *Der "Lebensborn e. V.": Ein Instrument nationalsozialistischer Rassenpolitik* (Stuttgart: Fischer, 1985), 49.

229. First mentioned by Ackermann, *Heinrich Himmler,* 36; see also Longerich, *Heinrich Himmler,* 84; Trimondi and Trimondi, *Hitler, Buddha, Krishna,* 27.

230. Nietzsche, *Wille zur Macht,* 133.

231. Madhav M. Deshpande, "Aryan Origins: Arguments from the Nineteenth-Century Maharashtra," in *The Indo-Aryan Controversy: Evidence and Inference in Indian History,* ed. Edwin F. Bryant and Laurie L. Patton (London: Routledge, 2005), 407; Rosalind O'Hanlon, "Caste and Its Histories in Colonial India: A Reappraisal," in "New Directions in Social and Economic History: Essays in Honour of David Washbrook," special issue, *Modern Asian Studies* 51, no. 2 (2017): 448; Rosalind O'Hanlon, "Maratha History as Polemic: Low Caste Ideology and Political Debate in Late Nineteenth-Century Western India," *Modern Asian Studies* 17, no. 1 (1983): 5–6, 8; Deshpande, "Aryan Origins," 421.
232. Martin A. Ruehl, "'In This Time without Emperors': The Politics of Ernst Kantorowicz's *Kaiser Friedrich der Zweite* Reconsidered," *Journal of the Warburg and Courtauld Institutes* 63 (2000): 187–242.
233. Ibid., 217, 240.
234. Franz Haiser, *Freimaurer und Gegenmaurer im Kampfe um die Weltherrschaft* (Munich: J. F. Lehmann, 1924).
235. See Trimondi and Trimondi, *Hitler, Buddha, Krishna,* 27–31, 243–4.
236. Erwin Baur, Eugen Fischer, and Fritz Lenz, *Grundriß der menschlichen Erblichkeitslehre und Rassenhygiene,* 2 vols. (Munich: J. F. Lehmann, 1921). For a discussion of these eugenicists in their context, see Weingart, Kroll, and Bayertz, *Rasse, Blut und Gene.* Also see Haiser, *Freimaurer und Gegenmaurer,* 66, 71.
237. Barton Scott, *Spiritual Despots,* 38–9; Dumont, *Homo Hierarchicus,* 292; Dorothy M. Figueira, "The Nazi *Kṣatriya* Ethos," in *The Afterlives of the Bhagavad Gita: Readings in Translation,* ed. Dorothy M. Figueira (Oxford: Oxford University Press, 2023), 205–6.
238. Trimondi and Trimondi, *Hitler, Buddha, Krishna,* 27–31, 243–4.
239. Haiser, *Freimaurer und Gegenmaurer,* 104.
240. Ibid., 66, 73.
241. Ibid., 77.
242. Ibid., 52.
243. Ibid., 71.
244. Figueira, "Nazi *Kṣatriya* Ethos"; Vishwa Adluri and Joydeep Bagchee, *The Nay Science: A History of German Indology* (Oxford: Oxford University Press, 2014).
245. Luna Sabastian, "Spaces on the Temporal Move: Weimar *Geopolitik* and the Vision of an Indian Science of the State, 1924–1945," *Global Intellectual History* 3, no. 2 (2018): 243; Figueira, "Nazi *Kṣatriya* Ethos," 206.
246. Figueira, "Nazi *Kṣatriya* Ethos," 211–22; Karla Poewe and Irving Hexham, "Jakob Wilhelm Hauer's New Religion and National Socialism," *Journal of Contemporary Religion* 20, no. 2 (2005): 206; Adluri and Bagchee, *Nay Science,* 267–77.
247. Figueira, "Nazi *Kṣatriya* Ethos," 225–8; Padfield, *Himmler,* 402.
248. Longerich, *Heinrich Himmler,* 352–69. See also Gudrun Schwarz's groundbreaking work on SS wives, in *Eine Frau an seiner Seite: Ehefrauen in der "SS-Sippengemeinschaft"* (Hamburg: Hamburger Edition, 1997); Jochen Böhler and Robert Gerwarth, eds., *The Waffen-SS: A European History* (Oxford: Oxford University Press, 2017).
249. Longerich, *Heinrich Himmler,* 368–82, 461–4.
250. Heinrich Himmler, "Das Blut und die Einheit des Reiches (1938)," in Heinrich Himmler, *Heinrich Himmler: Geheimreden, 1933 bis 1945, und andere Ansprachen,* ed. Bradley F. Smith and Agnes F. Peterson (Frankfurt am Main: Propyläen Verlag, 1974), 54.
251. Heinrich Himmler, "SS-Familien und Rekrutierung (1936)," in *Geheimreden,* 63.
252. Heinrich Himmler, "Lernen von den Engländern (1942)," in *Geheimreden,* 187; Heinrich Himmler, "Rede vor den SS Gruppenführern zu einer Gruppenführerbesprechung im Führerheim der SS-Standarte 'Deutschland' am 08.11.1938," in *Geheimreden,* 32; Himmler, "Der Ehrendienst (1936)," in *Geheimreden,* 78.
253. Heinrich Himmler, "Rede vor Gauleitern und anderen Parteifunktionären am 29.2 [*sic*].1940," in *Geheimreden,* 125–6; Padfield, *Himmler,* 289; Longerich, *Heinrich Himmler,* 264.

254. Himmler, "Rede vor Gauleitern," 127.
255. Heinrich Himmler, "Sterilisation und 'Beseitigung' des 'Untermenschentums' (1940)," in *Geheimreden*, 197.
256. Alfred Rosenberg, ed., *Handbuch der Romfrage: Unter der Mitwirkung einer Arbeitsgemeinschaft von Forschern und Politikern* (Munich: Hoheneichen, 1940), 23; Rosenberg, *Mythus*, 183; Alfred Rosenberg, *Houston Stewart Chamberlain als Verkünder und Begründer einer deutschen Zukunft* (Munich: Bruckmann, 1927), 38; Alfred Rosenberg, "Kollektivismus: Die Bauernvernichtung in der Sowjetunion," *Völkischer Beobachter*, December 31, 1929, in Alfred Rosenberg, *Kampf um die Macht: Aufsätze von 1921–1932*, ed. Thilo von Trotha (Munich: Zentralverlag der NSDAP, F. Eher, 1940), 695; Joseph Goebbels, *Die Tagebücher von Joseph Goebbels*, ed. Elke Fröhlich, 31 vols. (Munich: G. K. Saur, 1993), part 1, 7:317; part 2, 5:91; also see Joseph Goebbels, "Winston Churchill," February 2, 1941, in Joseph Goebbels, *Die Zeit ohne Beispiel: Reden und Aufsätze aus den Jahren 1939/40/41* (Munich: Zentralverlag der NSDAP, F. Eher Nachf., 1941), 382; Rosenberg, *Houston Stewart Chamberlain*, 41.
257. Alfred Rosenberg, "Um Deutschlands Weltgeltung," October 30, 1933, in *Blut und Ehre*, 356.
258. Alfred Rosenberg, *Letzte Aufzeichnungen: Ideale und Idole der nationalsozialistischen Revolution* (Göttingen: Presse Verlag, 1955), 218.
259. Rosenberg, *Mythus*, 519–120.
260. Alfred Rosenberg, "Vom Meister der Schule zum Meister des Lebens," October 1934, in *Gestaltung der Idee: Blut und Ehre II. Band: Reden und Aufsätze von 1933–1935*, ed. Thilo von Trotha (Munich: Zentralverlag der NSDAP, F. Eher, 1939), 168–9.
261. Alfred Rosenberg, "An die deutsche Wehrmacht," in *Gestaltung der Idee*, 302.
262. Rosenberg, *Mythus*, 597.
263. Ibid., 596.
264. Alfred Rosenberg, "Die Überwindung des Gentleman," *Völkischer Beobachter*, June 30, 1940, in Alfred Rosenberg, *Tradition und Gegenwart: Reden und Aufsätze 1936–1940; Blut und Ehre, VI. Band*, ed. Karlheinz Rüdiger (Munich: Zentralverlag der NSDAP, Franz Eher Nachf.), 488.
265. Alfred Rosenberg, "Der deutsche Ordensstaat," in *Gestaltung der Idee: Blut und Ehre II. Band: Reden und Aufsätze von 1933–1935*, ed. Thilo von Trotha (Munich: Zentralverlag der NSDAP, F. Eher, 1939), 80, 84.
266. Geoff Eley, *Nazism as Fascism: Violence, Ideology, and the Ground of Consent in Germany 1930–1945* (London: Routledge, 2013), 42. For a historiographical overview of the consent-coercion debate, see Richard J. Evans, "Coercion and Consent in Nazi Germany," *Proceedings of the British Academy* 151 (2007): 53–81; Norbert Frei, "People's Community and War: Hitler's Popular Support," in *The Third Reich between Vision and Reality: New Perspectives on German History, 1918–1945*, ed. Hans Mommsen (Oxford: Berg, 2001), 59–77.
267. For Nazi propaganda, see Ian Kershaw, "Volksgemeinschaft: Potenzial und Grenzen eines neuen Forschungskonzepts," *Vierteljahrshefte für Zeitgeschichte* 59, no. 1 (2011): 1–17; Tim W. Mason, *Arbeiterklasse und Volksgemeinschaft: Dokumente und Materialien zur deutschen Arbeiterpolitik, 1936–1939* (Opladen, Germany: Westdeutscher Verlag, 1975). For a rebuttal, see Wildt, "'Volksgemeinschaft,'" 102–9. For a discussion, see Martina Steber and Bernhard Gotto, eds., *Visions of Community in Nazi Germany: Social Engineering and Private Lives* (Oxford: Oxford University Press, 2014). For coercion, see Eley, *Nazism as Fascism*, 74. On the exclusion of Jews and others, see Detlev Peukert's classic: *Volksgenossen und Gemeinschaftsfremde: Anpassung, Ausmerze und Aufbegehren unter dem Nationalsozialismus* (Cologne: Bund, 1982); see also Frank Bajohr, "Dynamik und Disparität: Die nationalsozialistische Rüstungsmobilisierung und die 'Volksgemeinschaft,'" in Bajohr and Wildt, *Volksgemeinschaft*, 89–90; Ulrich Herbert, "Arbeiterklasse und Gemeinschaftsfremde: Die Gesellschaft des NS-Staates in den Arbeiten Detlev Peukerts," in *Detlev Peukert und die NS-Forschung*, ed. Rüdiger Hachtmann and Sven Reichardt (Göttingen, Germany: Wallstein, 2015), 39–48; Götz Aly, *Warum die Deutschen? Warum die Juden? Gleichheit, Neid und Rassenhass, 1800–1933* (Frankfurt am Main: S. Fischer, 2011), 133–43, 150–2, 164–73, 290–1; Wildt, *Volksgemeinschaft als Selbstermächtigung*.

268. Hitler, "13 November 1930," 104.

269. See Fernando Esposito, "Revolution and Eternity: Introductory Remarks on Fascist Temporalities," *Journal of Modern European History* 13, no. 1 (2015): 35.

270. See Richard Bourke and Quentin Skinner, eds., *Popular Sovereignty in Historical Perspective* (Cambridge: Cambridge University Press, 2016); Hedwig Richter, *Demokratie: Eine deutsche Affäre*: Vom 18. *Jahrhundert bis zur Gegenwart* (Munich: C. H. Beck, 2020), 234.

271. Clark, *Time and Power*, 207–8.

272. Benoy Kumar Sarkar, *The Political Philosophies since 1905*, vol. 2, *The Epoch of Neo-Democracy and Neo-Socialism (1929–)*, part 1 (Lahore, India: Motilal Banarsidass, 1941), 53.

Chapter Four: The Hindu Crown

1. See, paradigmatically, Sumathi Ramaswamy, "Visualising India's Geo-Body: Globes, Maps, Bodyscapes," *Contributions to Indian Sociology* 36, no. 1 and 2 (2002): 151–89; Manu Goswami, *Producing India: From Colonial Economy to National Space* (Chicago: University of Chicago Press, 2004); Diana L. Eck, "The Imagined Landscape: Patterns in the Construction of Hindu Sacred Geography," *Contributions to Indian Sociology* 32, no. 2 (1998): 165–88. On Savarkar, see Janaki Bakhle, "Country First? Vinayak Damodar Savarkar (1883–1966) and the Writing of *Essentials of Hindutva*," *Public Culture* 22, no. 1 (2010): 183.

2. Vinayak Damodar Savarkar, *Hindu Rashtra Darshan (A Collection of the Presidential Speeches Delivered from the Hindu Mahasabha Platform)* (Bombay: L. G. Khare, 1949), 50.

3. Ibid., 54.

4. Ibid., 48.

5. Ramsay MacDonald, introduction to *Fundamental Unity of India (From Hindu Sources)*, by Radhakumud Mookerji (London: Longmans, Green, 1914), vii–viii.

6. For British paramountcy in India, see Hira Singh, *Colonial Hegemony and Popular Resistance: Princes, Peasants and Paramount Power* (New Delhi: Sage, 1998), 177–84, 188–213; Ian Copland, *The British Raj and the Indian Princes: Paramountcy in Western India, 1857–1930* (Bombay: Orient Longman, 1982).

7. Cf. Joya Chatterji, "Nationalisms in India, 1857–1947," in *The Oxford Handbook of the History of Nationalism*, ed. John Breuilly (Oxford: Oxford University Press, 2013), 242–62.

8. Sheldon Pollock, *The Language of the Gods in the World of Men: Sanskrit, Culture, and Power in Premodern India* (Berkeley: University of California Press, 2006).

9. For Indianization theories, see I. W. Mabbett, "The 'Indianization' of Southeast Asia: Reflections on the Historical Sources," *Journal of Southeast Asian Studies* 8, no. 2 (1977): 143–61.

10. Sheldon Pollock, "The Death of Sanskrit," *Comparative Studies in Society and History* 43, no. 2 (2001): 392–426.

11. Ibid., 116–17.

12. Susan Bayly, "Imaging 'Greater India': French and Indian Visions of Colonialism in the Indic Mode," *Modern Asian Studies* 38, no. 3 (2004): 703–44; William Dalrymple, *The Golden Road: How Ancient India Transformed the World* (London: Bloomsbury Publishing, 2024).

13. Marieke Bloembergen, "Borobudur in the Light of Asia: Scholars, Pilgrims, and Knowledge Networks of Greater India," in *Belonging across the Bay of Bengal: Religious Rites, Colonial Migrations, National Rights*, ed. Michael Laffan (London: Bloomsbury, 2017): 37. See also Mark R. Frost, "That Great Ocean of Idealism: Calcutta, the Tagore Circle, and the Idea of Asia, 1900–1920," in *Indian Ocean Studies: Cultural, Social and Political Perspectives*, ed. Shanty Moorthy and Ashraf Jamal (New York: Routledge, 2009), 250–79.

14. See Carolien Stolte and Harald Fischer-Tiné, "Imagining Asia in India: Nationalism and Internationalism (ca. 1905–1940)," *Comparative Studies in Society and History* 54, no. 1 (2012): 67–8; Sugata Bose, *A Hundred Horizons: The Indian Ocean in the Age of Global Empire* (Cambridge,

MA: Harvard University Press, 2006), 31, 275–7; Prasenjit Duara, "The Discourse of Civilization and Pan-Asianism," *Journal of World History* 12, no. 1 (2001): 99–130.

15. See Mabbett, "'Indianization' of Southeast Asia"; Kishor K. Basa, "Indian Writings on Early History and Archaeology of Southeast Asia: A Historiographical Analysis," *Journal of the Royal Asiatic Society* 8, no. 3 (1998): 395–410.

16. Jolita Zabarskaitė, *"Greater India" and the Indian Expansionist Imagination, c. 1885–1965: The Rise and Decline of the Idea of a Lost Hindu Empire* (Berlin: De Gruyter, 2023).

17. Cf. Bayly, "Imagining 'Greater India,'" 715–17. For "Greater India" and Hindutva today, see Arkotong Longkumer, *The Greater India Experiment: Hindutva and the Northeast* (Stanford, CA: Stanford University Press, 2021).

18. Cf. Bayly, "Imagining 'Greater India,'" 710; Zabarskaitė, *"Greater India,"* 24–57. Shamasastry's Sanskrit transcript was first published in installments in the *Mysore Review* and the *Indian Antiquary* in 1906–1910. It was translated into English and published in book form as Rudrapatna Shama Sastri, *The Arthásastra of Kautilya* (Bangalore: Government Press, 1915).

19. Benoy Kumar Sarkar, *The Positive Background of Hindu Sociology: Introduction to Hindu Positivism* (1937; repr., Delhi: Motilal Banarsidass, 1985), 223–5, quote at 225.

20. Ibid., 220–2.

21. Sarkar, trans., *The Sukranîti* (Allahabad, India: Panini Office, 1914).

22. Sarkar, *Positive Background,* 220–2, 245–51; Benoy Kumar Sarkar, *The Beginning of Hindu Culture as World-Power (A.D. 300–600)* (Shanghai: Commercial Press, 1916); Benoy Kumar Sarkar, *The Folk-Element in Hindu Culture: A Contribution to Socio-Religious Studies in Hindu Folk-Institutions* (1917; repr., New Delhi: Oriental Books Reprint Corporation, 1972).

23. Sarkar, *Positive Background,* 221; Kashi Prasad Jayaswal, *Hindu Polity: A Constitutional History of India in Hindu Times,* 5th ed. (1924; repr., Bangalore: Bangalore Printing and Publishing, 1978).

24. Jayaswal, preface to the second edition of *Hindu Polity,* viii; Jayaswal, *Hindu Polity,* 352. Jayaswal first laid out this view in *An Introduction to Hindu Polity: A Paper Read to the Third Hindi Conference, Calcutta, 1912; Reprinted from the Modern Review, May to September 1913* (Calcutta: Brahmo Mission Press, 1913), 1, 27.

25. Vinayak Damodar Savarkar, *Six Glorious Epochs of Indian History,* trans. S. T. Godbole (1963; repr., Bombay: Bal Savarkar, 1971), 7.

26. K. M. Panikkar, *The Ideas of Sovereignty and State in Indian Political Thought* (Bombay: Bharatiya Vidya Bhavan, 1963), 4–5.

27. Christophe Jaffrelot, *Religion, Caste, and Politics in India* (Delhi: Primus Books, 2010), 22.

28. Ibid.; Jayaswal, *Hindu Polity,* 348.

29. Benoy Kumar Sarkar, "Democratic Ideals and Republican Institutions in India," *American Political Science Review* 12 (1918): 591.

30. Pollock, *Language of the Gods,* 221–58; André Wink, *Land and Sovereignty in India: Agrarian Society and Politics under the Eighteenth-Century Maratha Svarājya* (Cambridge: Cambridge University Press, 1986), 11–51.

31. Ramesh Chandra Majumdar, "The Śailendra Empire (Up to the End of the Tenth Century A.D.)," *Journal of the Greater India Society* (hereafter *JGIS*) 1, no. 1 (1934): 16; Ramesh Chandra Majumdar, *Ancient Indian Colonies in the Far East,* vol. 2, *Suvarnadvipa,* part 1, *Political History* (Dhaka, India: Asoke Humar Majumdar Ramna, 1937), 37–48.

32. For ancient Indian (Hindu, Jain, and Buddhist) cosmology, see Pollock, *Language of the Gods*; Klaus Konrad, *Die altindische Kosmologie: Nach den Brāhmaṇas dargestellt* (Bonn, Germany: Indica et Tibetica Verlag, 1986); Willibald Kirfel, *Die Kosmographie der Inder: Nach den Quellen dargestellt* (Bonn, Germany: Kurt Schröder, 1920).

33. Radhakumud Mookerji, *Indian Shipping: A History of the Sea-Borne Trade and Maritime Activity of the Indians from the Earliest Times* (Bombay: Longmans, Green, 1912).

34. Ibid., x; Sarkar, *Positive Background,* 220–2.

35. Mookerji, *Indian Shipping*, ix.

36. Ibid., 12, 39.

37. Ramesh Chandra Majumdar, "The Decline and Fall of the Śailendra Empire," *JGIS* 1, no. 2 (1934): 12–24; Edward Gibbon, *The History of the Decline and Fall of the Roman Empire*, 6 vols. (London: W. Strahan & T. Caddell, 1776–1788).

38. Cf. Satadru Sen, *Benoy Kumar Sarkar: Restoring the Nation to the World* (New Delhi: Routledge, 2014), 116; Bayly, "Imagining 'Greater India,'" 719.

39. Carl Schmitt, *Land and Sea: A World-Historical Meditation*, trans. Samuel Garrett Zeitlin (Candor, NY: Telos Press, 2015), 79–83.

40. Samuel Garrett Zeitlin, introduction to Schmitt, *Land and Sea*, xlii–xliii.

41. Carl Schmitt, *Der Nomos der Erde im Völkerrecht des Jus Publicum Europaeum* (Cologne: Greven Verlag, 1950).

42. Ibid., 144; Carl Schmitt, *Der Leviathan in der Staatslehre des Thomas Hobbes: Sinn und Fehlschlag eines politischen Symbols* (Hamburg: Hanseatische Verlagsanstalt, 1938), 119–20.

43. O. C. Gangoly, "Relation between Indian and Indonesian Culture," *JGIS* 7, no. 1 (1940): 51.

44. Ibid., 51, 60; O. C. Gangoly, "The Cult of Agastya: And the Origin of Indian Colonial Art," *Rupam*, no. 25 (1926): 6.

45. Gangoly, "Relation between Indian," 60.

46. Ibid., 59. For the identification of *karmabhumi* and Bharatvarsha, see Pollock, *Language of the Gods*, 194–6.

47. Benoy Kumar Sarkar, "Miscellany: 'Greater India' in Indonesia," *Calcutta Review* 75, no. 1 (1940): 77.

48. Ibid., 76.

49. Majumdar, *Ancient Indian Colonies*, 2:1:17.

50. Kalidas Nag, "Sylvain Lévi and the Science of Indology," *JGIS* 3, no. 1 (1936): 6 (italics in the original).

51. Kalidas Nag, "Obituary Notice: Gabriel Ferrand," *JGIS* 2, no. 2 (1935): 169; George Cœdès, "Le Royaume de Çrīvijaya," *Bulletin de l'École française d'Extrême-Orient* 18, no. 1 (1918): 1–36.

52. Ibid., 3.

53. Ramesh Chandra Majumdar, "IV. Les Rois Šailendra de Suvarnadvîpa," *Bulletin de l'École française d'Extrême-Orient* 33, no. 1 (1933): 140–1, quote at 140; Devaprasad Ghosh, "Migration of Indian Decorative Motifs," *JGIS* 2, no. 1 (1935): 39; Gangoly, "Relation between Indian," 54.

54. Himansu Bhusan Sarkar, "Comment and Criticism: 'The Study of Javanese Literature in India,'" *JGIS* 3, no. (1936): 190.

55. Ramesh Chandra Majumdar, "The Malays," *JGIS* 3, no. 1 (1936): 95.

56. Cf. Bayly, "Imagining 'Greater India,'" 728; Carolien Stolte, "Orienting India: Interwar Internationalism in an Asian Inflection, 1917–1937" (PhD diss., University of Leiden, 2013), 95.

57. Himansu Bhushan Sarkar, "Ten Old-Javanese Copper-Plates from Sidotěka of the Śaka Year 1245," *JGIS* 2, no. 2 (1935): 132.

58. Senarath Paranavitana, "The Kāliṅga Dynasty of Ceylon," *JGIS* 3, no. 1 (1936): 57.

59. Gangoly, "Relation between Indian," 54.

60. Majumdar, *Ancient Indian Colonies*, 2:1:120.

61. Ramesh Chandra Majumdar, *Hindu Colonies in the Far East*, 2nd rev. and enlarged ed. (Calcutta: K. L. Mukhopadhyay, 1963), 16, quote at 31.

62. Subhas Chandra Bose, *The Indian Struggle 1920–1942*, in Subhas Chandra Bose, *Netaji: Collected Works*, ed. Sisir Kumar Bose and Sugata Bose, 12 vols. (Calcutta: Netaji Research Bureau, 1980–2007), 2:151.

63. J. Przyluski, "The Terminal Stūpa of the Barabuḍur," *JGIS* 3, no. 1 (1936): 169.

64. Senarath Paranavitana, "Two Royal Titles of the Early Sinhalese, and the Origin of Kingship in Ancient Ceylon," *Journal of the Royal Asiatic Society of Great Britain and Ireland*, no. 3 (1936): 449–51; Senarath Paranavitana, "Ploughing as a Ritual of Royal Consecration in

Ancient Ceylon," in *R. C. Majumdar Felicitation Volume,* ed. Himansu Bhusan Sarkar (Calcutta: Firma K. L. Mukhopadhyay, 1970), 36.
65. Gangoly, "Relation between Indian," 54.
66. Kalidas Nag, "Greater India: A Study in Indian Internationalism," *Greater India Society Bulletin,* no. 1 (1926).
67. Ibid., 17, 20.
68. Ibid., 40, 34.
69. Ibid., 11–12 (italics in original).
70. Radhakumud Mookerji, *A New Approach to the Communal Problem* (Bombay: Padma Publications, 1943), front matter, 1–2; Radhakumud Mookerji, *Nationalism in Hindu Culture* (London: Theosophical Publishing House, 1921), 70.
71. Radhakumud Mookerji, *Fundamental Unity of India (From Hindu Sources)* (London: Longmans, Green, 1914), 107 (italics in original).
72. Ibid., 107–10.
73. Mookerji, *Indian Shipping,* 12, 45, 152.
74. Przyluski, "Terminal Stūpa," 169.
75. "Draft Resolution of the Hindu Mahasabha," Cripps Mission Papers, Hindu Mahasabha, IOR/L/PJ/10/8, p. 8, British Library, London.
76. Bose, *Indian Struggle,* 1–2.
77. Vincent Arthur Smith, *The Early History of India, from 600 B. C. to the Muhammadan Conquest* (Oxford, Clarendon Press, 1904), 5.
78. Vincent Arthur Smith, *The Oxford History of India, from the Earliest Times to the End of 1911* (Oxford, Clarendon Press, 1919), x, ix–x; Mookerji credited at xiii.
79. Mookerji, *Fundamental Unity,* 128.
80. Radhakumud Mookerji, *Akhand Bharat* (Bombay: Hind Kitabs, 1945), 5; Mookerji, *New Approach,* 3.
81. Mookerji, *Akhand Bharat,* 6, 59.
82. Chaman Lal, *Hindu America: Revealing the Story of the Romance of the Surya Vanshi Hindus and Depicting the Imprints of Hindu Culture on the Two Americas* (Bombay: New Book, 1940); Har Bilas Sarda, *Hindu Superiority: An Attempt to Determine the Position of the Hindu Race in the Scale of Nations* (Ajmer, India: Rajputana Printing Works, 1906), 190, 406–7.
83. Dayananda Sarasvati, *An English Translation of the Satyarth Prakash, Literally: Exposé of Right Sense (of Vedic Religion) of Maharshi Swami Dayanand Saraswati, "The Luther of India"; Being a Guide to Vedic Hermeneutics,* trans. Durga Prasad (1875; repr., Lahore, India: Virganand Press, 1908), 282; M. S. Golwalkar, *We, or: Our Nationhood Defined* (Nagpur, India: Bharat Publications, 1939), repr. in Shamsul Islam, *Golwalkar's We or Our Nationhood Defined: A Critique* (New Delhi: Pharos, 2006), 55; Vinayak Damodar Savarkar [A Maratha, pseud.], *Essentials of Hindutva* (Nagpur, India: V. V. Kelkar, 1923), 15.
84. Martha C. Nussbaum, *The Clash Within: Democracy, Religious Violence, and India's Future* (Cambridge, MA: Harvard University Press, 2007), 53–4.
85. Sarda, *Hindu Superiority,* 192.
86. Ibid., 190; Lal, *Hindu America,* 4.
87. Sarda, *Hindu Superiority,* 188–9; Lal, *Hindu America,* 1–7.
88. Thomas R. Trautmann, *Aryans and British India* (New Delhi: Yoda Press, 2006), 50.
89. Edward Pococke, *India in Greece, or: Truth in Mythology; Containing the Sources of the Hellenic Race, the Colonisation of Egypt and Palestine, the Wars of the Grand Lama, and the Bud'histic Propaganda in Greece* (London: Griffin, 1852), 165–5, 174–6.
90. Ramón Mena, *Synthesis of Mexican Archaeology for the Summer School of the National University* (Mexico [City]: Secretaria de Educacion Publica, 1924), 54; Lal, *Hindu America,* 5–6. For context, see Robert Wauchope, *Lost Tribes and Sunken Continents: Myth and Method in the Study of American Indians* (Chicago: University of Chicago Press, 1962); Robert E. Bieder, *Science*

Encounters the Indian, 1820–1880: The Early Years of American Ethnology (Norman: University of Oklahoma Press, 1989), 221–3. For India, see M. N. Roy, *M. N. Roy's Memoirs* (Bombay: Allied Publishers, 1960), 43.

91. Lal, *Hindu America.* Nehru's library is preserved at his former residence at Teenmurti Bhavan, New Delhi, which today houses the Nehru Memorial Museum and Library. The staff assured me that all books on display are Nehru's own.

92. Savarkar cited Mookerji in 1963: Savarkar, *Six Glorious Epochs,* 37.

93. Mookerji, *Fundamental Unity,* 15–16.

94. Ibid., 20–24; Savarkar, *Essentials of Hindutva,* 6, 11–12.

95. Mookerji, *Fundamental Unity,* 16–17; Savarkar, *Essentials of Hindutva,* 11–12.

96. Mookerji, *New Approach*, 29.

97. Ibid., 30.

98. Mookerji, *Fundamental Unity,* 27.

99. Mookerji, *Nationalism in Hindu Culture,* 23.

100. Savarkar, *Essentials of Hindutva,* 100, 73.

101. Mookerji, *Nationalism in Hindu Culture,* 69–71.

102. Ibid., 70–3.

103. Radhakumud Mookerji, *Chandragupta Maurya and His Times (Sir William Meyer Lectures, 1940–41)* ([Madras]: University of Madras, 1943); Radhakumud Mookerji, *Asoka (Gaekwad Lectures)* (London: Macmillan, 1928); Radhakumud Mookerji, *Harsha (Calcutta University Readership Lectures, 1925)* (London: Oxford University Press, 1926), quotes at 9, 28.

104. Mookerji, *Nationalism in Hindu Culture,* 89–102, quote at 90f1.

105. Mookerji, *Fundamental Unity,* 89–107.

106. James Mill, *History of British India,* 2nd ed., 6 vols. (1817; repr., London: Baldwin, Cradock, and Joy, 1820), 2:144–5.

107. Ibid., 148.

108. Ibid., 150–1.

109. Mookerji, *Nationalism in Hindu Culture,* 73.

110. Benoy Kumar Sarkar, *The Political Institutions and Theories of the Hindus: A Study in Comparative Politics* (Leipzig: Markert & Petters, 1922), 58–9.

111. Vinayak Damodar Savarkar, *The Story of My Transportation for Life: A Biography of Black Days of Andamans,* trans. V. N. Naik (1927 in Marathi; trans., Bombay: Sadbhakti Publications, 1950), 67.

112. Savarkar, *Essentials of Hindutva,* 106.

113. Stolte, "Orienting India," 33–6; Stolte and Fischer-Tiné, "Imagining Asia in India," 85–6.

114. Cf. Stolte and Fischer-Tiné, "Imagining Asia in India," 85.

115. Savarkar, *Essentials of Hindutva,* 25.

116. Ibid., 15, 24.

117. Ibid., 22.

118. Ibid., 23.

119. Shruti Kapila, *Violent Fraternity: Indian Political Thought in the Global Age* (Princeton, NJ: Princeton University Press, 2021), 108–10.

120. Savarkar, *Essentials of Hindutva,* 19.

121. Ibid., 17.

122. Ibid., 22–3.

123. Ibid., 25, 27.

124. Ibid., 28 ("Sindhu" in Nagari script in the original).

125. Ibid., 27. For the philological contention recently revived by Manan Ahmed Asif, *The Loss of Hindustan: The Invention of India* (Cambridge, MA: Harvard University Press, 2020), 34–5, see Arvind Sharma, "On Hindu, Hindustān, Hinduism and Hindutva," *Numen* 49, no. 1 (2002): 1–4; Paul Thieme, "Sanskrit *Sindhu-/Sindhu-* and Old Iranian *hindu-/Hindu-*," in *W. B.*

Henning Memorial Volume, ed. Mary Boyce and Ilya Gershevitch (London: Lund Humphries, 1970), 447–50.

126. Savarkar to Rash Behari Bose, August 18, 1938, reel no. 23, serial no. 1, p. 238, Veer Savarkar Papers. Cf. my reading of this letter with Stolte, "Orienting India," 35; and Stolte and Fischer-Tiné, "Imagining Asia in India," 85–6.

127. Savarkar to Bose, November 14, 1938, reel no. 23, serial no. 1, p. 415, Veer Savarkar Papers.

128. Ibid., 416; cf. Stolte, "Orienting India," 35.

129. Savarkar to Bose, 417.

130. Louis Dumont, *Homo Hierarchicus: The Caste System and Its Implications*, complete rev. English ed. (1966; repr., Chicago: University of Chicago Press, 1980), 72–3.

131. Ernst H. Kantorowicz, *The King's Two Bodies: A Study in Mediaeval Political Theology* (Princeton, NJ: Princeton University Press, 1957). See Milinda Banerjee, "The Royal Nation and Global Intellectual History: Monarchic Routes to Conceptualizing National Unity," in *Transnational Histories of the "Royal Nation,"* ed. Milinda Banerjee, Charlotte Backerra, and Cathleen Sarti (Cham, Switzerland: Palgrave Macmillan, 2017), 37; A. Azfar Moin, *The Millennial Sovereign: Sacred Kingship and Sainthood in Islam* (New York: Columbia University Press, 2012), 266.

132. Benoy Kumar Sarkar, "Democratic Ideals and Republican Institutions in India," *American Political Science Review* 12, no. 4 (1918): 584.

133. See Banerjee, "Royal Nation," 22.

134. Milinda Banerjee, *The Mortal God: Imagining the Sovereign in Colonial India* (Cambridge: Cambridge University Press, 2018), 123.

135. Vinayak Damodar Savarkar, "Choose, oh Indian Princes!" Leaflet reprinted in Valentine Chirol, *Indian Unrest*, a reprint, revised and enlarged, from *The Times*, with an introduction by Sir Alfred Lyall (London: Macmillan, 1910), 195–6; see also Savarkar, *Story of My Transportation*, 348.

136. Savarkar, *Essentials of Hindutva*, 11; Vinayak Damodar Savarkar [An Indian Nationalist, pseud.], *The Indian War of Independence of 1857* (S.l.: s.n., 1909), 61, quote at 234; Vinayak Damodar Savarkar, *Hindu-Pad-Padashahi, or: A Critical Review of the Hindu Empire of Maharashtra* (Madras: P. G. Paul, 1925), 176–7.

137. Savarkar, *Essentials of Hindutva*, 11–12.

138. Savarkar, *Six Glorious Epochs*, 10.

139. Ibid., 11.

140. For Mughal imperial language, see Moin, *Millennial Sovereign*; see also David Gilmartin, "Imperial Sovereignty in Mughal and British Forms," *History and Theory* 56, no. 1 (2017), 85–7; C. A. Bayly, *Indian Society and the Making of the British Empire* (Cambridge: Cambridge University Press, 1988), 13–15; John F. Richards, "The Formation of Imperial Authority under Akbar and Jahangir," in *The Mughal State, 1526–1750*, ed. Muzaffar Alam and Sanjay Subrahmanyam (Oxford: Oxford University Press, 2000), 126–7.

141. Lauren Benton, *A Search for Sovereignty: Law and Geography in European Empires, 1400–1900* (Cambridge: Cambridge University Press, 2009), 225, 245–8, 251f88.

142. Ibid., 245.

143. Bernard Cohn, "Representing Authority in Victorian India," in *The Invention of Tradition*, ed. Eric Hobsbawm and Terence Ranger (1983; repr., Cambridge: Cambridge University Press, 2012), 167–91. On the *darbars*, see Singh, *Colonial Hegemony*, 177–180.

144. Mookerji, *Fundamental Unity*, 102.

145. Savarkar, *Six Glorious Epochs*, 439; Savarkar, *Essentials of Hindutva*, 11; Savarkar, *Indian War of Independence*, 234; Savarkar, *Hindu-Pad-Padashahi*, 176–7.

146. Savarkar, *Indian War of Independence*, 6, 227.

147. Ibid., 56–8.

148. Ibid., 395.

149. Ibid., 233.

150. Ibid., 234. On this point, see Salmoli Choudhuri, "Theology of the 'Absent King' and the Possibility of Rabindranath Tagore's Political Thought," *Political Theology* 23, no. 1–2 (2021): 48, who argues that it was the emptiness of the throne in 1857 (Bahadur Shah Zafar's willingness to abdicate) that allowed the Mughal emperor to incarnate the rebellion.
151. Savarkar, *Indian War of Independence*, 105, 234.
152. Ibid., 62.
153. Ibid., 234.
154. Ibid., 8.
155. Savarkar, *Six Glorious Epochs*, 1, in fact opens with an explicit rejection of Puranic history.
156. For the flag, see Savarkar, *Indian War of Independence*, 61; Savarkar, *Six Glorious Epochs*, 450. For the banner, see Savarkar, *Hindu-Pad-Padashahi*, 30–1. For the drum, see Savarkar, *Indian War of Independence*, 61. For the umbrella, see Savarkar, *Essentials of Hindutva*, 11.
157. Savarkar, *Hindu-Pad-Padashahi*, 9.
158. Savarkar, *Indian War of Independence*, 10.
159. Benoy Kumar Sarkar, "The Political Philosophy of Ramdas the Guru of Shivaji the Great," *Calcutta Review* 57, no. 2 (1935): 157–68.
160. M. G. Ranade, *Rise of the Maratha Power* (Bombay, India: Punalekar, 1900); Benoy Kumar Sarkar, *The Sociology of Population* (Calcutta: N. M. Ray-Chowdhury, 1936), 3.
161. See Prachi Deshpande, *Creative Pasts: Historical Memory and Identity in Western India, 1700–1960* (New York: Columbia University Press, 2007), 127–8.
162. Anne Feldhaus, "Maharashtra as a Holy Land: A Sectarian Tradition," *Bulletin of the School of Oriental and African Studies, University of London* 49, no. 3 (1986): 532, 546; C. A. Bayly, *Origins of Nationality in South Asia: Patriotism and Ethical Government in the Making of Modern India* (New Delhi: Oxford University Press, 1998), 21–27.
163. Sarkar, "Political Philosophy of Ramdas," 161–2.
164. Ibid., 161, 164, 167.
165. Ibid., 164.
166. Ibid., 161.
167. Ibid., 164.
168. Savarkar, *Six Glorious Epochs*, 406.
169. Ibid., 164, 166–7.
170. Savarkar, *Hindu-Pad-Padashahi*, 3.
171. Ibid., 27.
172. Ibid., 338.
173. Ibid., 65, 141.
174. Ibid., 229, 232.
175. Ibid., 240.
176. Ibid., 230–1.
177. Ibid., 83.
178. Ibid., 92.
179. Ibid., 287.
180. Brian H. Hodgson, *Papers Relative to the Colonization, Commerce, Physical Geography. etc., etc., of the Himalaya Mountains and Nepal* (Calcutta: Calcutta Gazette Office, 1857), 234, quoted in Richard Burghart, "The Formation of the Concept of Nation-State in Nepal," *Journal of Asian Studies* 44, no. 1 (1984): 106 (square brackets in the original).
181. Savarkar, *Essentials of Hindutva*, 68 ("Attock" and "Cuttack" in Nagari script in original).
182. Vinayak Damodar Savarkar, "Hindu sanghatanatmak Nepali andolan ka prarambh," in *Savarkar Samagra*, 10 vols. (Delhi: Prabhat Prakashan, 2000–3), 9:518–19.
183. Vinayak Damodar Savarkar, "The Nepal Movement (1925 A.D)," in *Selected Works of Veer Savarkar*, 4 vols. (Chandigarh, India: Abhishek Publications, 2007), 3:481.
184. Savarkar, "Hindu sanghatanatmak," 9:525–6, 9:537.
185. Ibid., 9:537.

186. Ibid.
187. Benton, *Search for Sovereignty*, 2–4, quote at 2.
188. Savarkar, *Six Glorious Epochs*, 399.
189. Savarkar, *Indian War of Independence*, 233.
190. Savarkar, *Story of My Transportation*, 355.
191. Ganesh Damodar Savarkar, "Pratham avritti ki prastavna," in Savarkar, *Savarkar Samagra*, 9:507–8.
192. [G. M.?] Puckle, report, December 27, 1941, in "Demonstration of Keen Interest in the Kingdom of Nepal in the Letters and Presidential Address of Mr. V. D. Savarkar, President Elect of the All-India Hindu Mahasabha Session at Bagchalpur. Representation from the Afghan Consul General Regarding the Mention of Afghanistan in the Presidential Address of Mr. Savarkar," n.d., p. 7, Progs., Nos. 187-F/1942, External Affairs Department, Frontier Branch, National Archives of India, New Delhi.
193. Savarkar, "Hindu sanghatanatmak," 513.
194. Savarkar, "Nepal Movement," 481.
195. Savarkar, "Hindu sanghatanatmak," 528, 526.
196. Ibid., 535.
197. Ibid., 527.
198. Savarkar, *Story of My Transportation*, 355.
199. Savarkar, "Hindu sanghatanatmak," 515.
200. Savarkar, "Nepal ko shalya chubhne lagaa," in *Savarkar Samagra*, 9:605; similarly, see "Weekly Report of the Intelligence Bureau, Home Department, Government of India, Dated New Delhi, Saturday, the 18th October 1941," "File 230/35 - Weekly Reports of the Director, Intelligence Bureau, Home Department, Government of India, Nos. 1–49," p. 118, IOR/L/PJ/12/483, British Library.
201. Savarkar, "Hindu sanghatanatmak," 538.
202. Savarkar, *Indian War of Independence*, 118; Savarkar, *Essentials of Hindutva*, 114–15.
203. Ganesh Savarkar, "Pratham avritti," 506.
204. Siegfried Wolf, "Die Konstruktion einer kollektiven Identität: Vinayak Damodar Savarkar und sein Hindutva-Konzept" (PhD diss., Ruprecht-Karls Universität Heidelberg, 2009), 60. For *History of the Sikhs*, see Savarkar, *Hindu-Pad-Padashahi*, viii; Savarkar, *Six Glorious Epochs*, 396. For *History of the Nepalese Nationalist Movement*, see Puckle, report, 7.
205. Savarkar, *Indian War of Independence*, 119–20.
206. Ibid., 62; Savarkar, *Essentials of Hindutva*, 115.
207. Savarkar, *Indian War of Independence*, 120.
208. Vinayak Damodar Savarkar, "Awaken Nepal (1926 A.D.)," in *Selected Works*, 3:486.
209. Ibid., 486.
210. Burghart, "Formation of the Concept," 106.
211. Axel Michaels, "The King and the Cow: On a Crucial Symbol of Hinduization in Nepal," in *Nationalism and Ethnicity in a Hindu Kingdom: The Politics of Culture in Contemporary Nepal*, ed. David Gellner (Amsterdam: Harwood Academic, 1997), 80. For the *Muluki Ain*, see Burghart, "Formation of the Concept," 101–25; Simon Cubelic and Rajan Khatiwoda, "Nepalese Monarchy in an Age of Codification: Kingship, Patriotism, and Legality in the Nepalese Code of 1854," in Banerjee, Backerra, and Sarti, *Transnational Histories*, 67–86.
212. John Whelpton, "Political Identity in Nepal: State, Nation, and Community," in Gellner, *Nationalism and Ethnicity*, 40, 49.
213. Michaels, "King and the Cow," 93.
214. Whelpton, "Political Identity in Nepal," 49.
215. Michaels, "King and the Cow," 94.
216. Ramananda Chatterjee, Padamraj Jain, and Jagatnarainlal on behalf of the members of the All-India Hindu Mahasabha to Bhim Shamsher Jung Bahadur Rana, p. 1, p. 3, "Coll 21/30 Visit of Maharaja and Family to India: Courtesies and Facilities for Distinguished

Nepalese Personages Passing through India," IOR L/PS/12/3041, India Office Records and Private Papers, British Library.

217. O. K. Caroe, report, July 31, 1941, , p. 3, Progs., Nos. 187-F/1942, External Affairs Department, Frontier Branch, National Archives of India; Geoffrey L. Betham, January 29, 1942, p. 32, Progs., Nos. 187-F/1942, External Affairs Department, Frontier Branch, National Archives of India.

218. Quoted in Michaels, "King and the Cow," 93–4.

219. J. B. Howes to G. A. Falconer, June 12, 1944, "Copy of a Secret Report Dated 2-6-44: 'Hindu Mahasabha and Nepal,'" in "The Hindu Mahasabha and Nepal. Code 61 file 5172," FO 371/41782, National Archives, Kew, UK.

220. Ibid.

221. "Copy of a D.C. No. 4-C/42, dt/-15-8-44, from THE BRITISH LEGATION, Nepal, to J.B. Howes Esq., Under Secy., E.A. Deptt., New Delhi: The Hindu Mahasabha and Nepal," in G. Ahmed, "Copy of a Secret Report Dated 2-6-44: Hindu Mahasabha and Nepal," p. 12, and E. Leighton, June 6, 1944, "Extract from C.I.O. Calcutta's Report Dated the 17th June, 1944," pp. 3–4, both in "Activities of Hindu Mahasabha—Proposed formation of a Mahasabha in Nepal—Dropped," Home (Political), 9/10, National Archives of India.

222. "Weekly Report of the Director, Intelligence Bureau, Home Department, Government of India, Dated New Delhi, Saturday, the 7th March 1942," "File 230/35 - Weekly Reports of the Director, Intelligence Bureau, Home Department, Government of India, Nos. 1–51," p. 30, IOR/L/PJ/12/484, British Library.

223. Puckle, report, 7.

224. Falconer to Howes, August 14, 1944, FO 371/41782, National Archives, Kew, UK.

225. "Weekly Report of the . . . 18th October 1941," 119.

226. Savarkar, "Nepal Movement," 482.

227. Betham, January 29, 1942, 32.

228. "Report on Nepal for 1945," in "Coll 21/51 Nepal: Annual Reports on Political Situation 1935–1946," p. 16, IOR L/PS/12/3063A, British Library.

229. Cypher telegram, H. M. M. Nepal to Government of India, External Affairs Department and Secretary of State for Foreign Affairs, July 14, 1945, in "Coll 21/40 Effect of Indian Constitutional Reforms on Relations of HMG with Nepal," IOR L/PS/3051, British Library.

230. E. J. Beveridge, "Extracts from the Calcutta S.B. Daily Notes, Paragraph No. 65, Dated the 9th March 1945," March 16, 1945, pp. 1–2, Progs., Nos. 67-C.A., 1945 (Secret), External Affairs Department, Central Asia Branch, National Archives of India.

231. Secretary External Affairs Department, July 14, 1941, in "Ext 3913/41 Letter to Maharaja of Nepal regarding treatment of Hindus in Bengal," IOR/L/PS/12/533, British Library.

232. Geoffrey L. Betham, "Aide Memorie of a Conversation I Had with General Bahadur on the Evening of August 19th, 1942," in "Coll 21/76 Communications with India: Breakdown during Congress Disturbances," pp. 2–3, IOR/L/PS/12/3090, British Library.

233. Betham, January 29, 1942, 33; Betham, "Aide Memorie," 3.

234. "Copy of a letter from V.D. Savarkar, President All-India Hindu Mahasabha, to Shriman Raja Kamakhya Narayan Singh, Raja of Ramgarh, President Bihar Provincial Hindusabha, Ramgarh," p. 22, Progs., Nos. 187-F/1942, External Affairs Department, Frontier Branch, National Archives of India.

235. Weekly Report of the . . . 18th October 1941," 118.

236. Nandini Gondhalekar and Sanjoy Bhattacharya, "The All India Hindu Mahasabha and the End of British Rule in India, 1939–1947," *Social Scientist* 27, no. 7/8 (1999): 54–5.

237. *The History of the Bhagalpur Struggle: The 23rd Session of the A.I.H. Mahasabha 1941* (Bangalpur, India: Madhukari, 1942); "Weekly Report of the Director, Intelligence Bureau, Home Department, Government of India, Dated New Delhi, Saturday, the 10th January 1942," p. 8, IOR/L/PJ/12/484, British Library.

238. Vinayak Damodar Savarkar, "Extract from the Undelivered Presidential Address at the 23rd Session of the All-India Hindu Mahasabha, Bhagalpur, 1941, by V. D. Savarkar," pp. 4–5, Progs., Nos. 187-F/1942, External Affairs Department, Frontier Branch, National Archives of India; Muhammad Shafi Khan to Caroe, January 13, 1942, Progs., Nos. 187-F/1942, External Affairs Department, Frontier Branch, National Archives of India; "Weekly Report of the Director, Intelligence Bureau, Home Department, Government of India, Dated New Delhi, Saturday, the 3rd January 1942," p. 4, IOR/L/PJ/12/484, British Library.

239. Savarkar, "Extract," 4.

240. Caroe to Betham, January 13, 1942, p. 5, Progs., Nos. 187-F/1942, External Affairs Department, Frontier Branch, National Archives of India.

241. "Weekly Report of the . . . 3rd January 1942," 4.

242. Muhammad Ali Jinnah, "Qu'id-e-Azam Explains Political Situation," *The Dawn* 2, no. 1 (1942): 8; Caroe, letter, January 16, 1942, p. 10, Progs., Nos. 187-F/1942, External Affairs Department, Frontier Branch, National Archives of India.

243. Vinayak Damodar Savarkar, "The Following Statement Is Issued by Barrister Mr. V. D. Savarkar, President of the Hindu Mahasabha, in Connection with the Chinese Moslems," in "Hindu Mahasabha," reel no. 52, file no. 1032, p. 6, Qaid-e-Azam Papers, IOR Neg 10811/4, British Library.

244. Ibid., 6.

245. Savarkar, "A Mere Dream!," *Mahratta,* May 29, 1942, in *Selected Works,* 3:526–7.

246. Vinayak Damodar Savarkar, "The Following Statement Has Been Issued by Barrister Savarkar, the President of the Hindu Mahasabha, Regarding the Resolutions Passed by the Moslem League," August 27, 1941, in "Coll 117/D1; Hindu Mahasabha," p. 170, IOR/L/PJ/8/683, British Library.

247. See Manu Bhagavan, "Princely States and the Hindu Imaginary: Exploring the Cartography of Hindu Nationalism in Colonial India," *Journal of Asian Studies* 67, no. 3 (2008): 881–995; "'Sinister Meaning of Pakistan': Mr. K. M. Munshi's Criticism," *Times of India,* June 24, 1942, 7.

248. Betham, January 29, 1942, 32.

249. Sunil Purushotham, *From Raj to Republic: Sovereignty, Violence, and Democracy in India* (Stanford, CA: Stanford University Press, 2021), 109–10, quote at 4.

250. Vinayak Damodar Savarkar, "Hindu Districts of Andhra Should be Reannexed to Andhra," February 1, 1942, in *Historic Statements,* ed. S. S. Savarkar and G. M. Joshi (Bombay: Popular Prakashan, 1967), 32–4. For Hyderabad in the imperial endgame, see Purushotham, *From Raj to Republic*; for the Mahasabha's antagonism toward it, see Bhagavan, "Princely States," 889–94.

251. M. K. Gandhi, *The Indian States' Problem* (Ahmedabad, India: Navajivan Press, 1941), 672–5.

252. Sunil Purushotham, "Federating the Raj: Hyderabad, Sovereign Kingship, and Partition," *Modern Asian Studies* 54, no. 1 (2020): 193.

253. Gandhi, *Indian States' Problem,* 672.

254. Ibid., 674.

255. "PZ 953/41 'Future Emperor of India' by V D Savarkar (in the Khyber Mail)," February 10, 1941, p. 1, IOR/L/PS/12/484, Political and Secret Department Records, India Office Records and Private Papers, British Library; similarly, see Vinayak Damodar Savarkar, "Academically: Who Is Likely to be Free Hindusthan's Future Emperor?," in *Hindu Sanghatan: Its Ideology and Immediate Programme* (Bombay: N. V. Damle, 1940), 201–18.

256. "Appeal for Assistance in Establishing a Hindu Newspaper: Letter from Ashutosh Lahiri to the Maharaja of Alwar, 15 May 1947: Ashutosh Lahiri Papers, Subject File No. 2, NMML," in Sucheta Mahajan, ed., *1947,* vol. 10 of *Towards Freedom: Documents on the Movement for Independence in India,* ed. Sabyasachi Bhattacharya, 2 parts (New Delhi: Oxford University Press, 2013–2015), 10:2:2429.

257. "States Must Join India and Establish Democracy: Letter From Jawaharlal Nehru to the Maharajah of Alwar, 12 May 1947, *SWJN*, VOL: II, p. 255," in Mahajan, *Towards Freedom*, 10:2:2428; see also Ian Copland, *State, Community and Neighbourhood in Princely North India, c. 1900–1950* (Basingstoke, UK: Palgrave Macmillan, 2005), 101.
258. Syed Azhar Husain Zaidi, *The New Nazis, an Account of the Vast Incredible Plan of the R.S.S.S., the Hindu Mahasabha, the Akali Sikhs and Some Rulers of Indian States in the East Punjab, and Rajputana to Exterminate the Muslims*, n.d., p. 20, Mss Eur F164/31, British Library.
259. Ian Copland, *The Princes of India in the Endgame of Empire, 1917–1947* (Cambridge: Cambridge University Press, 1997), 235–6, 206.
260. Zaidi, *New Nazis*, 30.
261. "CURRENT dossier re R.S.S.S. (Rashtriya Swayam Sevak Sangh or Hindu National Volunteer Corps and THE HINDU MAHASABHA," January 6, 1948, p. 2, and Colonel C. M. Tarver to Phillip C. Vickery, February 13, 1948, in "Political Matters: Hindu Mahasabha (Indian Political Party)," WO 208/5005, National Archives, Kew, UK; Arun Bose, "Bid to Divert Anti-Communal Drive against Democratic Forces: Conspiracy to Shield the Guilty at the Top?," *People's Age*, February 3, 1948, 12; Zaidi, *New Nazis*, 36–7.
262. Cf. Ian Copland, "Crucibles of Hindutva? V. D. Savarkar, the Hindu Mahasabha, and the Indian Princely States," *South Asia: Journal of South Asian Studies* 25, no. 3 (2002): 215; Copland, *State, Community, Neighbourhood*, 101–4; Bhagavan, "Princely States," 881–915.
263. See Nicholas Dirks, *The Hollow Crown: Ethnohistory of an Indian Kingdom* (Cambridge: Cambridge University Press, 1988); Joya Chatterji, "Princes, Subjects and Gandhi: Alternatives to Citizenship at the End of Empire," in *Gandhi's Moral Politics*, ed. Naren Nanda (Abingdon, UK: Routledge, 2017), 108–15.
264. B. S. Moonje, "Baroda Hindu Sabha Conference, Presidential Address [April 1944]," in *The Making of India and Pakistan: Select Documents*, ed. R. S. Bakshi, 6 vols. (New Delhi: Deep & Deep, 1997), 3:563.
265. Cf. Bhagavan, "Princely States," 883, 893.
266. Savarkar, "Extract," 4.
267. Cf. Bhagavan, "Princely States," 882, 888, 891. See also Savarkar, "Hindu Districts of Andhra, 33.
268. "Draft Resolution," 8–9.
269. "The All India Hindu Mahasabha Working Committee Meeting, New Delhi—8th. to 10th February 1947," in *The Indian Annual Register: An Annual Digest of Public Affairs of India Recording the Nations' Activities Each Year in Matters Political, Economic, Industrial, Educational, Social, Etc.*, ed. Nripendra Nath Mitra, 2 vols. (Calcutta: Annual Register Office, 1947), 1:183.
270. Moonje and L. B. Bhopatkar to Cabinet Delegation, April 15, 1946, p. 2, in "1/6/3; Cabinet Mission; Minor Parties and Interests, Hindu Mahasabha, Christians, Women, Labour; Radical and Democratic Party, Shiahs, Individuals e.g. Mirza Ismael Cowasjee Jehangir," IOR/L/PJ/10/51, British Library; Wavell to Amery, January 2, 1945, p. 1, "Private and Secret Weekly Letters between the Secretary of State for India and the Viceroy (Printed)," IOR/L/PO/10/22, British Library.
271. "All India Hindu Mahasabha Working Committee Meeting," 182.
272. On federation, see, for instance, Karuna Mantena, "Popular Sovereignty and Anti-Colonialism," in *Popular Sovereignty in Historical Perspective*, ed. Richard Bourke and Quentin Skinner (Cambridge: Cambridge University Press, 2016), 297–319. See also "'Give Federation a Chance': Mahasabha Appeal," *Times of India*, December 31, 1938, p. 230, IOR/L/PJ/8/683, British Library.
273. Moonje and Bhopatkar to Cabinet Delegation, April 15, 1946, p. 2; Savarkar to Amery, July [*illeg.*], 1944, pp. 56–7, IOR/L/PJ/8/683, British Library; "No Communal Unity Possible so Long as Britain Has Power: S. P. Mookerjee's Presidential Address," *Hindustan Times*, 15 December 1944, p. 47, IOR/L/PJ/8/683, British Library.

274. "A. I. Akhand Hindustan Conference," in Mitra, *Indian Annual Register,* 2:228; Mookerji, *Akhand Bharat,* 12–13; Mookerji, *New Approach,* 38–43, 54.
275. "A. I. Akhand Hindustan Conference," 229.
276. "Draft Resolution," 8.
277. "'Give Federation a Chance.'"
278. Ayesha Jalal, *The Struggle for Pakistan: A Muslim Homeland and Global Politics* (Cambridge, MA: Harvard University Press, 2014), 31.
279. Purushotham, *From Raj to Republic,* 55.
280. Ayesha Jalal, *The Sole Spokesman: Jinnah, the Muslim League, and the Demand for Pakistan* (Cambridge: Cambridge University Press, 1985).
281. Ibid., quote at 242.
282. Ibid., 241–65.
283. Choudhary Rahmat Ali, *Pakistan: The Fatherland of the Pak Nation* (1935; repr., Cambridge: Foister and Jagg, 1947), 320, 327.
284. Ibid., 309–10.
285. Kapila, *Violent Fraternity,* 242.
286. Vallabhbhai Patel, January 15, 1946, cited in Kapila, *Violent Fraternity,* 237.
287. Ibid., 239.
288. D. S. Deshpande to Savarkar, January 8, 1938, reel no. 12, serial no. 1, p. 11, Veer Savarkar Papers; see also Savarkar's presidential address at the 22nd session of the Akhil Bharat Hindu Mahasabha in Madura in 1940: Savarkar, *Hindu Rashtra Darshan,* 203.
289. "The All-India Mahasabha Working Committee, New Delhi, 22nd & 23rd January, 1944," in Bakshi, *Making of India and Pakistan,* 3:535.
290. Walter Andersen, "The Rashtriya Swayamsevak Sangh: II: Who Represents the Hindus?," *Economic and Political Weekly* 7, no. 12 (1972): 635, 638; see also Kannan Srinivasan, "A Subaltern Fascism?," in *Fascism: Essays on Europe and India,* ed. Jairus Banaji (Gurgaon, India: Three Essays Collective, 2013), 107–17.
291. Report dated November 20, 1941, in "Hindu Mahasabha—Bengal Provincial," serial no. 51, file no. 169/38, part 6 (1938), pp. 1611–12, Intelligence Branch Files, State Archives of West Bengal, Kolkata.
292. Moonje [to Linlithgow?], September 12/13, 1941, p. 172, IOR/L/PJ/8/683, British Library; Moonje to Linlithgow, September 26, 1940, p. 220, IOR/L/PJ/8/683, British Library.
293. Report dated November 20, 1941, 1611–12.
294. "Extract from Central Intelligence Officer, Lahore's Daily Report, Dated the 29th December, 1943," January 3, 1944, in "Activities of Hindu Mahasabha - Proposed Formation of a Mahasabha in Nepal - Dropped," 9/1, Home (Political), National Archives of India, New Delhi.
295. Ashutosh Lahiry, "10th of May—Independence Day," April 22, 1946, reel no. 4, file no. C-97/1946, p. 690, Akhil Bharat Hindu Mahasabha Papers, Nehru Memorial Museum and Library; Vishwar Savarkar, "Veer Savarkar, I.N.A.'s Source of Inspiration," in *Savarkar Commemoration Volume,* ed. Sudhakar Raje (Bombay: Savarkar Darshan Pratishthan, 1989), 148; Jyoti Trehan, *Veer Savarkar: Thought and Action of Vinayak Damodar Savarkar* (Delhi: Deep & Deep, 1991), 66. For a discussion, see Marzia Casolari, *In the Shade of the Swastika: The Ambiguous Relationship between Indian Nationalism and Nazi-Fascism* (Bologna, Italy: Il Libre de Emil, 2011), 177–180.
296. See Joya Chatterji, *Bengal Divided: Hindu Communalism and Partition, 1932–1947* (Cambridge: Cambridge University Press, 1994), 227, 249–59.
297. "Weekly Report of the Director, Intelligence Bureau, Home Department, Government of India, Dated New Delhi, Saturday, the 28th November 1942," p. 131, IOR/L/PJ/12/484, British Library.
298. "May 1947," in Mitra, *Indian Annual Register,* 1:66.
299. Jalal, *Sole Spokesman,* 237.

300. Chatterji, *Bengal Divided,* 240–50.
301. "Mahasabha Resolution on H. M. G's Plan," in Mitra, *Indian Annual Register,* 1:256.
302. Savarkar to Mukherjee, "Bengal—A Hindu Majority Province," March 21, 1947, in *Selected Works,* 3:540.
303. Vinayak Damodar Savarkar, "Before They Vivisect India, Let Us Vivisect Their Pakistan First," May 23, 1947, in *Selected Works,* 3:539–40. A slightly different version of the text is preserved as a telegram from Savarkar to Mukherjee for publication in Bengal: "Bengal Hindus Persist with Demand for Partition: Telegram from V. D. Savarkar to S. P. Mookerjee, 15 May 1947: S. M. Mookerjee Papers, File No. 141, Instalment II to IV, NMML," in Mahajan, *Towards Freedom,* 10:1:1204–5.
304. Savarkar, "Before They Vivisect," 539.
305. "Bengal Hindus Persist," 10:1:1204–5.
306. Savarkar, "Before They Vivisect," 539.
307. Savarkar, "Problems before Hindudom after Bloodless (!) Vivisection," *Mahratta,* September 25, 1947, in *Selected Works,* 3:534.
308. Vinayak Damodar Savarkar, "Nehru's Nightmare—Hindu Raj," *Mahratta,* September 25, 1947, in *Selected Works,* 3:539.
309. Savarkar, "Problems before Hindudom," 532.
310. Quote from *Hindu Outlook,* September 30, 1947, in Mohan Kumaramangalam, "A Patriot's Notebook," *People's Age,* October 26, 1947, 16.
311. "Mahasabha Resolution," 1:256.
312. "Who Plotted Against Nehru Govt. in Delhi?," *People's Age,* October 26, 1947, 8.
313. "Form a Strong National Government," *Hindu Outlook,* September 30, 1947, in Kumaramangalam, "A Patriot's Notebook," 16.
314. "Hindu Mahasabha: Part II," in "War Staff 'WS' Series Files: File WS 13130," p. 5, IOR/L/WS/1/746, British Library (bold in original).
315. "Mahasabha Resolution," 1:256.
316. "Partition Proceedings, vol., 6, Bengal Boundary Commission, chapter 2: 'A.-- Report of Non-Muslim Members,'" p. 75, in "Copies Taken from the Microfilm (IOR Pos 3658) of the Reports, Dated Jul–Aug 1947, of the Members of the Bengal and Punjab Boundary Commissions," Mss Eur Photo Eur 211, British Library.
317. "Hindu Mahasabha: Part II."
318. "Hindu Mahasabha: Part III," p. 8, IOR/L/WS/1/746, British Library.
319. Savarkar to N. C. Chatterji, December 28, 1947, in *Selected Works,* 3:544–5.
320. Vinayak Damodar Savarkar, "Hindu Crisis: Suppressed Statement by Veer Savarkar," *The Word* 9, no. 3 (1947): 35. Reprinted, with minor deviations, in Savarkar, "Problems before Hindudom," 533.
321. Savarkar, "Problems before Hindudom," 534–5.
322. Dhananjay Keer, *Savarkar and His Times* (Bombay: A. V. Keer, 1950), 381.
323. Vinayak Damodar Savarkar, "Message on the Inauguration of the Bharatiya Republic," January 24, 1950, in *Historic Statements,* 228–9.
324. Madhav Sadashiv Golwalkar, *Bunch of Thoughts* (Bangalore: V. Prakashan, 1966), 93.
325. Vinayak Damodar Savarkar, "If We Win We Should March Upto [*sic*] Peking," December 29, 1962, in *Historic Statements,* 241–2.

Chapter Five: After the Dualism of Pakistan

1. See Shruti Kapila, *Violent Fraternity: Indian Political Thought in the Global Age* (Princeton, NJ: Princeton University Press, 2021), 229–71.
2. "Anekta mein ekta," in a 1953 article by Deendayal Upadhyaya, in *Rashtra Chintan* (1968; repr., Lucknow, India: Lokhit Prakashan, 2007), 26.

3. For example, Henry Thomas Colebrooke, "On the Philosophy of the Hindus: Part IV; On the Vedánta [From the Transactions of the Royal Asiatic Society, Vol. ii. pp. 1–39]," in *Miscellaneous Essays of Henry Thomas Colebrooke*, new ed. with notes by E. B. Cowell (1827; repr., London: Trübner, 1873), 1:393; Monier Monier-Williams, *Buddhism, in Its Connexion with Brāhmanism and Hindūism, and in Its Contrast with Christianity* (New York: Macmillan, 1889), xvii.

4. On the colonial "construction" of Hinduism, see Brian K. Pennington, *Was Hinduism Invented? Britons, Indians, and the Colonial Construction of Religion* (Oxford: Oxford University Press, 2005); David N. Lorenzen, "Who Invented Hinduism?," *Comparative Studies in Society and History* 41, no. 4 (1999): 630–59; Richard King, *Orientalism and Religion: Postcolonial Theory, India, and "the Mystic East"* (London: Routledge, 1999). On the "invention" of "religion," see Tomoko Masuzawa, *The Invention of World Religions, or: How European Universalism was Preserved in the Language of Pluralism* (Chicago: University of Chicago Press, 2005); Talal Asad, *Genealogies of Religion: Discipline and Reasons of Power in Christianity and Islam* (Baltimore: Johns Hopkins University Press, 2009); Russell T. McCutcheon, *Manufacturing Religion: The Discourse on Sui Generis Religion and the Politics of Nostalgia* (New York: Oxford University Press, 1997).

5. McCutcheon, *Manufacturing Religion*, 58–9. For the complicity of the discipline of religious studies in the formation of the new concept of religion(s), see Michael Bergunder, "What Is Religion? The Unexplained Subject Matter of Religious Studies," *Method & Theory in the Study of Religion* 26 (2014): 257–8.

6. Masuzawa, *Invention of World Religions*, 120.

7. Ibid., xiii; Michael Bergunder, "'Östliche' Religionen und Gewalt," in *Religion, Politik und Gewalt: Kongressband des XII. Europäischen Kongresses für Theologie 18.-22. September 2005 in Berlin*, ed. Friedrich Schweizer (Gütersloh, Germany: Gütersloher Verlagshaus, 2006), 136–7.

8. See King, *Orientalism and Religion*.

9. Stefan Arvidsson, *Aryan Idols: Indo-European Mythology as Ideology and Science*, trans. Sonia Wichmann (Chicago: University of Chicago Press, 2006), 37.

10. Ruth Harris, *Guru to the World: The Life and Legacy of Vivekananda* (Cambridge, MA: Belknap Press of Harvard University Press, 2022), 8, attributes the coinage of the term "global idealist moment" to the late Chris Bayly. For an overview of reform movements in India, see Kenneth W. Jones, *Socio-Religious Reform Movements in British India* (New Delhi: Cambridge University Press, 1989).

11. Indira Sarkar, "The Milieu of Comte and Renan in the Poetry of Nabin Sen," *Calcutta Review* 107, no. 3 (1948): 14–15.

12. Ibid., 21.

13. Ibid., 14.

14. For Dara Shukoh's monotheistic religion, see Supriya Gandhi, *The Emperor Who Never Was: Dara Shukoh in Mughal India* (Cambridge, MA: Harvard University Press, 2020).

15. Michael Bergunder, "Religionsvergleich in der nordindischen Nirguna-Bhakti des 15. bis 17. Jahrhunderts? Die Sant-Tradition und ihre Vorstellung von 'Hindus' und 'Muslimen,'" in *Religion in Asien? Studien zur Anwendbarkeit des Religionsbegriffs*, ed. Peter Schalk (Uppsala, Sweden: Uppsala Universitet, 2013), 43, 67, 76; Jones, *Socio-Religious Reform*, 10–14.

16. Carl Schmitt, *Der Begriff des Politischen: Mit einer Rede über das Zeitalter der Neutralisierungen und Entpolitisierungen* (Munich: Duncker & Humblot, 1932).

17. Luna Sabastian, "Women, Violence, Sovereignty: 'Rakshasa' Marriage by Capture in Modern Indian Political Thought," *Modern Intellectual History* 19, no. 3 (2022): 776.

18. See Aldred's account of his trial, in Guy Aldred, ed., *Rex v. Aldred: London Trial, 1909, Indian Sedition, Glasgow Sedition Trial, 1921* (Glasgow: Strickland Press, 1948); see also Ole Birk Laursen, "Anarchist Anti-Imperialism: Guy Aldred and the Indian Revolutionary Movement, 1909–14," *Journal of Imperial and Commonwealth History* 46, no. 2 (2018): 286–303.

19. Dhananjay Keer, *Savarkar and His Times* (Bombay: A. V. Keer, 1950), 84n1.

20. Lala Ganpat Rai to Aldred, July 1, 1947, "Delhi's Advocate's View," *The Word* 8, no. 12 (1947): 147; G. V. Damle to Aldred, June 16, 1947, *The Word* 9, no. 6 (1948): 67; Savarkar to Aldred, June 22, 1947, *The Word* 9, no. 6 (1948): 67.
21. Anand Vihari to Aldred, July 15, 1947, *The Word* 9, no. 6 (1948): 68.
22. Savarkar to Aldred, June 22, 1947, 67; M. R. Deshpande to Aldred, September 17, 1947, *The Word* 9, no. 6 (1948): 68; Pandit Babhale to Aldred, June 9, 1947, *The Word* 9, no. 6 (1948): 68; N. [Nathuram] V. Godse to Aldred, March 12, 1947, *The Word* 9, no. 6 (1948): 68.
23. V. D. Paranjape to Aldred, December 2, 1949, "News from India: N. V. Godse: Final Commentary," *The Word* 11, no. 6 (1950): 49.
24. Guy Aldred, "Britain's Scrap of Paper," *The Word* 8, no. 12 (1947): 148.
25. "Calcutta: Reactions to Gandhiji's Death: Congress Ministry Shields Mahasabha: Shanti Sena Leads Three Lakh Funeral Procession, Congress Leaders and Ministers Absent," *People's Age*, February 3, 1948.
26. Keer, *Savarkar and His Times*, 370–1.
27. Ibid., quote at 379.
28. "Gandhi Murder Trial: Official Account of the Trial of Godse, Apte, and Others for Murder and Conspiracy; With Verbatim Reports of Speeches by Godse and Savarkar," *The Word Quarterly* 1, no. 1 (1950); V. D. Paranjap [Paranjape] to Aldred, December 4, 1948, "Gandhi Murder Trial," *The Word* 10, no. 4 (1949): 49. For an account of the trial and judgement, see A. G. Noorani, *Savarkar and Hindutva: The Godse Connection* (New Delhi: LeftWord Books, 2002), 95–134.
29. Om P. Kahol to Aldred, August 19, 1950, *The Word* 11, no. 12 (1950): 130.
30. E. G. Macfarlane, "Is Savarkar Reactionary?," *The Word* 9, no. 12 (1948): 134.
31. Savarkar to Aldred, May 1, 1947, reel no. 33, file no. B 15/142, p. 56, Veer Savarkar Papers; also quoted, though without citing the source, in Vishwanath Prasad Varma, *Modern Indian Political Thought* (Agra, India: Lakshmi Narain Agarwal, 1961), 473.
32. Savarkar to Aldred, May 1, 1947, 56.
33. "Petition by Vinayak D Savarkar, a Prisoner in the Andaman Islands, for an Amnesty to All Political Offenders," 1917, file 806, IOR/L/PJ/6/1525, Public and Judicial Department Records, India Office Records and Private Papers, British Library, London.
34. Savarkar to Narayan Damodar Savarkar, July 7, 1920, Cellular Jail, Port Blair, in Vinayak Damodar Savarkar, *An Echo from Andamans: Letters Written by Veer Savarkar during His Captivity to His Brother Dr. Savarkar* (Pune, India: Venus Book Stall, 1947), 476.
35. Ibid., 477.
36. Keer, *Savarkar and His Times*, 235, 410.
37. Dhananjay Keer to Aldred, May 18, 1950, "Hindu Protests," *The Word* 11, no. 8 (1950): 84; Dhananjay Keer, "Comrade of Hindusthan and Friend of Humanity Guy Alfred Aldred," *The Word* 9, no. 5 (1948): 54, originally published in "Diwali Special 1947," special issue, *Free Hindusthan*, November 15, 1947.
38. See, for example, V. S. Godbole, *Rationalism of Veer Savarkar* (Thane, India: Itihas Patrika Prakashan, 2004), 69; Siegfried Wolf, "Vinayak Damodar Savarkar's 'Strategic Agnosticism': A Compilation of His Socio-Political Philosophy and Worldview," *Heidelberg Papers in South Asian and Comparative Politics*, no. 51 (2010): 17; Matthew Lederle, *Philosophical Trends in Modern Maharashtra* (Bombay: Popular Prakashan, 1976), 280.
39. Vinayak Damodar Savarkar [A Maratha, pseud.], *Essentials of Hindutva* (Nagpur, India: V. V. Kelkar, 1923), 128.
40. Ibid.
41. Indira Sarkar, "Milieu of Comte," 128.
42. T. L. Vaswani, *Creative Revolution* (Madras: Ganesh, 1922), 42 (italics in the original).
43. See Andrew Sartori, *Bengal in Global Concept History: Culturalism in the Age of Capital* (London: University of Chicago Press, 2008).
44. Benoy Kumar Sarkar, *The Folk-Element in Hindu Culture: A Contribution to Socio-Religious Studies in Hindu Folk-Institutions* (1917; repr., New Delhi: Oriental Books Reprint

Corporation, 1972), xi, xiv, 23–4, 175; Benoy Kumar Sarkar, *Chinese Religion through Hindu Eyes: A Study in the Tendencies of Asiatic Mentality* (Shanghai: Commercial Press, 1916), 145, 292–3.

45. Benoy Kumar Sarkar, *The Political Philosophies since 1905*, vol. 2, *The Epoch of Neo-Democracy and Neo-Socialism (1929–)*, part 3 (Lahore, India: Motilal Banarsidass, 1942), 2:3:58.

46. Ibid., 2:3:53.

47. Ibid., 2:3:60.

48. Ibid., 2:3:60.

49. Ibid., 2:3:55.

50. Ashutosh Lahiry, "Explanatory Note," n.d., reel no. 4, C-107/1946, p. 1109, Akhil Bharat Hindu Mahasabha Papers.

51. "All India Hindu Mahasabha Working Committee, New Delhi, 6th October, 1944," in *The Making of India and Pakistan: Select Documents*, ed. R. S. Bakshi, 6 vols. (New Delhi: Deep & Deep, 1997), 3:658.

52. Lahiry, "Explanatory Note," 1109; Supriya Gandhi, *The Emperor Who Never Was: Dara Shukoh in Mughal India* (Cambridge, MA: Harvard University Press, 2020), 1–8; Vinayak Damodar Savarkar, *Six Glorious Epochs of Indian History*, trans. S. T. Godbole (1963; repr., Bombay: Bal Savarkar, 1971), 382, 400–1. For the initial overture in Savarkar, *Essentials of Hindutva*, 39, see Janaki Bakhle, "Country First? Vinayak Damodar Savarkar (1883–1966) and the Writing of *Essentials of Hindutva*," *Public Culture* 22, no. 1 (2010): 169–171.

53. Bergunder, "'Östliche' Religionen," 145, 150.

54. Munis D. Faruqui, "Dara Shukoh, Vedanta, and Imperial Succession in Mughal India," in *Religious Interactions in Mughal India*, ed. Vasudha Dalmia and Munis D. Faruqui (Delhi: Oxford University Press, 2014), 30–64.

55. Bergunder, "'Östliche' Religionen," 150.

56. Gandhi, *Emperor Who Never Was*, 7; Faruqui, "Dara Shukoh," 32–3.

57. Savarkar, *Six Glorious Epochs*, 402.

58. Ashutosh Lahiry, "Resolution," n.d., reel no. 4, C-107/1946, pp. 1107–8, Akhil Bharat Hindu Mahasabha Papers.

59. Ashutosh Lahiry, "Shree Ashutosh Lahiry, General Secretary of All India Hindu Mahasabha Has Issued the Following Statement," August 18, 1948, reel no. 4, C-88/1945-49, p. 259, Akhil Bharat Hindu Mahasabha Papers.

60. Ashutosh Lahiry, "Shree Ashutosh Lahiry, General Secretary of All India Hindu Mahasabha Has Issued the Following Statement," September 10, 1948, reel no. 4, C-88/1945-49, p. 306, Akhil Bharat Hindu Mahasabha Papers.

61. Ibid., 305.

62. Report, New Delhi, Hindu Mahasabha Bhawan, September 30, 1949, reel no. 4, C-88/1945-49, pp. 70–1, Akhil Bharat Hindu Mahasabha Papers.

63. Ashutosh Lahiry, "Sri Ashutosh Lahiry, General Secretary, All India Hindu Mahasabha in Course of a Press Statement Says," November 15, 1949, reel no. 4, C-88/1945-49, p. 68, Akhil Bharat Hindu Mahasabha Papers; Lahiry to Nathuram Godse, November 10, 1949, reel no. 4, C-88/1945-49, p. 69, Akhil Bharat Hindu Mahasabha Papers.

64. Lahiry to Godse.

65. Yasmin Khan, "Performing Peace: Gandhi's Assassination as a Critical Moment in the Consolidation of the Nehruvian State," *Modern Asian Studies* 45, no. 1 (2011): 57–80.

66. K. M. Munshi, *Akhand Hindustan* (Bombay: New Book, 1942), 33, 54–5; partially quoted in Manu Bhagavan, "Princely States and the Hindu Imaginary: Exploring the Cartography of Hindu Nationalism in Colonial India," *Journal of Asian Studies* 67, no. 3 (2008): 903; Taushif Kara, "The Problem of Taqiyya: Invisible Subjects in Indian Political Thought" (Political Thought Intellectual History Seminar, University of Cambridge, March 13, 2023); Savarkar, *Essentials of Hindutva*, 85–9, 102.

67. Kapila, *Violent Fraternity*, 8.

68. See Faisal Devji, "Jinnah and the Theatre of Politics," *Asiatische Studien / Études Asiatiques* 67, no. 4 (2013): 1182; Kara, "Problem of Taqiyya."

69. See Bhagavan, "Princely States," 883; Munshi, *Akhand Hindustan*, 33, 176–7.

70. Munshi, *Akhand Hindustan*, 207.

71. Anthony Elenjimittam, *Philosophy and Action of the R.S.S. for the Hind Swaraj* (Bombay: Laxmi, 1951), 184.

72. Deendayal Upadhyaya, *Integral Humanism* (New Delhi: Bharatiya Janata Sangh, 1965). When italicized, *Integral Humanism* refers to the book.

73. Cf. Jyotirmaya Sharma, *A Restatement of Religion: Swami Vivekananda and the Making of Hindu Nationalism* (New Haven, CT: Yale University Press, 2013); see also Christophe Jaffrelot, introduction to *Hindu Nationalism: A Reader*, ed. Christophe Jaffrelot (Princeton, NJ: Princeton University Press, 2007), 7, 14, 16–17. For an extreme position blaming Vivekananda for Hindutva, see Jyotirmaya Sharma, *Hindutva: Exploring the Idea of Hindu Nationalism* (New Delhi: Penguin Books, 2006). For a defense, see William Radice, ed., *Swami Vivekananda and the Modernization of Hinduism* (Delhi: Oxford University Press, 1998); Shamita Basu, *Religious Revivalism as Nationalist Discourse: Swami Vivekananda and New Hinduism in Nineteenth Century Bengal* (New Delhi: Oxford University Press, 2002).

74. See B. K. Kelkar, "Deendayalji, RSS and Hindu Nationalism," in *Deendayal Upadhyaya's Integral Humanism: Documents, Interpretation, Comparisons*, ed. Devendra Swarup (New Delhi: Deendayal Research Institute, 1992), 109–15.

75. Deendayal Upadhyaya, "Mai 1952 mein Deendayal ji dvara prastut Jansangh ka vimukhi siddhant," in *Akhand Bharat aur Muslim Samasya* (Noida, India: Jagriti Prakashan, 1992), 30.

76. Ibid., 30.

77. Geeta Puri, *Bharatiya Jana Sangh: Organisation and Ideology: Delhi: A Case Study* (New Delhi: Sterling Publishers, 1980), 61.

78. Thomas Blom Hansen, *The Saffron Wave: Democracy and Nationalism in Modern India* (Princeton, NJ: Princeton University Press, 1999), 109–10; "Appendix V: The Original 'Pratahsmaran' or 'Bharat Bhakti Stotra—Text and Translation," in Partha Banerjee, *In the Belly of the Beast: The Hindu Supremacist RSS and BJP of India: An Insider's Story* (Delhi: Ajanta Books International, 1998), 153.

79. Arkotong Longkumer, *The Greater India Experiment: Hindutva and the Northeast* (Stanford, CA: Stanford University Press, 2020), which deals with the Northeast in the Hindu nationalist imagination, is an exception.

80. Puri, *Bharatiya Jana Sangh*, 12–13.

81. Syed Azhar Husain Zaidi, *The New Nazis, an Account of the Vast Incredible Plan of the R.S.S.S., the Hindu Mahasabha, The Akali Sikhs and Some Rulers of Indian States in the East Punjab, and Rajputana to Exterminate the Muslims*, n.d., p. 20, Mss Eur F164/31, British Library, 5–6; *The Hindustan Times*, February 3, 1948.

82. Syama Prasad Mukherjee, quoted in B. N. Jog, *Politics for Nation's Sake*, vol. 6 of *Pt. Deendayal Upadhyay Ideology and Perception* (New Delhi: Suruchi Prakashan, 2014), 73.

83. Upadhyaya, "Mai 1952 mein," 30.

84. Bharatiya Jana Sangh, "Principles and Policies," in *Bharatiya Jana Sangh, 1952–1980: Party Document*, vol. 1, *Policies and Manifestoes*, 2nd updated ed. (1965–1971; repr., New Delhi: Bharatiya Janata Party, 2005), 34; "1954 [Election Manifesto]," in Sangh, *Bharatiya Jana Sangh*, 1:277.

85. Deendayal Upadhyaya, "April 1964 mein Deendayal Upadhyaya aur Da. Rammanohar Lohiya dvara prakashit sanyukt vaktavya," in *Akhand Bharat aur Muslim*, 29. See also Craig Baxter, *The Jana Sangh: A Biography of an Indian Political Party* (Philadelphia: University of Pennsylvania Press, 1969), 250.

86. Deendayal Upadhyaya, "Deendayal ji dvara Mai 1965 mein hi Pune mein diye gaye bhashan ke kuch ansh," in *Akhand Bharat aur Muslim*, 23–4.

87. Deendayal Upadhyaya, "Selected Thoughts," in *Pt. Deendayal Upadhyaya: A Profile*, ed. Sudhakar Raje (New Delhi: Deendayal Research Institute, 1972), 184.

88. "1951 [Election Manifesto]," in Sangh, *Bharatiya Jana Sangh,* 1:292.
89. Upadhyaya, "Deendayal ji dvara Mai 1965," 23.
90. Deendayal Upadhyaya, "Can We Afford to Compromise on Kashmir?," in *Political Diary* (Bombay: Jaico Publishing House, 1968), 41.
91. Deendayal Upadhyaya, "Mai 1952 mein," 30.
92. Deendayal Upadhyaya, "Akhand Bharat aur Muslim Samasya," in *Akhand Bharat aur Muslim,* 6.
93. B. D. Graham, *Hindu Nationalism and Indian Politics: The Origins and Development of the Bharatiya Jana Sangh* (Cambridge: Cambridge University Press, 1990), 86; Shailendra Sengar, *Life and Works of Deen Dayal Upadhyaya* (New Delhi: Anmol Publications, 2015), 13.
94. Ram Madhav, *The Hindutva Paradigm: Integral Humanism and Quest for a Non-Western Worldview* (Chennai: Westland Non-Fiction, 2021), viii.
95. A recent exception, though one focused on the political economy of *Integral Humanism,* is John Abraham, "In Search of Dharma: Integral Humanism and the Political Economy of Hindu Nationalism," *South Asia: Journal of South Asian Studies* 42, no. 1 (2019): 16–32.
96. Upadhyaya, *Integral Humanism,* 1–12, quote at 5.
97. Ibid., 13–30, quote at 18.
98. Ibid., 31–49., quote at 32.
99. Ibid., 60–81, quote at 76.
100. Walter Andersen, "The Rashtriya Swayamsevak Sangh: III: Participation in Politics," *Economic and Political Weekly* 7, no. 13 (1972): 677. For the text of the constitution, see Rashtriya Swayam Sevak Sangh, *The Constitution of the Rashtriya Swayamsevak Sangh (Translated from the Original in Hindi)* (New Delhi: Rashtriya Swayamsevak Sangh, 1949), 1 (italics mine). I am grateful to Neha Chaudhary for making a copy of the RSS Constitution available to me.
101. Upadhyaya, *Integral Humanim,* 20, 37–39, 46,
102. Ibid., 52.
103. Ibid., 46–8.
104. Sartori, *Bengal in Global Concept,* 121 (italics in original).
105. Upadhyaya, *Integral Humanism,* 19; Deendayal Upadhyaya, *Ekatma Manavvad* (Noida, India: Jagriti Prakashan, 2008), 26.
106. Upadhyaya, *Integral Humanism,* 18.
107. Upadhyaya, *Ekatma Manavvad,* 26.
108. The Hindi translation of "humanism" is derived from *manav,* "human." While Deendayal opted for *manavvad,* literally the "human doctrine," his contemporaries could also choose from *manavtavad, manavta,* "humanity, the quality of being human," or *manushya jati ki seva,* "the service of humanity": R. C. Pathak, ed., *Bhargava's Standard Illustrated Dictionary of the English Language (Anglo-Hindi Edition),* 11th ed., thoroughly revised and enlarged (Varanasi, India: Bhargava Book Depot, 1965), 383.
109. See P. S. Sastri, "Indian Thought," *Revue Internationale de Philosophie* 10, no. 37 (3) (1956): 285; John G. Arapura, *Radhakrishnan and Integral Experience: The Philosophy and World Vision of Sarvepalli Radhakrishnan* (London: Asia Publishing House, 1966), 56.
110. Arapura, *Radhakrishnan and Integral Experience,* 289, 290.
111. Ashok Modak, "Two Exponents of Humanism: M. N. Roy and Deendayal," in Swarup, *Deendayal Upadhyaya's Integral Humanism,* 141, 145–6; Sengar, *Life and Works,* 13.
112. Koenraad Elst, *Decolonizing the Hindu Mind: Ideological Development of Hindu Revivalism* (New Delhi: Rupa, 2007), 402; Upadhyaya, *Integral Humanism,* 81.
113. Sartori, *Bengal in Global Concept,* 142–4.
114. Bipin Chandra Pal, "Indian Nationalism: Hindu Standpoint," in *Voices of Indian Freedom Movement,* ed. J. C. Johari, vol. 3, *Voices of Extremist and Militant Nationalism,* part 2 (New Delhi: Akashdeep Publishing House, 1993), 405.
115. Elenjimittam, *Philosophy and Action,* 34.
116. Sartori, *Bengal in Global Concept,* 144.

117. D. B. Thengadi, "Integral Humanism—A Study," in *The Integral Approach,* 3rd ed., by Madhav Sadashiv Golwalkar, Deendayal Upadhyaya, and Dattopant Bapurao Thengadi (New Delhi: Surushi Prakashan, 1991), 100.
118. Bharatiya Jana Sangh, "Principles and Policies," 44.
119. Deendayal Upadhyaya, "Akhand Bharat: Dhyey aur sadhan," in *Rashtra Chintan,* 26–9.
120. Ibid., 26.
121. Ibid., 28.
122. Ibid., 28–9.
123. Ibid., 29.
124. Keshav Baliram Hedgewar, "Vichar-dhara," in *Rashtriya Svayaṃ Sevak Sangh: Tattva aur vyavahar* (Lucknow, India: Lokahita Prakashan, 1972).
125. M. S. Golwalkar, "Sagh shiksha varg (1938)," in *Sri Guruji Samagra,* 12 vols. (New Delhi: Suruchi Prakashan, n.d.), 4:8–9.
126. M. S. Golwalkar, "Chirtan [*sic*] ki or dhyan," in *Sri Guruji Samagra,* 2:9–10, 5; M. S. Golwalkar, "Yah hindurashtra hai," in *Sri Guruji Samagra,* 2:10–11.
127. M. S. Golwalkar, "Statement 1," in appendix VIII of *Justice on Trial: A Collection of the Historic Letters between Sri Guruji and Government (1948–49),* 3rd ed. (Bangalore: Prakashan Vibhag, 1962), 69–71.
128. M. S. Golwalkar, "Atmiyata ka bodh," in *Sri Guruji Samagra,* 3:23–4.
129. In 1963, Golwalkar disowned *We,* and the RSS has since followed suit, claiming it was a translation of a work by Ganesh "Babarao" Savarkar. See Dhirendra K. Jha, "Guruji's Lie: The RSS and MS Golwalkar's Undeniable Links to Nazism," *The Caravan: A Journal of Politics & Culture,* July 31, 2021, https://caravanmagazine.in/history/rss-golwalkar-links-nazism.
130. See C. A. Bayly, "India, the Bhagavad Gita and the World," in *Political Thought in Action: The Bhagavad Gita and Modern India,* ed. Shruti Kapila and Faisal Devji (Cambridge: Cambridge University Press), 20–1; Sartori, *Bengal in Global Concept,* esp. 135.
131. For the motto, see publisher's preface to Upadhyaya, *Akhand Bharat aur Muslim,* 3. Also see Upadhyaya, "Akhand Bharat aur Muslim," 21.
132. Upadhyaya, "Akhand Bharat aur Muslim," 6.
133. Ibid., 5.
134. Ibid., 6.
135. Ibid., 5, 14–15.
136. Ibid, 14; Bharatiya Jana Sangh, "Principles and Policies," 34.
137. Upadhyaya, "Akhand Bharat aur Muslim," 14.
138. Upadhyaya, "Selected Thoughts," 184.
139. Upadhyaya, "Akhand Bharat aur Muslim," 6, 15.
140. Ibid., 9.
141. Ibid., 9, 16.
142. "1951 [Election Manifesto]," 291.
143. Bharatiya Jana Sangh, "Principles and Policies," 37–9; Bharatiya Jana Sangh, *Election Manifesto 1967* (Delhi: Arjun Press, 1967), 5; Motilal A. Jhangiani, *Jana Sangh and Swatantra: A Profile of the Rightist Parties in India* (Bombay: Manaktalas, 1967), 46.
144. Bharatiya Jana Sangh, "Principles and Policies," 45, 37.
145. Shashi Tharoor, *Why I Am a Hindu* (London: Hurst, 2018), 157.
146. Upadhyaya, "Akhand Bharat aur Muslim," 7, 15–16.
147. Ibid., 15–16; Upadhyaya, "Mai 1952 mein," 31.
148. See, for example, P. K. Das, *Modern Vedanta: Ghandi's Philosophy Compared with the Philosophies of Vivekananda, Raman Mahershi, Tagore, Aurobindo Ramatirtha, Radha Krishanan and Deen Dayal Upadhyaya* (Meerut, India: Rahul Publishing House, 2001), 299–322. As examples of the ubiquitous coupling of Upadhyaya and Gandhi, see Deendayal Research Institute titles such as P. Parameswaran, ed., *Gandhi, Lohia and Deendayal* (New Delhi: Deendayal Research

Institute, 1978); Satyavrata Sinha, "Gandhi, Lohia and Deendayal," in Raje, *Pt. Deendayal Upadhyaya,* 67–74; Keshava Prasad Singh, "Economic Thought of Gandhi, Lohia, Deendayal," in Swarup, *Deendayal Upadhyaya's Integral Humanism,* 122–32. For a reappropriation of Gandhi as a Hindu nationalist, see Shyam Kartik Mishra, *Deen Dayal Upadhyay: Thoughts Revisited in Contemporary India* (New Delhi: Kunal Books, 2017), 102.

149. M. S. Golwalkar, *Homage to the Mahatma* (Bangalore: Prakashan Vibhag Rashtriya Swayamsevak Sangh, 1969), 3–4.

150. Upadhyaya, "Akhand Bharat aur Muslim," 15.

151. Ibid., 9.

152. Ibid., 8.

153. See Bergunder, "'Östliche' Religionen," 136–7.

154. See ibid., 140–1.

155. Upadhyaya, "Akhand Bharat aur Muslim," 21.

156. Upadhyaya, *Integral Humanism,* 52.

157. See David Gilmartin, "Imperial Sovereignty in Mughal and British Forms," *History and Theory* 56, no. 1 (2017): 85–7.

158. Upadhyaya, "Akand Bharat aur Muslim," 8–9, 11.

159. Ibid., 8.

160. Ibid., 20–1.

161. Ibid., 21.

162. Ibid., 8 (English in the original).

163. Ibid., 16–17.

164. Upadhyaya, "Mai 1952 mein," 30.

165. Upadhyaya, "Akhand Bharat aur Muslim," 16.

166. Ibid.," 21–2.

167. Ibid., 19.

168. Upadhyaya, *Integral Humanism,* 38. Upadhyaya engaged with William McDougall's classic, *The Group Mind* (Cambridge: Cambridge University Press, 1920).

169. Upadhyaya, *Integral Humanism,* 32.

170. Upadhyaya, "Mai 1952 mein," 30; Upadhyaya, *Integral Humanism,* 19–20.

171. Upadhyaya, *Integral Humanism,* 30.

172. Ibid., 19.

173. Ibid., 26.

174. Ibid., 40–6.

175. Ibid., 32.

176. M. S. Golwalkar, preface to the first edition of *We, or: Our Nationhood Defined* (1939; repr., Nagpur, India: Bharat Prakashan, 1947), 1.

177. Adolf Hitler, *Mein Kampf: Eine kritische Edition,* ed. Christian Hartmann, Thomas Vordermayer, Othmar Plöckinger, and Roman Töppel, 2 vols. (1925–1926; repr., Munich: Institut für Zeitgeschichte, 2016), 2:1007.

178. M. S. Golwalkar, "Challenge of the Times," in *Bunch of Thoughts* (1966; repr., Bangalore: Vikrama Prakashan, 1968), 24.

179. Ibid., 25.

180. Upadhyaya, *Integral Humanism,* 46.

181. Ibid., 44–5.

182. Ibid., 40.

183. Ibid., 50.

184. Ibid., 46–7.

185. Ibid., 40–1.

186. Ibid., 46.

187. Ibid., 56–9.

188. Ibid., 52.
189. Ibid., 22.
190. Ibid., 6–7.
191. Ibid., 47–8.
192. Ibid., 61.
193. See Meera Nanda, *Prophets Facing Backward: Postmodernism, Science and Hindu Nationalism* (Delhi: Permanent Black, 2004), 54.
194. Upadhyaya, *Integral Humanism,* 61.
195. For the RSS view of the state, see Jaffrelot, *Hindu Nationalism,* 139.
196. Shruti Kapila, "Ambedkar's Agonism, Sovereign Violence and Pakistan as Peace," *Comparative Studies of South Asia, Africa and the Middle East* 39, no. 1 (2019): 184–95.
197. Upadhyaya, *Integral Humanism,* 11–12.
198. Ibid., 11–12.
199. Ibid., 8.
200. Ibid., 10.
201. Ibid., 76.
202. Elenjimittam, *Philosophy and Action,* 75.
203. Golwalkar, "Challenge of the Times," 19.
204. Ibid., 16–17.
205. Ibid., 19.
206. Ibid., 20 (italics in original).
207. Dattopant Bapurao Thengadi, *Spectrum: Occasional Speeches, Writings and Interviews* (Bombay: Bharatiya Shram Shodh Mandal, 1984), 23.
208. Ibid., 26.
209. Ibid., 47.
210. Bani Deshpande, *The Universe of Vedanta* (Bombay: Indian Institute of Socialist Studies, 1974).
211. *Marxism on Vedanta: Papers of the Conference on "The Universe of Vedanta," 6–7 May 1975* (New Delhi: People's Publishing House, 1976).
212. Balarama Murty, "Metaphysical Idealism Twisted and Presented as Dialectical Materialism," in *Marxism on Vedanta,* 162.
213. Thengadi, *Spectrum,* 30.
214. Ibid., 68.
215. Ibid., 30–9.
216. Guy Aldred, "Why Kahol Was Interned," *The Word* 11, no. 9 (1950): 99.
217. Thengadi, *Spectrum,* 40.
218. Ibid., 41.
219. Ibid., 42.
220. Faisal Devji, *Muslim Zion: Pakistan as a Political Idea* (Cambridge, MA: Harvard University Press, 2013), 228–40, quote at 237.
221. Faisal Devji, "A Minority of One," *Global Intellectual History* 7, no. 6 (2022): 1058–64.
222. Devji, *Muslim Zion,* 231–2.
223. Devji, "Minority of One," 1061.
224. "1951 [Election Manifesto]," 285.
225. Bharatiya Jana Sangh, "Principles and Policies," 7–8.
226. "1951 [Election Manifesto]," 285 (bold in the original).
227. Upadhyaya, *Integral Humanism,* 53–4.
228. Ibid., 55 (Hindi words in Nagari script in the original).
229. Ibid.
230. M. S. Golwalkar, "Vision of Our Work," in *Bunch of Thoughts,* 62–3.
231. Ibid., 61.
232. M. S. Golwalkar, "The Technique That Succeeds—I," in *Bunch of Thoughts,* 341.

233. Deendayal Upadhyaya, *Jagadguru Shri Shankaracharya* [in Hindi] (1947; repr., New Delhi: Prabhat Prakashan 2018).
234. Ibid., 17.
235. Ibid., 30, 33.
236. Ibid., 32.
237. Ibid.
238. Ibid., 31–2.
239. Ibid., 31–2.
240. Ibid., 22–3, 32.
241. Ibid., 22–3, quote at 27.
242. Ibid., 24.
243. See Brian A. Hatcher, "Bourgeois Vedānta: The Colonial Roots of Middle-Class Hinduism," *Journal of the American Academy of Religion* 75, no. 2 (2007): 308–9; see similarly Sartori, *Bengal in Global Concept,* 80; see also Ankur Barua, "The Absolute of Advaita and the Spirit of Hegel: Situating Vedānta on the Horizons of British Idealisms," *Journal of Indian Council of Philosophical Research* 34, no. 1 (2017): 9.
244. See Hatcher, "Bourgeois Vedānta," 308. For Raja Rammohan Roy's householder ideal, see Bruce Carlisle Robertson, *Raja Rammohan Ray: The Father of Modern India* (Delhi: University of Oxford, 1995), 78, 174.
245. Upadhyaya, *Integral Humanism,* 27.
246. Shubh Mathur, *The Everyday Life of Hindu Nationalism: An Ethnographic Account* (New Delhi: Three Essays Collective, 2008), 93.
247. Upadhyaya, *Jagadguru Shri Shankaracharya,* 50–1.
248. Ibid., 51.
249. Upadhyaya, "Akhand Bharat aur Muslim," 19.
250. Dattopant Bapurao Thengadi, *Third Way,* ed. Bhanu Pratap Shukla, 2nd ed. (1995; repr., Bangalore: Sahitya Sindhu Prakashana, 1998), 99, 212; cf. Elst, *Decolonizing the Hindu Mind,* 402, 495n160, 500, 500n179, who trivializes the connection.
251. Samuel Moyn, *Christian Human Rights* (Philadelphia: University of Pennsylvania Press, 2015), 75, 67.
252. Ibid., 36.
253. Elst, *Decolonizing the Hindu Mind,* 499.
254. Jacques Maritain, *True Humanism,* trans. Margot Robert Adamson (1936 in French; London: Centenary Press, 1938), 81.
255. Ibid., 81, 84; see Moyn, *Christian Human Rights,* 54.
256. Maritain, *True Humanism,* 84 (italics mine).
257. Jacques Maritain, "Integral Humanism and the Crisis of Modern Times," *Review of Politics* 1, no. 1 (1939): 15–16.
258. Maritain, *True Humanism,* 118.
259. Ibid., 157.
260. Ibid., 160 (italics in original).
261. Ibid., xii.
262. Ibid., 100 (italics in origial).
263. Ibid., xvi.

Epilogue

1. Ram Madhav, *The Hindutva Paradigm: Integral Humanism and Quest for a Non-Western Worldview* (Chennai: Westland Non-Fiction, 2021), 124.
2. See Christophe Jaffrelot, *Modi's India: Hindu Nationalism and the Rise of Ethnic Democracy,* trans. Cynthia Schoch (Princeton, NJ: Princeton University Press, 2021).
3. Sunil Ambedkar, *The RSS: Roadmaps for the 21st Century* (New Delhi: Rupa, 2020), vii–viii.

4. M. S. Golwalkar, "Atmiyata ka bodh," in *Sri Guruji Samagra,* 12 vols. (New Delhi: Suruchi Prakashan, n.d.), 3:29.
5. Ambedkar, *RSS,* 81–2.
6. See Christophe Jaffrelot, "The Hindu Nationalist Reinterpretation of Pilgrimage in India: The Limits of Yatra Politics," *Nations and Nationalism* 15, no. 1 (2009): 7–11.
7. Pranay Kumar, "Akhand Bharat: Understanding the Inevitable," *Organiser,* December 14, 2021, https://organiser.org/2021/12/14/15818/bharat/akhand-bharat-understanding-the-inevitable/. Curiously, the article has since been renamed "Akhand Bharat: Understanding the Cultural Concept of Akhand Bharat that Respects Sovereignty," though it is undeterredly bent on folding Pakistan and Bangladesh back into India (as of April 11, 2024).
8. Ambedkar, *RSS,* 23–4.
9. Ibid., 88.
10. Uday Mahurkar and Chirayu Pandit, *Veer Savarkar: The Man Who Could Have Prevented Partition* (New Delhi: Rupa, 2021).
11. Ibid.
12. "'Savarkar Wrote about Hindu-Muslim Unity', RSS Chief Addresses Launch of 'Veer Savarkar' Book," *Republic World,* October 12, 2021, YouTube video, 15:40, https://www.youtube.com/watch?v=A9Eba5FTlTU.
13. "1954 [Election Manifesto]," in Bharatiya Jana Sangh, *Bharatiya Jana Sangh, 1952–1980: Party Document,* vol. 1, *Policies and Manifestoes,* 2nd updated ed. (1965–1971; repr., New Delhi: Bharatiya Janata Party, 2005), 277.
14. See Luna Sabastian, "India's Citizenship Amendment Act: Partition's Fulfilment or Its Undoing?," criticalasianstudies.org Commentary Board, June 3, 2024, https://doi.org/10.52698/PRUV6217.
15. See Christophe Jaffrelot, *Les nationalistes hindous: Idéologie, implementation et mobilisation des années 1920 aux années 1990* (Paris: Press de la Fondation nationale des sciences politiques, 1993); enlarged and updated in the English version: Christophe Jaffrelot, *The Hindu Nationalist Movement and Indian Politics, 1925 to the 1990s: Strategies of Identity Building, Implantation and Mobilisation (With Special Reference to Central India)* (London: Hurst, 1996); Peter van der Veer, *Religious Nationalism: Hindus and Muslims in India* (Berkeley: University of California Press, 1994); Thomas Blom Hansen, *The Saffron Wave: Democracy and Nationalism in Modern India* (Princeton, NJ: Princeton University Press, 1999).
16. See Shruti Kapila, "Modi Asked 'What Next' at Ayodhya: A New Date, Grander Ritual for an Official Hindu State," *ThePrint* (blog), January 23, 2024, https://theprint.in/opinion/modi-asked-what-next-at-ayodhya-a-new-date-grander-ritual-for-an-official-hindu-state/1934612/.
17. Karan Thapar, "'Only Political Hindus Are Happy': Shankaracharya on Ayodhya Ram Temple Consecration," *The Wire,* January 17, 2024, https://thewire.in/religion/full-text-only-political-hindus-are-happy-shankaracharya-on-ayodhya-ram-temple-consecration.
18. Ibid.

ACKNOWLEDGMENTS

It took ten years to write this book, and I could not have done it alone. Adam made it all possible, and I can't begin to thank him. Maia was my reward. I thank my family for their love and support: Leena has always been my greatest champion and interlocutor; my mother and father gave me strength and inspired my passion for Indian history and religion; my late grandparents roused my interest in academia and the history of National Socialism, and they would have been so proud; Birte and Mika, Jan and Silke, and Iris and Nils provided a haven away from it all. For her mentorship and the indelible intellectual stamp she left on me, I thank Shruti Kapila, and for their intellectual camaraderie, Leila Essa, Taushif Kara, Lydia Wassan, Mayte Sastre, Charlotte Johann, Salmoli Choudhuri, Isa Zirden, Umme Lalani, Nastasha Sartore, Chris Sandal-Wilson, and Samuel Zeitlin. Faisal Devji, Martin Ruehl, and Pradip Kumar Datta provided invaluable feedback. Thank you to my editor, Joseph Pomp; production manager Jamie Armstrong; copyeditor Laura Larsen; and the team at Harvard University Press. A big thank you also to my anonymous peer reviewers. This work was supported by the Smuts Memorial Fund, managed by the University of Cambridge in memory of Jan Christiaan Smuts. Further funding was provided by the Studienstiftung des Deutschen Volkes and the University of Cambridge's Clare Hall.

Chapter 2 reprints, with minor edits, "Savarkar's Miscegenous Hindu Race," *Comparative Studies of South Asia, Africa, and the Middle East* 44, no. 1 (2024): 66–79. Chapter 3 reprints, with minor edits, "Volk against Kaste: Non-Democratic Popular Sovereignty in Nazi Germany," *Journal of Modern History* 96, no. 4 (2024): 842–80.

INDEX